‘An excellent book which demonstrates vividly the extraordinary significance and complexity of a wide range of contested issues surrounding the nature, scope and implications of religious freedom today – written by a distinguished team of scholars from multiple legal, religious and other perspectives, it is a richly-documented and invalubale resource.’

Professor Norman Doe, Director of the Centre for Law and Religion,
The School of Law and Politics, Cardiff University, United Kingdom

‘A timely and judicious collection of essays by established stars and erudite newcomers to the burgeoning international study of religious freedom. The new taxonomy of freedom of, for, from, and within religion is a valuable heuristic to map out the new issues facing persons and peoples of faith throughout the world. And several of the essays, especially on the treatment of religious pastors, proselytism, properties, and prisoners, are major new contributions. This collection deserves a place in every religious freedom library.’

John Witte, Jr., Center for the Study of Law and Religion,
Emory University School of Law, USA

# Religious Freedom and the Law

This volume presents a timely analysis of some of the current controversies relating to freedom *for* religion and freedom *from* religion that have dominated headlines worldwide. The collection trains the lens closely on select issues and contexts to provide detailed snapshots of the ways in which freedom *for* and *from* religion are conceptualized, protected, neglected, and negotiated in diverse situations and locations. A broad range of issues, including migration, education, the public space, prisons, and health care, are discussed, drawing examples from Europe, the United States, Asia, Africa, and South America. Including contributions from leading experts in the field, the book will be essential reading for researchers and policy-makers interested in law and religion.

**Brett G. Scharffs** is Rex E. Lee Chair and Professor of Law, and Director of the International Center for Law and Religion Studies, J. Reuben Clark Law School, Brigham Young University, and a Member of the Steering Committee of the International Consortium for Law and Religion Studies (ICLARS).

**Asher Maoz** is Dean of the Peres Academic Center Law School, Israel; Vice President of the Honorary Committee, The International Association for the Defense of Religious Liberty (AIDLR); and a Member of the Steering Committee of ICLARS.

**Ashley Isaacson Woolley** is an Independent Editorial Associate, International Center for Law and Religion Studies, J. Reuben Clark Law School, Brigham Young University.

## ICLARS Series on Law and Religion

Series Editors:

*Silvio Ferrari, University of Milan, Italy, Russell Sandberg, Cardiff University, UK, Pieter Coertzen, University of Stellenbosch, South Africa, W. Cole Durham, Jr., Brigham Young University, USA, and Tahir Mahmood, Amity International University, India*

The *ICLARS Series on Law and Religion* is a new series designed to provide a forum for the rapidly expanding field of research in law and religion. The series is published in association with the International Consortium for Law and Religion Studies, an international network of scholars and experts of law and religion founded in 2007 with the aim of providing a place where information, data and opinions can easily be exchanged among members and made available to the broader scientific community. The series aims to become a primary source for students and scholars while presenting authors with a valuable means to reach a wide and growing readership.

Other titles in this series:

**Free Exercise of Religion and the United States Constitution**
The Supreme Court's Challenge
*Mark P. Strasser*

**Religious Freedom and the Australian Constitution**
Origins and Future
*Luke Beck*

**Islam, Law and the Modern State**
(Re)imagining Liberal Theory in Muslim Contexts
*Arif A. Jamal*

**Atheist Exceptionalism**
Atheism, Religion, and the United States Supreme Court
*Ethan G. Quillen*

**Lutheran Theology and Secular Law**
The Work of the Modern State
*Edited by Marie A. Failinger and Ronald W. Duty*

**Religious Freedom and the Law**
Emerging Contexts for Freedom for and from Religion
*Edited by Brett G. Scharffs, Asher Maoz and Ashley Isaacson Woolley*

For more information about this series, please visit:
www.routledge.com/ICLARS-Series-on-Law-and-Religion/book-series/ICLARS

# Religious Freedom and the Law

## Emerging Contexts for Freedom for and from Religion

**Edited by**
**Brett G. Scharffs, Asher Maoz and Ashley Isaacson Woolley**

Routledge
Taylor & Francis Group
LONDON AND NEW YORK

First published 2019 by Routledge

2 Park Square, Milton Park, Abingdon, Oxfordshire OX14 4RN
52 Vanderbilt AVenue, New York, NY 10017

*Routledge is an imprint of the Taylor & Francis Group, an informa business*

First issued in paperback 2019



*British Library Cataloguing-in-Publication Data*
A catalogue record for this book is available from the British Library

*Library of Congress Cataloging-in-Publication Data*
Names: Scharffs, Brett G., author. | Maoz, Asher, author. | Woolley, Ashley Isaacson, 1982– author.
Title: Religious freedom and the law: emerging contexts for freedom for and from religion / Brett G. Scharffs, Asher Maoz and Ashley Woolley.
Description: Abingdon, Oxon [UK]; New York: Routledge, 2018. |
Series: ICLARS series on law and religion | Includes index.
Identifiers: LCCN 2017039542 | ISBN 9781138555785 (hbk) |
ISBN 9781315149707 (ebk)
Subjects: LCSH: Freedom of religion. | Freedom of religion (International law) | Religion and law.
Classification: LCC K3258 .S33 2018 | DDC 342.08/52–dc23
LC record available at https://lccn.loc.gov/2017039542

ISBN: 978-1-138-55578-5 (hbk)
ISBN: 978-0-367-48127-8 (pbk)

Typeset in Galliard
by codeMantra

# Contents

*Notes on contributors* ix

Introduction: Freedom of/for/from/within religion: conceptually inseparable rights 1
BRETT G. SCHARFFS, ASHER MAOZ AND ASHLEY ISAACSON WOOLLEY

PART I
Freedom for and freedom from religion 13

1 Freedom 'for' religion: (yet) another view of the Cathedral 15
RICHARD W. GARNETT

2 The ministerial exception: an inquiry into the status of religious freedom in the United States and abroad 25
THOMAS F. FARR

3 The ministerial exception: theological and legal perspectives from Finland and Europe 39
PAMELA SLOTTE

4 Freedom from religion in international human rights law 56
FRANCES RADAY

5 Is there a right to freedom *from* religion? 63
DAVID POLLOCK

PART II
Emerging social contexts 77

6 Immigration as an experience of fundamental rights and religious freedom 79
PIERRE C. NOËL

7 Health-care conscience and competing sexual liberty claims 87
SISTER RENÉE MIRKES

8 Preventing religious fundamentalism through higher education of faith leaders 96
CLEMENS STEINHILBER

9 Religious freedom and places of worship: religious buildings in Europe and the United States 111
MARIA LUISA LO GIACCO

10 The religious precinct: the inequalities of equality law in religious property 124
SARAH HAYES

11 Freedom of/for/from/within religion in prison: a taxonomy of the Strasbourg jurisprudence 144
JEROEN TEMPERMAN

PART III
Emerging regional contexts 155

12 Islamic Preaching Board Laws of Kano, Borno, and Niger States: a constitutional and human rights assessment 157
AHMED SALISU GARBA

13 Freedom of religious beliefs or religious freedom? The recent case law of the Polish Constitutional Tribunal 172
PIOTR SZYMANIEC

14 Christonormativity as religious neutrality: a critique of the concept of state religious neutrality in Germany 182
ARMIN LANGER

15 Freedom of religious conscience and persuasion: international law, domestic practice, and perspectives from Asia 196
LI-ANN THIO

16 Religious equality in the Peruvian Constitution 217
OSCAR DÍAZ MUÑOZ

*Index* 223

# Notes on contributors

**Oscar Díaz Muñoz has** a PhD in Law from the University of Zaragoza (Spain) and a Licentiate in Law from the Pontifical Catholic University of Peru. He is advisor and former Secretary to the Constitutional Tribunal of Peru and Professor of Constitutional Law in the Graduate School at the University of San Martín de Porres (Peru). His publications include *El derecho fundamental de libertad religiosa: Jurisprudencia y doctrina constitucional* (2014), *El derecho constitucional de libertad religiosa del menor: Familia, escuela y tratamientos médicos* (2010), *La moción de censura en el Perú* (1997), and numerous articles on constitutional law and human rights, appearing in various books and law journals in Peru and other countries.

**Thomas F. Farr** is President of the Religious Freedom Institute, an NGO working to advance religious freedom worldwide. A leading authority on international religious freedom, Farr is also a senior fellow at the Institute for Studies of Religion at Baylor University. He served for 28 years in the US Army and the US Foreign Service. In 1999, he became the first director of the State Department's Office of International Religious Freedom. He taught for 10 years at Georgetown University's School of Foreign Service, and directed Georgetown's Religious Freedom Research Project. His major works include *World of Faith and Freedom: Why International Religious Liberty is Vital to American National Security* (Oxford University Press 2008); *Religious Freedom and Gay Rights: Emerging Conflicts in North America and Europe*, co-edited with Timothy Shah and Jack Friedman (Cambridge University Press 2016); and 'Diplomacy in an Age of Faith' in Foreign Affairs (2008). Farr received a BA from Mercer University and a PhD from the University of North Carolina.

**Ahmed Salisu Garba** attended the University of Jos, Faculty of Law, earning First and Second Degrees in 2004 and 2011, respectively. Called to the Nigerian Bar in 2005, he now teaches law at the Bauchi State University, Gadau, in Nigeria. A PhD candidate at the Faculty of Law, Bayero University, Kano, Nigeria, he is working on the regulation of religious preaching in Nigeria with a focus on Islamic Preaching Board Laws. He was a visiting scholar at the University of Iowa College of Law in the United States from August to December 2013.

**Richard W. Garnett** is the Paul J. Schierl/Fort Howard Corporation Professor of Law and Concurrent Professor of Political Science at the University of Notre Dame. He is the founding Director of the Notre Dame Law School's Program on Church, State, and Society, which explores the societal role and legal status of religious institutions, communities, and authorities. He earned his BA in philosophy from Duke University and his

JD from Yale Law School. He served as law clerk to the late Chief Justice of the United States, William H. Rehnquist, and to the late Chief Judge of the US Court of Appeals for the Eighth Circuit, Richard S. Arnold.

**Sarah Hayes** is associate vicar of St. Germain's Church in Birmingham, England, a community-focused Anglican church. She holds an LM (Distinction) in Canon Law from Cardiff University and a BA (Hons) in Politics and Modern History from Manchester University. She recently completed doctoral research at Oxford Brookes University on the impact of wider community use on the relationship between state and religions' laws around religious buildings. Prior to her research role, Sarah provided legal support to not-for-profit organizations developing physical, organizational, and human resources. She became a solicitor in 1990 and remains on the roll. Sarah brings to academic research practical experience of the law and her specialist knowledge of religious communities' structures and the wider economic, political, and legal contexts within which third-sector organizations work.

**Armin Langer** holds a BA in Philosophy and Religious Studies from the Eötvös Lorand University in Budapest, a BA in Jewish Theology from the University of Potsdam, and an MA in Jewish Theology from the University of Potsdam. He studied Talmud at the Conservative Yeshiva in Jerusalem. He is the author of *Ein Jude in Neukölln* (Aufbau 2016), an autobiographical work on Jewish identity politics in Germany, and co-editor of Fremdgemacht & Reorientiert: jüdisch-muslimische Verflechtungen (Yilmaz-Günay 2018). He is co-founder and coordinator of the intercultural Salaam-Shalom Initiative, established by Jews and Muslims in Berlin to promote peaceful coexistence and solidarity through projects that raise awareness of social and institutional exclusions in mainstream German society. Several of Langer's articles on anti-Semitism and anti-Muslim racism have been published in German, Hungarian, English, and Arabic in print and online newspapers, including *die ZEIT*, *Frankfurter Rundschau*, and *Deutsche Welle*.

**Maria Luisa Lo Giacco** is Associate Professor in Law and Religion, Department of Law, University of Bari Aldo Moro. She has a PhD in Ecclesiastical and Canon Law from the University of Naples 'Federico II' (1996). She is a Doctor in Canon Law, Lateranense Pontifical University, Rome (2008). Previously, she taught Ecclesiastical Comparative Law and later, Law and Religion in the Mediterranean Area. Her research interests are law and religion in Europe, comparative law, religious freedom, family law, and pilgrimage. Her recent publications include *Le competenze delle Regioni in materia ecclesiastica* (Bari 2004), *Pellegrini, romei e palmieri. Il pellegrinaggio fra diritto e religione* (Bari 2008), *La famiglia e i suoi soggetti. Temi giuridici* (Bari 2008), 'Religione e cultura nell'adozione internazionale', *Diritto & Religioni* (2015), and 'Hidden Meanings of the Words "Religion" and "Religious" in Legal Discourse', *Semiotica: Journal of International Association for Semiotic Studies* (2016).

**Asher Maoz** is the Founder and Dean of the Peres Academic Center Law School. He was for many years on the Faculty of Law at Tel-Aviv University and taught at several universities in the United States, Europe, and Australia. Professor Maoz holds the degrees of LLB and LLM, both *summa cum laude* (Hebrew University), M.Comp.L. (University of Chicago), JSD (Tel-Aviv University), and Doctor Honoris Causa (Ovidius University, Romania). He is the founding Editor-in-Chief of *Law, Society and Culture*; a former editor of the Tel-Aviv University Law Review; a member of the Scientific Board, *Review*

*Dionysina;* a member of the Academic Council of The International Academy for Jewish Leadership; and a member of the Academic Council, Shalem College, Jerusalem. He was Chair of the Law Commission for Journalists' Privileges; served as academic advisor to the Knesset Constitution, Law and Justice Committee on adopting a constitution for the State of Israel; and serves with many other organizations. Professor Maoz is the author of numerous publications on the intersections of law and religion. He is Vice President of the Honorary Committee of the International Association for the Defense of Religious Liberty (AIDLR), a member of the G20 Interfaith Forum Advisory Council and member of the organizing committee of the Forum, and a member of the Steering Committee of ICLARS.

**Sister Renée Mirkes,** O.S.F., PhD, is a member of the Franciscan Sisters of Christian Charity, Manitowoc, Wisconsin. She serves as Director of the Center for NaProEthics (the ethics division of the Pope Paul VI Institute, Omaha, Nebraska) and was editor of its ethics publication, *The NaProEthics Forum*, from 1996 to 2002. She received her master's degree in moral theology from the University of St. Thomas, Houston, Texas, and her doctorate in theological ethics from Marquette University, Milwaukee, Wisconsin. In her current position, she focuses on procreative and birth ethics through consultations, publications, and public speaking. To these commitments Sister Renée brings experience in clinical ethics as well as broad experience in bioethics. She has published articles in *The Journal of Philosophy and Medicine*, *Ethics & Medics*, *New Blackfriars*, *The Thomist*, *Linacre Quarterly*, *The American Catholic Philosophical Quarterly*, *Catholic Answer*, *Our Sunday Visitor*, *The NaProEthics Forum*, *National Catholic Bioethics Center Quarterly*, *Ethics and Medicine*, *Catholic World Report*, and *The Catholic Response*.

**Pierre C. Noël** is Professor titulaire and former Dean of the Faculty of Theology and Religious Studies (2009–2016) at the University of Sherbrooke in Québec, Canada. He has been at Sherbrooke since 2002. His research interests are in theology and religious law, and his teaching focuses on ecumenical issues and interfaith dialogue. He received a bachelor's in Theology and a master's in Theology from the University of Sherbrooke, and a PhD in Theology from Laval University in Québec City. He did post-doctoral study specializing in religious law at the Catholic University of Leuven in Belgium and the University of Tübingen in Germany.

**David Pollock** (MA, Oxford 1964) is a board member and past Chair of Humanists UK (previously the British Humanist Association) and of the Rationalist Association, publishers of *New Humanist* magazine. He was President of the European Humanist Federation (2006–2012) and chaired the Advisory Board (of NGOs) to the European Parliament Platform for Secularism in Politics. He represented the International Humanist and Ethical Union at the Council of Europe (2012–2017). He takes a special interest in public policy on the place of religion and belief in society in a context of human rights, equality, and non-discrimination. His writings on the subject are at www.thinkingabouthumanism.org. He has spoken at EU, European Parliament, Council of Europe, and OSCE conferences and has given oral evidence to committees of both the UK Parliament and the Parliamentary Assembly of the Council of Europe. He was given the Distinguished Service to Humanism Award at the 2011 World Humanist Congress in Oslo.

**Frances Raday** is a member of the United Nations Working Group on Discrimination against Women in law and in practice. She assumed her function on 1 May 2011. She is a former member of CEDAW. Professor Raday is currently the Director of the Concord Research Centre for Integration of International Law in Israel at Haim Striks Law School, Colman. She is Professor Emerita, Hebrew University, Lieberman Chair for Labour Law; Honorary Professor, University College London; and Doctor Honoris, University of Copenhagen. She has held academic appointments at Oxford University, University of Southern California, Tulane University, and University of East Africa. She is the author of numerous academic books and articles on human rights, labor law, and feminist legal theory. She has acted as legal counsel on precedent-setting human rights cases in Israel's Supreme Court, including advancing women's constitutional right to equality in political representation, participation in religious ceremony, religious court procedures and divorce, and combatting employment discrimination in retirement age, sexual harassment, and promotion.

**Brett G. Scharffs** is Rex E. Lee Chair and Professor of Law and Director of the International Center for Law and Religion Studies at Brigham Young University Law School. He received a BS/BA in international business and an MA in philosophy at Georgetown University and, as a Rhodes Scholar, earned a B.Phil in philosophy at Oxford. He received his JD from Yale Law School, where he was senior editor of the *Yale Law Journal*. He is a recurring Visiting Professor at Central European University in Budapest and at the University of Adelaide Law School. He has for several years helped organize certificate training programs in religion and the rule of law in China and Vietnam and has taught and helped organize programs at several Indonesian universities on Sharia and human rights. Author of more than 100 articles and book chapters, he has made more than 300 scholarly presentations in 30 countries. His casebook, *Law and Religion: National, International and Comparative Perspectives* (with W. Cole Durham, Jr., 2nd English edition forthcoming 2018), has been translated into Chinese and Vietnamese, with Turkish, Burmese, Arabic, Russian, and Spanish in process. He is the author, with Elizabeth Clark, of *Religion and Law in the USA*, a 2016 contribution to Wolters Kluwer's *International Encyclopaedia of Laws*.

**Pamela Slotte,** D.Theol., is Associate Professor (tenure track) in Minority Studies at Åbo Akademi University and an Academy of Finland Academy Researcher (2013–2018), as well as Vice-Director of the Centre of Excellence in Law, Identity and the European Narratives (2018–2025) at the University of Helsinki. She is trained in theology and law, and is Adjunct Professor of theological ethics with philosophy of religion at Åbo Akademi University and Adjunct Professor of religion and law research at the University of Helsinki. She is Principal Investigator in the HERA-funded project *Protestant Legacies of Nordic Law: Uses of the Past in the Construction of the Secularity Law* (2016–2019). Her recent publications include the co-edited volume *Revisiting the Origins of Human Rights* (Cambridge University Press 2015), as well as 'Whose Justice, What Political Theology? On Christian and Theological Approaches to Human Rights in the 20th and 21st Centuries', in Martti Koskenniemi, Monica Garcia-Salmones Rovira, and Paolo Amorosa, eds, *International Law and Religion: Historical and Contemporary Perspectives* (Oxford University Press 2017).

**Clemens Steinhilber** holds law degrees from Heidelberg (first examination in law 2012, doctorate 2016), Krakow (LLM 2012), and Paris Sud (D.U. Gratianus 2015) Universities. He served as legal clerk (*Juristischer Vorbereitungsdienst*) at the Higher Regional Court of Berlin (*Kammergericht*) with rotations at the German Federal Chancellery (*Bundeskanzleramt*) and the German Federal Constitutional Court (*Bundesverfassungsgericht*). He has been a lecturer in the Faculties of Law at Montpellier I and Paris Sud University as well as at Humboldt-University Berlin. He was recently appointed a judge of the Sozialgericht Berlin.

**Piotr Szymaniec** earned a PhD in law (2012) and a degree of Habilitated Doctor of Law (*doktor habilitowany nauk prawnych*) (2017) from the University of Wroclaw. He is Associate Professor and Rector's Representative for Research and International Cooperation at the Angelus Silesius University of Applied Sciences in Wałbrzych (Poland). He is the author of more than 70 publications, including *Republikanizm dla społeczeństwa handlowego. Myśl polityczno-prawna Adama Fergusona* ('Republicanism for a Commercial Society. The Political and Legal Thought of Adam Ferguson') (2013), *Koncepcje wolności religijnej. Rozwój historyczny i współczesny stan debaty w zachodniej myśli polityczno-prawnej* ('Concepts of Religious Freedom: Historical Development and the Present Status of the Debate in Western Legal and Political Thought') (2017), *Religionsfreiheitsraum im Polen, Tschechien und im Deutschland. Rechtliche Analyse* ('The Space of Religious Freedom in Poland, the Czech Republic, and Germany: Legal Analysis') (co-author, 2017), *Zasada proporcjonalności a ochrona praw podstawowych w państwach Europy* ('The Principle of Proportionality and the Protection of Fundamental Rights in the European States') (editor and co-author, 2015), and *Wymiary wolności religijnej we współczesnej Europie* (*'Dimensions of Religious Freedom in Contemporary Europe'*) (2017).

**Jeroen Temperman** is Professor of International Law and Religion and Deputy Head of the Department of International and European Union Law at Erasmus School of Law, Erasmus University, Rotterdam, the Netherlands. He is also the Editor-in-Chief of *Religion & Human Rights* and a member of the Organization for Safety and Cooperation in Europe's Panel of Experts on Freedom of Religion or Belief. He has authored, among other books, *Religious Hatred and International Law* (Cambridge University Press 2016) and *State–Religion Relationships and Human Rights Law* (Martinus Nijhoff 2010) and edited *Blasphemy and Freedom of Expression* (Cambridge University Press 2017) and *The Lautsi Papers* (Martinus Nijhoff 2012).

**Li-ann Thio,** BA Oxford (Hons); LLM (Harvard); PhD (Cambridge), Barrister (Gray's Inn), is Provost Chair Professor at the Faculty of Law, National University of Singapore, where she teaches and writes on constitutional and administrative law, law and religion, public international law, and international and comparative human rights law with an Asian focus. Her publications include *Managing Babel: The International Legal Protection of Minorities in the 20th Century* (Brill 2005), *A Treatise on Singapore Constitutional Law* (Academy Publishing 2012), and *Constitutionalism in Asia* (Hart 2014, with Kevin Tan, Wen-Chen Chang, and Jiunn-rong Yeh). She was a Nominated Member of the Singapore Parliament (11th Session, 2007–2009) and formerly General Editor of the *Asian Yearbook of International Law*, editor of the *International Journal of Constitutional Law*, and Chief editor of the *Singapore Journal of International and Comparative Law*. She is the current Chief Editor of the *Singapore Journal of Legal Studies* and an Advisory Board member of the *Max Planck Encyclopedia of Comparative Constitutional Law*.

**Ashley Isaacson Woolley** holds an AB (*summa cum laude*) in Romance Languages and Literatures from Harvard University, a Master of Theological Studies from Harvard

Divinity School, and a JD from Stanford Law School. She is an independent writer and editor whose clients include major law schools in the United States. Among other projects, she served as content and format editor for the international *Encyclopedia of Law and Religion* (Brill-Nijhoff 2016) and Associate Editor for *Intellectual Property in Asia* (Springer 2009).

# Introduction

## Freedom of/for/from/within religion: conceptually inseparable rights

*Brett G. Scharffs, Asher Maoz and Ashley Isaacson Woolley*

On 8–11 September 2016, a conference was held at St. Hugh's College of Oxford University with the theme 'Freedom of/for/from/within Religion: Differing Dimensions of a Common Right?' It was the fourth biennial conference of the International Consortium for Law and Religion Studies (ICLARS), a worldwide professional learned membership society devoted to the academic study of law and religion. Plenary sessions were organized around each of these four prepositions – of, for, from, and within[1] – with breakout sessions developing and elaborating upon each. In all, more than a hundred papers were presented by scholars from 40 countries. Seldom has a conference theme been as successful as this one in triggering thoughtful and innovative ways of approaching issues that have already been the subject of frequent attention.

From this conference have emerged two volumes of select papers that reflect, develop, and elaborate on the conference proceedings. This is the first of those volumes, focusing broadly on freedom *for* and *from* religion. The second book, edited by W. Cole Durham, Jr., Javier Martínez-Torrón, and Donlu Thayer, will focus on freedom *of* religion and freedom *within* religion, as well as on issues of a theoretical and conceptual character.

***

Prepositions (such as *of*, *for*, *from*, and *within*) are among the most frequently used words in the English language, commonly appearing up to ten times in a sentence, and are especially ubiquitous in legal texts.[2] But it is fair to say that prepositions do not get the attention they deserve. Their primary task is to reduce ambiguity and increase the precision and clarity of sentences.[3] It is not surprising, then, that there is insight to be had from paying close attention to prepositions.

As a general matter, a preposition introduces a relationship between two entities or concepts or sets of entities or concepts. While the entities or concepts may remain the same, using different prepositions can significantly alter the meaning of the phrase. Recall US President Franklin D. Roosevelt's 1941 State of the Union Address, remembered as the 'Four Freedoms' speech. There he alternated between freedom *of* and freedom *from*, saying the people everywhere in the world ought to enjoy freedom *of* speech and freedom *of* religion

1 It is worth noting at the outset, as we elaborate later, that this division is somewhat arbitrary; issues involving religious freedom cannot be neatly divided along these lines.

2 Kamariah Yunus, 'Colligations of Prepositions: Essential Properties of Legal Phraseology', (2016) 5 *International Journal of Applied Linguistics & English Literature* (6) 199–208.

3 Yunus at 199.

(two good things) and freedom *from* want and freedom *from* fear (two bad things).[4] If the prepositions were reversed, President Roosevelt's meaning would have been inverted as well.

Consider the concepts 'freedom' and 'religion'. These two words are often linked, usually by the preposition *of.* When the preposition varies, it may reflect certain attitudes, presuppositions, and assertions about the relationship. The connotations of freedom *for* religion are deferential and accommodating, while the connotations of freedom *within* religion direct our attention to institutional issues involving the autonomy or self-direction of religious groups. Freedom *from* religion is the most modern concept in the relationship between 'freedom' and 'religion'. It invites us to focus on the absence of religion or religious pressure or, at the extreme, hostility toward religion as toxic, undesirable, and to be avoided.

## Freedom *of* religion

*Of* is the most traditional connector between 'freedom' and 'religion'. But what exactly does the preposition 'of' tell us about the relationship between freedom and religion?

There are many dictionary definitions of *of* which might make sense in the phrase 'freedom of religion'.[5] First, *of* expresses the relationship between a part and a whole, as in, for example, 'the days of the week'. In this sense, freedom is a part and religion is the whole. Religion cannot be whole without freedom; freedom is a part of, and included in, a complete understanding of religion. On this definition, and perhaps as an oversimplified conceptualization, we might imagine religion as a large circle (the whole) and religion as a small circle within it (the part), as illustrated in Figure 1.

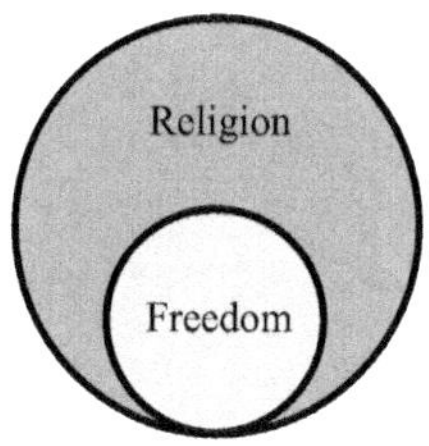


*Figure 1*

While rich in suggestion and implication, this definition is somewhat of a philosophization: it does not capture the usual sense of the phrase 'freedom of religion'.

Alternatively, *of* can express the relationship between a general category or type and the thing being specified that belongs to such a category: for example, 'the city of London'. Here, 'London' is one type of 'city'. In contrast with the first definition, here freedom would be a general category or concept, and religion would be one thing that belongs within this category. In other words, religion would be one type of freedom. Again rich in suggestion and implication, this meaning, too, does not exactly capture our usual use of the phrase 'freedom of religion'. Nevertheless, it comes close, if we think of 'freedom of religion' as a part of the larger category of 'freedom'. In this model, freedom of religion is not *sui generis*, but instead

4 Franklin D. Roosevelt, 1941 State of the Union Address, https://fdrlibrary.org/four-freedoms (accessed 7 August 2017).

5 See, for example, 'of', *Oxford Living Dictionaries*, https://en.oxforddictionaries.com/definition/of and 'of', *Merriam-Webster Dictionary*, www.merriam-webster.com/dictionary/of (accessed 14 July 2017).

one among many species of freedom or liberty.[6] On this definition, and again perhaps as an oversimplification, freedom could be conceptualized as a large circle, with religion (Figure 2) or freedom of religion (Figure 2a) as one of several components of that concept.

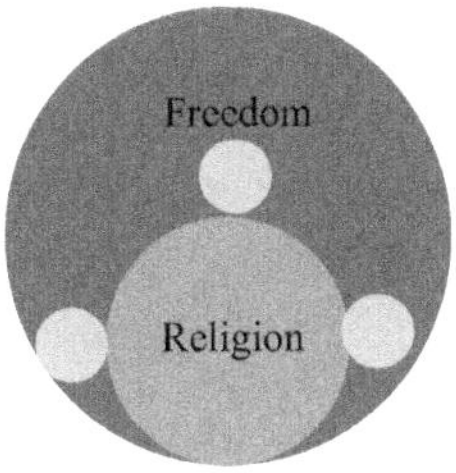


*Figure 2*

*Figure 2a*

Alternatively, *of* can indicate an association between two entities, typically one of belonging, in which the first is the head of the phrase and the second is something associated with it, as in 'the son of a friend'. This definition suggests that 'religion' is an entity associated with 'freedom'. Unlike the first and second definitions, this definition indicates that 'freedom' and 'religion' are two separated ideas or entities, each of which can exist without the other. This definition of *of* creates a picture of freedom and religion as two separate concepts that do not overlap each other, but which are connected by a bond between the two, as illustrated in Figure 3.

*Figure 3*

Another possibility is that *of* indicates the component material, parts, or elements, as in 'throne of gold'. These are not two separate entities that can have boundaries drawn around them and their relationship analyzed. Rather, one is integral to the other. Religion is the material that constitutes and defines the freedom (Figure 4).

*Figure 4*

These general definitional relations between freedom and religion are, of course, quite abstract. Looking to legal dictionaries that define 'freedom of religion', we find, unsurprisingly,

6 See Richard W. Garnett, 'Positive Secularism and the American Model of Religious Liberty', (2010) 11 *Engage* (1) 126–127, www.fed-soc.org/library/doclib/20100331_GarnettEngage11.1.pdf (accessed 8 August 2017).

more pragmatic and less conceptual definitions. One law dictionary defines freedom of religion as 'the freedom to practice or change one's own religion or not to believe in or practice a religion at all'.[7] This definition comes close to capturing the agreed-upon meaning of freedom of religion in many constitutions and international human rights norms.

But before we discuss what freedom of religion is in the legal sense, we should consider what freedom of religion is not. In the 2016 Fourth ICLARS Conference, David Novak explained that freedom of religion in the United States and Canada is not what in pre-modern times was called *libertas ecclesiae* or the 'liberty of the Church'.[8] Those terms reflect a system in which the church and the state were two interrelated institutions that jointly governed society; the church was monolithic just as the state was monolithic. The First Amendment to the US Constitution upended that model with its prohibition on established religions. However, Novak also pointed out that the radical secularist interpretation of the First Amendment as the 'freedom *from* religion' is not consistent with the First Amendment, which prohibits Congress not from making any law 'respecting religion', but respecting 'an establishment of religion'. Rather, Professor Novak suggested that freedom of religion is the freedom of religious communities and their adherents to be ultimately committed to an absolute authority beyond the relative authority of the state; in other words, freedom of religion is freedom from the totalizing authority of the state.

This view of freedom of religion is reflected in the First Amendment to the US Constitution, which is framed as a prohibition on government action: 'Congress shall make no law respecting an establishment of religion, or prohibiting the free exercise thereof.' The notion of freedom of religion as essentially freedom from state authority is less explicit in international law. To take just one example, Article 18 of the Universal Declaration of Human Right (UDHR) declares,

> Everyone has the right to freedom of thought, conscience and religion; this right includes freedom to change his religion or belief, and freedom, either alone or in community with others and in public or private, to manifest his religion or belief in teaching, practice, worship and observance.

It is notable that unlike the First Amendment, this formulation and many others like it worldwide are not framed in terms of a limitation on government, but in terms of a positive right.

## Freedom *for* religion

Freedom *for* religion is by comparison a much less common phrase. In fact, while there are thousands of references to 'freedom of religion' in US case law,[9] there is only one case in the history of federal court cases that uses the phrase 'freedom for religion', and it is a direct quote from a non-native English speaker.[10] Nevertheless, in scholarly discussions

7 *Bouvier Law Dictionary Freedom of Religion*, The Wolters Kluwer Bouvier Law Dictionary Desk Edition, https://advance.lexis.com/api/permalink/a551a1d7-4b9b-40be-9805-0277fec63612/?context=1000516 (accessed 14 July 2017).

8 David Novak, *What is Religious Freedom?*, Fourth Conference of the International Consortium of Law and Religion Studies, St Hugh's College, Oxford University, 8 September 2016, in W. Cole Durham, Jr., Javier Martínez Torrón, and Donlu Thayer, eds (Routledge forthcoming).

9 As of 31 July 2017, there were 5,934 federal cases and 3,537 state cases mentioning the phrase 'freedom of religion'.

10 *Wu Xiong Tao v. Holder*, 367 Fed. Appx. 898 (10th Cir. 2010). ('Tao testified that he came to the United States because "some people from [his] hometown" had advised him that it was a "country of democracy and of human rights" and it would provide "freedom for religion".')

some commentators have begun to recognize this formulation as valuable, with one even suggesting that it represents the 'American model of religious liberty'.[11]

Dictionary definitions of *for* that seem relevant to the phrase 'freedom for religion' include 'with respect to' or 'concerning', for example 'a stickler for detail', or purpose, such as 'a grant for studying medicine'.[12] Therefore, the phrase 'freedom for religion' can mean either 'freedom with regard to or concerning religion' or 'freedom for the purpose of or on behalf of religion'.

Both of these suggestions imply that freedom should be in the service of, or positively facilitate, religion. Again, as an oversimplification, if we were to try to diagram the relationship, freedom might reside along religion, with an arrow suggesting that freedom's job is to serve or facilitate religion, as illustrated in Figure 5.

*Figure 5*

The articulation 'freedom for religion' is likely to treat religion as something positive and special, and view religious freedom as being designed to ensure the function of religion. The idea is not that the government should demand religious observances or establish a state religion; it is, instead, that a political community should commit to positive secularity.[13] Positive secularity means that the government recognizes the value and importance of religion in the society and to people, and while maintaining a secular legal order and government, treats religion positively and makes laws that facilitate the smooth operation and development of religious groups.

Specific usage of the word *for* in the context of government confirms the meaning of *for* as indicating purpose or service to another, as in the phrase 'government of the people, by the people, and for the people'.[14] In contrast with freedom *of* religion, which might indicate a neutral attitude toward religious freedom, freedom *for* religion might treat religion as a uniquely positive good. While this was the prevailing view of religion historically in America, for example, it has come under scrutiny and even attack in recent years, eliciting book-length defenses of the idea that religion is and should be treated as special under the US Constitution.[15]

Richard Garnett argues that freedom *for* religion 'represents the American experiment in "healthy secularism" at its best; it is the one that people should be rooting for'.[16] Furthermore, he suggests that

> the government, under this approach, will not only refrain from discriminating against religion, it will take special care to accommodate and facilitate it – though always in

11 Garnett at 126.

12 See 'for', *Merriam-Webster Dictionary*, www.merriam-webster.com/dictionary/for (accessed 16 July 2017).

13 Here, we do not intend to refer to the French *laïcité*, a strict separation of church and state, but to the notion of 'positive secularism' endorsed by Garnett, consistent with the definition of 'freedom for religion' that is implied by the meaning of 'for'.

14 Abraham Lincoln, 'Gettysburg Address', 19 November 1863.

15 See, for example, Kathleen Brady, *The Distinctiveness of Religion in American Law: Rethinking Religion Clause Jurisprudence* (Cambridge University Press 2015).

16 Garnett at 127.

a way that respects the distinction between "church" and "state" and the liberty of individual conscience.[17]

The Conference sessions on freedom *for* religion focused on these themes of whether religion is special and deserves particular protection, especially in specific contexts such as the ministerial exception, religious freedom of corporations, freedom of religion in specialized settings such as religious buildings in Europe and the United States, and religious freedom in prisons.

## Freedom *from* religion

While freedom *for* religion treats religion positively, freedom *from* religion tends to take a neutral or even an opposite approach. *From* indicates physical separation or an act or condition of removal, abstention, exclusion, release, subtraction, or differentiation.[18] In other words, freedom *from* religion means the freedom to be separated from religion. In our oversimplified schemata, a diagram of freedom *from* religion might be represented by freedom escaping the grasp of religion, as represented in Figure 6, or by the familiar metaphor of a wall of separation between church and state, as in Figure 7.

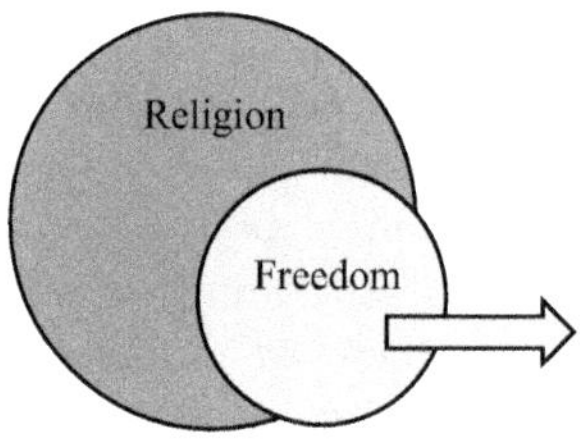


*Figure 6*

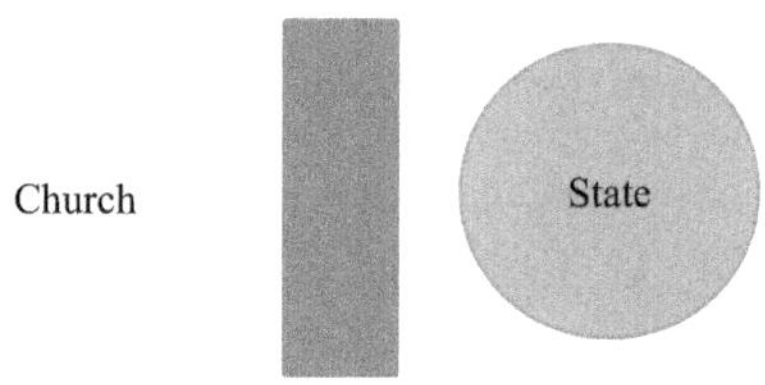


*Figure 7*

The wall metaphor, of course, is ambiguous. In Roger Williams' vision,[19] the 'garden of the church' was to be separated from the 'wilderness of the world', so the wall might be viewed as

17 Garnett at 127.

18 See 'from', *Merriam-Webster Dictionary*, www.merriam-webster.com/dictionary/from (accessed 17 July 2017).

19 See Roger Williams, 'Mr. Cotton's Letter Lately Printed, Examined and Answered', in *The Complete Writings of Roger Williams* vol. 1 (Russell & Russell 1963), 108 ('When they [the church] have opened a gap in the hedge or wall of separation between the garden of the church and the wilderness of the world, God hath ever broke down the wall itself, removed the Candlestick, etc., and made His Garden a wilderness as it is this day. And that therefore if He will ever please to restore His garden and Paradise again, it must of necessity be walled in peculiarly unto Himself from the world, and all that be saved out of the world are to be transplanted out of the wilderness of the World.'). See also Mark De Wolfe Howe, *The Garden and the Wilderness: Religion and Government in America Constitutional History* (University of Chicago Press 1967).

facilitating both freedom *of* and freedom *for* religion. Thomas Jefferson's use of the metaphor,[20] in contrast, seems more concerned with protecting the state from the corrupting influence of powerful religious establishments such as he observed while serving as US Ambassador to France, a picture that fits more closely with the idea of freedom *from* religion.[21]

Advocates of freedom *from* religion will accept religion as a social reality, but will view it at least sometimes as a danger to the common good, and may advocate that its practice be confined to private or personal life.[22] Concern for freedom from religion is most likely to arise in places where there is a powerful and dominant religion, which might take the form of an official established church or a favored religious group. Social science research suggests that in countries where there is a dominant religious group representing more than 70% of the population (with the exception of Catholic-majority countries), there are high or very high restrictions on religious freedom, both in the form of formal legal restraints and in the form of social hostilities.[23]

The goal of freedom *from* religion will likely be a robust form of secularism that seeks to minimize religion's influence in public life and on the policy-making process. The Establishment Clause of the First Amendment certainly represents a strain of freedom *from* religion in that it prohibits the government from making any law 'respecting an establishment of religion', and it requires the lawmaking process to be carefully neutral toward different religious groups and, more controversially, as between religion and non-religion. The Establishment Clause can be interpreted to mean two things: (1) no preferential treatment of religion and/or (2) no preferential treatment of a specific religion.

Although the freedom from religion formulation will incline toward negative views of religion, it will usually still protect the internal domain of conscience, what international law refers to as the *forum internum* or 'internal forum', while being quite permissive of limitations on religious practice or manifestations of religion that take place in the *forum externum* or 'external forum'. We should expect freedom from religion to articulate a sharp division between private and public life, and while religion will be protected, it will be relegated to the private sphere. In addition, the role of law and government will be to maintain and police the boundary between private religion and public life. Although certainly it is possible to imagine variations of freedom from religion as still accommodating religion in public life to a certain degree, we would not

20 See Thomas Jefferson, Letter to the Danbury Baptists, 1 January 1802 ('Believing with you that religion is a matter which lies solely between Man & his God, that he owes account to none other for his faith or his worship, that the legitimate powers of government reach actions only, & not opinions, I contemplate with sovereign reverence that act of the whole American people which declared that their legislature should "make no law respecting an establishment of religion, or prohibiting the free exercise thereof", thus building a wall of separation between Church & State. Adhering to this expression of the supreme will of the nation in behalf of the rights of conscience, I shall see with sincere satisfaction the progress of those sentiments which tend to restore to man all his natural rights, convinced he has no natural right in opposition to his social duties.').

21 Identifying Jefferson's wall with freedom *from* religion might itself be an oversimplification or even a mistake, however. At the University of Virginia, Jefferson did not object to the use of school buildings for religious worship as long as all denominations were treated equally. See Mark Beliles and David Barton, 'Thomas Jefferson and Religion at the University of Virginia', https://wallbuilders.com/thomas-jefferson-religion-university-virginia/#FN43 (accessed 31 July 2017) ('Jefferson not only sought to ensure that students would study about God, he also made provision for them to worship God. In the early planning stages of the University, he had stipulated "that a building… in the middle of the grounds may be called for in time in which may be rooms for religious worship"; later, he specifically ordered that in the University Rotunda, "one of its large elliptical rooms on its middle floor shall be used for… religious worship" and that "the students of the University will be free and expected to attend".').

22 Garnett at 127.

23 Brett G. Scharffs, 'Religious Majorities and Restrictions on Religion', (2016) 91 *Notre Dame Law Review* (4) 1419.

expect this relationship between freedom and religion to be supportive of, for example, some special religious claims for exceptions to general rules on the basis of conscientious objection.

The plenary session of the conference on freedom *from* religion focused on the meaning of the phrase, while breakout sessions focused on freedom of religion and non-discrimination, whether security requires freedom from religion, the challenge of migration to freedom of religion, and freedom of religion and secularism.

## Freedom *within* religion

*Within* means inside, and freedom *within* religion simply means the freedom inside the religion itself.[24] A schematic might depict a single circle with both freedom and religion being included, as depicted in Figure 8.

*Figure 8*

The basic idea here is what we often refer to as religious autonomy, or the liberty inside religious institutions, that churches have the right of self-determination and the right to self-management. Two particular issues related to the right of freedom within religion are governmental intervention in church affairs, especially conflicts that arise concerning church doctrine and employment decisions. From a non-discrimination viewpoint, firing someone on the basis of religion looks like discrimination on the basis of religion, but for a religious group, the ability to use religious criteria in personnel issues is a fundamental part of religious freedom.

Several points are important to emphasize. The first is that freedom within religion implies that religious institutions have the right of self-determination free from the influence or intervention of government. Self-determination for a religious institution includes selecting its religious leaders and determining its theology and doctrine. Nevertheless, in a number of countries religious groups are required to operate under the government's supervision.[25]

24 See 'within', *Merriam-Webster Dictionary*, www.merriam-webster.com/dictionary/within (accessed 17 July 2017).

25 A few more dramatic examples include the Israeli government's involvement in selecting the Chief Rabbinate as well as the Druze Religious Council and religious court judges (see Asher Maoz, 'Religious Human Rights in the State of Israel', in Johan D. van der Vyer and John Witte, Jr., eds, *Religious Human Rights in Global Perspectives: Legal Perspectives* (Martinus Nijhoff 1996), 349)), and strict government control of Muslim religious personnel and activities in many Muslim-majority nations. Tibetan Buddhists in China cannot freely choose their religious leaders. In the Eleventh Panchen Lama controversy in 1995, the Tibetan Buddhists followed the Tibetan traditional means to identify Gedhun Choekyi Nyima, a six-year-old boy, as the Eleventh Panchen Lama. However, the Chinese government denounced the decision and selected a different boy, Gyaincain Norbu, as the new Panchen Lama, and he has not been seen in public since that time. Chinese party control over religious groups besides Tibetan Buddhists is also commonplace. See Melvyn C. Goldstein, *The Snow Lion and the Dragon: China, Tibet, and the Dalai Lama* (University of California Press 1997).

Second, freedom within religion implies that religious institutions should have the freedom to determine how their organizations function and who conducts those functions. For example, religious institutions typically believe that certain religious functions must be conducted by people who are spiritually qualified. In a recent case, the US Supreme Court officially recognized a 'ministerial exception' from employment non-discrimination laws that provides religious groups a zone of autonomy within which they can hire and fire ministers based on religious criteria without being held liable for violating employment non-discrimination laws.[26] In a series of employment cases, the European Court of Human Rights has also recognized the importance of, while placing limits upon, church autonomy with respect to hiring and firing personnel.[27]

One major aspect of freedom within religion is the freedom of people or groups within a religion not to respect rulings of the religious establishment. One example of a lack of freedom within religion is the millet system, a feature of the Ottoman Empire that is still in effect in many countries, which applies religious jurisprudence to personal law based on an individual's religious heritage, whether or not they are themselves religious, and to subgroups within religious communities. For example, Jews in Israel are subject to the Chief Rabbinate and to the rabbinical courts even if they do not practice Judaism. And although the law does not define which strand of Judaism should govern, the composition of the Chief Rabbinate is Orthodox; Reform and Conservative conversion within Israel is not recognized, and rabbis of these strands of Judaism cannot perform legal marriages.[28]

***

This volume brings together a selection of timely papers from the Fourth ICLARS Conference analyzing the current controversies relating to freedom *for* religion and freedom *from* religion that have dominated headlines worldwide and brought to the attention of the public vital issues connected to religious freedom. To take only one example, as immigrants now pour into other nations from conflict-ridden regions of the world, religious tensions are at the heart of every stage of the process: from fleeing religious violence at home, to facing the politics of immigration in host countries that invoke religious identity and difference, to attempting to integrate into the host country while maintaining one's

26 *Hosanna-Tabor Evangelical Lutheran Church & School v. Equal Employment Opportunity Commission*, 565 U.S. 171 (2012).

27 See *Siebenhaar v. Germany*, App. No. 18136/02 (ECtHR, 3 February 2011); *Eweida and Others v. The United Kingdom*, App. Nos 48420/10, 59842/10, 51671/10, and 36516/10 (ECtHR, 15 January 2013), *Fernández Martínez v. Spain*, App. No. 56030/07 (ECtHR Grand Chamber, 12 June 2014), and *Travaš v. Croatia*, App. No. 75581/13 (ECtHR, 4 October 2016).

28 Asher Maoz, 'The Application of Religious Law in a Multi-Religion Nation State: The Israeli Model', in Rossella Bottoni, Rinaldo Cristofori, and Silvio Ferrari, eds, *Religious Rules, State Law, and Normative Pluralism: A Comparative Overview* (Springer 2016), 209 and Asher Maoz, 'Israel', in Gerhard Robbers, W. Cole Durham, Jr., and Donlu Thayer, eds, *Encyclopedia of Law and Religion* (Brill-Nijhoff 2016). Another interesting example is that of the Eastern (Greek) Orthodox Patriarchate of Jerusalem. In 2005 Patriarch Irenaios was accused of being pro-Israeli and of selling church land to Israelis. He was ousted by the Holy Synod of Jerusalem and replaced by Patriarch Theophilos. To assume his civil functions, the new Patriarch needed the recognition of the governments of both Israel and Jordan. While Jordan recognized Theophilos, Israel refused to do so, and Theophilos applied to the Israeli Supreme Court to force the government to recognize him. Finally Israel granted his petition; Irenaios petitioned the court but lost the case.

own religious identity – and, conversely, host countries' attempts to integrate migrants with different cultural backgrounds while preserving the country's own unique culture.

This collection of papers trains the lens closely on select issues and contexts to provide detailed snapshots of the ways in which freedom *for* and *from* religion are conceptualized, protected, neglected, and negotiated in diverse situations and locations at the present time.

**Part I: Freedom *for* and *from* religion** focuses on specific issues relating to freedom *for* and *from* religion. Richard Garnett highlights the diversity of perspectives among the ICLARS scholars, then emphasizes the importance of caring for the cultural infrastructures that are essential to freedom *for* religion as articulated in both the Second Vatican Council and US constitutional law. Thomas Farr's and Pamela Slotte's chapters focus on recent developments for the ministerial exception to employment laws, a classic freedom *for* religion issue, while Frances Raday and David Pollock advocate freedom *from* religion and grapple with the meaning and implications of that freedom.

**Part II: Emerging social contexts** focuses on emerging issues in a variety of social contexts, including immigration, health care, education, places of worship, and prisons. Pierre Noël urges attention to the religious aspects of the immigration process from start to finish, pointing to religious involvement as a key to the successful integration of immigrants. Sister Renée Mirkes addresses the tensions between access to health care and physicians' rights of conscience, arguing that it is not a zero-sum game; courts and society can and should find ways to protect both simultaneously. Clemens Steinhilber analyzes religious fundamentalism's clash with modernity, positing that higher education of faith leaders is one method of integrating and de-radicalizing potentially fundamentalist religious communities. Maria Luisa Lo Giacco recommends embracing construction of minority religious buildings as part of a natural process of social and architectural development over time. Sarah Hayes addresses issues involving religious precincts, defined as places in which both worship and community-oriented activities take place, and demonstrates how equality law paradoxically creates new inequalities in these spaces. Finally, Jeroen Temperman provides a comprehensive survey of European Court of Human Rights jurisprudence concerning religious freedom in prisons.

**Part III: Emerging regional contexts** shifts attention from social contexts to regional contexts. One of the remarkable features of ICLARS as a scholarly body is its broad international scope. Here we include chapters that focus on regions of Africa, Europe, Asia, and Latin America. Ahmed Salisu Garba educates us about laws regulating Islamic religious preaching in some Nigerian states and suggests a judicial standard of review for future cases involving such laws. Piotr Szymaniec's chapter describes and interprets the seemingly divergent rulings of the Polish Constitutional Tribunal on matters of religious freedom, including offense to religious feelings, conscientious objection to performing medical procedures, and ritual slaughter, seeking a unifying principle that may harmonize the decisions. Armin Langer evaluates religious neutrality laws such as those in Germany's Berlin State that forbid public displays of religion or religious garb in government schools, offices, etc. Langer argues that such laws, far from enforcing neutrality, actually reinforce the pervasive Christonormativity embedded in Europe.[29] Li-Ann Thio analyzes the legal

29 Langer's arguments in the European context echo Justice Brennan's dissent in the US Supreme Court case of *Goldman v. Weinberger*, 475 U.S. 503 (1986). Asher Maoz makes a related argument about the shifts over time in the Supreme Court's interpretation of the Establishment Clause, raising the idea that it did not advocate total divorce between government and religion, and in a way reflects religious – specifically Christian – demand to separate religion from state intervention. 'State and Religion in Israel', in Menachem Mor, ed., *International Perspectives on Church and State* (Creighton University Press 1993), 239.

protection afforded to religious proselyting in select Asian nations, including countries with Buddhist, Hindu, and Muslim majorities, as well as in multi-religious Singapore. Finally, Oscar Díaz Muñoz traces the development of religious freedom in the Peruvian Constitution from colonial times to the present day, with particular emphasis on the notion of 'healthy secularity', by which the state is neutral among the various religions, but values religion and maintains collaborative relations with religious groups.

One pattern that becomes clear from the juxtaposition of these contexts is that often, freedom *for* and freedom *from* religion manifest themselves as conceptually inseparable rights. A religious group's interest in hiring ministers based on religious criteria (*for*) is inseparably connected to an employee's interest in non-discriminatory employment (*from*). Any consideration of a physician's right to refuse to provide care that violates his or her conscience (*for*) requires consideration of a patient's ability to receive medical care without the interference of religion (*from*). Government attempts to curb extremism by controlling religious expression (*from*) rub up against individual and collective freedoms of religious expression (*for*). And state attempts at neutrality toward religion or among religions (*from*) may in practice benefit majority religions to the detriment of minority religions (*for*).

Indeed, the many issues surrounding religious freedom cannot be neatly separated into the categories *of*, *for*, *from*, and *within*. For the ICLARS gathering, the purpose of this division and the focus on these prepositions was to prompt innovative thought and debate, not to propose a permanent theoretical framework for religious freedom issues. For that reason, neither the Conference talks nor the resulting articles in this volume adhere strictly to that framework; rather, the focus is on the authors' unique insights in their specific contexts that arise from, but are in no case dependent upon, the chosen prepositions.

# Part I

# Freedom for and freedom from religion

# 1 Freedom 'for' religion

## (yet) another view of the Cathedral

*Richard W. Garnett*[1]

In the early 1890s, the French Impressionist Claude Monet composed a series of more than 30 paintings of the towering Gothic Rouen Cathedral in Normandy, France. The artist had rented rooms and set up a studio across the street, with the aim of capturing – over many months – how the fog, rain, dust, and especially – as always, for Monet – the light both affected and carried the appearance, and especially the colors, of the structure's windows, statues, portals, and arches. As one critic has noted, 'By focusing on the same subject through a whole series of paintings, Monet was able to concentrate on recording visual sensations themselves. The subjects did not change, but the visual sensations – due to changing conditions of light – changed constantly.'[2]

I imagine him waking up each morning and, as he throws open the window shutters, wondering, 'What will I see today?'

About 80 years later, in one of the most-cited American law review articles ever, 'One View of the Cathedral', Guido Calabresi and his coauthor Douglas Melamed borrowed the inspiration behind Monet's Cathedral Series in an effort to provide a unified theory of rights, or 'entitlements', and how they are protected by legal rules.[3] They noted, among other things, that some phenomena, like 'legal relationships', are 'too complex to be painted in any one picture'.[4]

The theme of the Fourth ICLARS Conference suggests that much the same thing can be said about 'religious freedom'. While Monet composed around 30 'views' of *his* Cathedral, the Conference participants presented about a hundred of *ours*. And while he took advantage of changing seasons, weather, air, and light to emphasize and illuminate the many features and facets of his subject, we used four prepositions – *of*, *for*, *from*, and *within* – to engage and unpack the different dimensions of ours. Our subject was the moral, human, and legal

1 Paul J. Schierl/Fort Howard Corporation Professor of Law and Concurrent Professor of Political Science, University of Notre Dame. I am grateful to Cole Durham, Brett Scharffs, Donlu Thayer, and Ashley Woolley for their advice, support, and patience.

2 Robert Pelfrey, *Art and Mass Media* (Kendall Hunt 1996), 166.

3 See Guido Calabresi and A. Douglas Melamed, 'Property Rules, Liability Rules, and Inalienability: One View of the Cathedral', (1972) 85 *Harvard Law Review* (6) 1089, fn 2. Many other legal scholars have borrowed from Monet, or from Calabresi and Melamed, for titles. See, e.g., Eyal Zamir, 'Contract Law and Theory: Three Views of the Cathedral', (2014) 81 *University of Chicago Law Review* (4) 2077; Paul Horwitz, 'Religion and American Politics: Three Views of the Cathedral', (2009) 39 *University of Memphis Law Review* (4) 973; Lucian Arye Bebchuk, 'Property Rights and Liability Rules: The Ex Ante View of the Cathedral', (2001) 100 *Michigan Law Review* (3) 601; and Richard A. Epstein, 'A Clear View of the Cathedral: The Dominance of Property Rules', (1997) 106 *Yale Law Journal* (2) 2091.

4 Calabresi and Melamed at 1128.

right to religious freedom. And these four everyday, unremarkable words provided – like four different windows or, perhaps, four different tables outside a café across the street from the Cathedral – different vantage points, from which we can see shades and details that, depending on the light, might be less visible to a colleague watching from another window or sitting at another table. By comparing notes on and sketches of what we saw, we created the possibility of a richer, more complete picture of the whole.

What's more, these four unassuming connection-words provided us with many more than just four views of religious freedom. Each preposition has many possible meanings, particularly among scholars of diverse linguistic and other backgrounds. We do not all share the same perspective that each preposition provides on religious freedom or that each suggests between 'religion' and 'freedom'. For example, the English preposition 'for' can be translated into Spanish as both *por* and *para*. In turn, each of those Spanish words encompasses a variety of different English prepositions and phrases.

Context also matters. Take 'freedom *from* religion' for example. As a lawyer working in the early twenty-first-century United States, I tend to associate 'freedom *from* religion' with the aggressive anti-religious stance of some activist groups[5] and with the view that one has a right to not be confronted or offended by, or even to encounter, unwelcome religious arguments, practices, and symbols in the public square.[6] However, someone from another jurisdiction or environment might well understand it as the freedom of religious dissenters and minorities not to be coerced or persecuted by the state in the name of official religious orthodoxy or the demands of political unity.[7] This person's view of the Cathedral from the 'freedom from' window is different than mine.

Similarly, there are lawyers and scholars for whom 'freedom *within* religion' has to do with the authority, and perhaps even the obligation, of the state to regulate the internal goings-on of more traditional religious institutions and communities, so as to bring their practices and rules more in line with those of the liberal state, and to guarantee the 'freedoms' of those who may be trapped in or oppressed by those communities.[8] For me, though, the 'freedom *within*' table at the café affords a direct view – and, in a way, the opposite view – of the crucial right of church autonomy,[9] of the ancient idea of the 'freedom

5 The Freedom From Religion Foundation comes to mind as an example of such a group. See https://ffrf.org/.

6 See Eric W. Treene, 'Religion, the Public Square, and the Presidency', (2001) 24 *Harvard Journal of Law and Public Policy* (2) 582 ('Religious symbols and garb are often unwelcome in the public square.'). See also *Freedom from Religion Foundation, Inc. v. Connellsville Area School District*, 127 F. Supp. 3d 283 (W.D. Pa. 2015) (noting that 'direct, unwelcome contact' with a religious symbol in public can supply the injury-in-fact required by the Constitution's 'standing' requirement).

7 Cf. *West Virginia State Board of Education v. Barnette*, 319 U.S. 624 (1943), 642 ('If there is any fixed star in our constitutional constellation, it is that no official, high or petty, can prescribe what shall be orthodox in politics, nationalism, religion or other matters of opinion or force citizens to confess by word or act their faith therein.'). See generally, e.g., Shima Baradaran-Robinson, Brett G. Scharffs, and Elizabeth Sewell, 'Religious Monopolies and the Commodification of Religion', (2005) 32 *Pepperdine Law Review* (4) 885.

8 See, e.g., Jessie Hill, 'Ties That Bind? The Questionable Consent Justification for Hosanna-Tabor', (2015) 109 *Northwestern University Law Review* (2) 563 and Madhavi Sunder, 'Piercing the Veil', (2003) 112 *Yale Law Journal* (6) 1399.

9 See, e.g., Paul Horwitz, 'Defending (Religious) Institutionalism', (2013) 99 *Virginia Law Review* (5) 1049; Michael P. Moreland, 'Institutional Conscience and Moral Dilemmas: Why "Freedom of Conscience" Is Bad for "Church Autonomy"', (2009) 7 *Georgetown Journal of Law and Public Policy* (1) 217; Gerard V. Bradley, 'Church Autonomy in the Constitutional Order: The End of Church and State?', (1989) 49 *Louisiana Law Review* (5) 1057; and Douglas Laycock, 'Towards a General Theory of the Religion Clauses: The Case of Church Labor Relations and the Right to Church Autonomy', (1981) 81 *Columbia Law Review* (7) 1373.

of the church',[10] and of the Supreme Court's clear, welcome embrace in the *Hosanna-Tabor* case of the ministerial exception.[11] In other words, to consider religious freedom through the lens of 'within' is to see the incompetence and the lack of jurisdiction on the part of the state when it comes to church polity and religious affairs.[12] From here, the light does not reveal, to me, a warrant for a progressive rescue mission or for an ambitious state-sponsored renovation scheme of traditional teachings and practices.

Turning to 'freedom *for* religion', one could ask at least three different questions, each revealing new perspectives on religious freedom: The first is, 'What is religious freedom *for*?' What are we trying to do when we enact and entrench protections for this 'first freedom'?[13] Is the *purpose* of our legal religious freedom regimes to, say, advance the very practical goal of promoting civil peace – perhaps even civic virtue?[14] Is it to 'reduce[] human suffering'[15] or 'relie[ve]... special mental torment'?[16] Is it to manage religious diversity, mute religious strife, or dampen religious division?[17] Or, as John Garvey contended 20 years ago in *What Are Freedoms For?*, is its purpose to promote real human flourishing and to make it easier to pursue what is, in fact, a 'good thing' for human persons, namely, the search for transcendence?[18]

A second possibility: maybe the benefit of the 'freedom *for*' perspective is that it reminds us that it is *freedom* we should aim to provide for religious persons, groups, and communities – not merely toleration, or a relatively safe haven at the margins, at the pale's edge, and in private. In other words, we might come to see that to pursue 'freedom *for* religion' is to refuse to settle for privatization, for *laïcité*, for conditional access to civic life or political participation, or for a 'naked public square'.[19]

10 See, e.g., Richard W. Garnett, '"The Freedom of the Church": (Towards) an Exposition, Translation, and Defense', (2013) 21 *Journal of Contemporary Legal Issues* (1) 33; Steven D. Smith, 'Freedom of Religion or Freedom of the Church?', in Austin Sarat, ed., *Legal Responses to Religious Practices in the United States* (Cambridge University Press 2012), 249; and Richard W. Garnett, 'The Freedom of the Church', (2007) 4 *Journal of Catholic Social Thought* (1) 59.

11 *Hosanna-Tabor Evangelical Lutheran Church & School v. EEOC*, 565 U.S. 171 (2012).

12 See, e.g., Steven D. Smith, 'Discourse in the Dusk: The Twilight of Religious Freedom', (2009) 122 *Harvard Law Review* (7) 1869; Carl H. Esbeck, 'Establishment Clause Limits on Governmental Interference with Religious Organizations', (1984) 41 *Washington & Lee Law Review* (2) 347; and Note, 'Religious Exemptions Under the Free Exercise Clause: A Model of Competing Authorities', (1980) 90 *Yale Law Journal* (2) 350.

13 Michael W. McConnell, 'Why Is Religious Liberty the "First Freedom"?', (2000) 21 *Cardozo Law Review* (4) 1243.

14 See, e.g., George Washington, 'Farewell Address', 19 September 1796, in Michael W. McConnell, John H. Garvey, and Thomas C. Berg, *Religion and the Constitution* (4th edn, Wolters Kluwer 2016), 18.

15 Douglas Laycock, 'Religious Liberty and the Culture Wars', (2014) *University of Illinois Law Review* (3) 839 at 842.

16 John H. Garvey, 'Free Exercise and the Values of Religious Liberty', (1986) 18 *Connecticut Law Review* 779 at 799.

17 Garvey, 'Free Exercise and the Values of Religious Liberty' at 799 ('[R]eligious liberty reduces social conflict[.]'). Cf. Richard W. Garnett, 'Religion, Division, and the First Amendment', (2004) 94 *Georgetown Law Journal* 1666.

18 John H. Garvey, *What Are Freedoms For?* (Harvard University Press 1996). See also John H. Garvey, 'An Anti-Liberal Argument for Religious Freedom', (1996) 7 *Journal of Contemporary Legal Issues* 275 at 283 ('The best reasons for protecting religious freedom rest on the assumption that religion is a good thing.').

19 See generally, e.g., Richard John Neuhaus, *The Naked Public Square* (William B. Eerdmans 1984). Cf. Douglas Laycock, 'Religious Liberty as Liberty', (1996) 7 *Journal of Contemporary Legal Issues* (2) 313.

Or, finally, the invitation to consider 'freedom *for* religion' as one dimension of the right to religious freedom is perhaps an invitation to ask, 'What are the necessary or helpful conditions that contribute to making religious freedom a healthy reality? What is needed 'for' religious freedom to work, even to thrive?'

***

The Declaration on Religious Freedom, *Dignitatis humanae* (the 'Declaration'), issued 50 years ago at the close of the Second Vatican Council, took what was seen by many at the time as a major step: the Declaration affirmed that 'the human person has a right to religious freedom' and that this right 'has its foundation in the very dignity of the human person as this dignity is known through the revealed word of God and by reason itself'.[20] That is, the Council fathers insisted, the 'right to religious freedom has its foundation not in the subjective disposition of the person, but in his very nature'.[21] Freedom of religion, then, is justified in terms of moral anthropology – in terms of an account of who we really are, and what we're really for – and not in terms of political convenience, benefit, or necessity. It is a pre-political possession, and not a state-granted concession.[22]

This idea that religious freedom is a fundamental human right, one that every person, precisely because he or she is a person, enjoys – like the idea that human rights are not mere conventions but are instead implications of the truth about what human persons really are – is a familiar, if not an entirely uncontroversial, one.[23] For many today, even if not for all, what Michael Perry has called 'the morality of human rights' *is* morality.[24] On this point, the Declaration could be read as simply echoing the 1948 Universal Declaration of Human Rights, which proclaimed, among other things, that '[a]ll human beings are born free and equal in dignity and rights' and that '[e]veryone has the right to freedom of thought, conscience and religion.'[25]

Some other passages in the Declaration, however, may be less familiar and are, perhaps, more controversial. At first, these passages might not seem to 'fit' well with North American traditions of 'church-state separation' and official 'neutrality'. In my view, however, they are intriguing and could help us understand what it means to say, or to embrace, 'freedom *for* religion' – not as authoritative religious texts but as arguments, offered to 'all people of good will', about the entailments of the human right to religious freedom.[26]

20 Pope Paul VI, *Dignitatis humanae* (7 December 1965), para. 3, www.vatican.va/archive/hist_councils/ii_vatican_council/documents/vat-ii_decl_19651207_dignitatis-humanae_en.html (accessed February 2018).

21 *Dignitatis humanae* at para. 3.

22 Cf. Richard W. Garnett, 'Christian Witness, Moral Anthropology, and the Death Penalty', (2003) 17 *Notre Dame Journal of Legal Ethics & Public Policy* (2) 541 at 543 (using 'moral anthropology' to mean 'an account of what it is about the human person that does the work in moral arguments about what we ought or ought not to do and about how we ought or ought not to be treated').

23 Cf., e.g., Andrew Brown, 'Do Human Rights Exist?', *The Guardian*, 20 October 2010 ('The essential point about human rights is that there is no evidence whatsoever that they actually exist.'), www.theguardian.com/commentisfree/andrewbrown/2010/oct/20/human-rights-exist (accessed February 2018).

24 Michael J. Perry, 'The Morality of Human Rights: A Nonreligious Ground?', (2005) 54 *Emory Law Journal* (5) 97.

25 Universal Declaration of Human Rights (1948).

26 Although the Declaration on Religious Freedom was, as a declaration and not a letter, addressed to particular groups or people, papal encyclicals are routinely addressed to, *inter alia*, 'all people of good will'. See, e.g., Pope Benedict XVI, *Caritas in veritate* (29 June 2009), http://w2.vatican.va/content/benedict-xvi/en/encyclicals/documents/hf_ben-xvi_enc_20090629_caritas-in-veritate.html (accessed February 2018).

Consider, first, these passages:

> Since the common welfare [or, the 'common good'] of society consists in the entirety of those conditions of social life under which men [and women] enjoy the possibility of achieving their own perfection in a certain fullness of measure, and also with some relative ease, it chiefly consists in the protection of the rights… of the human person.[27]
>
> The protection and promotion of the inviolable rights of [the person] ranks among the essential duties of government. Therefore, government is to assume the safeguard of the religious freedom of all its citizens, in an effective manner, by just laws and by other appropriate means. Government is also *to help create conditions favorable to the fostering of religious life*, in order that the people may be truly enabled to exercise their religious rights and to fulfill their religious duties.[28]
>
> Government therefore ought indeed to take account of the religious life of the citizenry *and show it favor*, since the function of government is to make provision for the [common good].[29]

Taken together, these passages make a claim that is an interesting and perhaps unsettling one, particularly for someone engaged in the law-and-religion enterprise in the United States: that it is the business and duty of government to promote and secure the 'common good' of society, and this task includes not only preventing violations of persons' rights, but also helping to create conditions in society that are 'favorable to the fostering of religious life'.[30] A government that is doing its job, in other words, is not blind or indifferent to the existence and the flourishing of the 'religious life of the citizenry'.[31] Instead, such a government will, again, 'take account of the religious life of the citizenry *and show it favor*'.[32]

Constitutional law in the United States can take on board pretty easily the Declaration's statements about the foundations of religious freedom in the objective dignity of the human person.[33] But what about this latter claim, about 'creating conditions' and 'showing favor'? Is this an atavistic or reactionary call for throne-and-altar arrangements, or an anachronistic embrace of the old notion of *cura religionis*, that is, that it is the business, and indeed the duty, of civil authorities to look after the true faith?[34]

I do not believe so.[35] Still, there does seem to be a disconnect, and perhaps some dissonance, between the Declaration's argument about 'creating conditions' and 'showing favor', and the position of the US Supreme Court regarding the First Amendment to the Constitution. James Madison – 'the father of the Constitution' – famously insisted

27 *Dignitatis humanae* at para. 6.

28 *Dignitatis humanae* at para. 6 (emphasis added).

29 *Dignitatis humanae* at para. 3 (emphasis added).

30 *Dignitatis humanae* at para. 6 (emphasis added).

31 *Dignitatis humanae* at para. 3.

32 *Dignitatis humanae* at para. 3 (emphasis added).

33 See generally, e.g., Maxine Goodman, 'Human Dignity in Supreme Court Constitutional Jurisprudence', (2006) 84 *Nebraska Law Review* (3) 740.

34 See F. Russell Hittinger, 'Political Pluralism and Religious Liberty: The Teaching of *Dignitatis Humanae*', in *Universal Rights in a World of Diversity – The Case of Religious Freedom*, Pontifical Academy of Social Sciences, Acta 17 (2012), 48 ('"Care of religion" is a term of art in Catholic history. It means that the sovereign bears a responsibility and a right to care for, to protect, and to promote a religion.').

35 As Hittinger notes, in the Declaration, the *cura religionis* has become *cura iuris ad libertatem religiosam*. Hittinger at 45 fn 17.

that religion is 'wholly exempt from [the] cognizance' of government and that government attempts to support it could only result in perversion and corruption.[36] The Court's so-called '*Lemon* test' requires that all state actions have a 'secular purpose', that public policies not 'advance' or 'support' religion, and that laws and regulations not excessively 'entangle' government and religion (or, we might add, the 'religious life of the citizenry').[37] To these requirements has been added an additional prohibition against 'endorsing' religion or making 'adherence to a religion relevant in any way to a person's standing in the political community'.[38] And the First Amendment has been said to demand 'wholesome', but still 'strict', neutrality.[39]

In his recent, important book, Andrew Koppelman defends 'American religious neutrality' as 'coherent and attractive'.[40] It turns out, though, that the coherence and attractiveness of the regime Koppelman defends depends substantially on its *not* being entirely 'neutral' toward religion. The government is not required, by Koppelman's understanding of neutrality, to be religion-blind or indifferent to religion, and it is certainly not required to be leery of or hostile to it. Instead, 'American religious neutrality' permits governments and officials to regard religion – at a high level of generality – as a good thing, and to act accordingly.[41] In his account, the state is to be 'silent about religious truth',[42] but this silence may be accompanied or complemented by policies – like religion-based accommodations from generally applicable laws, or even-handed tax exemptions – that both reflect and communicate the view that 'religion as such… [is] valuable.'[43]

Maybe one way to put the matter is to say that the religious liberty regime in the United States aims to be 'neutral' with respect to the truth of (most) religious claims precisely because it is *not* 'neutral' – it does not aim to be neutral, it should not be neutral – regarding the good of religious freedom. As I have written,

> [t]he line that separates "secular" purposes from others is not always clear but, in any event, it is clear that the protection and promotion of religious freedom "counts" as such a purpose.... It is not the case that the [Constitution] forbids or calls for skepticism regarding efforts by political authorities to improve the religious-freedom landscape or to make it possible for people and institutions to exercise religion.[44]

Religious freedom is not what results from the operationalization through law of hostility toward religion. It is not simply a mechanism for conflict-avoidance or division-dampening. It is, instead, a valuable and necessary feature of any attractive legal regime because it reflects, promotes, and helps to constitute human flourishing. So yes, the state should remain 'neutral' with respect to (most) religious questions – primarily because

36 James Madison, 'Memorial and Remonstrance against Religious Assessments', 20 June 1785, Papers 8:298–304, para. 1, http://press-pubs.uchicago.edu/founders/documents/amendI_religions43.html (accessed February 2018).

37 See *Lemon v. Kurtzman*, 403 U.S. 602 (1971).

38 *County of Allegheny v. ACLU*, 492 U.S. 573 (1989), 594.

39 *School District of Abington Township, Pennsylvania. v. Schempp*, 374 U.S. 203 (1962), 222 and 225.

40 Andrew Koppelman, *Defending American Religious Neutrality* (Harvard University Press 2013), 1.

41 Koppelman at 19. See also Garvey, 'An Anti-Liberal Argument for Religious Freedom' at 283.

42 Koppelman at 25.

43 Koppelman at 7.

44 Richard W. Garnett, 'Accommodation, Establishment, and Freedom of Religion', (2014) 67 *Vanderbilt Law Review En Banc* 39 (2014), 47.

the resolution of such questions, assuming for now that they can be identified, is outside the jurisdiction of civil authorities – but it may and should affirm enthusiastically that religious freedom is a good thing and that it should be not only protected but also nurtured by law and policy.

The Declaration on Religious Freedom similarly rejects the centuries-old notion that the 'secular' authority was charged by God with the direct care of true religion itself.[45] On this view, it was the obligation of the 'secular' authority not to keep itself somehow separate from religion but to 'defend the faith', even as it respected the appropriate (but usually contested) domain and independence of religious authorities.[46] This way of thinking has been abandoned in Western governments, including in those nations that retain what John Adams might have called 'mild and equitable' religious establishments.[47] It has also been abandoned by most religious communities and authorities.

As I understand the Declaration, the government's function with respect to religion is 'secular'. Its task is not to care directly for the true religion but is, instead, in John Courtney Murray's words, 'confined to a care of the free exercise of religion within society – a care therefore of the freedom of the Church and of the freedom of the person in religious affairs'.[48] This task is 'secular' because 'freedom in society... [is] a secular value – the sort of value that government can protect and foster by the instrument of law.'

Again, the Declaration affirms that governments should 'help create conditions favorable to the fostering of religious life' and 'take account of the religious life of the citizenry and show it favor'.[49] This stance is not 'neutral' toward religion. It is, however, consistent with an attractive and 'healthy secularity'.[50] As Pope Emeritus Benedict XVI put it,

> healthy secularity... involves the effective autonomy of earthly realities, not indeed from the moral order but from the ecclesiastical sphere.... [It] implies that the state does not consider religion merely as an individual sentiment that may be confined to the private sphere alone. On the contrary, since religion is organized in visible structures,... it should be recognized as a form of public community presence.[51]

How might all this work in practice? How might secular, political authorities care for 'the freedom of the person in religious affairs', 'create conditions favorable to the fostering of religious life', and 'take account of the religious life of the citizenry and show it favor' in a

45 John Courtney Murray, S.J., 'The Declaration on Religious Freedom', in *War, Poverty, Freedom: The Christian Response* (Paulist Press 1966), 3, www.library.georgetown.edu/woodstock/murray/1966c#1 (accessed February 2018).

46 Murray at 3.

47 John Adams, 'Diary, with Passages from an Autobiography', in Charles Francis Adams, ed., *The Works of John Adams* vol. 2, 293 at 399 (Little, Brown & Co. 1850–1856). See generally John Witte, Jr., '"A Most Mild and Equitable Establishment of Religion": John Adams and the Massachusetts Experiment', (1999) 41 *Journal of Church & State* (2) 213.

48 Murray at 3.

49 *Dignitatis humanae* at para. 6.

50 For more on what Pope Emeritus Benedict XVI and others have called 'healthy' or 'positive' secularity, see, e.g., Zachary R. Calo, 'Christianity, Islam, and Secular Law', (2013) 39 *Ohio Northern University Law Review* (3) 879 and Richard W. Garnett, 'Religious Freedom, Church Autonomy, and Constitutionalism', (2009) 57 *Drake Law Review* (4) 901.

51 Pope Benedict XVI, 'Address to the Participants in the 56th National Study Congress Organized by the Union of Italian Catholic Jurists', 9 December 2006, www.ewtn.com/library/PAPALDOC/b16layjurists.htm (accessed February 2018).

way that is broadly consistent both with American First Amendment doctrine and democratic constitutionalism more generally?[52]

Part of the answer is easy: governments 'foster[]... religious life'[53] by not obstructing or unduly limiting it, and – in the United States, anyway – by enforcing (legislatively, judicially, and in the course of administration and regulation) the Constitution's no-establishment rule and anti-discrimination norm.[54] Another part of the answer is, admittedly, more controversial today: governments should broadly and generously accommodate religiously motivated activity, through exemptions and otherwise, even when it does not have to, consistent with the requirements of justice and public order and with the rights of others. As the Supreme Court put it more than 60 years ago, it 'follows the best of our traditions' to 'respect the religious nature of our people and accommodate[] the public service to their spiritual needs'.[55]

The Constitution of the United States and the American constitutional tradition allow and invite, even when they do not require, governments and officials to 'single out' religion for 'special constitutional protection'.[56] Again, American governments are not required to settle for formal or religion-blind neutrality. They can and should take positive steps to ensure meaningful 'freedom *for* religion'. They may do so even when these steps come at some cost. Just as we

> all have a stake in efficient and transparent markets, functioning courts, and clean air[,]... we all benefit, whatever our religious tradition and whether or not we embrace or practice a religious faith at all, from practices and commitments – like the accommodation of religion – that place limits on the state, on its demands, and on its authority.[57]

What other 'conditions' are favorable to religious freedom, and in what other ways (if any) may governments 'show... favor' to 'the religious life of the citizenry'?[58] Once again, the question is not whether governments like ours are charged with the *cura religionis* – the identification and care of the true religion. They are not. But they could well be charged with the care of *religious freedom*.[59] How might they fulfill this charge?

I have proposed elsewhere that governments should build, maintain, and nurture the 'infrastructure' of religious freedom.[60] Jack Balkin has argued that the freedom of speech requires 'more than mere absence of government censorship or prohibition to thrive; [it] also requires institutions, practices and technological structures that foster and promote [it]'.[61] That is to say, certain institutions – newspapers, political parties, interest groups,

52 *Dignitatis humanae* at para. 6.
53 *Dignitatis humanae* at para. 6.
54 See generally Richard W. Garnett, 'Religious Freedom and the Nondiscrimination Norm', in Sarat, ed. at 194.
55 *Zorach v. Clausen*, 343 U.S. 306 (1952), 313.
56 Michael W. McConnell, 'The Problem of Singling Out Religion', (2000) 50 *DePaul Law Review* (1) 1 at 3.
57 Garnett, 'Accommodation, Establishment, and Freedom of Religion' at 49.
58 *Dignitatis humanae* at para. 3.
59 See Hittinger.
60 See Richard W. Garnett, 'Religious Accommodations and – and Among – Civil Rights: Separation, Toleration, and Accommodation', (2015) 88 *Southern California Law Review* (2) 493 and Richard W. Garnett, 'Do Churches Matter? Towards an Institutional Understanding of the Religion Clauses', (2008) 53 *Villanova Law Review* (2) 273.
61 Jack M. Balkin, 'The Infrastructure of Religious Freedom', *Balkinization*, 5 May 2007, https://balkin.blogspot.com/2007/05/infrastructure-of-religious-freedom.html (accessed February 2018).

libraries, universities, and so on – play an important structural, or infrastructural, role in clearing out and protecting the civil-society space within which the freedom of speech can be well exercised.[62] The same thing can be said about religious freedom. Just as the '[f]reedom of speech… depends on an infrastructure of free expression,'[63] the freedom of religion depends on an infrastructure of religious freedom. Its infrastructure consists of obvious components, like open and functioning courts, legal accommodations, thriving communications networks, etc., but also a web of independent, thriving, distinctive, self-governing (in their appropriate spheres) institutions. In this light, the Supreme Court's *Hosanna-Tabor* decision, which vindicated the right of religious groups, communities, and associations to choose their own ministers, leaders, and teachings, can be seen as a welcome judicial reinforcement of religious freedom's infrastructure and of the conditions that are useful, or even necessary, for its health. As I have said elsewhere, '[t]he freedom of religion is not only lived and experienced through institutions, it is also protected, nourished, and facilitated by them.'[64] The political community can protect religious freedom appropriately only if there are at work in society free associations and authorities that are not merely political.

In a recent essay, Gerard Bradley reminds us that 'religious freedom is… an achievement of a sound political and juridical culture.'[65] To rephrase, 'religious liberty is a cultural achievement'. And, he suggests, it is one that 'history and current events show to be uncommon, and fragile'. Without the 'right cultural stuff', he warns, 'a scheme overridingly committed to each one's free quest for religious truth is likely to derail into an enabler of individual self-invention, individuality for its own sake, subjectivity, or identity.' Far from providing a strong and necessary infrastructure for religious freedom, this sort of subjectivity 'corrodes the undercarriage of religious liberty[.]'

The Declaration speaks of the 'conditions' in which religious freedom thrives,[66] but it has little to say about what those conditions are, beyond a legal regime that protects the rights of persons, families, and communities. However, other documents of the Second Vatican Council – including *Gaudium et spes*, promulgated the same day as *Dignitatis humanae* – brimmed with references to the importance of culture.[67] What would a well-functioning cultural infrastructure for religious freedom, one that complemented institutions, official practices, and the legal regime, look like?

A cultural infrastructure conducive to religious freedom would include citizens who are informed, and formed to appreciate, not only that religious freedom is a fundamental human right but also that respecting that right sometimes – not always, but sometimes – requires creating exemptions for religiously motivated conduct from well-intended and otherwise valid laws and regulations. This appreciation, and a willingness to act in accord with it, cannot be taken for granted and should not be assumed to arise and thrive unaided or unencouraged. 'Liberty', as Learned Hand reminded us, 'lies in the hearts of men and

62 See generally Paul Horwitz, *First Amendment Institutions* (Harvard University Press 2013).

63 Jack M. Balkin, 'Two Ideas for Access to Knowledge: The Infrastructure of Free Expression and Margins of Appreciation', *Balkinization*, 30 April 2007, https://balkin.blogspot.com/2007/04/two-ideas-for-access-to-knowledge.html (accessed February 2018).

64 Garnett, 'The Freedom of the Church' at 41.

65 Gerard Bradley, 'Religious Liberty and the Common Good', *Public Discourse*, 9 May 2017 (quoting Pope Emeritus Benedict XVI, 'Religious Freedom, the Path to Peace' (1 January 2011)), www.thepublicdiscourse.com/2017/05/19244/ (accessed February 2018).

66 See *Dignitatis humanae* at para. 6.

67 See generally, e.g., *Gaudium et spes* (7 December 1965), www.vatican.va/archive/hist_councils/ii_vatican_council/documents/vat-ii_const_19651207_gaudium-et-spes_en.html (accessed February 2018).

women; when it dies there, no law, no court can save it.'[68] A culture that has uncritically absorbed, and that too enthusiastically promotes, the view that respect for religious freedom consists only of those concessions that cause no inconvenience, and is not, instead, what is owed by a political community to human dignity, is probably not one in which the conditions are favorable for religious life.

Furthermore, a culture favorable for religious life should be proactive, not merely reactive. It should not settle for identifying and lifting the burdens on religion that, given religious diversity, even well-meaning laws will inevitably impose. It should, instead, resolve to proactively create and care for 'conditions for the fostering of religious life', the conditions within which 'people may be truly enabled to exercise their religious rights and to fulfill their religious duties.'[69] Such a resolution need not involve abandoning the well-established rule in American constitutional law that civil governments' legislation should have a 'secular purpose'[70]; it simply recognizes that non-coercive support for the conditions – or infrastructure – that make it possible for people to pursue a human good and enjoy a human right has an appropriately 'secular' purpose.

***

Does the 'sound political and juridical culture'[71] that is required for religious freedom – that is part of its vital infrastructure – exist in the United States today? It is difficult to say. Increasingly, it seems more that our 'culture wars' are undermining and eroding support for religious freedom than it does that our culture is demonstrating and buttressing our commitment to it.[72] As Paul Horwitz put it, describing and evaluating what he calls the '*Hobby Lobby* Moment', 'American religious liberty is in a state of flux and uncertainty'; what's more, he suggests, '[t]he problem is social and political, not judicial.'[73]

The Cathedral of Notre Dame at Rouen has endured lightning, fire, hurricanes, bombs, and revolutionaries. Its pointed arches and flying buttresses helped preserve it so that it could, among other things, invite Monet's experiments with light, time, and perspective. The view from the 'freedom *for* religion' window suggests that we attend carefully to religious freedom's various and vital supports.

68 Learned Hand, *The Spirit of Liberty* (Knopf 1952), 144.
69 *Dignitatis humanae* at para. 6.
70 See generally Andrew Koppelman, 'Secular Purpose', (2002) 88 *Virginia Law Review* (1) 87.
71 Bradley.
72 See generally, e.g., Laycock.
73 Paul Horwitz, 'The *Hobby Lobby* Moment', (2014) 128 *Harvard Law Review* (1) 154. Horwitz observes, with respect to the 'legal and political culture', that '[t]he ground has shifted from underneath [religious-accommodations laws].' Horwitz, 'The *Hobby Lobby* Moment' at 172.

# 2 The ministerial exception

## An inquiry into the status of religious freedom in the United States and abroad

*Thomas F. Farr*

> We hold these truths to be self-evident: that all men are created equal; that they are endowed by their Creator with certain unalienable rights; that among these are life, liberty and the pursuit of happiness.
>
> US Declaration of Independence

> Congress shall make no law respecting an establishment of religion, or prohibiting the free exercise thereof.
>
> First Amendment to the US Constitution

***

In 2005, the government of the United States sued Hosanna-Tabor, a Lutheran church school, for the prejudicial firing of a teacher who was also a minister. After several years of battle in the lower courts, the US Supreme Court in 2012 unanimously rejected the government's position by affirming a legal doctrine called the 'ministerial exception'. That doctrine forbids the state from interfering in the relationship between religious institutions and their ministers, even when certain other important claims, such as unjust employment discrimination, are at stake.[1]

In *Hosanna-Tabor*, the Court ruled that the ministerial exception was required by both religion clauses of the First Amendment – the Free Exercise and Non-Establishment Clauses, respectively. As such, it appears to be a victory for proponents of religious freedom.

But is that, in fact, the case?

In this essay, I reflect on the *Hosanna-Tabor* ruling and its implications for religious freedom in light of developments in contemporary American culture and law. I hypothesize that *Hosanna-Tabor*, far from indicating a deepening of religious freedom, mirrors a broader movement by progressives on the Court to restrict that right. Following influential segments of American public opinion, the progressive justices may be drawing a more restrictive boundary between private belief and public expressions of religion in public life – especially in politics. Whether, and how, such a boundary should be drawn has been contested for many decades in American law and culture. *Hosanna-Tabor* may reflect a repositioning and strengthening of what some have long contended is a necessary 'wall of separation' between religion and political life.[2]

1 *Hosanna-Tabor Evangelical Lutheran Church & School v. Equal Employment Opportunity Commission*, 565 U.S. ___ (2012).

2 Historian Daniel Dreisbach observes, 'Occasionally a metaphor is thought to encapsulate so thoroughly an idea or concept that it passes into the vocabulary as the standard expression of that idea. Such is the case with the graphic phrase "wall of separation between Church and State", which in the twentieth century has

I will examine these issues in three parts: first, an overview of the key principles underlying what I take to be the traditional American understanding of religious freedom; second, an interpretation of what may be afoot with the ministerial exception as defended by the Court in *Hosanna-Tabor*; and third, a brief assessment of the implications of any new boundary, drawn by the Court or otherwise, for US and Western foreign policy in the lands of Islam.

## The American understanding

Two overarching principles may fairly be said to characterize the traditional American understanding of the meaning and the value of religious freedom. First, ***religion*** has distinct, intrinsic, and universal value for free individuals and free societies, including both its interior spiritual value for individuals, and its public contributions to limited government, civic virtue, and the determination by free and equal citizens of the common good and the extent to which the common good should be reflected in law and public policy.[3]

Second, the value of religion for individuals, groups, and society at large warrants broad and vigorous protections for religious freedom. Those protections should provide, for those who object on grounds of religious conscience, exemptions from otherwise neutral laws of general applicability.[4] More importantly, however, protection should also be provided to the free exercise of religion by individuals and groups in the public life of the nation, especially those who wish to engage in the ***political*** process with religious or religiously informed moral arguments. Properly limited and properly encouraged, public manifestations of religion in society and politics can generate distinct benefits for everyone.[5]

### *The importance of religion*

From their earliest settlements in the seventeenth century to the founding of the United States in the late eighteenth, Americans were on balance a religious people. It is true that, despite their mainly Protestant religious orientation, the way settlers and colonials

---

profoundly influenced discourse and policy on church-state relations.' Quoted in Philip Hamburger, *Separation of Church and State* (Harvard University Press 2002), 2 fn 2.

3 On the importance of religion in the American founding era, see generally James H. Hutson, *Religion and the Founding of the American Republic* (Library of Congress 1998); Michael Novak, *On Two Wings: Humble Faith and Common Sense at the American Founding* (Encounter Books 2002); Ellis Sandoz, ed., *Political Sermons of the American Founding Era* (2nd edn, Liberty Fund 1998); Mark A. Noll, *America's God: From Jonathan Edwards to Abraham Lincoln* (Oxford University Press 2002); Thomas S. Kidd, *God of Liberty: A Religious History of the American Revolution* (Basic Books 2010); and Daniel L. Dreisbach, *Reading the Bible with the Founding Fathers* (Oxford University Press 2017). See also Alexis De Tocqueville, *Democracy in America*, trans. Gerald Bevan (Penguin Books 2003), 336–352; Matthew Franck, 'Christianity and Freedom in the American Founding', in Timothy Samuel Shah and Allen D. Hertzke, eds, *Christianity and Freedom: Historical Perspectives* vol. 1 (Cambridge University Press 2016), 264–289; Paul Johnson, *A History of the American People* (HarperCollins 1997), 204–211; Walter A. McDougall, *Freedom Just Around the Corner: A New American History* (HarperCollins 2004), 507–512; and Andrew Preston, *Sword of the Spirit, Shield of Faith: Religion in American War and Diplomacy* (Alfred A. Knopf 2012), 77–121.

4 The locus of the dispute over exemptions is Justice Scalia's opinion for the majority in *Employment Division, Department of Human Resources of Oregon v. Smith*, 494 U.S. 872 (1990).

5 See Thomas Farr, 'Is Religious Freedom Necessary for Other Freedoms to Flourish?' in *Big Questions Online*, The John Templeton Foundation, 7 August 2012, www.bigquestionsonline.com/2012/08/07/religious-freedom-necessary-other-freedoms-flourish/ (accessed 22 June 2017).

practiced Christianity varied widely and at times even yielded intra-religious persecution.[6] Religion-state arrangements were diverse and included Anglican establishments in the south, Congregational establishments in the north, and colonies that rejected establishments, such as Pennsylvania and Rhode Island.[7]

However, incidents of persecution and differences over religion-state arrangements did not stem from disagreements over the intrinsic value of religion. To the contrary, all the colonies privileged some version of Protestant Christianity in order to advance and protect the public good. Whether they had established sects or not, they were as one in believing that religion was a primary source of public morality and civic virtue, as well as other social goods, and required special protection.[8]

During and after the Revolutionary War, Americans settled on a constitutional experiment grounded in popular sovereignty and limited government. Citizens and states, suspicious of concentrations of power, granted to the national government a limited number of enumerated powers, checked and balanced by the separated branches, by the residual powers of the states, and by the Bill of Rights. As Chief Justice John Roberts succinctly puts it, the government of the United States 'possesses only limited powers; the states and the people retain the remainder.'[9]

The new American constitutional experiment relied on religion in numerous ways. Here are four: first, the founding generation venerated the role of the religious conscience in human nature and human prospering. Most agreed with Thomas Jefferson and James Madison in defining religion as 'the duty which we owe to our Creator and the manner of discharging it'.[10] They understood conscience as a primary means by which people discerned and carried out their duty to God. Conscience helps discern truths about God himself, and about God's will for the individual and for the common good. It orients individuals toward the natural moral goods that are to be pursued and against evils that are to be avoided. The duty of following one's religious conscience is so important that, as Madison put it, the duty is 'precedent, both in order of time and degree of obligation to the claims of Civil Society'.[11]

Second, the core American democratic principle of limited government and the need for checks and balances are supported by a fundamental Christian concept: the inherent sinfulness of man, which is the root cause of the corruptions endemic to concentrations of power. Even the saints cannot be trusted with unchecked political or religious power.[12] Moreover, both the theory and practice of limited government are supported by the commitment of religious citizens to an authority beyond the state and by the important role of religious communities in the voluntary institutions of civil society. The latter role is strengthened both by the persistence characteristic of those with spiritual motives and by the provision of services that, in

6 Kevin S. Hasson, *The Right to Be Wrong: Ending the Culture War over Religion in America* (Encounter Books 2005), 39–44.

7 Kidd at 40–55 and Noll at 114–137.

8 Steven D. Smith, *The Rise and Decline of American Religious Freedom* (Harvard University Press 2014), 78–79.

9 Richard W. Garnett and John M. Robinson, '*Hosanna-Tabor*, Religious Freedom, and the Constitutional Structure', 2011–2012 *CATO Supreme Court Review* 307.

10 James Madison, 'Memorial and Remonstrance against Religious Assessments', in Robert A. Rutland and William M.E. Rachal, eds, *The Papers of James Madison* vol. 8 (University of Chicago Press, 1973), 295.

11 Madison at 295.

12 Kidd at 76–77 and Dreisbach at 46 and fn 119. Dreisbach notes the many places in the Federalist Papers where Christian concepts of man's fallen nature appear to be reflected in discussions of why state powers must be limited.

their absence, government and secular agencies would be required to provide – for example, early education, colleges and universities, hospitals, care of the poor, elderly, and orphans, services for immigrants, and relief to victims of natural disasters.[13]

Third, most Americans believed that the new republic would fail without a virtuous citizenry, and that a central source of virtue was religion. They came to accept that religion's contribution to the common good in law and public policy was not through establishments and religious monopolies but through the free and peaceful contention of citizens' moral arguments derived primarily from religion. In this sense, the ban on a religious establishment was similar to the constitutional guarantee of a free press.[14] Just as government should not control the press, whose job is to help mold public opinion, so too it should not control religion, whose task is, *inter alia*, to mold public morality and to influence citizens' views of public policy. This view was perhaps best expressed by the first president, George Washington, in his 1796 farewell address: 'Of all the dispositions and habits which lead to political prosperity', he told the new nation, 'religion and morality are indispensable supports.'[15]

The reason for the First Amendment's ban on an established religion was therefore to protect religion and its free exercise from the state, not the reverse. Here the founding generation's understanding of the value of religion comports with modern democratic theory, in which democracy is understood to be a system that regulates competition among citizens and groups over differing conceptions of the common good.[16] At the Founding, religion was understood as the most significant repository of conceptions of the good and therefore critical to the health of the republic. Most believed that religious conceptions of the good were derived from objective and universal truths about mankind (including human equality), rather than from human invention.

Fourth, a major contribution of religion to the American constitutional settlement came from Thomas Jefferson's radical religious truth claim, in the Declaration of Independence, that 'all men are created equal, that they are endowed by their Creator with certain unalienable rights'. Thus did the most heterodox and religiously skeptical of the Founders lay the religious predicate for American democracy itself. Drawing on scriptural sources he at times professed to disdain, in particular the belief that all human beings are created in the image and likeness of God, that God loves each, and that *for this reason* Christians are called to love others, Jefferson's truth claim established a secure grounding for human equality in the new Republic.[17]

Over the course of the pre-revolutionary period, the ideas of protecting the 'free exercise of religion' and rejecting establishments of religion began slowly to emerge as aspirational norms, especially in those colonies that had already rejected formal establishments.[18] By the late eighteenth century, the growth and increased influence of

13 See generally Corwin Smidt, ed., *Religion as Social Capital: Producing the Common Good* (Baylor University Press 2003) and Robert D. Putnam, *Bowling Alone: The Collapse and Revival of American Community* (Simon and Schuster 2000), 65–79.

14 Michael W. McConnell, 'Religion and Its Relation to Limited Government', (2010) 33 *Harvard Journal of Law & Public Policy* (3) 947.

15 George Washington, 'Farewell Address', 19 September 1796, www.presidency.ucsb.edu/ws/?pid=65539.

16 Alfred Stepan, 'Religion, Democracy, and the "Twin Tolerations"', (2000) 11 *Journal of Democracy* (4) 37.

17 Kidd at 142. Of course, the grounding of equality in the Declaration was challenged, both by public figures and by the reality of slavery. See Kidd at 131–137 and 143–146.

18 Michael W. McConnell, 'The Origins and Historical Understanding of Free Exercise of Religion', (1990) 103 *Harvard Law Review* (7) 1436–1437.

dissenting Evangelical sects combined with the American revolution against England and elements of the Enlightenment[19] to yield something new in Western history – indeed, in the history of the world: the idea that religion is a necessary element in the achievement of liberal democracy, ordered liberty, and equality, and that the freedom to practice religion must therefore be protected by the state and against the intrusions of the state.

In sum, colonial belief in the supreme importance of religion, the individual conscience in pursuing the duty of religion, and the role of both in supporting limited government and producing laws and public policies to elevate the common good led to the ban on an establishment of religion. Although the Establishment Clause applied only to the national government, Southern states cast aside their own establishments during the period of the Revolution and founding, and gradually the Northern establishments disappeared as well. As they abandoned religious establishments, however, Americans were not sanctioning the separation of religion from politics. By ending their Erastian settlements, i.e. state control of doctrine and funding and government meddling in religious communities, they were endeavoring to protect religion itself. In so doing, they were laying the groundwork for supporting the idea of the 'free exercise of religion'.

### *The importance of free exercise*

At least four key aspects of religious freedom in the American Constitution highlight both the significance of religion and the benefits that were associated with protecting its free exercise.

First, in the First Amendment the framers employed, and the states ratified, protection for the 'free exercise of religion', not for the 'rights of conscience'. Both phrases appeared in early drafts, which makes it clear that both were considered. A good deal of evidence shows that colonial Americans understood religious freedom as including conduct as well as belief. According to First Amendment scholar and jurist Michael McConnell, the framers' choice of 'free exercise' over 'rights of conscience' shows that they intended to grant Constitutional protection for public religious conduct, as well as for the conscientious beliefs that give rise to religious conduct.[20]

Second, the free exercise provision was intended to protect the religious conscience and religion-related conduct, not secular conscience and conduct. The framers of course knew that all people, including the non-religious, had consciences and could be motivated in important decisions by legitimate, non-religious reasons. They also knew that secular beliefs and expressions were protected by the First Amendment's guarantee of free speech. But in guaranteeing the 'free exercise of religion', the framers were attempting to provide special protection for both the interior religious conscience and religiously inspired action in the public sphere. Until recently, the Supreme Court has accepted this view of what is protected under the Free Exercise Clause.[21] Religion, in short, has long been understood in American law and culture as something identifiable, distinct from other motives for action, and deserving of special protection.

19 Gertrude Himmelfarb, *The Roads to Modernity: The British, French, and American Enlightenments* (Knopf 2004), 212–217.

20 McConnell, 'Origins and Historical Understanding' at 1488–1500.

21 1491.

Third, the guarantee of free exercise was extended to religious communities as well as individuals. Professor McConnell observes,

> [An] important difference between the terms 'conscience' and 'religion' is that 'conscience' emphasizes individual judgment, while 'religion' also encompasses the corporate or institutional aspects of religious belief.... [The use of the phrase] 'free exercise of religion' suggests that government may not interfere with the activities of religious bodies, even when the interference has no direct relation to a claim of conscience.[22]

Fourth, early colonists either posited or experienced a positive relationship between religious freedom and economic prosperity. For example, immigration to Pennsylvania was among the highest in the colonies, a circumstance attributed in significant part to the religious toleration established there by William Penn, and with immigration came prosperity.[23] Penn himself justified greater religious freedom on economic grounds. He appealed to the English king to grant greater religious freedom with the argument that it would bring greater prosperity.[24]

This understanding of the meaning and value of free exercise and non-establishment remained dominant in American culture until well into the nineteenth century, and in the courts until the mid-twentieth century. A standard modern counter-narrative focuses on President Thomas Jefferson's 1802 letter to the Danbury Baptists, in which he endorsed a 'wall of separation between church and state'.[25] According to this narrative, the Founders intended the Establishment Clause to codify a wall of separation that would protect the state from religion and keep religion out of political life.[26] That interpretation has been thoroughly dissected and disproven by Philip Hamburger's magisterial study, *Separation of Church and State*. Hamburger demonstrates that the idea of separating religion from political life first emerged with any force during the nineteenth century among Protestant groups reacting to the surge of Catholic immigrants from Ireland and elsewhere in Europe.[27] According to Hamburger, separation of religion from public life was an idea completely rejected by the Founders.

Ironically, Protestant support for separation, while it originated in the desire to restrict Catholics, was joined by late nineteenth-century anti-Christian secularists. These groups, recognizing that separation was not present in the Constitution, tried and failed to secure a separationist constitutional amendment.[28] Although the Supreme Court referred to Jefferson's wall in its 1879 *Reynolds* decision,[29] separation reached the status of judicial doctrine only with the 1947 *Everson* decision. *Everson* led to rulings barring religion from some

22 1490.

23 1430.

24 Anthony Gill and Timothy Samuel Shah, 'Religious Freedom, Democratization, and Economic Development: A Survey of the Causal Pathways Linking Religious Freedom to Economic Freedom and Prosperity and Political Freedom and Democracy', presented at the Annual Meeting of the Association for the Study of Religion, Economics, and Culture, Washington, DC, 13 April 2013, www.asrec.org/wp-content/uploads/2015/10/Gill-Shah-Religious-freedom-democratization-and-economic-development.pdf.

25 Daniel Dreisbach, *Thomas Jefferson and the Wall of Separation between Church and State* (New York University Press 2002), 1–8.

26 Dreisbach at 1–8.

27 Hamburger at 191–284.

28 296–302.

29 *Reynolds v. United States*, 98 U.S. 145 (1879).

public spaces and to court (and academic) theories requiring 'secular reasons' for laws.[30] But inconsistencies and disagreements in the courts and within American society have kept the boundaries of religious free exercise relatively undefined and still contested, at least until now.

## Hosanna-Tabor

To summarize thus far, two principles buttress the American understanding of religious freedom: that religion itself is necessary for the success of the American experiment in ordered liberty, and that the free exercise of religion should be privileged in the political processes of American life, including a ban on religious establishment as a means of protecting free exercise. That understanding, never without challenge and never perfectly implemented, remained reasonably clear in law, and to some extent in culture, into the mid-twentieth century.

In recent years, however, American courts, including the Supreme Court, appear to be moving to separate religion from public life – especially from the realm of politics where, I have argued, it was firmly placed by the founding generation. In so doing, the courts appear to be following powerful elements in American society whose interests would be served by muting or removing traditional religious ideas and actors from political discourse. While there are long-term reasons for this development, including secularization, the more immediate rationale is recent shifts in public opinion toward normalizing sexual freedom and same-sex marriage.

I contend that these shifts, whatever merit they may have as public policy, have had a distinctly negative impact on religious freedom, with effects that may be intended by some, but not all, Americans. As we shall see, their primary effect is to undermine the core meaning of the First Amendment – that religious ideas and actors in public life are necessary for the health of American democracy. Such actors have, at a minimum, a right to contend in political life for their religiously informed conceptions of the common good on an equal basis with other ideas and actors and, if they are persuasive, to prevail. The First Amendment's purpose is undermined, and American democracy harmed, if these arguments, and their equal opportunity to form the basis for law and public policy, are arbitrarily banned from public life.

Four recent examples will illustrate the direction of the judiciary. First, in 2008 a California referendum known as Proposition 8 defined marriage in California law as the union of one man and one woman. In 2010, a federal judge overruled the referendum in part because those who voted for traditional marriage had done so on religious and moral grounds. According to this ruling, religious and moral grounds cannot meet the rationality standards set by the modern court.[31] The appeals court concurred in overturning the referendum.[32] In 2013 the Supreme Court ruled that the sponsors of the referendum lacked standing to defend it, and left lower court rulings in place.[33]

Second, in a series of opinions over the past two decades the Supreme Court has developed a pattern of decisions that suggests a new constitutional doctrine centered on unlawful 'animus'. Those who oppose contemporary judicial rulings on sexual rights and same-sex marriage, or who support laws and public policies that reflect traditional sexual morality and civic virtue, are said to be motivated by 'animus' against homosexuals or other sexual

30 *Everson v. Board of Education*, 330 U.S. 1 (1947). On the requirement for 'secular reasons', see *Lemon v. Kurtzman*, 403 U.S. 602 (1971).

31 *Perry v. Schwarzenegger*, 704 F.Supp.2d 921 at 940 (N.D. Cal. 2010), 132–135.

32 *Perry v. Brown*, 671 F.3d 1052 (9th Cir. 2012).

33 *Hollingsworth v. Perry*, 570 U.S. ___ (2013). The State of California refused to defend the referendum, leaving it to the sponsors to attempt to do so.

minorities.[34] Most who oppose such rulings or support such policies (although not all) are religious persons or institutions. They argue that they are not motivated by animus, but by religiously informed moral norms that have existed for millennia, and which they believe are derived from reason as well as faith.[35]

The Court has effectively written these people (and others motivated on these issues solely by secular beliefs) out of the democratic process by attributing to them 'animus', a 'bare desire to harm', and 'a purpose… to demean', 'to injure', and 'to disparage'.[36] As First Amendment scholar Stephen Smith has observed, the 'animus' in question often amounts to moral disapproval of homosexual conduct. It need not (and often does not) entail a desire to harm anyone.[37] More importantly, the judicial practice of imputing negative motives to (primarily) religious actors in American society, and holding their expressions unconstitutional as a result, might reasonably be interpreted as an arbitrary means of elevating and protecting sexual freedoms by removing from the field of political debate those (often) religious or religiously inspired ideas that support other, more traditional forms of public morality.

Third, the most recent of these rulings, *Obergefell v. Hodges* (2015), created a right to same-sex marriage by overturning all state laws establishing marriage as a union of one man and one woman.[38] Although the *Obergefell* decision purported to protect the rights of opponents who disagreed on religious grounds, it did so only by citing a right to maintain beliefs about traditional sexual morality and marriage, and to teach them within religious communities, a right that comports with the scope of the *Hosanna-Tabor* decision on the ministerial exception. Conspicuously absent was the right to bring those beliefs to bear in public debate over law and public policy, and, if the arguments deriving from those beliefs are as persuasive as they historically have been, to prevail.

Fourth, in 2016 the Supreme Court refused to hear a case in which Washington state regulations require all pharmacies to stock and dispense abortion-inducing drugs. The Stormans, a religious family who owns a pharmacy, sued the state, noting that the drugs were readily available from other sources and claiming that the regulations violate their right to religious free exercise. The district court found for the Stormanses, but the appeals court overturned. In June 2016, the Supreme Court refused to take up the case and allowed the regulations to take effect. Justice Alito's dissent noted that 'there is much evidence that the impetus for the adoption of the [pharmacy] regulations was hostility' to the pharmacists' religious beliefs.[39]

There is, in fact, considerable evidence that hostility to traditional religious views is growing among influential cultural institutions and political leaders in American society, especially in the arena of sexual freedom, marriage, and abortion. The examples are many, but I will cite a few that are both representative and increasing in number:

- In 2014, Mozilla Corporation forced its new CEO, Brenden Eich, to resign because he had made a donation to the California Proposition 8 campaign in favor of defining marriage as a union of one man and one woman. Even the private holding of traditional

34 See *Romer v. Evans*, 517 U.S. 620 (1996), *Lawrence v. Texas*, 539 U.S. 558 (2003), *United States v. Windsor*, 570 U.S. (2013), and *Obergefell v. Hodges*, 576 U.S. ___ (2015).

35 See generally Sherif Girgis, Ryan T. Anderson, and Robert P. George, *What Is Marriage: Man and Woman – A Defense* (Encounter Books 2012).

36 *Windsor* at 19, 21, and 25.

37 Steven D. Smith, 'The Jurisprudence of Denigration', (2014) 48 *U.C. Davis Law Review* (2) 680–681.

38 576 U.S. ___.

39 *Stormans, Inc. v. Wiesman*, 579 U.S. ___ (2016) (Alito, J., dissenting).

religious views on sex, marriage, and the family is considered unacceptable in some large American corporations.[40]

- Students at major American college campuses are demanding 'safe spaces' where they can avoid the 'trauma' of being exposed to views with which they disagree. Often, the offending views concern religiously informed sexual morality.[41] In such cases, students are being insulated from religious ideas that they (and their administrations and faculties) find objectionable. Free exercise is being stripped of its meaning in institutions of higher learning. Religious ideas are excluded from debates and discussions concerning virtue or the common good.
- A California senate bill would have required private religious colleges, as a condition of receiving state aid, to accept sexual behavior by their students that is morally abhorrent to Christian, Muslim, and orthodox Jewish teachings. The bill has been amended, but a determination to coerce religious institutions of higher learning into accepting state-enforced codes of sexual morality is increasingly apparent in the United States.[42]
- The 2011 Affordable Care Act as passed by the US Congress had no requirement that health insurance plans include contraception or abortifacients. However, the Health and Human Services agency mandated that such services be provided by some employers. Although thousands of existing health plans were exempted, faith-based NGOs such as Christian colleges and the Catholic Little Sisters of the Poor were not. This is an example of the 'administrative state' employing regulatory power to coerce religious actors to change their beliefs or, facing crippling fines, depart from public life.
- A 2014 essay by a University of Pennsylvania Professor in the *Chronicle of Higher Education* argued that religious colleges should no longer be accredited because they 'draw lines around what is regarded as acceptable teaching and research'. Note the monistic premise: teaching and research must be 'acceptable' to contemporary standards or driven from the field.[43]
- Major American corporations, as well as professional sports leagues, have threatened boycotts on states such as Arizona, Georgia, Indiana, and Mississippi, whose legislatures had passed religious freedom statutes designed, *inter alia*, to protect businesses such as florists and photographers from being compelled to participate in same-sex marriage ceremonies. In all cases, Republican governors acceded to the threats and either vetoed or watered down the legislation.[44]
- In 2015, the city government of Houston, Texas, citing a local equal rights ordinance, subpoenaed five local ministers to determine whether their sermons were critical of

40 Nick Bilton and Noam Cohen, 'Mozilla's Chief Felled by View on Gay Unions', *New York Times*, 4 April 2014, A1.

41 See, for example, Kirsten Powers, *The Silencing: How the Left Is Killing Free Speech* (Regnery Publishing 2015), 76–88.

42 Sen. Bill 1146, 2015–2016 Reg. Sess., 30 September 2016.

43 Peter Conn, 'The Great Accreditation Farce', *The Chronicle of Higher Education*, 30 June 2014.

44 See Sarah Fowler, 'Nation Reacts to Mississippi's "Religious Freedom" Bill', *The Clarion-Ledger*, 15 April 2016, www.clarionledger.com/story/news/2016/03/31/national-reactions-religious-freedoms-bill/82463028/; Hunter Schwarz, 'Indiana Is the Battle over "Religious Freedom" Arizona Never Was', *The Washington Post*, 26 March 2015, www.washingtonpost.com/news/the-fix/wp/2015/03/26/indiana-is-turning-into-the-battle-over-religious-freedom-that-arizona-never-was/?utm_term=.8943b59961ae; Catherine E. Shoichet and Halimah Abdullah, 'Arizona Gov. Jan Brewer Vetoes Controversial Anti-Gay Bill, SB 1062', CNN Politics, 26 February 2014, www.cnn.com/2014/02/26/politics/arizona-brewer-bill; and Ralph Ellis and Emanuella Grinberg, 'Georgia Gov. Nathan Deal to Veto "Religious Liberty" Bill', CNN, 28 March 2016, www.cnn.com/2016/03/28/us/georgia-north-carolina-lgbt-bills/ (all accessed 11 May 2017).

same-sex relations.[45] In Iowa, a Civil Rights Commission policy on 'Sexual Orientation and Gender Identity Public Accommodation' required churches not to consider these characteristics in hiring 'where qualifications are not related to a bona fide religious purpose'. The defining of religious purpose was left with the Civil Rights Commission.[46] These initiatives were in the end altered, but are increasingly typical of efforts to coerce religious organizations into accepting state-enforced codes of sexual morality.

- The influential American Bar Association has amended its Model Rules of Professional Conduct to recommend sanctions on any attorney who practices law in a way that constitutes 'discrimination on the basis of… sexual orientation [or] gender identity'. UCLA law professor Eugene Volokh has written that the ABA rule is intended to 'limit lawyers' expression of viewpoints that it disapproves of.'[47]
- A Christian ethicist, David Gushee, recently wrote a warning to Christian communities, urging them to accept the new sexual morality: 'Neutrality is not an option. Neither is polite half-acceptance. Nor is avoiding the subject. Hide as you might, the issue will come and find you.'[48]
- The US Commission on Civil Rights has issued a report that includes a statement from Chairman Martin Castro that '[t]he phrases "religious liberty" and "religious freedom" will stand for nothing except hypocrisy so long as they remain code words for discrimination, intolerance, racism, sexism, homophobia, Islamophobia, Christian supremacy or any form of intolerance.'[49]
- In a recent speech at the Women in the World Summit, Hillary Clinton spoke of the court-established right to abortion: 'Laws have to be backed up with resources and political will', she explained. To the extent they oppose the right to abortion, she said, 'deep-seated… religious beliefs… have to be changed.' This alarming assertion suggests an intent to coerce even at the level of belief.[50]

These examples are illustrative of a growing trend in American society – to remove from public discourse the ideas and reasons provided by traditional religious individuals and communities. Of course, the arguments of those who oppose orthodox Christian, Jewish, and Muslim views on sexuality, abortion, or anything else are entitled to equal respect in the American constitutional system, which includes freedom of speech. But they are not entitled to eliminate from consideration the arguments of those who oppose them. This

45 Josh Sanburn, 'Houston Pastors Outraged after City Subpoenas Sermons over Transgender Bill', *Time*, 17 October 2014, http://time.com/3514166/houston-pastors-sermons-subpoenaed/ (accessed 11 May 2017).

46 Josh Hersberger, 'Regulating the Pulpit: Is Iowa Just the Beginning?', Church Law Institute, 12 July 2016, http://churchlawinstitute.com/regulating-the-pulpit-is-iowa-just-the-beginning/ and David Pitt and Timothy Meinch, 'Civil Rights Commission Revises Church Exemption Language', *The Des Moines Register*, 8 July 2016, www.desmoinesregister.com/story/news/2016/07/08/civil-rights-commission-revises-church-exemption-language/86879100/ (both accessed 11 May 2017).

47 Eugene Volokh, 'A Speech Code for Lawyers, Banning Viewpoints that Express "Bias", Including in Law-Related Social Activities', *The Washington Post*, 10 August 2016.

48 David Gushee, 'On LGBT Equality, Middle Ground Is Disappearing', Religion News Service, 22 August 2016, http://religionnews.com/2016/08/22/on-lgbt-equality-middle-ground-is-disappearing/ (accessed 11 May 2017).

49 Martin R. Casto, 'Commissioners' Statements and Rebuttals', in US Commission on Civil Rights, *Peaceful Coexistence: Reconciling Nondiscrimination Principles with Civil Liberties*, September 2016, www.usccr.gov/pubs/Peaceful-Coexistence-09-07-16.PDF (accessed 11 May 2017).

50 Hillary Clinton, Keynote Address at the 2015 Women in the World Summit, New York, 23 April 2015.

anti-pluralist, authoritarian trend, encouraged by the courts, is dangerous for the free exercise of religion and dangerous for democracy.

Against this background, let us turn to the hypothesis that the Court's decision in *Hosanna-Tabor* may signal that progressives on the Court are responding to public opinion by shaping new, more restrictive, and more defensible boundaries between private and public religion. While the decision on ministerial exception has no direct bearing on issues of sexual freedom, it could have the effect of shrinking the public zone of free exercise for those with religiously informed views on sexual morality.

### *The Hosanna-Tabor decision*

Cheryl Perich was a 'called teacher' in the Hosanna-Tabor Evangelical Lutheran Church and School. According to church doctrine, a 'called' teacher is a commissioned minister with theological training, whereas a 'lay' teacher need not receive theological training or even be Lutheran. Perich developed narcolepsy and began the school year of 2004 on disability leave. After a few months, she informed the school that she was able to report for work. The school, which hired lay teachers only when called teachers were not available, responded that a lay teacher was already under contract to fill Perich's position. After a series of conversations, the school asked Perich to resign, she refused, and she was fired.

Perich filed a charge with the US Equal Employment Opportunity Commission (EEOC). She claimed she been terminated in violation of the Americans with Disabilities Act (ADA), a federal law that prohibits an employer from discriminating against a qualified individual on the basis of a disability. The EEOC, representing the US government, brought suit in federal court. Hosanna-Tabor responded by invoking the 'ministerial exception', arguing that the suit was barred by the First Amendment's guarantee of religious free exercise.

Because the claim of ministerial exception appeared to entail employment discrimination under the popular ADA, many expected the court to rule in favor of Perich or, at the least, to see a court divided between its 'conservative' and 'progressive' factions. Progressives such as Justices Ginsburg and Kagan were expected to conclude that Hosanna-Tabor had unjustly discriminated against Perich in ways that secular associations could not. As one legal scholar put the question, 'Why are churches allowed to engage in what would otherwise be illegal discrimination in their dealings with ministers?'[51]

Many were surprised when the Court ruled unanimously that the ministerial exception was required by both religion clauses of the Constitution, and that the core meaning of the exception was to ensure 'that the authority to select and control who will minister to the faithful is the church's alone'.[52]

An important part of the ruling rejected the government's argument that the Court's 1990 *Smith* decision prohibited the firing of Perich. In *Smith*, the Court had ruled that neutral laws of general applicability could, in fact, restrict the free exercise of religion. In *Hosanna-Tabor*, the government argued that the ADA, like the law at issue in *Smith*, was a neutral law of general applicability and was sufficient to overcome any exemption or ministerial exception. The justices rejected that argument, ruling that 'Smith involved government regulation of only outward physical acts.' The issue at hand concerned internal church decisions, so Smith

51 Richard W. Garnett, 'Religion and Group Rights: Are Churches (Just) Like the Boy Scouts?' (2007) 22 *St. John's Journal of Legal Commentary* (2) 521.

52 *Hosanna-Tabor* at 5 and 19–20.

did not apply.[53] Here, the concurrence of progressive justices, such as Ruth Bader Ginsburg and Elena Kagan, was surprising. Both were known as supporters of the *Smith* standard that neutral laws of general applicability could restrict free exercise.

Was the decision a temporary detour from an otherwise secularist path, or was it, as some religious freedom advocates earnestly hoped, evidence that the Court was recommitting itself to vigorous legal protections for the free exercise of religion? The latter view found support when, in 2014, the Court declared that a family business called Hobby Lobby – a national chain of arts and crafts stores – was in fact entitled to protection under the Free Exercise Clause of the First Amendment.[54]

I suggest that *Hosanna-Tabor* was neither a detour nor a reaffirmation of a judicial commitment to free exercise. The concept of a ministerial exception, however broadly the position of 'minister' is defined, by its nature reaches only the internal governance of religious groups. The exception need not have any practical applicability to the critical public aspects of free exercise, especially the question of whether a law or public policy influenced by religious ideas (such as a law based on religiously informed arguments concerning marriage) constitutes an establishment of religion. In short, affirming the *internal* free exercise right of a church or other religious organization to choose its ministers does not enhance or otherwise affect the *public* free exercise right of that church or organization to enter into the political life of the nation, and to prevail, in debates over laws and public policies concerning the common good.

During earlier periods of American history, the *Hosanna-Tabor* ruling may rightly have been understood as a confirmation of a threshold principle: the internal autonomy of religious communities must be protected *precisely because they have a constitutionally mandated public role in securing American democracy and in shaping public debates over the common good.* But in the twenty-first century, *Hosanna-Tabor* may indicate the affirmation by Court progressives of a growing US political labeling of religious freedom as 'freedom of worship', a usage that can, and often does, mean a constriction of free exercise, whether for individuals or groups, to the private sphere.

There are many examples of this usage and its critics.[55] Some insist it has no substantive meaning and simply constitutes a synonym for free exercise,[56] but I believe the evidence suggests otherwise. In a major speech on human rights at Georgetown University in 2012, for example, Secretary of State Hillary Clinton declared that people 'must be free to wor-

53 14–15.

54 An additional Court decision of June 2017 has been acclaimed as a victory for free exercise. In *Trinity Lutheran Church of Columbia, Inc. v. Comer, Director, Missouri Department of Resources*, the Court ruled (7–2) that the Missouri constitutional prohibition on the use of state funding for religious entities did not permit the state to deny funding for a church playground. I read this decision much as I read *Hosanna-Tabor*, i.e., as an example of Court progressives (in this case, only three of them – Kennedy, Kagan, and Breyer) permitting 'free exercise' of religion in a case with no direct applicability to public religious engagement. For a rousing approbation of the decision and a different analysis of its free exercise implications, see Matthew J. Franck, 'Paving a Playground, and Weeding the Unruly Garden of Religious Liberty', *The Public Discourse*, 29 June 2017, www.thepublicdiscourse.com/2017/06/19675 (accessed 27 July 2017).

55 See, for example, Wesley J. Smith, 'Freedom of Worship's Assault on Freedom of Religion', *First Things*, 13 July 2012, www.firstthings.com/web-exclusives/2012/07/freedom-of-worships-assault-on-freedom-of-religion and John J. Miller, 'Freedom of Worship Is Not Enough', *Wall Street Journal*, 10 June 2016, www.wsj.com/articles/freedom-of-worship-isnt-enough-1465511901 (both accessed 11 May 2017).

56 See this defense of the Obama Administration usage from the editors of *Commonweal*: www.commonwealmagazine.org/blog/freedom-worship-vs-freedom-religion (accessed 11 May 2017).

ship, associate, and to love in the way that they choose'.[57] This elevation of sexual freedom to the level of a fundamental human right, while in the same sentence employing the more restricted expression for religious freedom, is unlikely to have been a rhetorical coincidence.

Equally important is the uniform, bold, and consistent support by Court progressives for the rulings establishing sexual freedoms and same-sex marriage as fundamental rights in the United States, as well as for the new proposition that 'animus' toward and moral disapproval of such conduct are unconstitutional motives. Underlying this judicial abhorrence for the motives of (mainly) religious opponents of the new sexual freedom is the proposition, penned by Justice Anthony Kennedy, who is also the author of the animus doctrine, that '[a]t the heart of liberty is the right to define one's own concept of existence, of meaning, of the universe, and of the mystery of human life.'[58] If liberty is thus conceived, so too is the right to define or redefine one's self – including one's gender, source of being, or source of dignity. So understood, liberty leaves little room for those who view gender, being, and dignity as given by God. Such beliefs may survive, but only in the private precincts of the conscience, or in houses of worship.

The *Hosanna-Tabor* opinion provides an opportunity for the Court to reinforce the idea of religious freedom as essentially a private matter by creating a new boundary (a readjusted wall of separation) between private and public/political free exercise rights. Inside the boundary – that is, when the (more or less) private affairs of religious communities, such as their choices of ministers and the interior consciences of their adherents, are at stake – free exercise protections may enthusiastically be affirmed by progressives, even to the detriment of some non-discrimination laws, without affecting the ongoing removal of traditional religious norms from considerations of law and public policy.

Outside the boundary lies the space where, in the past, Americans have engaged in lively, contentious debates over conceptions of the common good and where religious justifications could be offered freely. Today, as we have seen, many have come to accept the idea that the 'free exercise' of religion, whatever it means, does not mean that traditional religious ideas might prevail as the basis for laws and policies. For some, the mere expression of these ideas is inherently discriminatory.[59] The ministerial exception thus may illustrate a new private free exercise safe zone constructed by progressives on the Court and elsewhere in American society, rather than what it had once been – a threshold element of a vigorous understanding of religious liberty in American *public* life.

The reactions to *Hosanna-Tabor* of some progressives suggest they are unwilling even to go this far because of the implications of the decision for more sweeping modern concepts of discrimination. They wish, for example, to protect the rights of employees or job candidates to sue religious employers who reject them because employees' or candidates' views on sex or marriage do not comport with core religious teachings. Under *Hosanna-Tabor*'s ministerial exception standard, such suits would be difficult to win if the employee or applicant could be construed as a minister. However, this opposition from the Left, as it were, could enable progressives on the Court to position a new doctrine – which we might call in shorthand the 'free exercise of worship' – as centrist, rather than a full-throated rejection of traditional conceptions of free exercise.

57 Hillary Clinton, 'Remarks on the Human Rights Agenda for the 21st Century', Georgetown University, 14 December 2009, www.state.gov/secretary/20092013clinton/rm/2009a/12/133544.htm (accessed 11 May 2017).

58 *Planned Parenthood of Southeastern Pennsylvania v. Casey*, 505 U.S. 833 (1992).

59 See generally Brian Leiter, *Why Tolerate Religion?* (Princeton University Press 2013) and Micah Swartzman, 'What If Religion Is Not Special?', (2012) 79 *University of Chicago Law Review* (4) 1351–1427.

If, then, *Hosanna-Tabor* indicates a modern Supreme Court's shrinking of religious free exercise to 'worship', ministerial decisions, and other internal matters, the consequences are likely to be significant for believers and non-believers alike. They implicate not only the trajectory of free exercise, which I have argued was a pillar of American democracy, but also the aims of American foreign policy, including its will and capacity to advance religious freedom in the lands of Islam.

## Conclusion: the global implications of separating religion from politics

I will conclude by noting briefly that there is a huge 'religious freedom deficit' in most Muslim-majority nations, a deficit that contributes to instability, failed states, economic stagnation, suppression of women's rights, stillborn democracies, and the rise of violent Islamist extremism.[60] Our studies at Georgetown's Religious Freedom Project have not only confirmed the religious freedom deficit, but have demonstrated its powerful connection to these debilitating and destructive pathologies.[61]

More to the point, we have also produced compelling evidence that the *advance* of religious freedom in Muslim-majority nations can undermine these pathologies and even reverse them. Religious freedom, in short, can contribute to stability, economic development, democratic consolidation, the equality of women, pluralism, and the undermining of violent Islamist extremism.

However, Muslim-majority societies will not accept, let alone embrace, religious freedom if it means the privatization of Islam. I take this as a given. Unfortunately, our growing incapacity in Western democracies to understand religious freedom as a *public* matter reduces dramatically our ability to convince Muslim societies that religious freedom can advance their own interests. In short, it is difficult to sell a product in which you no longer believe.

60 The Pew Research Center's annual reports on *Global Restrictions on Religion* routinely show the Muslim-majority nations of the Middle East and North Africa with the highest restrictions. See www.pewforum.org/2015/02/26/regions-and-countries/.

61 For a full list of the publications of the Religious Freedom Project at Georgetown, see https://berkleycenter.georgetown.edu/rfp/publications/all.

# 3 The ministerial exception

## Theological and legal perspectives from Finland and Europe

*Pamela Slotte*

The issue of so-called ministerial exceptions from generally applicable laws has been widely and rather passionately debated in recent times. This essay approaches the issue by means of a succinct inquiry into the question of to what extent religious communities are, can, and should be exempt from general law. In elaborating on this issue, the article offers an account of two concrete examples of how governance through law in matters of faith is being conceptualized and approached: in the Evangelical Lutheran Church of Finland and in the jurisprudence of the European Court of Human Rights.[1]

### The future legal arrangements of the Evangelical Lutheran Church of Finland

The Evangelical Lutheran Church of Finland, a majority church, is currently revisiting its legal relations to the State and making decisions on how its activities ought to be regulated in law in the future.[2] This is one dimension of an extensive review of all aspects and activities of the Church's organization and administration. The goal is to improve the Church's ability to carry out its foundational tasks in the future and to make sure that it is able to respond in an adequate way to the needs and challenges of the contemporary age. Is this, for example, best secured by the Church holding status under public law, or not? The overall work is headed by a special 'ELFC Committee for the Future' (*Kirkon tulevaisuuskomitea*) appointed by the General Synod of the Evangelical Lutheran Church.[3]

1 This essay was written as part of the author's personal Academy of Finland Academy Research Fellow project 'Management of the Sacred – A Critical Inquiry' (2013–2018). The essay in part expands some thoughts from a co-written article published in the *Oxford Journal of Law and Religion*. In it, we raised certain general theoretical questions that pertain to the matter of a ministerial exception, and we offered an overview of how the matter is being handled in international human rights law, within the United Nations and the European human rights systems. Pamela Slotte and Helge Årsheim, 'The Ministerial Exception – Comparative Perspectives', in Special Issue on the Ministerial Exception, (2015) 4 *Oxford Journal of Law and Religion* (2) 171–198.

2 I refer the reader to the recording of the speech by Lisbet Christoffersen at the Fourth ICLARS Conference in Oxford, 8–11 September 2016, for a good overview of the current Nordic situation as regards state-religion relationships. Available at www.iclrs.org/index.php?pageId=4&linkId=225&contentId=21&blurbId=67428 (accessed 28 October 2016). For a more comprehensive account, see also Lisbet Christoffersen, Svend Andersen, and Kjell Å. Modéer, eds, *Law and Religion in the 21st Century: Nordic Perspectives* (Djøf Publishing 2010).

3 Kirkkohallitus, *Kirkon tulevaisuuskomitean mietintö*, Suomen ev.-lut. Kirkon julkaisuja 47 (Kirkkohallitus 2016), 3, http://sakasti.evl.fi/sakasti.nsf/0/EE4CA05F09EA5A22C2257E70003B1F1B/$FILE/Kirkon%20tulevaisuuskomitea_Mietint%F6.pdf (accessed 27 October 2016).

At present, a Church Act (*Kirkkolaki* (1054/1993)) regulates relations with the State and the order and administration of the Evangelical Lutheran Church of Finland. Here the order of enactment is central: the Church itself decides on the content of the Act collectively through its General Synod. The Finnish Parliament can only approve or reject an ecclesiastical bill. As stated in the Church Act,

> The Church has the exclusive right to make legislative proposals for the enactment of the Church Act in all matters which concern solely its own affairs. It has the same right to propose amendments and repeal of the Church Act.[4]

Thus, we are talking about a collective internal law, recognized by the State,[5] which is expressive of the Church's self-understanding as both a social community and importantly a community of believers, and hence linked to the theological underpinnings of the Church. The confession of the Church is mentioned in the first paragraph of the Act, where it is also stated that it is further elaborated in the Church Order (*Kirkkojärjestys* (1055/1993)).[6] There is also a Church Election Order (*Kirkon vaalijärjestys* (416/2014)) that further specifies some of the rules on elections in the Church Act.[7] The last two regulative instruments are subject to the exclusive authority of the General Synod.[8]

4 Church Act (*Kirkkolaki*) 26.11.1993/1054, Chap. 2 Sec. 2(1). Translation taken from *Ahtinen v. Finland*, App. No. 48907/99 (ECtHR, 23 September 2008), § 17. The Constitution of Finland 11.6.1999/731, § 76 reads as follows:

> Provisions on the organization and administration of the Evangelic Lutheran Church are laid down in the Church Act. The legislative procedure for enactment of the Church Act and the right to submit legislative proposals relating to the Church Act are governed by the specific provisions in that Code. In church law is enacted the constitution and administration of the Evangelical Lutheran Church. As concerns the order of enactment of church law and the initiative concerning church law, that which is in force is laid down in the aforementioned law separately.

Available at www.finlex.fi/sv/laki/kaannokset/1999/en19990731.pdf (accessed 27 October 2016). See also, for example, Kimmo Kääriäinen, 'Religion and State in Finland', (2011) 24 *Nordic Journal of Religion and Society* (2) 155–171, 160–161 and Pekka Leino, *Kirkko ja perusoikeudet* (doctoral dissertation) (Suomalainen Lakimiesyhdistys 2003), 103–109.

5 What we see expressed here is a so-called 'East Nordic' understanding of the Church with its own internal order. It differs from how the situation developed after the Protestant Reformation in the West Nordic countries. See, for example, Lisbet Christoffersen, 'The Argument for a Narrow Conception of "Religious Autonomy"', (2015) 4 *Oxford Journal of Law and Religion* (2) 278–302, 279.

6 As is stated in Chapter 1 of the Church Act,

> Section 1. Confession: The Evangelical Lutheran Church of Finland professes the Christian faith which is based on the Bible and which has been expressed in the three creeds of the old church and in the Lutheran Confessions. The confession of the Church is articulated in more detail in the Church Order.
>
> Section 2. Task: In accordance with its confession, the church preaches God's word and administers the sacraments and also otherwise seeks to spread the Christian message and realize neighborly love.

7 For a compilation of the laws and other regulations of the Evangelical Lutheran Church of Finland as it stood on 1 January 2016, see http://sakasti.evl.fi/sakasti.nsf/0/84759E9DB769A9A6C2257D94002752D4/$FILE/Kirkkolainsaadanto_2016_netti.pdf (accessed 25 October 2016).

8 See, for example, Leino at 170–173. There are also other laws that have been enacted exclusively for the purpose of being applied in the Evangelical Lutheran Church of Finland, for example the Law on the Collective Labor Agreements of the Evangelical Lutheran Church (*Laki evankelis-luterilaisen kirkon virkaehtosopimuksista*) 20.12.1974/968. With regard to these, the previously mentioned order of enactment does not apply. Kirkkohallitus, 'Kirkkolainsäädännön kodifioinnin esitysluonnos', 22 March 2016, 10, available at http://sakasti.evl.fi/sakasti.nsf/0/FF04BB5160743CC8C2257F85002195AE/$FILE/Kodifiointiehdotus%20 2016,%20maaliskuu.pdf (accessed 25 October 2016).

As a majority church, the Evangelical Lutheran Church is very much intertwined with the Finnish State, which is manifested in the legal arrangements. For example, many parts of general administrative law and labor law apply to the Church. 'Worldly law' actually forms part of the law of the Church itself; the Church Act makes explicit references to relevant generally applicable laws. To take but one example, both officeholders and contractual employees – depending on whether their employment relationship is based on public law or not (and also ordained ministers can stand in an employment relationship) – have certain recourse to the judicial review of secular courts, either administrative or civil, in matters that concern their employment.[9] Certain employment matters – although not, for example, the issue of whether someone should or should not be ordained in the first place – can be and have upon appeal been dealt with in regular administrative or civil courts, and courts have at times ruled that discrimination has taken place, that proper procedures have not been followed, etc.[10]

This confirms, at least as far as the Evangelical Lutheran Church of Finland is concerned, what Russell Sandberg has noted: namely, that while 'religious law can be defined by reference to its purposes, sources, [and] subject-matter,'[11] in all these areas there are overlaps with general law.[12] Moreover, the Evangelical Lutheran Church assumes various functions related to public administration on behalf of the State, such as tasks in relation to the maintenance of the population register as well as funeral and burial services. All this may come with some cost of autonomy. However, the other side of the coin is that a change in status could eventually lead to less presence, less funding, and fewer possibilities to carry out the work of the Church, as this work is identified to its relevant parts as a 'low-threshold' majority church[13] that seeks to make it easy for people to partake in church activities and make everyone feel welcome.

The alternative future scenarios that the Committee for the Future initially put forward regarding the Church's legal status and relations and legal code would have potentially expanded or limited the Church's ability to decide fully independently what are the Church's 'own matters', regarding personnel issues or other matters. The first option would have been to carry on more or less as before. A second option was a more succinct so-called 'framework law of the Church', in relation to which the initiative in accordance with the order of enactment would remain with the Church. A third option was to pursue a 'law of the Church', which would be enacted as a normal law by Parliament; hence, the initiative

9 See Church Act (*Kirkkolaki*) 26.11.1993/1054, Part II, Chaps. 5 and 6. Here, a change took place in 1997 when Cathedral Chapters became part of the internal administration of the Church. They were no longer considered independent judicial bodies, something required for purposes of securing legal protection as required under the Finnish Constitution § 21, or Article 6 of the European Convention on Human Rights. (They were later dealt with in *Ahtinen v. Finland*.) Opinions differ as to what it has meant. Pekka Leino, who is an expert on Finnish ecclesiastical law, finds that this change has limited the autonomy of the Church. Leino at 3. However, in a study conducted for the Committee for the Future, Juha Meriläinen observes that this change had few effects, in principle or in practice, for the Church. It simply meant the removal of the Cathedral Chapters as first instances of redress with regard to certain decisions by ecclesiastical bodies in their capacity as public authorities. Juha Meriläinen, 'Kirkon julkisoikeudellinen asema', 18 November 2015, 7, http://sakasti.evl.fi/sakasti.nsf/0/EE4CA05F09EA5A22C2257E70003B1F1B/$FILE/JuhaMeril%E4inen-Kirkonjulkisoikeudellinenasema.pdf (accessed 1 November 2016).

10 For a review of some recent cases, see Johannes Heikkonen and Pamela Slotte, 'Religion and Discrimination Law in the European Union: Finland', in Mark Hill, ed., *Religion and Discrimination Law in the European Union – La discrimination en matière religieuse dans l'Union Européenne: Proceedings of the Conference, Oxford, 29 September–2 October 2011 – Actes du Colloque, Oxford, 29 septembre – 2 octobre 2011* (European Consortium for Church and State Research 2012), 125–144.

11 Russell Sandberg, *Law and Religion* (Cambridge University Press 2011), 13.

12 Sandberg at 172–178.

13 See also Kirkkohallitus, *Kirkon tulevaisuuskomitean mietintö* at 135–139.

for legislative changes would lie with the State, although the Church would be invited to give its views on the proposed changes.[14] The last scenario would not give the Evangelical Lutheran Church quite the same influence over new legislation which concerns it. It is based on the idea of the State delegating authority and power to the Church.[15] On the other hand, the last scenario would potentially distinguish more clearly between state and religion.[16]

In March 2016, the plenary session of the National Church Council (*Kirkkohallitus*), one of the Church's central administrative bodies, deliberated a proposal that a new Church Act replace the Church Act of 1993 by 2020 at the latest.[17] As part of this, the legal system of the Church would be revised. It would include no drastic changes to the legal arrangement, being instead a structural reform aimed at simplifying and clarifying the current system. The proposal aims to combine three existing regulative instruments – the Church Act, the Church Order, and the Church Election Order – into one Church Act and one Church Order.[18]

Under this proposal, the Church Act would regulate only those matters that require regulation in ordinary law – by implication, those matters that have a connection to the State. Moreover, independently of issues of autonomy, the Constitution requires that the rights and duties of the individual and 'other matters that belong to the realm of law' be regulated in law. Thus, this also applies – 'with some flexibility perhaps' – to the regulation of the Church. While the Church Act would regulate matters on a level of principle, the Church Order would concretize those principles.[19] The Church Order could also include matters not covered by the Church Act, such as matters regarding the creed. In general, the Church Order would regulate matters in which the Church has 'legislative authority' *and* which do not require regulation in ordinary law.[20]

As regards matters of employment pertaining to ordained ministers and other staff, these would continue to be regulated extensively and with reference to generally applicable law in the Church Act. Certain other dimensions, such as the qualifications needed for ordination to ministry, would continue to be regulated in the Church Order.[21]

It is curious that the proposed new Church Act in Chapter 1, Section 5 still includes an order of enactment that repeats *verbatim* the current one:

14 Expert opinion to the Committee for the Future by Pekka Leino, 'Kirkon organisaatiota ja hallintoa suunnittelevalle ja kirkon tulevaisuutta pohtivalle Kirkon tulevaisuuskomitealle', 16 October 2015, 4–5. On file with the author.

15 Christoffersen, 'The Argument for a Narrow Conception of "Religious Autonomy"' at 289.

16 To understand what it could mean, Pekka Leino refers to the current Law of the Orthodox Church (*Laki ortodoksisesta kirkosta*) 10.11.2006/985, which he finds actually regulates in some detail a number of issues related to administration, economy, processes of appeal, the general duties of priests, deacons, organists, etc. Leino at 5. The Law of the Orthodox Church is available at www.finlex.fi/fi/laki/alkup/2006/20060985 (accessed 1 November 2016).

17 Kirkkohallitus, 'Kirkkolainsäädännön kodifioinnin esitysluonnos'. For a short summary, see also http://sakasti.evl.fi/sakasti.nsf/sp?open&cid=Content3F92AE (accessed 25 October 2016).

18 http://evl.fi/EVLUutiset.nsf/Documents/CBC92DE19F5E67AAC2257F620048543A?OpenDocument&lang=FI (accessed 26 October 2016) and Kirkkohallitus, 'Kirkkolainsäädännön kodifioinnin esitysluonnos' at 12–13.

19 Kirkkohallitus at 12. The status of the Church under public law partly determines what can be regulated in the Church Act and the Church Order, respectively. For example, the principle of the rule of law in Section 2 of the Constitution is important here. (Observation of Pirjo Pihjala, head of the Department of Administration of the National Church Council; on file with the author.)

20 Kirkkohallitus at 12–13.

21 Kirkkohallitus at 51–79 and 127–136.

> The Church has the exclusive right to make legislative proposals for the enactment of the Church Act in all matters which concern solely its own affairs. It has the same right to propose amendments and repeal of the Church Act.[22]

One would think that the Church Act would make known the Church's perspective on matters of 'shared' concern rather than matters that are 'solely' the Church's own, and which would be regulated in the Church Order.[23]

Various parties, such as the Employers' Office of the Church (*Kirkon työmarkkinalaitos*), the Bishops' Conference, the Cathedral Chapters, local congregations, and certain public authorities, have since been specially invited or otherwise allowed to give their opinions regarding the proposed changes. To mention just one important voice, in August 2016 the Bishops' Conference issued its statement in response to the request by the National Church Council. In it, the bishops note that the principled position of the Church and its relations to the State would not change because of the amendment of the law. What is at stake is primarily a legal-technical reform, the work on which has been carried out in awareness of what the Finnish Constitution and other relevant legislation requires. While adding some remarks that were partly of a critical nature, the bishops welcomed the overall proposed changes, finding that they satisfy current needs. Of interest here is that the bishops found that the reform would lead to something they have previously advocated for, namely, a more succinct Church Act. The Act would refer to generally applicable laws of the land that apply to the Church, and it would regulate separately only those matters in which the Church wants to 'deviate' from generally applicable law. In turn, the Church Order, over which the Church has full authority, would include rules concerning internal matters of the Church.[24]

The final report of the Committee for the Future was published in October 2016. It supports the position of the proposal by the National Church Council, stating that, in fact, 'the significant streamlining of the Church Act and the transfer of regulations to the Church Order... would increase the Church's autonomy,'[25] and also make internal decision-making easier.[26] It does not want to take a stand on the actual content of the proposal of the

22 'Kirkolla on yksinoikeus ehdottaa kirkkolakia kaikesta, mikä koskee ainoastaan kirkon omia asioita, sekä kirkkolain muuttamista ja kumoamista.' Kirkkohallitus at 158. Translation, as before, taken from *Ahtinen v. Finland*.

23 On the other hand, the phrasing has a historical pedigree. Its roots can be traced back to the first Church Act of the Evangelical Lutheran Church of Finland, the Church Act of 1869. At the time, Finland was a Grand Duchy of the Russian Empire. I am grateful to Pirjo Pihjala for pointing this out.

24 For the statement of the Bishops' Conference on the proposal for a new Church Act, see http://evl.fi/EVLUutiset.nsf/0/668C157713194B10C2258020003FD16B/$file/Kodifiointi_lausunto.pdf (accessed 26 October 2016). The Bishops' Conference together with the General Synod and the National Church Council are the important organs of the central administration of the Evangelical Lutheran Church of Finland. Kirkkohallitus, *Kirkon tulevaisuuskomitean mietintö* at 177. In correspondence with Pirjo Pihjala on 19 November 2016 (on file with the author), Pihjala interestingly observed the following regarding statements made by the Ministry of Justice and the Ministry of Education and Culture with regard to the draft: the Ministry of Justice considered it possible to develop the Church Law in such a way that the regulation of 'internal matters' would become a matter where the Church has legislative authority, *provided*, however, that the demands of the Constitution are taken into account. The Ministry of Education and Culture observed that it *may* be possible, also from the perspective of constitutional law, to move more of the regulation that relates to the administration and economy of the Church to the organs of the Church itself. According to Pihjala, this shows that drawing a line between the Church Act and the Church Order is not unambiguous.

25 Kirkkohallitus at 183; see also 56–57.

26 Kirkkohallitus at 175.

National Church Council and so interfere in its work. Yet, while the Committee for the Future sees that proposal as a step in the right direction, it would actually prefer an even 'lighter' Church Act.[27]

In addition, during the drafting of the proposal for the future vision of the Church, which, as noted, also includes matters other than law, it was likewise the case that various parties with a vested interest were heard, as were external experts. This also included a large online discussion to hear feedback from people working in the Church as well as from those in positions of trust within the Church.[28] Over 1,200 persons were invited to participate, and of these, 206, or about 17%, registered as participants.[29] In this discussion, everyone underlined the importance of church autonomy, and a law and an order for the Church were considered important in order to safeguard this autonomy. However, opinions differed as to what should be the Church's public law status in future, if indeed it should have one. Would it help the Church in its mission, and if so, in relation to which foundational tasks? In what respect is it to the advantage of the Church and in what respect is it not?[30]

Another important group whose points of view the Committee for the Future took extra care to gather were the young members of the Church.[31] In a course in comparative 'religious and religion law' in spring 2016, I also asked my students – most of whom were theology students who imagine that they will have a career in the Church – to reflect on the three earlier mentioned proposed future alternatives in their final essays. A clear majority of the students favored the status quo.[32]

As always, what is at stake here and elsewhere are differing views of how God acts in the world, which values are foundational to Christianity and more specifically Lutheranism, the view of man and life here and now, and the relationship to the surrounding society. These affect how one relates to worldly law and those articulations of justice and foundational values which national, regional, and international law give expression to. Does one find that there are overlaps, common denominators, values, and purposes (for example, because one believes that humans even in the postlapsarian phase gain insight into what is right and good)? Or is the basic perspective that of contrasting the Christian community with the worldly community, from which it follows that 'religious' life is and should be reserved for the faithful themselves? For example, some of my students feared that the Church is being secularized both from within and from without and that law, including non-discrimination law, plays an important part here. They are surely not alone in this.

27 Kirkkohallitus at 56.
28 Kirkkohallitus at 4–5.
29 See the report 'Suomen evankelis-luterilaisen kirkon työntekijöiden ja luottamushenkilöiden kuuleminen' by Kirkon tulevaisuuskomitea, available at http://sakasti.evl.fi/sakasti.nsf/0/EE4CA05F09EA5A22C2257E70003B1F1B/$FILE/Meri-AnnaHintsala-Verkkokeskustelu.pdf (accessed 25 October 2016).
30 Kirkon tulevaisuuskomitea at 27.
31 Kirkkohallitus at 5.
32 Importantly, with the exception of a couple of students, they clearly saw national, regional, and international law not as a threat but as a complement to the internal regulation of the Church. On the other hand, there were also some students who found, for example, non-discrimination law and human rights law deeply problematic from the perspective of what they called a traditional Christian Lutheran view based on the Bible and the Confessions, and which, importantly for them, includes not accepting female priesthood. Yet these students favored the current model, surely for the present public role they wish to retain for Christianity in Finland. However, within it, they wanted to undo particular legislation and increase the scope of what would count as internal matters exclusive to the Church itself. Moreover, they were concerned with the way decision-making in the Church is detrimental to conservative minority positions within it.

## The ministerial exception and 'secular' laws: who decides when exceptions are due?

The same diagnosis – that religious communities have to ponder how to relate to worldly law and that easy answers or a uniform position on the matter can be hard to find – can be made in many other, diverse cases. We need only to consider how the position of the Evangelical Lutheran Church of Finland seems to differ from that of the Hosanna-Tabor Evangelical Lutheran Church in the United States, whose position in employment matters and worldly law and judicial review in relation to these in the case of 'ministers' was scrutinized in the high-profile case of *Hosanna-Tabor Evangelical Lutheran Church and School v. Equal Employment Opportunity Commission.*[33] To take just one example, the two churches clearly differ as regards the extent to which 'Lutheran teachings require that disputes over ministry must be resolved internally', with the US church insisting on more autonomy in this area.[34]

The diversity of faith traditions, even among those who are closely related theologically, is certainly one reason for the manifoldness we witness in the field of religion and law. Even scholars of religion find it difficult to define what religion is.[35] It is no wonder that legislators and courts struggle to decide what it means to have freedom of, for, from, and within religion in a way that does not simply depict in a descriptive manner existing religious ways of being, but normatively and in a more generalizing fashion takes a stand on how freedom should be looked at and regulated in matters of faith, so as to provide tools for solving conflicts where interpretation stands against interpretation, 'fundamental right' against 'fundamental right', and so forth – as far as this essay is concerned, in questions that concern employees in churches, religious organizations, and other workplaces with a faith-based ethos.

The ministerial exception could be seen as a way to conceptualize and handle frictions between collective religious views of life and society's legislation. In an article co-written with Helge Årsheim in 2015, we note, by reference to Christopher Lund, that the ministerial exception can be defined as denoting 'a cluster of legal statutes and practices that allow certain exclusive exemptions from otherwise generally applicable laws to religious organizations'.[36]

Certainly, both perspectives are important here. Certain themes which are significant to a religious group, and which the group regulates, are of no obvious interest beyond the group itself. It is not that there would be no 'compelling state interest'; there really is no interest at all. Or, phrased differently, one might not share the religious group's position concerning a particular matter, but it is not something one finds that society's legislation should concern itself with – quite the reverse. This also shows in the great agreement within law and among experts regarding certain matters. Creeds, for example, are considered virtually unanimously matters

33 *Hosanna-Tabor Evangelical Lutheran Church and School v. Equal Employment Opportunity Commission*, 565 U.S. ___ (2012). The case has been the subject of ample commentary. For just a few reviews representing different opinions, see Douglas Laycock, 'Hosanna-Tabor and the Ministerial Exception', (2012) 35 *Harvard Journal of Law and Public Policy* (3) 339–362, 849 and Marie Ashe, '*Hosanna-Tabor*, the Ministerial Exception, and Losses of Equality: Constitutional Law and Religious Privilege in the United States', (2015) 4 *Oxford Journal of Law and Religion* (2) 199–223.

34 Laycock at 849.

35 Slotte and Årsheim at 2. For a short overview, see also Paul Weller et al., eds, *Religion or Belief, Discrimination and Equality: Britain in Global Contexts* (Bloomsbury 2013), 6–8.

36 Slotte and Årsheim at 5. See also Christopher C. Lund, 'In Defense of the Ministerial Exception', (2011) 90 *North Carolina Law Review* 1–72, 3.

only for the religious groups themselves. Of course, it is always important to ask to what extent that which we take as self-evident is expressive of a blindness toward some expressions of faith.

Likewise, at the other extreme, there are certain actions with purportedly religious motivations which cannot be tolerated at all, and states can legitimately prevent these. The question of a ministerial exception certainly does not belong in this category.[37]

Certain themes, perhaps quite a few – particularly for majority religions, we might want to add – are of overlapping interest to both the religious community and the generally applicable law, among which employment is a salient one. Many times, religious communities find worldly legislation on employment matters adequate, and they accept it. Then the question of ministerial exception is moot. Additionally, in some matters where interests overlap, the legislation may perhaps be primarily of a technical nature to the state and an exception, if desired, is then not connected to great concessions.

However, to a certain extent we are dealing here with legislation which in a particular way is seen as giving expression to societal values and principles of justice – and I am here speaking of something else than what is just 'popular' – like non-discrimination legislation. These situations are often labeled 'hard cases'.

It is clear that worldly authorities hold a trump card here.[38] We are speaking of 'exceptions' from generally applicable law. Yet simultaneously, it is not – or we do not want to make it – as easy as to simply allow worldly authorities to decide unilaterally when exceptions are due. There are various reasons for this; a topical way to make this point today is to point out ways in which ostensibly neutral and 'religiously disinterested' law in fact has its own biases about religion. Alvin Esau, for example, makes this point with reference also to the work of Benjamin Berger, who has held that 'law's modesty is always false.'[39] In fact, he goes a step further and assigns to law its own 'liberal' faith, which ultimately takes precedence in so-called hard cases:

> I would say that law has its *own* religion that may well clash with other religions. And 'law's religion,' as Berger has called it, will talk about accommodation and tolerance, but when the stakes are high enough, it will pull out its guns and enforce its own integrity. *Charter* values will trump church values. The 'rule of law' becomes at some stage the notion that 'law rules,' and indeed that 'law overrules' contrary claims by individuals and groups that their God rules and reigns. People who have a robust religion will live their lives within a

37 Cecile Laborde touched upon this in her speech at the Fourth ICLARS Conference in Oxford 8–11 September 2016. The recording is available at www.iclrs.org/index.php?pageId=4&linkId=225&contentId=21&blurbId=67428 (accessed 28 October 2016).

38 For example, Christoffersen has pointed out that in the East Nordic countries (Finland and Sweden) up until the end of the twentieth century, even if the majority churches were granted the right to develop internal norms, this was seen 'from a jurisprudential perspective as a delegation of state powers'. Christoffersen, 'The Argument for a Narrow Conception of "Religious Autonomy"' at 280.

39 Benjamin L. Berger, 'Law's Religion: Rendering Culture', (2007) 45 *Osgoode Hall Law Journal* (2) 277–314, 311, available at http://digitalcommons.osgoode.yorku.ca/ohlj/vol45/iss2/2 (accessed 1 November 2016). As Berger puts it, '[L]aw defines rights and uses power and violence to enforce its vision, its claim rapidly assumes the greater form – the comprehensive claim about religion.... what religion relevantly *is*. This is the essence of Robert Cover's insight that law is *jurispathic*: that, whether it intends it or not, the very nature of law is that it kills other normative arrangements and interpretations.' Berger wants to speak of law being 'epistemologically colonial'. Berger at 311–312. See also Robert M. Cover, 'The Supreme Court 1982 Term – Foreword: *Nomos* and Narrative', (1983) 97 *Harvard Law Review* (4).

theocracy, which simply means the rule of God. The rule of God may clash with the rule of law.[40]

The relevant question thus becomes not *whether* generally applicable laws should yield, but *whose* perspective should take precedence when it comes to deciding *which* questions and in *what* situations generally applicable law should yield.[41] There are those who assert that the interpretative prerogative should always belong to the religious groups themselves. These know best when the friction becomes so great that, from a religious perspective, they would be forced to make too significant sacrifices were they required to follow generally applicable law.[42] Nevertheless, not everyone reasons in this way.

At the beginning of the article co-written with Årsheim, we mention the central distinction between an internal and an external perspective regarding religion. Should religious traditions be conceptualized with the help of their own categories, vocabularies, and ways of reasoning, or should we approach them from the outside with the help of 'neutral' categories that are not at home in any specific tradition? The latter seems impossible to achieve, not least given the diversity among religions,[43] but also for reasons such as those pointed out by Esau and Berger, among others. We note that religious traditions form their own identities and provide self-definitions. The question is, though, whether these are sufficient in all situations and for all purposes, for example, when the task is to decide whether an exception should be made to generally applicable law.[44]

I want to argue that it is one thing to affirm as a matter of principle that, usually, an individual will have the best insight into who he or she is and wants. (Although we should not

40 Alvin J. Esau, '"Islands of Exclusivity" Revisited: Religious Organizations, Employment Discrimination and *Heintz v. Christian Horizons*', (2009–2010) 15 *Canadian Labour & Employment Law Journal* (3) 389–434, 429. See also Berger, who makes certain observations regarding law's religion in a Canadian constitutional context to tease out the cultural embeddedness of the legal approach. What Berger sheds light on resonates with other recent work trying to tease out implicit understandings of law that influence 'secular' adjudication in matters of faith: religion is seen as largely a private matter; the focus is on the individual, on choice and autonomy. Berger at 283.

41 I am simplifying here for the sake of the argument. This matter can be further qualified by asking at what level and stage decisions on exceptions for religion from generally applicable law should be made – either for specifically identified groups or particular activities or in general 'neutral' terms – and what the consequences of this are. Should it be done when a law is enacted or when it is interpreted? Marie Ashe, for example, finds the situation in the United States problematic, where after the 1990 Supreme Court decision in *Employment Division, Dept. of Human Resources of Oregon v. Smith*, 494 U.S. 872, and the subsequent Religious Freedom Restoration Act of 1993 (RFRA) and Religious Land Use and Institutionalized Persons Act of 2000 (RLUIPA), the statutory protection of religious liberty and accommodation for religion has drastically increased beyond what was earlier guaranteed under the US Constitution. Ashe at 209–210. See also, for example, Yossi Nehushtan, 'The Case for a General Constitutional Right to be Granted Conscientious Exemption', (2016) 5 *Oxford Journal of Law and Religion* (2) 230–254 and Rex Ahdar and Ian Leigh, *Religious Freedom in the Liberal State* (2nd edn, Oxford University Press 2013), 359–361, for a discussion of this.

42 This may come accompanied by the further assertion that this religious appraisal that accommodation is necessary cannot legitimately become the object of external assessment and judicial evaluation. Deference is required not only because, for example, the judiciary is poorly equipped when it comes to religious expertise, but also because this would be to venture into an area which is none of one's business. Mark O. DeGirolami, 'Religious Accommodation, Religious Tradition, and Political Polarization', (2017) 20 *Lewis & Clark Law Review* (4) 1127–1155.

43 Slotte and Årsheim at 2. See also Russell T. McCutcheon, ed., *The Insider/Outsider Problem in the Study of Religion: A Reader* (Cassell 1999), which through its selection of classic and contemporary contributions examines this matter from a variety of perspectives.

44 Slotte and Årsheim at 2.

underestimate the human ability of intentional or unintentional self-deception.[45]) What weight can or should be attributed to this in different situations is a different question, though. When we are dealing with a collective, the matter is rendered more difficult still by the fact that, as the short snapshots from current discussions within the Evangelical Lutheran Church of Finland and among my students show, an internal perspective is seldom completely uniform[46]; nor can we always unambiguously distinguish between an internal and an external perspective. Both as regards notions and values, and concrete regulation, there are overlaps, as I already noted with reference to Sandberg.

Now, religious traditions have different ways of viewing and localizing authority and making decisions. This naturally must be taken into account and respected.[47] Yet what this should or will mean in practice is not completely clear-cut, precisely for other reasons, such as those I have mentioned earlier. Various presentations at the Fourth ICLARS Conference in Oxford in September 2016 put forward ways to go about this.[48] Here, I merely wish to offer an overview of how the European human rights system currently handles these issues, in the context of which it has also dealt with a case concerning the Evangelical Lutheran Church of Finland, *Ahtinen v. Finland*.[49]

## The discussion within the European human rights system

On the question of the ministerial exception, where does the European human rights system stand after cases such as *Lombardi Vallauri v. Italy*,[50] the German cases of *Obst*, *Schüth*, and *Siebenhaar*,[51] the chamber and Grand Chamber judgments of *Fernández Martínez v. Spain*[52] and *Sindicatul "Păstorul cel Bun" v. Romania*,[53] the recent case of *Travaš v. Croatia*,[54] or indeed *Ahtinen v. Finland*? These are cases which have dealt with the character of a particular office or employment, the nature of the employment relationship, reasons for dismissal or non-renewal of contract, and related matters.

45 Here I refer the reader to the talk by Andrew Koppelman at the Fourth ICLARS Conference in Oxford 8–11 September 2016. The recording of the talk is available at www.iclrs.org/index.php?pageId=4&linkId=225&contentId=21&blurbId=67428 (accessed 28 October 2016).

46 See also, for example, Greg Walsh, 'Anti-Discrimination Legislation and Regulation of Employment Decisions of Religious Schools in Australia', in W. Cole Durham, Jr. and Donlu Thayer, eds, *Religion and Equality: Law in Conflict*, ICLARS Series in Law and Religion (Routledge 2016), 80–81.

47 This is, of course, also something law does. For example, the way that the ECHR is currently interpreted, an individual cannot make a claim to religious freedom against the community of which she forms a part, other than by exiting that community, nor against the religious community or organization for which she works and whose rules she has signed up to and must follow. In this respect, the perspective differs from the focus on the individual so central to human rights law. See, for example, *X v. Denmark*, App. No. 7374/76 (ECmHR, 8 March 1976), 158. See also, for example, Carolyn Evans, *Freedom of Belief under the European Convention on Human Rights* (Oxford University Press 2001), 85; Ahdar and Leigh at 392–393; Walsh at 84–85; and Laycock at 856.

48 For recordings of the talks at the conference, see www.iclrs.org/index.php?pageId=4&linkId=225&contentId=21&blurbId=67428 (accessed 28 October 2016). Some of the written presentations have also been published at www.iclrs.org/event.php/ICLARS+IV+(Oxford)+2016/Presentations/English (accessed 28 October 2016). For examples of what positions theorists take as far as religious exemptions to non-discrimination legislation are concerned, see also, for example, Ahdar and Leigh at 361–363.

49 App. No. 48907/99 (ECtHR, 23 September 2008).

50 App. No. 39128/05 (ECtHR, 20 October 2009).

51 *Obst* v. *Germany*, App. No. 425/03 (ECtHR, 23 September 2010); *Schüth v. Germany*, App. No. 1620/03 (ECtHR, 23 September 2010); and *Siebenhaar v. Germany*, App. No. 18136/02 (ECtHR, 3 February 2011).

52 App. No. 56030/07 (ECtHR, 15 May 2012; Grand Chamber, 12 June 2014).

53 App. No. 2330/09 (ECtHR, 31 January 2012; Grand Chamber, 9 July 2013).

54 App. No. 75581/13 (ECtHR, 4 October 2016).

Within the European human rights system, the matters at stake are conceptualized in terms of collective religious autonomy or church autonomy, and its scope and limits, rather than explicitly in terms of 'ministerial exceptions'.[55] It is not a surprising way of framing what is at stake. Rex Ahdar and Ian Leigh have defined 'religious group autonomy' as 'broadly speaking, the right of religious communities to determine and administer their own internal religious affairs without interference from the state'.[56] Adding to this, Julian Rivers has defined this autonomy as 'the power of a community for self-government under its own law'.[57]

Religious communities as such enjoy rights under the European Convention on Human Rights (ECHR). The European Court of Human Rights in Strasbourg considers religious autonomy to be an important part of the freedom of religion or belief and connects it with an idea of justified religious diversity, making clear that religious autonomy presupposes state neutrality, in the sense of non-interference and 'disinterest', to a certain extent. Religious communities can freely determine their own doctrines and also how they want to communicate these, for example, through rituals and worship. Communities can freely regulate membership, i.e. choose and exclude followers. This also goes for the persons whom they wish to entrust with religious tasks.[58] It is to be assumed that this may include voluntarily adhering to the standards of generally applicable law in certain respects, as the Evangelical Lutheran Church in Finland does.

However, in Europe, the organizational life and internal governance of religious communities is not completely beyond judicial scrutiny, and state interference can be justified on certain grounds. As Dominic McGoldrick has stated, comparing the situation in Europe to that in the United States, 'the legal black hole is decisively small and even within it some legal principles apply'.[59] In regard to the chamber judgment in the case of *Fernández Martínez v. Spain*, McGoldrick notes that the role of the Strasbourg court is to make sure that the foundational principles of general national law and the dignity of the individual are respected, and states must judiciously balance the rights and interests of the different parties.[60] What does this mean?

When it comes to matters of employment, it seems that religious associations or organizations with a faith-based ethos that function as employers (and I here use 'employer' and 'employee' in a generic sense for reasons of simplicity) cannot deviate from generally applicable law, including from labor law and non-discrimination law, to an extent that would disregard the fundamental rights of the employees.

Certainly, depending on the nature of the work, deviation from generally applicable norms may be acceptable practice when it comes to employees performing religious tasks. Moreover, religious organizations can demand loyalty – in some cases even a 'heightened' duty of loyalty – from those working for them, provided that the demands are not

55 Slotte and Årsheim at 10.

56 Ahdar and Leigh at 376, making reference to Mark E. Chopko, 'Constitutional Protection for Church Autonomy: A Practitioner's View', in Gerhard Robbers, ed., *Church Autonomy: A Comparative Survey* (Peter Lang Publishers 2001), 95–116, 96.

57 Julian Rivers, *The Law of Organized Religions: Between Establishment and Secularism* (Oxford University Press 2010), 334. Of course, we may ask what is meant by 'own law', for example, in light of how the Evangelical Lutheran Church of Finland sees the law of the land also in part as its own law.

58 See, e.g., *Hasan and Chaush v. Bulgaria*, App. No. 30985/96 (ECtHR, 26 October 2000), §§ 60 and 62, and *Fernández Martínez* (Grand Chamber), § 127.

59 Dominic McGoldrick, 'Religion and Legal Spaces – In Gods We Trust; in the Church We Trust, but Need to Verify', (2012) 12 *Human Rights Law Review* (4) 759–786, 783.

60 McGoldrick at 783.

'unreasonable' and concern issues that are central or indeed of crucial importance to the organization in question.[61] Still, by taking up employment in a religious organization, employees cannot be considered to have waived all their rights, like the right to freedom of expression[62] or the right to privacy or family life, in their entirety.[63]

Moreover, employees should enjoy procedural protection. They should have access to judicial review of decisions affecting them.[64] From this, it follows that when dealing with situations of conflict involving a private employer and its employees, states have a positive duty under the ECHR to make sure that employees have the opportunity 'to have a decision that concerns the terms of employment and its possible termination examined by a court of law'.[65] Examples here include the three German cases mentioned earlier, where the employees were dismissed on grounds of having acted in ways that contradicted the doctrines of the religious organizations for which they worked.

Importantly, and following Carolyn Evans and Anna Hood, it seems that the approach of the Court at this point in time may signal something more than 'simply' procedural safeguards. Evans and Hood want to speak of substantive limitations on employment autonomy,[66] for once a case ends up before the Strasbourg court, it will submit the actions of the state to scrutiny: have employees had the possibility to submit their cases for review by public authorities, and have national courts struck a fair balance between the rights, freedoms, and interests of employees and religious employers?[67] Have these taken into account the position of the employee in the organization, the nature of the work – where depending on its nature and status there may even have been a heightened duty of loyalty – the length of employment, the possibility to find other work, and so forth?

This evaluation may include taking into account religious law as part of valid law, to the extent that state law has recognized this, for example, following international agreements between the state and a church. The cases of *Fernández Martínez v. Spain* and *Sindicatul "Păstorul cel Bun" v. Romania* offer examples of this, as does the most recent case of *Travaś v. Croatia*. In this last case, the applicant challenged his dismissal as a layman teacher of religious education due to the fact that he had entered into a new civil marriage without a previous annulment of his earlier religious marriage. According to the applicant, the dismissal lacked a valid legal basis.[68] The Strasbourg court found that there was an international agreement between Croatia and the Holy See on education and cultural affairs,

61 See, for example, Merilin Kiviorg, 'Collective Religious Autonomy *versus* Individual Rights: A Challenge for the ECtHR?', (2014) 39 *Review of Central and East European Law* (3–4) 315–341, 330; Ioana Cismas, *Religious Actors and International Law* (Oxford University Press 2014), 131; and *Rommelfanger v. The Federal Republic of Germany*, App. No. 12242/86 (ECmHR, 26 June 1986), § 161.

62 See Kiviorg at 329 and *Rommelfanger*.

63 See Kiviorg at 332.

64 Slotte and Årsheim at 23. See, for example, *Rommelfanger* and Cismas at 131.

65 Slotte and Årsheim at 11.

66 Carolyn Evans and Anna Hood, 'Religious Autonomy and Labour Law: A Comparison of the Jurisprudence of the United States and the European Court of Human Rights', (2012) 1 *Oxford Journal of Law and Religion* (1) 81–107, 101–102 and 105–106. See also McGoldrick at 775; Ian Leigh, 'Human Rights Conflicts under the European Convention', (2012) 1 *Oxford Journal of Law and Religion* (1) 109–125, 119–120; and Cismas at 128 and 133.

67 See, for example, *Schüth* § 67, *Siebenhaar* § 45, and *Sindicatul "Păstorul cel Bun"* (Grand Chamber) § 159.

68 *Travaś* §§ 10–15. To be sure, before his dismissal, an attempt was made to find suitable tasks for him in the two schools where he had previously taught Catholic religious education. No such tasks could be found, however, which resulted in the applicant's dismissal. § 107. The applicant argued that the Agreement had not been implemented nationally in the correct manner. According to him, for example, certain issues pertaining to laymen teachers of religious education remained unresolved. § 60.

and an act ratifying this agreement – an international treaty – had come into force. This made the agreement, which among other things spelled out the terms of employment and the qualifications that teachers of religious education needed to meet, part of the law of the land.[69] The interference with what the applicant claimed was his right to private life and family life was lawful. (The Strasbourg court also made direct reference to relevant parts of the Code of Canon Law in its judgment.[70])

Returning to Finland, in the case of *Ahtinen v. Finland*, for example, a pastor in the Evangelical Lutheran Church of Finland disputed the presence of a valid legal basis for his transfer from one parish to another. However, the Strasbourg court, making reference among other things to the Church Act of 1993, found that the decision by the Cathedral Chapter in question was based on domestic law in force at the relevant time, and that the applicant's procedural rights had not been violated.[71]

We may, of course, also have cases where the state has been directly involved in a case,[72] and its actions – resulting in an interference – are submitted to the usual tests of legality, necessity, and proportionality. This test will *de facto* include careful scrutiny of many, if not most, of the aspects mentioned earlier; not least given the fact that it is difficult to pinpoint 'the boundaries between the State's positive and negative obligations', and similar 'applicable principles' apply, including a fair balance between different interests and rights.[73]

Now, certainly, the Strasbourg court does not want to take a stand on what is or is not religion, or indeed orthodoxy.[74] Apart from in 'very exceptional cases', it is not considered justified under Article 9 for states to assess the legitimacy of religious, or indeed other, beliefs or the means by which they are expressed.[75] Approval or disapproval should not be a standard criterion when deciding whether or not to afford religious freedom protection to individuals or groups. Yet perhaps what we are witnessing is partly a downplaying of what denoting something as religion or religious accomplishes in the context of European human rights law. It is not about relativizing religion *per se*, nor about denying that something is a religious matter, but that denoting something as religious – and the Strasbourg court may accept at face value the framing of a matter as put forward by the religious community itself[76] – does not necessarily move the matter completely beyond examination. Nor does it automatically posit it above other issues (values and interests) at stake, nor beyond the reach of generally applicable law.

69 *Travaš* § 79.
70 *Travaš* §§ 45, 91–92, and 94–95.
71 *Ahtinen* §§ 39–41 and 43.
72 Actually, this was deemed the situation in, for example, the Grand Chamber judgment of *Fernández Martínez*. The Strasbourg court found that the state authority had been directly involved in the process, which dealt with the non-renewal of an employment contract as teacher of Catholic religous education. *Fernández Martínez* (Grand Chamber) §§ 114–115.
73 *Fernández Martínez* (Grand Chamber) § 113, in reference to Article 8.
74 *Lombardi Vallauri* § 50.
75 *Manoussakis and Others v. Greece*, App. No. 18748/91 (ECtHR, 26 September 1996), § 47; *Hasan and Chaush*, § 78; *Leyla Şahin v. Turkey*, App. No. 44774/98 (Grand Chamber, 10 November 2005), § 107; *Refah Partisi (the Welfare Party) and Others v. Turkey*, App. Nos 41340/98, 41342/98, 41343/98, and 41344/98 (Grand Chamber, 13 February 2003), § 91; *Fernández Martínez v. Spain* (ECtHR), § 80; and *Fernández Martínez v. Spain* (Grand Chamber), § 128.
76 Hence, the Strasbourg court does not resort to reliance on such a narrow concept of religion that certain things simply do not qualify as such, nor need to be considered for a possible exception from generally applicable law. See Christoffersen, 'The Argument for a Narrow Conception of "Religious Autonomy"' at 286.

The situation under consideration, though in part 'religious' in nature, may still simultaneously be a 'non-religious matter' in certain respects and hence not fully beyond 'secular' law.[77] The two perspectives are not mutually exclusive.[78] As the Strasbourg court noted in the Grand Chamber judgment of *Sindicatul "Păstorul cel Bun" v. Romania* with regard to a group of priests of the Romanian Orthodox Church, it may be that some of the priests' duties could 'amount to an employment relationship rendering applicable the right to form a trade union within the meaning of Article 11'.[79] Referring to the standards of the International Labour Organisation (ILO), the Strasbourg court found that many characteristics of the employment relationships were *de facto* present alongside duties of a more spiritual or religious nature. This was so independently of how the parties themselves had framed the relationship in question, by way of contract or in another way.[80]

Moreover, in the Grand Chamber judgment of *Fernández Martínez v. Spain*, the Court did assess the quality of the original ecclesiastical decision, finding that it was sufficiently reasoned, was not arbitrary, and had been made for the purpose of exercising religious autonomy.[81]

In the same judgment, the Court also noted that to justify a religious community in reacting to a threat arising from actions of dissenters, the threat must be 'probable and substantial',[82] echoing the Grand Chamber ruling in *Sindicatul "Păstorul cel Bun" v. Romania*, where it stated that the threat had to be 'real and substantial'.[83] That ruling stated that religious communities have a right to react to what threatens 'their cohesion, image or unity',[84] or 'integrity', to pick up Cecile Laborde's terminology from her presentation

77 For further discussion of religious and secular views as regards so-called employment, see, for example, Ahdar and Leigh at 338–348. With reference to Esau, on a matter later revisited in the article I have referred to earlier, they distinguish between an 'instrumental' and an 'organic' approach to work, the former focusing narrowly on the specific work task of a person, the latter expecting the employee 'to participate in the mission of the organization as a whole in a way that cannot be confined to a job description'. Ahdar and Leigh at 338–339; Alvin Esau, '"Islands of Exclusivity": Religious Organizations and Employment Discrimination', (2000) 33 *University of British Columbia Law Review* (3) 719–827. According to Ahdar and Leigh, adopting the former approach leads to a narrow view of when exemptions are due to religious organizations. They seem to want to make the point that a religious view on work equals an organic approach, being most obvious, of course, in the case of religious ministers. Ahdar and Leigh at 339 and 373–374. Yet, presumably, we could think of instances where it is appropriate to talk of an 'instrumental' or 'organic' approach also in relation to other types of work than those which in one way or another are related to religion.

78 Even if, for example, the third-party intervener the European Centre for Law and Justice (the ECLJ) claimed this in the Grand Chamber case of *Sindicatul "Păstorul cel Bun"*, arguing, '[W]here, as in the present case, the facts in dispute were of a religious nature, the interference in issue could not be reviewed by means of a proportionality test weighing up the interests of religious communities against the interests which individuals could claim under Articles 8–12 of the Convention, since these Articles protected rights which the individual concerned had freely chosen not to exercise.' *Sindicatul "Păstorul cel Bun"* § 126.

79 § 141.

80 § 142. In that particular case, however, the Strasbourg court found that while there had been an inference with Article 11, such was justified if there was a real risk to the religious community's autonomy and the measure to safeguard this, in this case disallowing the registration of the applicants' union, was necessary. National courts had examined the situation and struck a fair balance. There was no violation. §§ 161–173.

81 *Fernández Martínez* (Grand Chamber), § 151. The dissenting judges would have wanted this coupled with an assessment of whether the so-called 'secular reaction' to that ecclesiastical decision was sufficient. Slotte and Årsheim at 23 and *Fernández Martínez* (Grand Chamber), dissenting opinion, § 35.

82 *Fernández Martínez* (Grand Chamber) § 129.

83 *Sindicatul "Păstorul cel Bun"* § 159.

84 § 165.

during the Fourth ICLARS Conference in Oxford.[85] However, the risk brought about by, for example, the actions of employees has to be real and substantial. Moreover, actions taken must not 'go beyond what is necessary to eliminate the risk' and may not serve any purpose 'unrelated to the exercise of the religious community's autonomy'.[86] This points to an external assessment being possible even with regard to what may be framed as 'religious matters', at least as far as the implications are concerned.

Likewise, in *Travaš v. Croatia*, the Strasbourg court, making reference to the case of *Fernández Martínez v. Spain*, stated that in addition to the fact that actions taken must be for the purpose of eliminating a risk related to the exercise of church autonomy, '[i]t should be remembered that such an autonomy is not absolute and cannot be exercised in a matter affecting the substance of the right to private and family life.' It is to certify that the aformentioned criteria are met that an in-detail and in-depth scrutiny and the balancing of different interests are of utmost importance.[87]

## Concluding discussion

Some commentators will surely see the position of the Strasbourg court as judicial second-guessing of and excessive meddling in internal religious governance, perhaps even arguing that when a community draws on both religious law and the generally valid law in going about its business, this should not be seen as opening the possibility of external judicial review.[88] Still, the position of the Strasbourg court is one position among many today. It is clear that within different jurisdictions, different (legal) conceptions of what constitutes 'law' and 'religion' (and the 'secular') are at play, resulting in very different conditions for religious communities. The exceptions from otherwise generally applicable law may be narrowly or widely construed.[89] Moreover, religious communities hold different views of what exceptions are needed and they seek to regulate their communal life accordingly, as the review of the discussion within the Evangelical Lutheran Church of Finland makes clear.

Reflecting on this diversity and acknowledging also the extent to which non-discrimination legislation has increased and been extended to new issues and groups, and also that religious diversity has increased within many states,[90] it seems that sticking to rigid categories of law and religion will not take us very far. This expansion and diversification of both the legal and the religious realms has consequences for how we might judge suggestions for how to go about identifying the space of justified religious autonomy and for how we allocate authority. Some will say that given the diversity, and also given the lack of trust toward the state that perhaps especially minority religious communities will exhibit, the way to deal with it all in a sensitive manner would be to hand over authority wholeheartedly to the communities themselves.

85 The recording of Laborde's talk is available at www.iclrs.org/index.php?pageId=4&linkId=225&contentId=21&blurbId=67428 (accessed 28 October 2016).

86 *Sindicatul "Păstorul cel Bun"* § 159. This is also repeated almost verbatim in *Fernández Martínez* (Grand Chamber), § 131.

87 *Travaš* § 102 and *Fernández Martínez* (Grand Chamber), § 13.

88 For a discussion on this with regard to the United States, see Ahdar and Leigh at 392.

89 Slotte and Årsheim at 1. This point was made by Esau, too, with reference to Berger.

90 Slotte and Årsheim at 5–6.

However, in relation to this, Saba Mahmood, in her recent book *Religious Difference in a Secular Age*, points out, with reference to Talal Asad, that asserting that religion belongs 'to a private sphere to be ruled by its own unique set of laws… amplifies the secular distinction between civil and religious jurisdictions', where in addition 'in the modern dispensation, secular law by virtue of its claim to universality necessarily appears neutral and, by contrast, religious law appears particular and partial.'[91] The view of secular law as universal and neutral is a very one-sided picture that seems difficult to retain in light of the actual diversity, and it may come at the cost of reification of unfeasible notions and distinctions.

What I am inclined to believe at the moment is that we are, in a way, left with a paradox. It is exactly the presumed legitimate inability to compromise that will activate the need for accommodation and ministerial exceptions. Yet as Isaac Weiner has pointed out, if we portray religion as 'absolutist, inflexible, [and] resistant to compromise', 'flexibility' and 'pragmatic compromise' in matters of religion will be viewed with skepticism, and this will favor rigid religious positions rather than those (individuals and groups) who in various ways 'negotiate their religious identities from within disciplinary power structures'.[92] Religious freedom, according to Weiner, is then turned 'into a tool for enforcing orthodoxy, allowing little space for difference and dissent, let alone inconsistency and inconstancy', 'collapsing internal heterogeneities into an idealized model of communal consent'.[93]

In light of this, the current position of the Strasbourg court does seem prudent, despite the criticism that so often also rightly has been directed at it. It seems that, in Europe at least, authority in matters of religion is, in fact, multi-located and multi-voiced. Depending on the concrete subject matter, it is also more or less clearly allocated with religious communities themselves or the governance is shared.[94]

Finally, I imagine that in the end, we do not get around the fact that it comes down to values and value choices at a general level and at a specific level in particular contexts. We have to take a stand, and to some extent fill that void of meaning at the heart of legal governance to which Zachary Calo was alluding in his talk at the Fourth ICLARS Conference in Oxford.[95] What are the concerns for which granting a ministerial exception may seem an adequate societal response? And when is it not acceptable? The values have to be articulated – be it about integrity, giving due recognition to minority positions, etc. – and choices have to be justified.

91 Saba Mahmood, *Religious Difference in a Secular Age: A Minority Report* (Princeton University Press 2016), 117, 127, and 131; Talal Asad, *Formations of the Secular: Christianity, Islam, Modernity* (Stanford University Press 2003), 228. Making a similar conceptual point, this time more specifically in the context of faith-based arbitration tribunals, Ayelet Shachar has talked of such deference of governance as 'privatized diversity', and pointed to its dangers. 'State, Religion, and the Family: The New Dilemmas of Multicultural Accommodation', in Rex Ahdar and Nicholas Aroney, eds, *Shari'a in the West* (Oxford University Press 2010), 115–133.

92 Isaac Weiner, 'On the Unreasonableness of Legal Religion', *The Immanent Frame*, 2015, http://blogs.ssrc.org/tif/2015/01/08/on-the-unreasonableness-of-legal-religion/ (accessed 29 October 2016).

93 A similar remark could be made with regard to a focus on 'integrity' as a way to identify that which deserves protection. Would such an emphasis rule out an ability or willingness to protect incoherent or inconsistent positions as incompatible with integrity?

94 Not surprisingly, the Strasbourg court acknowledges this lack of 'consensus' as a reason for giving deference to states in matters of state-religion relations, including in matters at issue in this essay. See, e.g., *Sindicatul "Păstorul cel Bun"* § 171.

95 The recording of Calo's talk is available at www.iclrs.org/index.php?pageId=4&linkId=225&contentId=21&blurbId=67428 (accessed 28 October 2016).

Yet boundaries have been drawn differently during different times in history and in different legal and religious contexts, and so it will remain.[96] The direction is not simply about moving toward more or less religious autonomy and exceptions. Instead, it is about continuously being aware of the complexity of the matters at hand and about making well-considered decisions which for the moment will hopefully come across as the 'legally correct' ones and be acceptable to those concerned, but which we, at least with the limited perspective of life here on earth, can take neither as absolute nor as unchangeable.

96 In this essay, I have not seen as my task to take a stand on whether religion deserves – or is best served by – this form of protection at all. For an overview of the current discussion as regards singling out religion for special protection, and the various positions that are taken in that discussion, see, for example, John Witte, Jr. and Joel A. Nichols, *Religion and the American Constitutional Experiment* (4th edn, Oxford University Press 2016), 282–288. Nor do I find the space here to think about how, if one can or should, one can justify similar exemptions for non-religious groups. See, for example, Peter Danchin, '*Hosanna-Tabor* in the Religious Freedom Panopticon', *The Immanent Frame*, 2012, http://blogs.ssrc.org/tif/2012/03/06/hosanna-tabor-in-the-religious-freedom-panopticon/ (accessed 30 October 2016).

# 4 Freedom from religion in international human rights law

*Frances Raday*

Freedom from religion is intrinsic to the human rights system. There are three attributes of the human rights system that rest on the implicit respect for freedom from religion. The first is the essentially secular character of the human rights regime, the second the universality of human rights, and the third the principle of non-distinction, which is essential to the enjoyment of universal human rights. These attributes are interrelated, interdependent, and indivisible.

The human rights idea has produced a regime of international human rights law, founded in the Universal Declaration of Human Rights (UDHR), signed in 1948 by almost all states in all regions with six abstentions and no rejections, and in the Vienna Declaration and Program of Action, adopted in 1993, which affirmed, 'All human rights are universal, indivisible and interdependent and interrelated'. Equality is the key to this universalistic human rights regime. At the very basis of the opening two articles of the Declaration is the paradigm of equality,[1] without distinction of any kind, such as race, color, sex, language, religion, political or other opinion, national or social origin, property, birth, or other status.

The human rights paradigm, with its roots in the rationalist secularism of the Enlightenment, has shifted the concept of human dignity from the transcendental realms of religious personhood to the political terms of human society. As historian Yehoshua Arieli writes, the modern concept of human rights is the product of secularism:

> The secular character of the normative system embodied in human rights doctrine is essential to its comprehension. All its premises, values, concepts and purposes relate to the homocentric world and to ways of thought freed from the transcendentalist premises and from the jurisdiction of religious authority. And so, the development of the doctrine of human rights is inseverably connected to the process of secularisation of Western society.[2]

The core of the human rights project is the dignity and worth of all human persons, and the equality of men and women. The shift toward human rights has taken place over 300 years, with its roots in the rationalist thinking of eighteenth-century Enlightenment philosophers, culminating in a new political paradigm committed to the human rights of all persons expressed in twentieth-century international and constitutional law.

1 Article 1. 'All human beings are born free and equal in dignity and rights. They are endowed with reason and conscience and should act towards one another in a spirit of brotherhood.'

Article 2. 'Everyone is entitled to all the rights and freedoms set forth in this Declaration, without distinction of any kind, such as race, colour, sex, language, religion, political or other opinion, national or social origin, property, birth or other status.'

2 Yehoshua Arieli, 'The Theory of Human Rights, its Origins and its Impact on Modern Society', in Daniel Gutwein and Menachem Mautner, eds, *Mishpat Ve-Historyah* (Merkaz Zalman Shazar le-Toldot Yisra'el 1999), 25 (in Hebrew).

The human rights transformation of the concept of personhood is clearly apparent in all that concerns the perception and treatment of the Other. Central to this transformation is a requirement to regard the Other as a subject of political philosophy, entitled to participate as of right in the formulation of social norms, rather than an object to be regulated by them. The Other's status as object has been used to express the reality of the members of marginalized groups, which have not traditionally belonged to the 'I' or the 'We' of society that formulate religious norms, political policy, and law. The Other, in this sense, has been the slave, the infidel, the black, the Jew, the homosexual, and the woman. As such, it is not the Other of Levi Strauss, or of Gigik. It is, rather, the Other of Simon de Beauvoir. What these groups have in common, where they are identifiable as the Other, is that they have been historically excluded, because of their group membership, from the social and political elites, who wield societal power.

The universality of the obligation to respect human rights requires a form of normative empathy, which constructs a positive ethical system and represents an advanced form of morality. The human rights transformation in the conception and perception of personhood, mandating recognition of the status of the Other as a full and equal member of the polis, purports nothing less than the requirement of an ethic of empathy for the Other in regulation of society by its political elites, irrespective of whether such empathy is intuitive or learned by individual members of the society. Universal human rights' premises are hence not culturally relativist. They presuppose the possibility of evaluating the basic good for all persons, with the understanding that all persons flourish under conditions of freedom and wither under oppression or inequality. The requirement of basic human rights for all members of humanity irrespective of their birth cultures has been accused of being a form of cultural imperialism. However, it can be countered that the universal human rights perspective is far more fully empathetic and less patronizing than cultural relativism. The empathetic perspective leads to recognition of the pain of the Other, if that Other is deprived of access to those capabilities considered essential for our own human well-being, as being no less important than our own pain would be. The empathetic ethos of human rights is a political projection of the cry of Shylock the Jew, in *The Merchant of Venice*: 'If you prick us, do we not bleed?'

At the core, then, of the human rights project is recognition of the dignity and worth of all human persons, without distinction on grounds of the previous categories of status which defined their life potential. This non-distinction principle differentiates human rights doctrine from religious dogma in a fundamental way, as it decentralizes the concept of 'We' and 'I' and instates all 'Others' as equally entitled. This shift of paradigm has been particularly potent as regards members of the aforementioned traditionally stigmatized or excluded groups. Inherent to religious belonging is the intrinsic dichotomy between 'we' and 'others'. It is in the religious DNA to distinguish between the believer and the infidel. Treatment of others may be magnanimous, as in the biblical injunction, 'You shall not wrong a stranger or oppress him, for you were strangers in the land of Egypt,' but it is not a recognition of equal entitlement in the polis. Furthermore, the religions have been uniformly patriarchal in their regulation of women's lives, excluding them from religious leadership, frequently silencing them in ritual, and awarding them inferior status in the family. The monotheisms continue to condemn and withhold recognition from LGBT individuals.

Thus, freedom from religion is intrinsic to the principle of non-distinction which is essential to the universality of human rights. It is also a precondition for pluralism of religious adherence, belief systems, and freedom of thought and conscience. It is to protect the universality of human rights, with entitlement of all persons without distinction, that freedom from religion must be prioritized not only in symmetry with freedom of religion but as the organizing principle within which freedom of religion functions.

## Freedom from religion in international human rights law

Freedom from religion, though not articulated as such, is guaranteed under the UDHR, Article 18:

> Everyone has the right to freedom of thought, conscience and religion; this right includes freedom to change his religion or belief, and freedom, either alone or in community with others and in public or private, to manifest his religion or belief in teaching, practice, worship and observance.

In a context which was not religio-centrist, it should have been enough to talk about freedom of belief, in addition to the right to equality, without the need to venture into discussion of freedom from religion at all. Indeed, the very concept of freedom from religion is a concession to the primacy of religious values. However, the starting point is indeed religio-centric and not a neutral playing field. The dominant discourse on religion is concerned with the boundaries of freedom of religion and not the boundaries of freedom of thought and conscience. The language of manifestation of religion or belief and of worship and observance uses terms which are primarily of religious significance.

The UDHR nevertheless provides authority for recognition of freedom from religion in international human rights law. In recognizing freedom of belief, alongside the specific recognition of freedom of religion and in the context of freedom of thought, conscience, and religion, the UDHR clearly guarantees freedom from the dominance of any one belief system, including religious belief systems. It gives concrete expression to this freedom from religion by recognizing the right to change a religion or belief, which is anathema for religions which prohibit apostasy or heresy. This catch-all freedom hence overrides the possibility of the restriction by religion or by any one religion of the freedom to teach, practice, worship, or observe any belief system, religious or non-religious.

Later endorsements of the right to freedom of thought, conscience, and religion in the International Covenant on Civil and Political Rights (ICCPR) and the 1981 Declaration on the Elimination of All Forms of Intolerance and of Discrimination Based on Religion or Belief notably do not explicitly guarantee the right to change religion. However, the Human Rights Committee interpreted the ICCPR broadly, restoring the ethos of the UDHR:

> The Committee observes that the freedom to 'have or to adopt' a religion or belief necessarily entails the freedom to choose a religion or belief, including the right to replace one's current religion or belief with another or to adopt atheistic views, as well as the right to retain one's religion or belief.[3]

Thus, for the enjoyment of freedom of religion or belief, the right to freedom from religion is an essential condition.

The imperative of freedom from religion is implicit in the human rights treaties. The clash between culture and religion on the one hand, and human rights on the other, is regulated in two of the human rights treaties, which establish a hierarchy of rights in which freedom of religion, whether specifically or as part of cultural and customary patterns of conduct or practices, is not regarded as justifying violation of other human rights. The

3 Human Rights Committee, General Comment 22 (1993), UN Doc CCPR/C/21/Rev.1/Add.4, § 5.

ICCPR declares, 'Freedom to manifest one's religion or beliefs may be subject only to such limitations as are prescribed by law and are necessary to protect public safety, order, health, or morals or the fundamental rights and freedoms of others.'[4] The Convention on the Elimination of all Forms of Discrimination Against Women (CEDAW) provides,

> States Parties shall take all appropriate measures... [t]o modify the social and cultural patterns of conduct of men and women, with a view to achieving the elimination of prejudices and customary and all other practices which are based on the idea of the inferiority or the superiority of either of the sexes or on stereotyped roles for men and women.[5]

International human rights bodies have explicitly called for eliminating the use of the right to freedom of religion or culture to justify discrimination against women.[6] The Human Rights Committee, the treaty body for the implementation of the ICCPR, has stated that where a clash occurs, for example between the right of ethnic minorities to practice their own culture and other human rights such as women's rights, the right to equality should prevail.

> Inequality in the enjoyment of rights by women throughout the world is deeply embedded in tradition, history and culture, including religious attitudes.... States parties should ensure that traditional, historical, religious or cultural attitudes are not used to justify violations of women's right to equality before the law and to equal enjoyment of all Covenant rights.... The rights which persons belonging to minorities enjoy under article 27 of the Covenant in respect of their language, culture and religion do not authorize any State, group or person to violate the right to equal enjoyment by women of any Covenant rights, including the right to equal protection of the law.[7]

Furthermore, the Human Rights Council's (HRC's) Special Rapporteurs on Freedom of Religion or Belief have repeatedly emphasized that freedom of religion cannot justify discrimination against women,[8] and the Special Rapporteur in the field of cultural rights includes religion in addition to culture as an invalid justification for discrimination against women: 'The justification for direct discrimination against women by reference to culture or religion – which, according to information provided to the Special Rapporteur, continues – should be eliminated.'[9]

4 Art. 18(3).

5 Art. 5.

6 See generally Frances Raday, 'Culture, Religion and Women's International Human Rights', in Fareda Banda and Lisa Fishbayne Joffe, eds, *Women's Rights and Religious Law: Domestic and International Perspectives* (Routledge 2016), 18–22.

7 Human Rights Committee, General Comment 28, 'Equality of Rights between Men and Women' (2000), UN Doc CCPR/C/21/REV 1/Add.10 5, § 32.

8 See, for example, Special Rapporteur on Freedom of Religion or Belief, Asma Jahangir, Parliamentary Assembly of the Council of Europe, Official Report of Debates, 2005 Ordinary Session (Fourth Part), 3 October 2005, 979; Report of the Special Rapporteur on Freedom of Religion, Abdelfattah Amor, 24 April 2009, UN Doc E/CN.4/2002/73/Add.2, § 29; and Heiner Bielefeldt, Statement to the Third Committee of the General Assembly on 21 October 2010, *Freedom of Religion or Belief: Thematic Reports of the U.N. Special Rapporteur 2010–2013* vol. III (Verlag für Kultur und Wissenschaft 2014), § 16, available at www.bucer.de/fileadmin/dateien/Dokumente/Buecher/Heiner_Bielefeldt-Freedom_of_Religion_or_Belief_2nd_ed-2010-2016.pdf.

9 Report of the Special Rapporteur in the Field of Cultural Rights, Ferida Shaheed, UN Doc A/HRC/23/24/Add.2, § 62.

## Religious challenges to the universality of human rights

The universality of human rights is being squarely challenged by institutionalized religious orthodoxies at both the international and the state political levels. The application of patriarchal religious law, whether in a hegemonic theocracy or a pluralistic system, compromises women's rights in both the private and the public spheres. Though patriarchy is strongly rooted in all traditionalist cultures, I focus here on religious patriarchy because religion is commonly recognized as an institutionalized belief system with a concentrated form of social or political power and there is a high level of deference to religious institutions, norms, and values which is not bestowed on cultural norms or values.

The challenge to the universality of human rights on grounds of traditionalism, religion, and conservatism has found expression over the past decade at the heart of the international human rights system: the HRC. A series of resolutions, heavily endorsed by Muslim-majority nations and passed by a majority of the HRC's 47 member states, has attempted to redraw the boundaries of human rights.[10] The first set of resolutions called for the interpretation of human rights in accordance with traditional values;[11] the second called for the prohibition of the defamation of religion;[12] and the third called for protection of the family, without inclusion of a guarantee for women's right to equality in the family.[13] These resolutions throw into question the universality of human rights, freedom of thought and expression, and women's right to equality.

The challenge to universality in the recent resolutions of the HRC is especially crucial for women and girls who, in addition to constituting a cross-cutting group in their identity as half of the holders of each of the threatened rights, are also in a stand-alone category of pervasive gender discrimination. Gender discrimination against women is preserved in traditionalist cultures and religions, and practiced both in the public sphere and in the family. The HRC resolutions on promotion of traditional values and protection of the family without strong guarantees for women's right to equality renege on the Vienna Convention's prioritizing of women's and girls' human rights as 'an inalienable, integral and indivisible part of universal human rights and... priority objectives of the international community'.

The UN human rights experts in the treaty bodies and the Special Procedures of the HRC have responded vigorously and repeatedly opposed the anti-universalist resolutions in the HRC, thus setting the political and professional branches of the UN human rights system on a collision course. To take just one example, the HRC's resolutions condemning 'defamation of religion' and calling on states 'to combat the defamation of religions' were roundly opposed by religious groups, human rights activists, free-speech activists, and several countries in the West, who argued that they amounted to an international blasphemy law. In the summer of 2011, the Human Rights Committee clarified that the prohibition of defamation of religion violates the right to freedom of expression: 'Prohibitions of displays of lack of respect for a religion or other belief system, including blasphemy laws, are incompatible with the Covenant.'[14] In 2011, the Organization of Islamic Cooperation (OIC), which

10 See Raday, 'Culture, Religion and Women's International Human Rights' at 20–22.

11 Human Rights Council, Resolution 16/3 'Promoting Human Rights and Fundamental Freedoms through a Better Understanding of Traditional Values of Humankind' (8 April 2011), UN Doc A/HRC/RES/16/3.

12 Human Rights Council, Resolution 13/16 'Combating Defamation of Religions' (15 April 2010), UN Doc A/HRC/RES/13/16 § 15.

13 Human Rights Council, Resolution 26/L.20 'Protection of the Family' (23 June 2014), UN Doc A/HRC/26/L20.

14 Human Rights Committee, General Comment 34, 'Article 19: Freedoms of Opinion and Expression' (12 September 2011), UN Doc CCPR/C/GC/34, § 13.

had sponsored the original resolution, changed its approach and introduced a new resolution to the HRC on 'Combating intolerance, negative stereotyping and stigmatization of, and discrimination, incitement to violence and violence against, persons based on religion or belief' that received unanimous support.

In response to the 2014 HRC resolution on the protection of the family, in which the right of women to equality in the family was omitted, the HRC Special Procedures Coordinating Committee expressed concern on behalf of its independent experts, calling on the HRC to ensure that, in all future resolutions, concept notes, and reports on the issue of the family, the right to equality between women and men – as well as between girls and boys – within the family would be explicitly included as a fundamental human right. In June 2015, after heated debate, the Resolution fell short of the reassertion of the right to equality for women in all aspects of family life, but it did include a recognition that equality between women and men and respect for all the human rights and fundamental freedoms of all family members are essential to family well-being and to society at large. In the same session, the HRC adopted a resolution in which it noted the Report of the Working Group on Discrimination against Women (WGDAW) on the theme of cultural and family life and called upon states to take all appropriate measures to eliminate discrimination against women in all matters relating to marriage and family relations, and to guarantee women's equality in law and in practice in family life, adding the proviso, 'in accordance with their respective international obligations and commitments' (an ambivalent addition in view of the religious reservations entered by states to CEDAW's requirements of equality in the family).[15]

The religious challenge to human rights in the HRC has thus been met with solid opposition from the UN human rights independent experts, demonstrating tension between the political and the professional branches of the UN human rights mechanisms. The professional independent experts have joined in reaffirming the universality of human rights and, with it, the barrier to encroachment of religious values and freedoms on individual human rights. This reaffirmation is also an affirmation of freedom from religion.

The political challenge to the universality of human rights at the United Nations accurately reflects the waves of backlash against universal human rights from religious institutions and lobbies in a critical mass of states. While some reformist strands of monotheism have converged with human rights doctrine, there remain enormous tensions between human rights doctrine and the norms of major religious communities worldwide.[16] There is a confrontational stance opposing human rights on the part of conservative religious institutions in most regions of the world, which reject the norms of equality and freedom where these infringe on religious dogma or sensibilities.[17] The elimination of state-sanctioned practices that violate human rights requires constitutional guarantees of the human rights they violate, without derogation for religious principles. In other words, the constitution must guarantee freedom from religion where religious principles violate human rights.[18]

15 See Frances Raday, 'CEDAW and Cultural and Religious Patriarchy: Jurisprudence of UN Human Rights Mechanisms', *Canadian Woman Studies* (forthcoming).

16 Raimundo Panikkar, 'Is the Notion of Human Rights a Western Concept?', (1982) 30 *Diogenes* (120) 75.

17 See Frances Raday, 'Secular Constitutionalism Vindicated', (2009) 30 *Cardozo Law Review* 2769.

18 See Frances Raday, 'Freedom from Religion Is Fundamental to the Human Rights System but It Is Under Threat', The London School of Economics and Political Science, http://blogs.lse.ac.uk/religionpublicsphere/2016/12/freedom-from-religion-is-fundamental-to-the-human-rights-system-but-it-is-under-threat.

## Secular constitutionalism

In legal terms, the right to freedom from religion can be best secured through secular constitutionalism or the relegation of the eschatological ideology of religions to the private sphere.[19] In contrast, deference to religious values in constitutions implants violation of universal human rights at the core of the constitutional system, variously excluding rights to equality, freedom of conscience or expression, and freedom of religious pluralism from full constitutional recognition.[20] The self-aware nature of the conflict with universal human rights of constitutional derogation clauses, which exempt religion from constitutional primacy, is demonstrated in the numerous reservations by states, on grounds of religion, to CEDAW's guarantees of equality for women.

Some academic and liberal commentators call instead for a more supportive, accommodating approach to religious beliefs and practices. They claim that secularism is not value-neutral but, in fact, imposes its own set of values, such as individualism over community and will over obligation. But this is a false symmetry, at least insofar as the values of a religion do not recognize the entitlement of others. In other words, liberal values leave space for religious individuals, but some religious value systems do not leave space for liberal individuals.[21] Furthermore, some religious communities, both in majoritarian and in minority populations, call for the autonomy of religious communities within a constitutional democracy and, since the basis of the community's claim to autonomy *vis-à-vis* the constitutional norms rests on the norms of equality and liberty, there is great irony in the community's reliance on the rights to equality and liberty to deny or reduce those rights for individuals.[22] Constitutional societies based on equality and liberty cannot tolerate enclaves in which any individuals are deprived of that equality and liberty.

## Freedom from religion: a human rights imperative

Freedom from religion is not merely the negative aspect of freedom of religion. It provides a space for pluralism and for the guarantee that human rights will be respected for all, without justification for discrimination based on religious norms. Freedom from religion is indispensable for the universality of human rights, including the right to freedom of religion itself.

19 See Raday, 'Secular Constitutionalism Vindicated'.

20 In many regions, structural impediments to human rights are embedded in the constitutional texts, which explicitly subjugate constitutional rights to religious principles or exclude family and customary law from constitutional review, whether throughout the legal system or on the basis of religious pluralism. See Frances Raday, *Women's Access to Justice*, www.ohchr.org/Documents/Issues/Women/WG/PresentationWomenAccessJustice.doc.

21 See Raday, 'Secular Constitutionalism Vindicated'.

22 See Raday, 'Secular Constitutionalism Vindicated'.

# 5 Is there a right to freedom *from* religion?

*David Pollock*

Is there – and if not, should there be – a right to freedom from religion?[1]

If you lived in Saudi Arabia, Pakistan, or Iran, you might welcome such a right with open arms. It is sobering to think that England used to be like them: that the Church of England was born in an orgy of destruction rivaling that of ISIS and that there followed a long-lasting persecution of Roman Catholics and discrimination against other non-Anglicans, including any who dared not to be religious: all were compelled by law to attend Anglican worship, could not be married or buried except courtesy of the established Church, and suffered curtailment of their civil rights well into the nineteenth century. We have come a distance since then, and we have done so without an explicit right to freedom from religion.

That said, the non-religious and religious non-conformists still have legitimate causes for complaint. Since people do not join clubs defined by what they are not, they lack organizations to stand up for their rights, and so they tend to be silent. Yet:

- They are the people who are not eligible for a wide range of teaching and public service jobs because the employers are religious organizations.
- They are the doctors who are forbidden to carry out abortions by the religious hospitals that employ them.
- They are the women who cannot get an abortion or have to go through hoops to do so.
- They are the taxpayers whose tax is paid to a church to support a religion they do not believe in and its political campaigning that they oppose.
- They are the scientists who cannot get European Union (EU) funding for their work because the EU, under pressure from allies of the Vatican, excludes research using human embryonic stem cells.
- They are the writers and artists who cannot get their work published or exhibited for fear of offending religious sensibilities.
- They are the same-sex couple who cannot get married or who risk being turned away at a hotel or registry office.
- They are the parents who find that the only school available to them is a religious one, or who cannot get their children into the local school because it is religious, or who find that even in their non-religious local school their children are expected to pray and are given religious education that ignores non-religious beliefs.

1 My paper is argued mainly from the legal position in Europe and particularly that in England (for the sake of simplicity I ignore here the other parts of the United Kingdom, but they are usually similar). The situation in other parts of the world, including the United States, is of course often different.

- They are the painfully and terminally ill who cannot end their lives because the churches – in England specifically the bishops in the House of Lords – forbid it.

More generally, they are all the people who resent the easy assumption, still too common, that religion is identical with virtue[2] and that there is therefore something not respectable about opposing any demand made by the churches or about criticizing anything labeled 'religion'. Is this not a case for a right to freedom from religion?

Natan Lerner, in the 2012 edition of his book *Religion, Secular Beliefs and Human Rights*,[3] claims there should be such a right, referring to 'the rather neglected right to freedom from religion' and proposing a 'tentative list' of the freedoms. They include, for example, freedom not to be coerced to belong to a religious faith or to perform any ceremony or act of a religious nature, not to be obliged to take a religious oath, not to be exposed to mandatory religious instruction, and not to have to reveal one's religion or belief in official documents. The last of his list is the right

> not to be exposed to religious propaganda, indoctrination or proselytism when forming part of a captive audience [including] the right not to be exposed to emblematic religious symbols, in obligatory schools, state judicial chambers, public hospitals or other places where a person is part of such a captive audience.[4]

What is notable about most of these is that they are – or should be – guaranteed already by the right to freedom of religion and belief – including, of course, the freedom not just to reject religion but to hold non-religious beliefs, such as Humanism. In some jurisdictions, this may still be a work in progress, but given General Comment 22 of the UN Human Rights Committee on Article 18 of the International Covenant on Civil and Political Rights (ICCPR) (which is essentially similar to Article 9 of the European Convention on Human Rights [ECHR])[5] and case law under the ECHR (which in particular has in

2 This may be the assumption underlying, for example, the BBC's unwillingness to allow Humanists to participate in its daily *Thought for the Day* slot, although representatives of all the major religions do so, as though only the religious have ethical insights of any value on current affairs.

3 (Martinus Nijhoff 2012).

4 The slightly odd complete list of relevant rights is as follows:

- a To have or not to have a religion or a belief and not to be coerced to belong to a religious community, church, or faith;
- b To opt out from any religious community, church, or faith with which one does not want to identify with or be a member of it (*sic*);
- c To be excluded from any official register identifying persons by religion or belief;
- d Not to be coerced to perform any ceremony or act of a religious nature;
- e Not to be obliged to take an oath related to religion;
- f Not to be exposed to religious indoctrination or mandatory religious instruction against one's will or the will of the parents or legal guardians of a minor;
- g Not to be buried in a religious ceremony;
- h Not to be coerced to reveal one's religion or belief in official documents;
- i Not to be exposed to religious propaganda, indoctrination, or proselytism when forming part of a captive audience. This includes the right not to be exposed to emblematic religious symbols in obligatory schools, state judicial chambers, public hospitals, or other places where a person is part of such a captive audience.

5 'Article 18 protects theistic, non-theistic and atheistic beliefs, as well as the right not to profess any religion or belief. The terms "belief" and "religion" are to be broadly construed. Article 18 is not limited in its application

several cases established the right to privacy about one's beliefs),[6] all but the last of Lerner's list would appear to be secure – and that also might have been covered but for the very dubious Grand Chamber judgment in the *Lautsi* case[7] and may yet emerge in other more deeply considered cases. (I revert later to Lerner's right not to be exposed to mandatory religious instruction.)

So what is there left that a right to freedom *from* religion could deliver that is not already provided by freedom *of* religion and belief?

Lerner generalizes, 'Everyone is entitled to be exempted from any duty, obligation, restriction or taxation imposed by religious norms and enacted by the state at the national or local levels'. This, especially with its mentions of restrictions or taxation imposed by religious norms, goes beyond his own list. Moreover, it could also be asked whether an entitlement to exemption is enough if what one is potentially exempt from would otherwise be a contravention of human rights. This would seem to follow from the logic of a recent High Court case in England[8] in which it was said, in effect, that a right to withdraw a child from religious education was not sufficient to render lawful a syllabus of religious education in state non-faith schools that would otherwise fail to meet the requirement under European Convention case law that such education be 'objective, critical and pluralistic'.

In the rest of this paper, I will put forward a catalogue of *desiderata* that might follow from a right to freedom from religion and will consider whether such a right is needed for their achievement or whether they might not better be established by extensions of the existing right to freedom of religion or belief or by other means, such as laws on equality and non-discrimination.

First, let me note that there is something odd about religion and belief in contrast to the other accepted freedoms – of movement, of assembly, to marry and raise a family, own property, and so on. They are by and large freedoms to live without constraint by others, especially by government, but their exercise does not in any essential way infringe the rights of others. In the same way, people covered by the various 'strands' of equality legislation – race, gender, sexuality, disability, age, and so on – do not as groups having those characteristics affect the rights or freedoms of those in other strands. But religion is different.

It is not that religion can be changed at will – it cannot, though it is mutable.

Rather, religions have intellectual content – they assert 'facts', make claims about values – and then not only organize their followers but often seek on grounds internal to their own religious systems to restrict the behavior of everyone else in ways that are potentially seriously damaging. Thus,

---

to traditional religions or to religions and beliefs with institutional characteristics or practices analogous to those of traditional religions.' Human Rights Committee, General Comment 22(48) (Art. 18) (20 July 1993), CCPR/C/21/Rev.1/Add.4 (27 September 1993), 1.

6 See, for example, *Sinan Işık v. Turkey*, App. No. 21924/05 (ECtHR, 2 February 2010), § 60; *Folgerø and Others v. Norway*, App. No. 15472/02 (ECtHR Grand Chamber, 29 June 2007), § 98; and *Hasan and Eylem Zengin v. Turkey*, App. No. 144804 (ECtHR, 9 October 2007), § 73.

7 *Lautsi and Others v. Italy*, App. No. 30814/06 (ECtHR Grand Chamber, 18 March 2011). For a devastating critique of the judgment, see Lorenzo Zucca, 'Lautsi: A Commentary on a Decision by the ECtHR Grand Chamber', (2013) 11 *International Journal of Constitutional Law* (1) 218–229; also my own analysis at www.thinkingabouthumanism.org under the tab 'Miscellany'.

8 *Fox and Others v. Secretary of State for Education* [2015] EWHC 3404 (Admin), § 79.

- Different religions make mutually incompatible and controversial claims about the nature of life and the world.
- Religions deliberately influence their followers' attitudes and behavior, often in ways which can be similarly controversial.
- Religions are in competition with each other: evangelists come to our front doors, set up television and radio stations, and run crusades to make converts.
- Religions are expressed through organizations, some of which are wealthy and powerful. They exercise that power in the name of their faith far outside the realm of religion – in influencing social attitudes and national and international policies (e.g. on free speech and on sexual and reproductive health and rights).
- Religious believers often feel under a duty to react strongly to any criticism or insult offered to their beliefs, prophets, or deities, however mild or reasonable.[9]

None of this is illegitimate (although some may deplore some of its effects), but it is different. No other human right, no other protected characteristic operates in this way. My freedom of movement does not limit or denounce yours. Protecting you as a member of one ethnic minority has no deleterious effect on me as a member of another. The nearest comparison is obviously with freedom of expression, but that protects only the act of expression, whereas freedom of religion confers a degree of protection and privilege on the content, not just the expression of religious claims, and on the behavior that results from them. By contrast, the claims of (say) political parties are not in themselves protected as a matter of human rights law, which provides only the (qualified) right to express them, and there is decidedly no legal protection for actions arising from political doctrines based merely on their being political doctrines.

Religion in other words is *sui generis*. And its effects are real. Insofar as religions – in the shape of individuals, churches, or religious lobby organizations – use their power and influence, albeit for what they see as the best of motives, to shape society to conform with their norms and doctrines, they can make life truly uncomfortable for non- and other-believers. I shall return to this.

So how might a right to freedom from religion be the solution to these difficulties? What would it mean? What would it deliver that we do not have already in human rights law in theory if not in practice or in foreseeable developments of it? I want to answer this question by looking at, first, the constitution of the state; second, laws influenced by religion; and third, the side effects of delivering freedom of religion and belief.

## The constitution of the state

The Westphalian settlement put an end in Europe to attempts by states to impose a single religion across the civilized world, but it took a long development after that for individual states first to concede a reluctant tolerance of other beliefs and much more recently to harden that into a right to freedom of belief. But this progress has applied principally to individuals and the way they choose to live, not to the state itself and its laws and official institutions. These have generally remained formally or informally wedded to a particular religion or Christian denomination.[10] Indeed, in most European states we still have a

9 This list is adapted from a longer version in my evidence to the Woolf Institute's Commission on Religion and Belief in British Public Life, for which see www.thinkingabouthumanism.org/religion/religion-and-belief-in-british-public-life/ (accessed July 2017).

10 Or just to religion as a category: for example, the English law on charities until the mid-twentieth century held that '[a]s between different religions, the law stands neutral, but it assumes that any religion is at least likely to be better than none.' *Neville Estates v. Madden* [1962] Ch. 832, 853.

residual theocracy – what Max Wallace calls 'soft theocracy'[11] – with established churches, state funding of religion, and so on. This, despite its alienating effect on what in many cases is now a majority of the population,[12] is still held to be compatible with the Universal Declaration of Human Rights and with the ECHR. However, the European Court of Human Rights in many judgments[13] has been edging toward a requirement for the state to be secular – that is, not wedded to or favoring any particular religion or belief.

So, supposing human rights fully embraced the principle of secularism and the secular state (where 'secular' means 'neutral' in matters of religion or belief, which is entirely compatible with a very religious society): what would that mean? It would free the non-religious and the other-religious citizen from implicit participation in and acknowledgement of a religion entrenched in the official laws and institutions of the state. It would demonstrate that the state accorded equal respect to all citizens, guarantee equal treatment, and reinforce equal access to official services. But – and this is vital – it would do so without infringing the freedom of belief of any follower of the previously favored religion. All it would do is remove privileges inherited from centuries before protection for human rights was established. Those privileges are often so encrusted with tradition that they seem untouchable, but they are typically enjoyed by shrinking minorities of the population[14] to the increasing irritation or incomprehension of the growing non-religious and non-Christian population.

Let me illustrate the effects by looking at England.[15] It would mean first that the Church of England was no longer established – which would have surprisingly little effect in everyday life, establishment being, in the words of Walter Bagehot, part of the 'dignified' rather than the 'efficient' constitution.[16] The 26 bishops who sit in Parliament as of right[17] would lose their seats. Religious observance would be removed from official occasions[18]: no prayers in Parliament or local councils, no religious observance on national occasions of celebration or mourning (the annual Remembrance Day ceremony at the Cenotaph was originally secular

11 Max Wallace, *The Purple Economy: Supernatural Charities, Tax and the State* (Australian National Secular Association 2007), 72.

12 The EU's Eurobarometer survey found as long ago as 2005 that in its then-25 member states, only 52% of people believed in God, while 18% rejected outright even the idea of 'some sort of spirit or life force'. *Eurobarometer Special Survey: Social Values, Science and Technology* (European Commission 2005), http://ec.europa.eu/public_opinion/archives/ebs/ebs_225_report_en.pdf (accessed September 2016).

13 See for example *Metropolitan Church of Bessarabia v. Moldova*, App. No. 45701/99 (ECtHR, 13 December 2001), §§ 116–117 and *Supreme Holy Council of the Muslim Community v. Bulgaria*, App. No. 39023/97 (ECtHR, 16 December 2004), § 93.

14 For example, the annual British Social Attitudes survey has for many years found under half the population saying they are Christian (41% in 2016), with well under one in six acknowledging the Church of England (15% in 2016). See www.bsa.natcen.ac.uk/media/39196/bsa34_full-report_fin.pdf at page 188 (accessed July 2017).

15 Elsewhere the effects would include reform of situations such as marriage and divorce being available only through religious authorities (as in Israel); courts requiring religious oaths (as in Greece, despite at least three findings against the practice at the European Court of Human Rights; see 'Oaths, the Greek Judicial System and Article 9 – Again', www.lawandreligionuk.com/2014/10/18/oaths-the-greek-judicial-system-and-article-9-again/ (accessed September 2016)); courtrooms displaying crucifixes (as in Italy; see 'Italian Judge Who Refused to Hear Cases Because of Crucifixes in Courtrooms Sacked', www.lifesitenews.com/news/italian-judge-who-refused-to-hear-cases-because-of-crucifixes-in-courtrooms) (accessed September 2016); and appointments of professors of philosophy, pedagogy, sociology, and political science at seven universities being subject to the local Roman Catholic bishop's consent (as in Bavaria, Germany; see www.concordatwatch.eu/topic-2891.834 (accessed September 2016)).

16 *The English Constitution* (1867).

17 A right that long antedates and does not depend on the establishment of the Church of England.

18 On occasion, there might be some subordinate participation by willing religious or belief groups.

but quickly hijacked by the Church of England[19]). State schools would not be compelled but forbidden to have daily religious worship, and the state would not finance religious schools. Official procedures would be secular – courts would not use religious oaths, and marriages would be solemnized by civil authorities, not by churches. Official buildings would not display crosses or other religious symbols (though few do and exceptions would have to be made, for example to avoid damage to historic buildings). More relevantly, the state would cease contracting out to religious bodies the provision of core public services. Religions, especially Christianity, would also lose their privileged position in the provision of pastoral care in 'closed' environments, such as universities, the armed services, hospitals, and prisons – something that is beginning to happen in England with (for example) a new policy of welcoming Humanist pastoral support workers in hospitals.

And, of course, there would be no official funding of religion as such. This is by and large already the current position in England, with the churches receiving financial support if at all only for secular purposes, principally for maintaining their historic buildings. Elsewhere in Europe, however, official funding is the norm, not the exception, with huge amounts of taxpayers' money providing a life support system for moribund churches.[20]

As to this first area of concern, therefore, it seems that adopting a secular constitution would avoid the need for a freestanding right to freedom from religion. This could be achieved by a gradual judicial and legislative extension of the obligation on the state by reason of freedom of religion and belief not to co-opt its population willy-nilly into religious observance or systematically to provide support, privileges, or power to one or more churches or to religions as a category. The religious institutions involved would predictably offer fierce resistance but – and this is vital – the freedom of religion and belief of their members would not be touched.

## Laws that originate in religious doctrine

There is another area where the inheritance from the Christian past still weighs heavily on the secular present, namely, laws that originate in religious doctrine and are still justified by it and by religious pressure. It is not straightforward in that, although such laws were and are plainly influenced or inspired by religion, plausible arguments in secular terms can usually be found in their defense. Their religious background, however, means that serious re-examination is justified to ensure that the secular case is convincing and not merely a disguised defense of residual theocracy. Moreover, such laws and policies are still being advocated, sometimes successfully, by powerful religious lobbies.

The laws and public policies in question mainly relate to the predominant concerns of religion: the beginning and end of life, sex and gender, heresy and blasphemy. They thus involve public ethical issues such as contraception, abortion, *in vitro* fertilization, genetic research,

19 See Norman Bonney, 'The Cenotaph: A Consensual and Contested Monument of Remembrance', October 2013, www.secularism.org.uk/uploads/cenotaph-a-consensual-and-contested-monument-of-remembrance.pdf

20 For example, in France, churches built before 1905 are owned and maintained by the State; Greece pays for the training, salaries, and pensions of Greek Orthodox clergy; in Italy, 0.8% of income tax goes to registered religions or to the State as nominated by each individual taxpayer – the Roman Catholic Church receives 87% of the total; the Evangelical-Lutheran Church of Finland receives 1.63% of the proceeds of corporation tax; and in Germany, direct annual subsidies to churches from individual Länder total EUR 460 million (*Der Spiegel,* 24 July 2010, www.spiegel.de/politik/deutschland/spardebatte-landespolitiker-wollen-kirchen-millionenzuschuesse-kuerzen-a-708309.html (accessed July 2017)).

all sexual behavior other than reproductive heterosexuality, marriage, divorce, illegitimacy, assisted dying and euthanasia, blasphemy and religious insult. Much progress has already been made with necessary reforms, but in most countries more – sometimes a lot more – remains to be done. It would be easy to produce a catalogue of examples (relatively few, to be fair, from Britain) ranging from restrictions on abortion in Ireland and Poland that have been condemned by the Strasbourg court, to criminalization of assisted dying for the incurably ill who wish to have the means to end painful and undignified lives; from restrictions on EU funding of research using human embryonic stem cells to laws against free speech about religion in Ireland, Poland, Greece, and elsewhere – including two states in the United States of America![21]

Re-examination would not necessarily see these laws repealed and policies changed, but it would see them reviewed and amended as necessary where they have no basis other than their religious roots. Members of faith groups have every right to live according to their own beliefs, but they cannot be allowed to command the law to impose their beliefs on others. Sadly some of them – maybe a small minority but an influential one – show remarkably little awareness of the freedoms and consciences of others. They are not being forced to have an abortion, but they are preventing others from doing so, even (recently in Ireland) at the cost of the mother's life. They are not being forced into a gay relationship, but they are stopping loving couples getting married, or even criminalizing their love. They are not being forced to benefit from treatments based on stem cell research, but they are trying to prevent the research and discovery of vital treatments for life-threatening inherited conditions. They are not being forced to die before their time, but they are forbidding others a merciful release from lives of intense and incurable suffering. To the extent that there is no compelling secular justification for these laws, they should be discarded.

But too often, religious lobbyists are powerful and effective in their attempts to impose their own notions of virtuous behavior on everyone else. To be fair, it is clearly not the majority of religious believers who seek to do so – assisted dying is supported by about 80% of the UK population almost regardless of religion[22] – but even mainstream leaders and institutions are usually unwilling to disown these religiously inspired lobbyists. Such lobbying is, of course, lawful and a legitimate exercise of freedom of speech, but it is aimed at imposing restrictions on the freedoms of others on the basis of the religious beliefs of the lobbyists and to the extent that it is successful it strengthens the case for a freestanding right to freedom from religion.

The most obvious examples are provided by campaigners against rights for the LGBTQI population and by the so-called 'pro-life' movement, which almost entirely for religious motives seeks with wide success in places like the United States to prevent women from accessing lawful abortion services or, as (appallingly) in El Salvador, to make abortion illegal even in cases of rape or incest.[23] These are only part of an increasingly well-organized international coalition of reactionary religious agents acting

21 Massachusetts and Michigan. Allan Turner, 'Two U.S. States Still Ban Blasphemy', *Houston Chronicle*, 2 August 2016, www.chron.com/news/houston-texas/article/Study-finds-laws-banning-blasphemy-and-apostasy-8987665.php (accessed September 2016). To be fair, those state laws are not enforced and would undoubtedly be found unconstitutional if they were.

22 A 2015 Populus poll of 5,000 people showed 82% support overall, including 79% of religious people. See 'Dignity in Dying Poll', March 2015, www.populus.co.uk/wp-content/uploads/2015/12/DIGNITY-IN-DYING-Populus-poll-March-2015-data-tables-with-full-party-crossbreaks.compressed.pdf (accessed July 2017).

23 A high school student in El Salvador was sentenced in March 2017 to 30 years' imprisonment after having a stillbirth. She had been repeatedly raped by a gang member and had not realized she was pregnant when she gave birth in a bathroom, aged 18. Medical experts were unable to establish whether the fetus died *in utero* or after delivery, and a female judge held that the failure to seek antenatal care amounted to murder. See

both in the United Nations and other treaty organizations as well as in individual countries. They are drawn from fundamentalists across the religious spectrum – Catholic, Evangelical, Mormon, Russian Orthodox, Muslim – but they work not in the name of their religions but under the thin disguise of defending religious liberty[24] or of supporting the 'traditional family' or 'traditional cultural values' – for which read patriarchal authority and suppression of freedom for minorities, such as (in particular) homosexuals.[25] Based mainly in the United States and in strongly Catholic countries, they are increasingly intervening in eastern European and African states.[26] The Center for Family and Human Rights (previously, and more honestly, the Catholic Family and Human Rights Institute) is ubiquitous and effective at the United Nations in New York,[27] with sophisticated lobbying against any move to establish sexual and reproductive health and rights, meantime raising funds from its supporters with alarmist propaganda.[28] It is not alone: in particular, it is joined by coalitions such as the International Organization of

---

www.theguardian.com/global-development/2017/jul/06/el-salvador-teen-rape-victim-sentenced-30-years-prison-stillbirth (accessed July 2017).

24 As Jay Michaelson has demonstrated, they are 'mainstreaming discrimination by rebranding it as religious liberty.... Religious liberty is meant to be a shield against state action, not a sword against minorities,' but that is how it is being used:

> Using the 'religious liberty' framework, the Christian Right now attacks access to contraception and abortion, same-sex marriage, and anti-discrimination laws – not on moral grounds (e.g., that contraception is morally wrong or that LGBTQ rights violate 'family values'), but because they supposedly impinge on the religious freedoms of others (e.g., by forcing employers to violate their religion by providing contraception coverage *[viz, in employee health insurance policies]*).... [T]his martyr narrative is a fantasy. School-prayer cases are not about individuals praying; they are about groups (including non-consenting individuals) being led in prayer by another. Gay rights cases are not about individuals or religious communities expressing opinions or engaging (or not) in private acts; they are about individuals and communities creating hostile environments for others by expressing their views, refusing services, or in other ways directly communicating a message of second-class status to LGBT people. And the current contraception battle is not about whether a church may exercise its conscience, but whether it may do so *at the expense of other parties' rights.* Yet in terms of Christian myth, the martyr narrative eclipses these inconvenient truths.

See www.politicalresearch.org/2013/05/28/redefining-religious-liberty/#sthash.koRDfKdT.h8mcMGR1.dpbs and the report to which this article is an introduction: *Redefining Religious Liberty: The Covert Campaign against Civil Rights*, www.politicalresearch.org/wp-content/uploads/downloads/2013/04/PRA_Redefining-Religious-Liberty_March2013_PUBLISH.pdf (both accessed July 2017).

25 The extent of such lobbying is described in detail in a recent report, *Rights at Risk*, from the Observatory on the Universality of Rights, www.oursplatform.org/wp-content/uploads/Rights-At-Risk-OURs-Trends-Report-2017.pdf (accessed July 2017). See also a report commissioned and published by the Norwegian government: *Lobbying for Faith and Family: A Study of Religious NGOs at the United Nations* (Norwegian Agency for Development Cooperation, February 2013), www.norad.no/globalassets/import-2162015-80434-am/www.norad.no-ny/filarkiv/vedlegg-til-publikasjoner/lobbying-for-faith-and-family.pdf (accessed July 2017).

26 See, for example, the report *Perspectives on Anti-Choice Lobbying in Europe*, www.heidihautala.fi/wp-content/uploads/2017/01/SRHR-Europe-Study-_-Elena-Zacharenco.pdf (accessed July 2017).

27 In March 2017, it formed part of the official US delegation to the 61st Session of the UN Commission on the Status of Women.

28 A recent fundraising email started,

> Without a doubt they are coming for your daughter and your son and your grandchildren. They don't have any children of their own. They are deliberately barren. So, they have set their sights on yours, your innocent girls and boys.
>
> From among our children they want to build an army that will subvert our world and create even more victims. They must subvert the family and the Church because the family and the Church are our sole protectors. The state cannot be counted on to help us. We are alone.
>
> Who is coming for our children?

the Family,[29] the World Youth Alliance, Human Life International, and Family Watch International. The result has been (in the words of the report from the Observatory on the Universality of Rights referenced earlier) 'the watering down of existing agreements and commitments; deadlock and conservatism in negotiations; sustained undermining of UN agencies, treaty monitoring bodies, and special procedures; and success in pushing through regressive language in international human rights documents'. Such determined and effective pressure for religiously inspired impositions on the non-religious and other-religious provides a strong *prima facie* case for a right to freedom from religion. A religious minority – or indeed, a religious majority – is not entitled, however convinced of its righteousness, to impose on the freedoms of others for religious reasons unless a good secular case can also be made out.

However, here again it is, I believe, preferable and in the end better to answer in kind by organizing equally effective campaigning, if possible by liberal religious actors as well as secular lobbyists, to fight against these attempts by a minority of zealots to impose their reactionary views at the expense sometimes even of their co-religionists.

## Burdens imposed on others by freedom of religion

The third and final argument for a right to freedom from religion that I wish to examine is that such a right would remove the burdens imposed on the non-religious (and often on the other-religious) in the course of delivering freedom of religion for the 'true believers'. There is sometimes an assumption that freedom of religion and belief means that religious sensibilities must in every case be accommodated – that religion carries all before it. That of course is not what it means: under the ECHR, there is absolute freedom of belief but only a qualified freedom to manifest it.

One of the qualifications serves to protect the rights and freedoms of others. Even legitimate delivery of freedom to manifest a religious belief can require some incidental compromise of the rights or freedoms of other people. But too often in delivering freedom of religion to the devout, the interests of those others involved are in practice given insufficient weight, especially when they – fellow employees, employers, customers, and service users – are non-religious. They may legitimately complain, and their objections will perhaps be

---

- UN Radicals
- UN Agencies
- International Planned Parenthood
- Human Rights Campaign
- Radical homosexuals

They use international institutions to impose their view on countries but most especially on children. They want to spread their devilish gospel of UN-style contraception, population control, p*rnography, abortion, gay rights, and all the other aspects of the sexual revolution that have caused untold sorrow in the United States and around the world.

They have billions of dollars and the awful might of governments behind them. And the body count grows ever higher. How many dead babies? A hundred million? More? How many dead from sexually transmitted diseases? Hundreds of millions. How many infected? How many divorces? How many addicted to violent p*rn?

There is really nothing to stop them ... except C-Fam and a handful of others.

C-Fam has been at this longer than most. At the UN, no other group has been there every day for twenty years like we have. Sure, lots of wonderful groups come to the UN, but then they all go home. We stay. We are there every day, seven of us, only seven that stand between the evil and your daughters and sons. The email ended: 'Please pray for us right now by name.' – C-FAM circular, 5 August 2016.

29 Previously the World Council of Families.

particularly acute when it is not individual religious freedom but that of organizations that is being protected.

Such is the case when:

- religious employers are permitted to discriminate against job applicants or candidates for promotion on grounds of religion. This is the case with a large minority of teaching posts in England and a proportion of some public service jobs in (for example) hospitals in many other countries;
- secular employers are obliged to make accommodations for religious employees that have deleterious effects for their other employees – e.g. if concessions over job duties or time worked are made without adequate compensating arrangements for those who have to fill the gap;
- women wanting emergency contraception are turned away by a pharmacist on grounds of religious exemption from professional duties;
- elderly same-sex couples are split up when the local authority's duty to house them is contracted out to a religious retirement home because it disapproves of their 'inherently disordered condition'.

So is this a case for a right to freedom from religion? I think not. The rights of non-religious people need to be defended on the basis of their own freedom of religion and belief. This is a question of the interpretation of freedom of religion and belief, not one of opposition to it. There is no easy solution by way of asserting a new right. Instead, tough arguments need to be had in multiple contexts with subtle distinctions of fact and circumstance over the boundaries between your and my and his and her rights.

This is where the distinction under the ECHR between manifestation of religion or belief and motivation by it is so valuable.[30] Not every act motivated by religion is a manifestation of it. It is well established that a pacifist cannot lawfully refuse to pay the proportion of taxes that goes to defense, although his religion may motivate him to do so.[31] Similarly, a Christian pharmacist's refusal to dispense contraceptives[32] and a Christian hotel owner's refusal to provide a room for a same-sex couple[33] are not manifestations of religion that deserve protection, but merely acts motivated by it.[34] Some consciences are very tender, but the law does not have to fall in with them – conscientious objection in war did not exempt objectors from alternative war work, and if they refused that, they went to jail.

These are often not easy questions: the territory is contested, and compromises are necessary on all sides. The United Kingdom, with its Equality Acts extending the law on equality and non-discrimination from employment and occupation, where the EU mandates legislation, to the provision of services and premises, has had to face problems that most other countries have not yet encountered. This is not the place for a detailed examination, and I

30 'Even where the belief in question attains the required level of cogency and importance, it cannot be said that every act which is in some way inspired, motivated or influenced by it constitutes a "manifestation" of the belief'. *Eweida and Others v. United Kingdom*, App. Nos 48420/10, 59842/10, 51671/10, and 36516/10 (ECtHR, 15 January 2013), § 82.

31 *Arrowsmith v. United Kingdom*, App. No. 7050/75 (ECmHR, 12 October 1978).

32 *Pichon and Sajous v. France*, App. No. 49853/99 (ECtHR, 2 October 2001).

33 *Bull and Bull v. Hall and Preddy* [2013] UKSC 73.

34 In terms of European discrimination law, they do not pass the tests of having a legitimate aim and being a proportionate response.

have written elsewhere on the matter,[35] but legislators wishing to provide for conscientious objection and religious exemptions from laws of general application need to think carefully through the consequences and, for example, draw distinctions between individuals and institutions, and among the latter between those with a primary purpose of advancing or practicing a religion (such as churches), those with a primary purpose of delivering a service, maybe to the general public, in a way based on religious principles (such as religious charities), and those with a primary purpose that is secular, despite their owners or managers wishing to act in a way consistent with their personal religious beliefs (such as businesses).

And among the latter two categories, another distinction is relevant: between those that are publicly funded to provide a public service, maybe under contract to a public authority, whose clients therefore have little or no choice but to come to them, and those that are independently offering a service to clients who choose to take it up.

A special case concerns the freedom – the human right – of parents to bring up their children according to their own beliefs. No one wishes to deny that right to parents, but theirs is not the only interest at stake. In Article 2 of the first protocol to the ECHR, the primary right is education – a reminder that children have rights too and there is a public interest at stake. The right of parents to bring up their children in their own beliefs is not unlimited – in the Article it comes in as a limit on what the state may do – nor is it a right to have the State do it for them. The state should not provide or fund the religious instruction of children,[36] whether in a single religion or in several at the option of parents, and should not therefore fund religious schools. (This is a policy for which there are many other good practical arguments, primarily the social and ethnic as well as religious divisiveness of separate schooling.) And any education about religion it provides in its own schools must be 'objective, critical and pluralistic'.[37]

Moreover, the state has a role in protecting the human rights of children even in privately funded schools: for example, in England, recent concerns about extremist influence in some Muslim schools have led to overdue official awareness of gross abuses of children's rights, not only in madrassahs providing supplementary education to Muslim children but also in full-time, ultra-Orthodox Jewish yeshivas, many operating unlawfully. The UN Convention on the Rights of the Child guarantees children's freedom of religion and belief which can sometimes require protection by the state from religious impositions by their parents.[38] All the more so should the state refrain from its own abuse of children's freedom of religion and belief, yet as the latest report from the UN Committee on the Rights of the Child[39] says, the United Kingdom is guilty of imposing religious worship on children in all state schools with no right for them (as opposed to their parents) to opt out until they reach the sixth form (i.e. are

35 See www.thinkingabouthumanism.org/religion/the-limits-to-legal-accommodation-of-conscientious-objection/ (accessed July 2017).

36 This is not an objection to education about religions and beliefs, which on balance is desirable in all schools subject to its being 'objective, critical and pluralistic' as required by European human rights law, and there is no right not to have education of this kind. See *Lautsi* at § 61, quoting *Bulski v. Poland*, App. Nos 46254/99 and 31888/02 (9 May 2006).

37 *Kjeldsen, Busk Madsen and Pedersen v. Denmark* App. Nos 5095/71, 5920/72, and 5926/72 (ECtHR, 7 December 1976), § 53; *Folgero v. Norway*, App. No. 15472/02 (ECtHR, 29 June 2007), §§ 84 and 89; and *Zengin v. Turkey* App. No. 1448/04 (ECtHR, 9 October 2007), §§ 54–55 and 63.

38 *R v. Secretary of State for Education ex parte Williamson* [2005] UKHL 15.

39 Committee on the Rights of the Child, Concluding Observations on the fifth periodic report of the United Kingdom of Great Britain and Northern Ireland, UN Doc CRC/C/GBR/CO/5, 12/07/16, http://tbinternet.ohchr.org/_layouts/treatybodyexternal/Download.aspx?symbolno=CRC/C/GBR/CO/5&Lang=En (accessed July 2017).

aged 16+). Schools indeed are another example of that special set of cases already noted where in a closed environment there may be no escape from religion. Just as in prisons, hospitals and the armed services, so in schools a right to some freedom from religion is entirely necessary.

## Conclusion

In sum, freedom from religion can be delivered partly by achieving a secular state, partly by a stringent review of laws that in origin are at least in part justified as imposing religious ethics, and partly by weighing fairly the rights of everyone affected by any claim for freedom to manifest religion. In every case, the degree of freedom from religion that can be justified is best delivered by a proper balancing of the freedom of religion and belief of the religious, the other-religious and the non-religious.

But is there a still wider right to freedom from religion? Should the public square be entirely free of religion – do we want to legislate for a secular society as against a secular state? Should religious arguments be barred in public debate rather than being answered and/or discounted to the extent that they are based only on religion? Should wearing religious dress and symbols be banned as incompatible with 'living together'[40] in society? Should street preachers be prosecuted for nuisance to the passing crowd? Should churches be required to remove their irritating doomsday propaganda from noticeboards facing the public street? Should governments refuse to engage with religious groups simply because they are religious? Should intolerant religion not be tolerated in a liberal democracy?[41] Should governments curtail freedom of religion in the name of freedom from religion in order to combat religious extremism?[42]

To all these questions, I would firmly say no, save (especially in the last two cases) for the limitations allowed under Article 9(2) of the ECHR and comparable provisions elsewhere. These proposals all go beyond those permitted limitations on religious manifestation – 'limitations… prescribed by law and… necessary in a democratic society in the interests of public safety, for the protection of public order, health or morals, or for the protection of the rights and freedoms of others'. They would tend to deny equality and protection from discrimination to religious minorities. They would curtail the freedom of religion and belief and freedom of expression of people with whom indeed we might disagree but who are our neighbors and to whom the public space belongs as much as it does to us. We are all members of society together: it may not always be comfortable, but the need to give and take is part of living in a community. Governments need to listen to all groups, including religious groups, not (*pace* Silvio Ferrari) because their 'power to mobilise significant groups of followers [is] too important to be ignored'[43] but because they are part of society and so have a right to be heard like anyone else (which is not in the least to say that a communitarian organization of society is desirable).

There is, however, an arguable case for a stronger form of secularism than that suggested earlier – one that would deliver an extensive freedom *from* religion but only in the official

40 As sanctioned by the ECtHR in *S.A.S. v. France*, App. No. 43835/11 (ECtHR Grand Chamber, 1 July 2014).

41 As proposed recently by Yossi Nehushtan in *Intolerant Religion in a Tolerant Liberal Democracy* (Hart Publishing 2016).

42 As suggested by Amos Guiora in *Freedom from Religion: Rights and National Security* (Oxford University Press 2013).

43 Silvio Ferrari, 'State Regulation of Religion in the European Democracies: The Decline of the Old Pattern', in Gabriel Motzkin and Yochi Fischer, eds, *Religion and Democracy in Contemporary Europe* (Alliance 2008), 109.

arenas of the state.[44] Under it, not only the organs of the state but every representative of it down to the most junior and even temporary or externally contracted employee[45] would be required in their official capacity to observe the strictest neutrality, in particular (in practice) by not wearing symbols, including items of dress, that are associated with a religion. This is exemplified by French *laïcité*, and it is based on the view that in official contexts, religion is to be seen as an ideological statement rather than a personal characteristic or preference. Religion can set itself up as an alternative – indeed, it claims, superior – source of authority to the state, and the state may in some circumstances legitimately respond by deciding that it has good reason not to allow this challenge to its authority within its own official sphere. While state neutrality is normally justified on grounds of fair dealing – and the perception of fair dealing – with individuals from (especially) minority religious groups, this stronger form of neutrality is founded on a view of religion as a potentially divisive force that might threaten the stability, peace, and good order of the state to the general detriment. This is patently not an argument open to states that have incorporated religion into their structures, but in some countries a history of damaging division on religious lines has led to a strong constitutional secularism that, while it cannot easily be justified under Article 9(2) of the ECHR, is potentially 'in line with underlying Convention values'.[46]

However, few states have a history and demography that can justify this *laïcité*-style secularism, and in open democratic societies where secularism (if it exists) is based on guaranteeing fair dealing with citizens of all religions and beliefs, dissenting religious groups, just like opposing political voices, should be answered with counter-arguments and social mobilization if they amount to a significant threat to one's values. Otherwise – as with street preachers – one may choose just to walk by.

Freedom from religion when justified is usually an aspect of the non- or other-believer's own freedom of religion and belief. It must not infringe the justifiable freedom of religion of others, just as reciprocally theirs must not infringe the freedom of the non-believer. That is not a prescription for easy answers: rather, there is no alternative to careful and multifaceted assessment of individual cases as they arise in light of established human rights principles and precedents.

44 I am indebted for most of the thoughts that follow to Ronan McCrea and his recent lucid and persuasive paper 'Secularism before the Strasbourg Court: Abstract Constitutional Principles as a Basis for Limiting Rights', (2016) 79 *Modern Law Review* (4) 678–705, while taking a more limited view (I believe) than him on the scope for this stronger form of secularism.

45 As in *Ebrahimian v. France*, App. No. 64846/11 (ECtHR, 26 November 2015).

46 McCrea at 704. As McCrea argues, *laïcité* nevertheless requires sharp delineation to ensure that it does not drift into unacceptable interference with individual rights to freedom of religion and belief.

# Part II

# Emerging social contexts

# 6 Immigration as an experience of fundamental rights and religious freedom

*Pierre C. Noël*

The recognition of fundamental rights of immigrant people in host countries is a strong indicator of those rights. To what extent are they actually fundamental rights? The International Convention on the Protection of the Rights of All Migrant Workers and Members of Their Families of 1990 (the 'Convention') drew immigrants' rights from the perspective of fundamental rights. Article 1 stipulates,

> The present Convention is applicable, except as otherwise provided hereafter, to all migrant workers and members of their families without distinction of any kind such as sex, race, colour, language, religion or conviction, political or other opinion, national, ethnic or social origin, nationality, age, economic position, property, marital status, birth and other status.

And Article 12 dealt with some aspects of religious freedom:

> 1. Migrant workers and members of their families shall have the right to freedom of thought, conscience and religion. This right shall include freedom to have or to adopt a religion or belief of their choice and freedom either individually or in community with others and in public or private to manifest their religion or belief in worship, observance, practice and teaching....
>
> 3. Freedom to manifest one's religion or belief maybe subject only to such limitations as are prescribed by law and are necessary to protect public safety, order, health or morals or fundamental rights and freedom of others.[1]

In short, approbation of the Convention means more or less that a country commits to recognize fundamental rights of non-citizens similarly to those of citizens. So far, only some countries (48) have signed the convention. Notably, the major destination countries for migrants in Europe and North America have not signed it. The reception of the Convention certainly corresponds with the extent to which fundamental rights of immigrants are already embodied in the national context, with those countries having legal norms already in place to protect immigrants' fundamental rights being more receptive to it.

1 International Convention on the Protection of the Rights of All Migrant Workers and Members of Their Families (1990), Res. 45/158, UN Doc. A/RES/45/158.

In an article on Argentina and immigration rights, Hines showed the innovation but also the relativeness of the Convention's ratification.[2] In fact, the 1994 Argentine Constitution, coming after the dictatorship period, reintroduced Article 25 of the former Constitution from 1853, which allowed foreigners to engage themselves in beneficial activities enumerated in the Constitution. Article 14 stipulates,

> All inhabitants of the Nation enjoy the following rights, in accordance with the laws that regulate their exercise, namely: of working in and practicing any lawful industry; of navigating and trading; of petitioning the authorities; of entering, remaining in, travelling through and leaving the Argentine territory; of publishing their ideas through the press without prior censorship; of using and disposing of their property; of associating for useful purposes; of freely practicing their religion, of teaching and learning.[3]

Various court decisions interpreted the concept of 'inhabitants' to encompass all foreigners present in the country.[4] Based on this constitutional disposition, a group of NGOs[5] and lawyers asked for a new law on immigration inspired by the Convention. This new law on immigration, promulgated in January 2004,[6] extends to all immigrants in the country constitutional and human rights protections, regardless of their legal status. The law recognizes all immigrants' rights to equal treatment, non-discrimination, and access to educational, medical, and social services.[7]

According to Hines, the main driver for such a legal acknowledgement of immigrants' rights is found in the South American normative context. Many South American countries saw significant migration during periods of dictatorship in the twentieth century and are today strongly dedicated to human rights.[8] Thus, immigration rights are seen through the scope of fundamental rights. Consequently, it is not surprising that among the states that ratified the Convention, a large number are from South America.

Even if the Argentine Constitution and Law 25.871 constitute a major promotion of human rights of immigrants in comparison to other nations, in practice there is a lack of regulations for its application, so it remains more or less ineffective.[9] Their application bumps into the same obstacles as in other countries that did not ratify the Convention, namely, the status of non-citizens before the law.

For the perspective of countries that did not ratify the Convention, we can take the example of Canada. Dauvergne, in a recent article, pointed out that the Canadian Supreme Court is reluctant to use international law when it deals with cases concerning non-citizens,[10] and the same is true for the Immigration and Refugee Board of Canada (IRB). According to Dauvergne, only five percent of the cases treated by the IRB made explicit references to

2 Barbara Hines, 'The Right to Migrate as a Human Right: The Current Argentine Immigration Law', (2010) 43 *Cornell International Law Journal* (3) 471–511.
3 1994 Constitution of Argentina, Art. 14.
4 See Hines at 477.
5 Among them there are some religious NGOs: Movimiento Ecuménico por los Derechos Humanos, Servicio de Paz y Justicia, and Fundación de la Comisión Católica de Migraciones.
6 Law No. 25.871, 17 December 2003.
7 Hines at 472–473.
8 Hines at 482.
9 Hines at 508.
10 See Catherine Dauvergne, 'International Human Rights in Canadian Immigration Law: The Case of the Immigration and Refugee Board of Canada', (2012) 19 *Indiana Journal of Global Legal Studies* (1) 307.

international human rights standards, and that is not a coincidence. Among many different motives, Dauvergne suggests that there is in Canada a resistance to the global phenomenon of the decline of citizenship rights in favor of the rise of international human rights.[11]

If we take the problem from another angle, that is the integration of immigrants in host countries, immigrants' own receptivity to the concept of fundamental rights constitutes in some way a scale of integration. A host country might measure the effective integration of immigrants according to their integration of fundamental rights. Do they recognize the religious freedom of everyone, even the right of not having a religious faith? In their cultural and religious practices, do they recognize the equality of men and women? In some way, we can say that an integrated immigrant shall stand beside other native citizens concerning fundamental rights.

But even at the integration level, the same division seems apparent. There is an absence of willingness to recognize the fundamental rights of migrants. The media coverage of the migration crisis in Europe has shown us migrants on one side asking for the recognition of their fundamental rights and, on the other side, host countries trying to deal with immigrants outside the framework of fundamental rights. For example, during the social debate on Quebec's Charter of Values three years ago, it was astonishing to see this division. Native Quebeckers were claiming, 'Let's protect our culture and laicity,' and 'In Quebec let's live by Quebec's values.' On the other side, we heard first- and second-generation migrants asking for their religious freedom saying, 'My hijab, my choice, my dignity', or 'My religion, my liberty'.

How fundamental are fundamental rights in host countries? Why is the immigrant's claim of fundamental rights not taken as such? In this paper I will try to bring new light to these questions by taking another approach. I propose to analyze the experience of immigration in itself, looking for the immigrant's experience of fundamental rights in the very process of migration. I will focus on its religious dimension using data from anthropological and sociological research done in North America. My hypothesis is that during the migration process, migrants are making an experience of fundamental rights, and more precisely of religious freedom. This experience goes beyond national interpretations of human rights, and it is a strong component of the integration process. After a brief North American contextualization, I will deal with the diverse moments of the migration process: the decision-making and the departure, the integration into a community, and the social involvement. To conclude, I will summarize the findings within the framework of immigration and fundamental rights.

## Immigration in North America

North American countries – Canada and the United States – figure among the most important immigration countries. Not only are they favorite destinations for migrants, they are also nations built on immigration. Canada and the United States have been pluralistic countries since the beginning – a Christian pluralism, but also since the nineteenth century an Asian pluralism and then more recently an African and Middle Eastern pluralism.

In both of those countries, we can see a great historical variety of religious denominations and practices. Nevertheless, until recently, the religious dimensions inside the migration process were not studied deeply. Rather, the focus was on the economic dimensions of migration, seeing the decision to migrate as a decision dealing solely with the improvement

11 See Dauvergne at 328.

of economic well-being.[12] As Benjamin Knoll explained it, the religious aspect was seen as only a marginalized variable.[13] It is only in the past two or three decades that the religious dimensions of migration began to be studied.

When we take a closer look at the migration process, it becomes clear that for migrants it represents something that pertains not only to economic well-being but to the wholeness of life. As Menjívar described it,

> Immigration involves crossing not only territorial borders, but also the physical, social, cultural, and psychological borders that shape and define relations, systems of meaning, membership, and worldviews of everyday experiences.[14]

The decision to migrate implies a risk that goes far beyond the day-to-day conduct of life. It puts at stake the personal narrative of the migrant and his worldview. This is why, according to Foner and Alba, religion can be seen as a social refuge for immigrants separated from their homelands.[15] In other words, Levitt said,

> Because religion is a global societal system as transnational in its operation as the economy or the nation-state, it is no surprise that migrants use religious institutions to live their transnational lives. Religion and, in particular, religious movements operating in broad geographic contexts, engage in increasingly homogenized forms of worship and organization creating global communities that locals then join.[16]

Such research reveals the religious dimensions of migration for the individual.

If we want to have a deeper understanding of the process, we should also take into consideration the specificity of the North American context. Some studies pointed out the great differences between European and North American countries concerning how religion as a belief system can play a major role for the integration of immigrants. They belong to different grand narratives.[17] Western European countries strongly rooted in laicity are less open to recognize such a role for religion in the immigration experience. On the contrary, in North America and especially in the United States, the very narrative of the State's birth crosses the religious narrative directly. To be American and to be religious are not mutually exclusive; some would argue that they are even dependent upon one another. As an example, one of the founders of the United States, James Madison, wrote the following on property in 1792:

> In its larger and juster meaning, [property] embraces every thing to which a man may attach a value and have a right;... In the former sense, a man's land,

12 See Jacqueline Hagan and Helen Rose Ebaugh, 'Calling Upon the Sacred: Migrants' Use of Religion in the Migration Process', (2003) 37 *International Migration Review* (4) 1145.

13 See Benjamin R. Knoll, 'And Who Is My Neighbor? Religion and Immigration Policy Attitudes', (2009) 48 *Journal for Scientific Study of Religion* (2) 313.

14 Cecilia Menjívar, 'Religion and Immigration in Comparative Perspectives: Catholic and Evangelical Salvadorans in San Francisco, Washington D.C. and Phoenix', (2003) 64 *Sociology of Religion* (1) 24–25.

15 See Nancy Foner and Richard Alba, 'Immigrant Religion in the U.S. and Western Europe: Bridge or Barrier to Inclusion?' (2008) 42 *International Migration Review* (2) 362.

16 Peggy Levitt, 'You Know, Abraham Was Really the First Immigrant: Religion and Transnational Migration', (2003) 37 *International Migration Review* (3) 848.

17 See Richard Alba and Nancy Foner, 'Comparing Immigrant Integration in North America and Western Europe: How Much Do the Grand Narratives Tell Us?', (2014) 48 *International Migration Review* (S1) 263–291.

> or merchandize, or money is called his property. In the latter sense, a man has a property in his opinions and the free communication of them. He has a property of peculiar value in his religious opinions, and in the profession and practice dictated by them.... Government is instituted to protect property of every sort; as well that which lies in the various rights of individuals, as that which the term particularly expresses.[18]

This understanding of individual liberties seems important for our present study. It leads us toward a larger understanding of religious liberty and its role in the development of the nation.

## Moments of the migration process

### *The decision-making and the departure*

If there are a growing number of studies concerning the religious experience of immigration in host countries, it is not the same for the first moments of the migration process, the decision-making, and the departure, where studies are few. For this perspective, we mainly use the works of Hagan and Ebaugh, who undertook an anthropological survey in Guatemala and the United States.[19] They followed groups of undocumented migrants from the very beginning to their arrival in the host country, participating in meetings as observers and conducting interviews with different actors.

Through data collected by Hagan and Ebaugh, we can identify several actions that testify to the religious dimensions or roots of the process in many cases. First at the individual level, the person making the decision to migrate engages in some spiritual reflection. Long before an eventual departure, he seeks counseling from a traditional pastor, who challenges him about his true motivations to migrate and whether he takes into account the welfare of his family left behind. The migrant takes part in an *ayuno*, an informal religious meeting held in a sacred location in the highlands of Guatemala. There he performs rituals and prayers, and the traditional pastor interprets dreams and makes prophecies. Then the migrant waits for positive signs and the permission of the pastor before making the final decision. Moreover, it is interesting to notice that many persons join these *ayunos*, including parents and family of those who have left. They are also looking for signs from God that everything is going well.

Once the decision is made, the spiritual dimension is ongoing. During the journey toward the host country, religious rituals are performed to ask for God's help or for thanksgiving. On this subject, Durand and Massey made an analysis of *retablos* along the Mexican border, small votive paintings expressing religious prayers.[20] Their study explores how migrants interpret their journeys as the will of God.

What comes out of this first moment of the migration process is its deep narrative dimension. The migrant understands his journey as part of a religious narrative involving the meaning of his life, family, and culture.

18 James Madison, 'Property', 29 March 1792, Papers 14:266–268, http://press-pubs.uchicago.edu/fournders/documents/v1ch16s23.html (accessed 30 September 2016).

19 Hagan and Ebaugh at 1145–1162.

20 Jorge Durand and Douglas S. Massey, *Miracles on the Border: Retablos of Mexican Migrants to the United States* (University of Arizona Press 1995).

### *Integration in a community*

The relations between immigrants and religious communities in North America appear to be reciprocal. On the one hand, migrants understand religious institutions as central in their lives.[21] On the other hand, religious communities are strong social actors for the integration of immigrants.

Concerning religious communities, a first relevant fact is that whatever their denomination, whether having a Judeo-Christian or an Asian origin, they insert themselves in civil society and conceive of their mission toward migrants in the same way. Foner and Alba noted that 'many studies point to the way immigrant religious groups adopt American forms and practices – for instance, using the English language, holding weekly services, or having a sermon as the focal point of the service.'[22] This American imitation among religious communities is important for our topic. It shows that groups agree to play by the rules of the religious market of the host nation.

The second relevant fact is the similarity of religious groups' involvement with immigrants. In her research on Salvadorian migrants, Menjívar showed that in three different cities and two different denominations, Catholic and Evangelical, the mission of churches regarding immigrants was more or less the same:

> Religion offers important psychological comfort for immigrants, however, it also plays an important institutional role – providing an anchorage for people undergoing the process of resettlement in foreign land.... Many churches offer the newcomers material and financial support, as well as legal counsel, access to medical care and housing, a lobby for less stringent immigration policies, and a welcome from the non-immigrant members.[23]

This observation about the multi-dimensional involvement of religious communities in migrants' experience in the host country is almost unanimous in every study. Religious communities not only deal with religious affairs but contribute to all aspects of the migrant's life.

Moreover, this experience of religious communities often constitutes the first place where migrants experience North American participatory democracy, being involved in the community's elections, membership lists, or board of directors.[24] In some way we can say that through these communities, migrants experience a global conception of their religious identity. It is not only a private and almost secret reality, but something fully integrated into social and political life.

From the migrant's point of view, the facts might sometimes be equivocal. For example, Foner and Alba noticed that 25%–30% of Taiwanese who arrived in America converted to Christianity, seeing in this religion an easy way to integrate. On the other hand, as Hagan and Ebaugh point out, immigrants often join the same church they attended in their home country in order to preserve continuity and to have access to a community of values. From both cases we can draw the conclusion, albeit perhaps an oversimplification, that migrants use religion as a means instead of an end.

21 See Menjívar at 22.
22 Foner and Alba at 367.
23 Menjívar at 25.
24 Foner and Alba at 364–365, quoting Helen Rose Ebaugh and Janet Saltzman Chafetz, *Religion and the New Immigrants: Continuities and Adaptation in Immigrant Congregations* (3rd edn, Altamira 2000).

It is clear that involvement in a religious community gives immigrants access to the host culture and public life. But it is not a one-way relationship. Immigrants also change these communities. They use religious institutions to 'reproduce and reassert important aspects of their home-country cultures – for example, incorporating ethnic practices in religious ceremonies.... "[They] share stories from their homeland, and pass on their religious and cultural heritage to the next generation".'[25] Furthermore, according to Foner and Alba there is a correlation between the emphasis on ethnic identity within a community and the immigrant's participation in local affairs and social or community development projects in the United States.[26] On a more spiritual level, the rituality of religious practices encourages immigrants to interpret their journeys in the host country as having transcendental meaning. Through diverse testimonies recorded by Menjívar in her survey, we see clearly the intersection of the migrant's individual narrative and the narrative of the religious community.[27] That is to say, not only is the migrant adopting the grand narrative of one religion, but this narrative is integrated into his own story. This reciprocal action of the host religious community on one side and the spiritual life of the migrant on the other side leads us to a more comprehensive understanding of the religious experience and consequently a more individual view of religious freedom.

### *Social involvement*

The last moment of the migration process is certainly the most important in regard to the topic of this paper. In fact, it consists in direct experience of human rights by being actively involved in human rights claims on immigration.

Upon their arrival, immigrants do not find religious communities that are solely dedicated to the integration of individual migrants. Rather, many religious groups in North America understand the immigration question as a high moral issue. For them, it is an issue like abortion and euthanasia that goes beyond state prerogatives, something rooted in divine will. Of course there are differences from one church to another. For example, Catholics tend to have stronger action at the national and transnational levels, and Evangelicals more at the local level. But the commitment looks the same.

Analyzing the involvement of different churches in the American debate on immigration, Benjamin Knoll reported on their official statements. For example, Catholic bishops made an official announcement in 2000: 'We bishops commit ourselves and all the members of our church communities to continue to the work of advocacy for laws that respect the human rights of immigrants and preserve the unity of the immigrant family.'[28] Using biblical references, mainline Protestant churches issued a similar statement:

> To make enforcement a central provision of our (American) immigration policy not only fails to honor our historic tradition of offering refuge to the oppressed, but also denies the call of Christ to welcome the stranger as if we were receiving Him as our guest.[29]

The turning point of those involvements is when they engage immigrants in public manifestations, in civic contestations of government policy. At that moment, immigrants experience

25 Foner and Alba at 363.
26 Foner and Alba at 363–364.
27 See, for example, the testimony of Isabel in Menjívar at 28.
28 Knoll at 315.
29 Knoll at 315.

an internal and individual experience of fundamental rights. The narrative of their church becomes their own narrative and vice versa. Foner and Alba, quoting Foley and Hoge, point out how religious leaders' appeals to ethnic identity to promote engagement in civic action for immigration rights 'paradoxically... integrate immigrants more deep into American civic and politic culture even as they preserve and reinforce their sense of difference'.[30]

## Conclusion

This brief incursion in the experience of immigrants gives us new insights concerning how fundamental rights and more specifically the freedom of religion are interpreted in the migration context. Immigrants perceive their fundamental rights as within the scope of international law and as having priority over national interpretations. This perception is deeply rooted in religious communities that welcome immigrants; as noted earlier, these communities view immigration rights as a moral issue superseding state prerogatives and as a divine commandment.

Religion is often deeply rooted in the individual experience of immigrants. First, immigrant creates a narrative that suggests that he is not simply reproducing the *status quo ante* of his religion. Rather, internalizing his religion, he uses his own narrative to reinterpret it, and sometimes to change or leave religion. In doing so, he is fulfilling the criteria of integrity, of sincere belief used by courts to identify real religious experience that qualifies for religious freedom protection. Second, a religious community's welcoming of an immigrant as a whole person gives him an understanding of another key feature of religious freedom: that the believer need not separate his religious life and his civil life, or his private sphere and his public sphere. His religious identity can be fully integrated to his life as a whole. Finally, the public involvement of the immigrant in the social debate on fundamental rights brings him to the core of his religious freedom – in other words, an understanding of the State's limited sovereignty in such matters. Putting together these three dimensions, we get a different understanding of what is at stake in the immigrant's claim for his fundamental rights. Turning back to the example of Quebec's Charter of Values, it seems clear to me that the Muslim woman who said, 'My hijab, my dignity' was not only claiming a sort of cultural status quo; she was also internalizing fundamental rights in the deepest way.

From another perspective, this brief study also gives insights at the level of grand narratives or worldviews. The interpretation of the migrant's fundamental rights will differ profoundly depending on the worldview in which it takes form. In other words, those interpretations depend on what we consider to be the epistemological foundations of freedom of religion as a fundamental right. Does religious liberty find its origins in the emancipation of the middle class at the Renaissance, or in other word in the birth of the 'free man' as we saw in the text of Madison? Does religious liberty find its origins in the French revolution and the secularization process? Or does religious liberty find its origins in the twentieth century's proclamation of human rights and, at the same moment, in the trauma of the Shoah? Answers to those questions give life to different interpretations. In this study, our interpretation is framed by the Madisonian perspective, which views religious freedom as an inalienable right regardless of citizenship, and requires governments to protect this liberty.

30 Foner and Alba at 364.

# 7 Health-care conscience and competing sexual liberty claims

*Sister Renée Mirkes*

There are emerging conflicts in what I call the second cycle of health-care conscientious objection in the United States. The first round, following *Roe v. Wade*, continues to involve religious health-care providers in conscientious objection to abortion, contraception, sterilization, and *in vitro* fertilization and is directed toward the protection of the basic human goods of life and procreation. Religious health-care providers are medical personnel who want to claim their First Amendment rights as not only the right to worship God on Sunday, but also the right to live out their faith on the other six days of the week.

The second round of conscientious objection in health care follows the federal legalization of sodomistic sex in 1990 and[1] of same-sex marriage in 2015,[2] and, for the past several decades, the introduction of state public accommodations/sexual orientation and gender identity (PA-SOGI) laws[3] – state statutes that prohibit sexual orientation and gender identity discrimination in public services/accommodations.

This new legal landscape has already impelled and will continue to impel religious health-care professionals to defend the basic goods of marriage and family as they conscientiously decline services that directly facilitate patients' same-sex relations or homosexual parenting.

## Clinical cases

### *Case 1*

A Connecticut woman in a homosexual relationship seeks treatment from a gynecologist for endometriosis and polycystic ovaries. Once these pathologies are successfully resolved, the patient returns to the gynecologist and requests Clomid to stimulate her ovaries. The clinician insists that although she had no moral reservations about improving the woman's health and well-being by treating her gynecological abnormalities, she does

1 *Lawrence v. Texas*, 539 U.S. 558 (2003), overruling *Bowers v. Hardwick*, 479 U.S. 186 (1986).

2 *Obergefell v. Hodges*, 576 U.S. ___ (2015).

3 California, Connecticut, Hawaii, Illinois, Iowa, Maine, Maryland, Massachusetts, Minnesota, New Hampshire, New Jersey, New Mexico, New York Oregon, Rhode Island, Vermont, Washington, Wisconsin, and Washington, D.C. prohibit discrimination on the basis of sexual orientation in public accommodations. See, for example, Cal. Civ. Code § 51b:

> All persons within the jurisdiction of this state are free and equal, and no matter what their sex, race, color, religion, ancestry, national origin, disability, medical condition, marital status, or sexual orientation are entitled to the full and equal accommodations, advantages, facilities, privileges, or services in all business establishments of every kind whatsoever.

have a moral objection to providing Clomid. The physician explains that since the only goal of giving Clomid would be to help the patient conceive a child, the physician would be morally complicit in facilitating a pregnancy outside a heterosexual marriage and in depriving the child of the complementary parenting of a mother and a father. Since providing this drug contradicts her religious convictions about the meaning of marriage and family, the physician advises the patient to seek the help of another gynecologist.[4]

### *Case 2*

An Iowa man in a same-sex relationship seeks help from his internist for problems related to erectile dysfunction. Since the patient is no longer able to have satisfying sex with his male partner, he requests that the doctor write a prescription for a medication that will address this problem. The physician explains that although she is willing to treat the underlying health conditions that may be contributing to his erectile dysfunction, she cannot in good conscience write a prescription for a drug that would directly facilitate sex outside a heterosexual marriage. For this reason, she helps the patient find another physician to help him meet his objective.[5]

### *Case 3*

A Washington man in a same-sex marriage seeks psychological counseling for emotional issues pertaining to the sexual relationship with his male partner. The clinical psychologist explains to the client that she has no problem helping him improve his psychological health, including resolution of emotional conflicts. She considers it a matter of professional and moral responsibility to provide sound counseling services irrespective of the client's sexual orientation. Nonetheless, the psychologist carefully delineates that to which she would object: providing counseling services whose direct goal is to affirm the client's sexual relationship with his male partner. Since such affirmation fails to comport with her deeply held beliefs and moral values, the clinician informs the client she cannot, in good conscience, counsel him.[6]

When cases like these involving alleged sexual orientation discrimination against conscientiously objecting health-care providers come to court, is there a general legal strategy that explains why judges hearing these cases tend to favor the sexual liberty claims? Yes.

When rights conflict, as they do in the three health-care cases just cited, instead of finding a way for sexual liberty and religious liberty to coexist, courts set up the case as a zero-sum direct conflict of rights. Instead of finding the least restrictive way to reconcile these conflicting rights, i.e. finding a way for sexual liberty and religious liberty claims to

4 This clinical scenario resembles circumstances in *North Coast Women's Care Medical Group v. San Diego County Superior Court*, 189 P.3d 959 (Cal. 2008).

5 A physician presented this clinical scenario to the Center for NaProEthics with the goal of discerning the moral dimensions of a treatment refusal.

6 This case mirrors the situation described in the Delaware statute legalizing same-sex civil unions (13 Del. Code § 207(a)):

> In the case of critical illness of one of the parties desiring to enter into a civil union, the physician attending such party may appear for the ill party and make an application for a civil union license for such party, if such physician first makes an affidavit and delivers it to the issuing officer stating that in the opinion of said physician the party for whom said physician is acting is at the point of death and that this person may lawfully enter into a civil union. The application for the civil union license shall be altered in such case to show that said physician acted as proxy and the affidavit of the physician shall be filled with the application.

Although assistance on the part of the attending physician is discretionary, it is possible that a refusal, allegedly based on sexual orientation, could run awry of a sexual public accommodations statute.

coexist, US courts are effectively holding that the homosexual patients' right to be free of discrimination trumps the religious liberty of health-care providers.

Chai Feldblum, a Georgetown University law professor and gay activist who helps draft federal legislation related to sexual orientation, agrees. She approvingly sums up the typical zero-sum mindset of the judges who try these sexual liberty/religious liberty conflict cases, stating that when religious and sexual liberty conflict, 'I'm having a hard time coming up with any case in which religious liberty should win.'[7]

The following statement of Baronelle Stutzman exposes the legal and logical error of Feldblum's opinion that sexual liberty claims must trump those of religious liberty:

> One thing I've loved about our country is that we protect the freedom of expression and the right to disagree over these kinds of issues without one side being threatened by the government over it. Rob and Curt [two homosexual employees who sued their employer, Baronelle, for alleged sexual orientation discrimination] have their beliefs about marriage and aren't being stopped by the state from living them out. I only ask for the same freedom to live out my beliefs about marriage.

Given the recent attacks on religious freedom in the United States, the bottom line is this: the days when religious health-care providers can take their right to practice conscientious medicine for granted are gone.

## Health-care rights of conscience are becoming an endangered species

### *The US Constitution cannot fully protect health-care rights of conscience*

It is true that the First Amendment expressly constrains government from enacting laws that infringe upon the free exercise of religion.[8] However, as the Supreme Court's 1990 decision in the landmark case *Employment Division v. Smith*[9] indicates, state laws of general applicability like PA-SOGI laws that impinge upon religious liberty may nevertheless be valid and may very well prevail against free exercise claims.

The decision in *Smith*, then, does not necessarily protect the First Amendment religious liberty of conscientiously objecting health-care professionals against claims from their homosexual patients based on state SOGI laws.

7 Maggie Gallagher, 'Banned in Boston: The Coming Conflict between Same-Sex Marriage and Religious Liberty', *The Weekly Standard*, 15 May 2006, www.weeklystandard.com/banned-in-boston/article/13329 (accessed May 2017).

8 See US Constitution, Amendment 1 ('Congress shall make no law respecting an establishment of religion, or prohibiting the free exercise thereof; or abridging the freedom of speech, or of the press; or the right of the people peaceably to assemble, and to petition the Government for a redress of grievances.'). Both the Free Exercise Clause and the Free Speech Clause may provide a basis for conscience safeguards. The Due Process Clause of the Fourteenth Amendment ('nor shall any Sate, deprive any person of life, liberty, or property, without due process of law') and the Equal Protection Clause of the Fourteenth Amendment ('nor [shall any state] deny to any person within its jurisdiction the equal protection of the laws') likewise provide a basis for conscience protections from the states. The Supreme Court has interpreted the Fourteenth Amendment to include First Amendment protections against the states. See, for example, *Cantwell v. Connecticut*, 310 U.S. 296 (1940).

9 494 U.S. 872 (1990).

### *The US Congress cannot fully protect conscience rights*

In 1993, the US Congress reacted to the implications of *Smith* by enacting, in bipartisan fashion, the Religious Freedom Restoration Act (RFRA).[10] The Act provides in part that

> Government may substantially burden a person's exercise of religion only if it demonstrates that application of the burden to the person –
>
> 1 is in furtherance of a compelling governmental interest; and
> 2 is the least restrictive means of furthering that compelling governmental interest.

This restriction on government authority applies 'even if the burden results from a rule of general applicability'. *Nota bene*: Each of the three health-care providers in the cases presented earlier did find a way to have both sexual liberty and religious liberty claims coexist by taking the least restrictive way to resolve the conflict. Each practitioner honored the patient's right to health care by referring the patient to another health-care provider, all the while maintaining the physician's right to practice according to her conscience.

However, in *City of Boerne v. Flores*,[11] the Supreme Court, in an opinion by Justice Anthony Kennedy, struck down the federal RFRA as an unconstitutional use of Congress's enforcement powers as it applies to the states. Hence, according to the Supreme Court, RFRA remains applicable to the federal government, but it does not apply to the states.[12]

### *'Right to privacy' protections threaten conscience rights*

The Due Process Clause of the Fourteenth Amendment has become a significant constitutional vehicle for defining a 'substantive sphere of liberty', a 'right to privacy' that allegedly lies in the penumbras of the Constitution and that presumably extends to a broad range of personal decisions including prevention of pregnancy, sexual relationships, and abortion, and now same-sex marriage.[13]

### *The regnant judicial interpretation of state PA-SOGI laws threatens freedom of conscience*

The first case earlier, involving the religious health-care provider who refused to provide Clomid to her infertile lesbian patient, is based on the California *Benitez* case.[14] Ultimately, the California Supreme Court ruled in favor of the lesbian patient who claimed sexual orientation discrimination because the physician refused to provide intrauterine insemination to facilitate her pregnancy within a lesbian relationship. The Supreme Court of California ruled that under California's Civil Rights Act (which includes a PA-SOGI provision), First Amendment religious liberty rights do not protect the conscientiously objecting physicians from patient claims of discrimination.

10 Pub. L. No 103–141, 107 Stat 1488 (1993), codified at 42 U.S.C.A. §§ 2000bb–2000bb-4.
11 521 U.S. 507 (1997).
12 In response, many states have passed their own RFRAs.
13 *Planned Parenthood v. Casey*, 505 U.S. 852 (1992).
14 *North Coast Women's Care Medical Group v. San Diego County Superior Court*, 189 P.3d 959 (Cal. 2008).

Without an exemption for moral or religious conscience written into PA-SOGI laws, the legislative and judicial preference for sexual liberty interests in public accommodations will likely trump the religious health-care providers' First Amendment rights of conscience and the free exercise of religion.

## The harms of coercing the conscience of health-care providers

If sexual liberty interests in public accommodations continue to be allowed to trump health-care providers' rights of conscience and religion, what will the harm be? Allowing the state to coerce physicians into violating their consciences harms the individual integrity of physicians, the integrity of the medical profession, and the very foundations of democracy and human rights upon which advocates of sexual liberty themselves stand alongside conscientious medical professionals.

### *Personal harms*

- To coerce a health-care provider's conscience is to threaten them with the Scylla of professional undoing, should they stand their ground, or the Charybdis of moral corruption, should they capitulate.[15]
- To require health-care workers to act contrary to their conscience is to strike at the heart of who they are:
  - by violating their very person – someone who, by nature, tends to the true and the good, and is only fulfilled by doing good and avoiding evil[16];
  - by deforming their inner moral self (character) with the vicious effects of bad choices;
  - by interrupting all the stages of their ability to act humanly, including the capacity to understand the moral principles of human nature, to reason from these principles, to judge according to them, and to choose and carry out these conscientious judgments in concrete acts;
  - by compromising their freedom for excellence and its dynamic quality of virtue that follows from their natural openness to truth, goodness, and happiness; and
  - by denying them the right to freely exercise their prudent conscience, an inalienable requirement of human dignity.

In sum, to coerce religious health-care providers to act against their conscience or prevent them from following their religious convictions so radically defaces their dignity,[17] freedom, and moral integrity as to imperil their quest for integral human happiness – not to mention endangering what they believe to be their eternal salvation.

15 Pope John Paul II argued that, when faced with the dilemma either of abandoning the medical profession or of compromising one's convictions, health-care providers should take the 'middle path' of conscientious objection which must be 'respected by all, especially legislators'. Address of John Paul II on the Occasion of the International Congress of Catholic Obstetricians and Gynaecologists, 18 June 2001, https://w2.vatican.va/content/john-paul-ii/en/speeches/2001/june/documents/hf_jp-ii_spe_20010618_obstetricians-gynaecologists.html (accessed May 2017) and *Evangelium vitae* (1995), §§ 72–74.

16 Cf. John Paul II, *Evangelium vitae*, § 74.

17 Douglas B. White and Baruch Brody, 'Would Accommodating Some Conscientious Objections by Physicians Promote Quality in Medical Care?', (2011) 305 *Journal of the American Medical Association* (17) 1804.

***Professional harms***

- To succumb to cooperation in the provision of a treatment they have judged to be immoral means health-care providers both confirm the patient in his wrongdoing and violate the premier norm of medicine: do no harm.
- Coercion of health-care rights of conscience discourages the affected professionals and their like-minded conscientious objectors from remaining in the medical profession, and new health-care recruits from entering the field. Elimination of conscientious objectors, 'morally serious persons'[18] who are 'unwilling to just follow orders',[19] not only stunts moral diversity within the health-care field but also smothers rich moral debate – an oft-cited means toward maintaining the purity of personal and professional integrity in the healing profession.
- Attempts to contravene conscience suppress personal autonomy, forcing the providers to bracket their religious convictions and park their moral beliefs outside their office.[20] Suppression of moral autonomy, in turn, causes moral distress and anxiety in the practitioners as they wrestle with their situation: 'Is protecting my professional standing worth forfeiting my moral integrity?' 'Is keeping my job worth sacrificing conscientious care as the hallmark of my personal and professional identity?' Anxious clinicians are also distracted ones, spending more time and energy worrying about their own affairs, and less time and energy focused on the needs of their patients.[21]
- To practice within an anti-conscience milieu slowly but inexorably breeds a callousness within the providers, replacing their wholesome empathy toward patients' vulnerabilities with an insalubrious attitude that 'patients do not deserve caring responses from their physicians.'[22]

18 A morally serious health-care worker certainly qualifies as a 'man of conscience' and, as such, can take as his models John Henry Cardinal Newman, Saint Thomas More, and Saint Thomas Becket who, within their professional lives, paid unequivocal 'obedience to that truth which must rank higher than every social authority and every kind of personal taste'. Cardinal Joseph Ratzinger, *Values in a Time of Upheaval* (Ignatius Press 2006), 87.

19 White and Brody at 1805.

20 Leon Kass warns that when the ends of medicine are not clearly defined or agreed upon, the practitioner is at risk of becoming a mere 'technician and engineer of the body, a scalpel for hire, selling his services upon demand'. *Toward a More Natural Science: Biology and Human Affairs* (The Free Press 1985), 158. Pope Benedict XVI encourages health-care workers to never lose sight of the fact that biomedical sciences are at the service of the human being and counsels them that anesthetizing their conscience will only reduce health-care services to 'a cold and inhuman character'. Address of His Holiness Benedict XVI to Members of the International Congress of Catholic Pharmacists, 29 October 2007, https://w2.vatican.va/content/benedict-xvi/en/speeches/2007/october/documents/hf_ben-xvi_spe_20071029_catholic-pharmacists.html (accessed May 2017). Margaret Somerville argues denial of conscience in the health-care setting does a great disservice not only to the individual medical professional but to the medical profession in general, where maintaining respect in the human encounter between health-care worker and patient demands mutual respect. 'Respect for Conscience Must Be a Social Value', Mercatornet, 17 October 2008, www.mercatornet.com/articles/view/respect_for_conscience_must_be_a_social_value/3897 (accessed May 2017).

21 Pope John Paul II underscores the psychophysical scope of patients' needs and their correlative requisites that health-care professionals practice not only biomedicine but the 'spiritual medicine' of compassionate human contact imitative of the gospel image of the Good Samaritan: the willingness even at great personal sacrifice to help those in need of healing, all the while witnessing 'to those higher values which have their firmest foundation in faith'. Speech of the Holy Father John Paul II to the Congress of the Catholic Doctors, 7 July 2000, https://w2.vatican.va/content/john-paul-ii/en/speeches/2000/jul-sep/documents/hf_jp-ii_spe_20000707_catholic-doctors.html (accessed May 2017).

22 White and Brody at 1805.

- To ask health-care providers to contravene their conscientious judgments has a boomerang effect: it provokes providers to take a similarly restrictive attitude toward the moral view of their patients, extinguishing, thereby, a key element of provider-patient respect and trust.
- To prohibit health-care rights of conscience, to constrict health-care providers' fidelity to core personal beliefs, is to encourage moral laxity toward other general professional responsibilities.

### *Public harms*

- To deny health-care rights of conscience violates what national and international human rights proclamations recognize as the basic civil right of every human being[23]: 'the right to freedom of thought, conscience and religion' including the freedom to 'manifest his religion or belief in teaching, practice, worship and observance'.[24]
- Coercion of conscience generates intolerance toward objectors and their system of objective morality[25]; intolerance vitiates civic peace and harmony[26] and can even lead to a tyranny of relativism, where every citizen's pursuit of the true and the good is held hostage by relativist and individualist tendencies to a 'sly selectiveness' that indirectly suppresses any ideas outside the mainstream of 'popular opinion' or elitist political ideology.[27]
- To the extent that laws of the state fail to give primacy to the free exercise of the conscientious judgments of its citizens, to that extent the state has overreached its authority, arrogating to itself the right to decide what is good and evil, and in the process failing to secure the fundamental rights of individuals against unjust encroachment by government and the majoritarian view.

23 Cardinal Ratzinger argues that when conscience and authority seem to be 'locked in struggle with each other', human freedom is rescued in an appeal 'to the classical principle of moral tradition that conscience is the *highest norm* which man is to follow even in opposition to authority'. 'Conscience and Truth', in *On Conscience* (Ignatius Press 2007), 12. See also Pope Paul VI, *Dignitatis humanae* (7 December 1965), 3, www.vatican.va/archive/hist_councils/ii_vatican_council/documents/vat-ii_decl_19651207_dignitatis-humanae_en.html and *Gaudium et spes* (7 December 1965), 79, www.vatican.va/archive/hist_councils/ii_vatican_council/documents/vat-ii_const_19651207_gaudium-et-spes_en.html (both accessed May 2017).

24 Universal Declaration of Human Rights, Art. 18.

25 Loyalty to conscience on the part of Christian believers not only puts them in solidarity with the same quest on the part of their non-Christian fellow-citizens but also, to the extent that an upright conscience prevails, facilitates just resolutions to societal problems, resolutions that follow from objective truths rather than 'blind choice'. *Gaudium et spes* at 16.

26 Pope John Paul II fuses societal respect for conscience with 'a force for peace'. Citizens' right to follow conscience, to judge and act in accord with truth, promotes 'unity rather than division; reconciliation rather than hatred and intolerance'. Seeking the truth together, 'with respect for the conscience of others', enables all people 'to go forward along the paths of freedom which lead to peace, in accordance with the will of God'. 'If You Want Peace, Respect the Conscience of Every Person', Message of His Holiness Pope John Paul II for the XXIV World Day of Peace, 1 January 1991, http://w2.vatican.va/content/john-paul-ii/en/messages/peace/documents/hf_jp-ii_mes_08121990_xxiv-world-day-for-peace.html (accessed May 2017).

27 Aleksandr I. Solzhenitzsyn, *A World Split Apart* (Harper & Row 1978), 30. NYU law professor Jeremy Waldron's observation that it 'infuriates' his fellow liberals that some intellectuals continue 'to actually argue on matters that many secular liberals think should be beyond argument, matters that we think should be determined by shared sentiment or conviction' and 'refuse to take the liberal position for granted' is a good example of Solzhenitzsin's 'sly selectivity'. Jeremy Waldron, 'Secularism and the Limits of Community', New York University School of Law Public Law & Legal Theory Research Paper Series, Working Paper No. 10–88, December 2010, 16–17.

- Promoting an anemic sense of conscience and conscientious objection in health care (and in other professions) could help to derail even the most liberally enlightened state and push it toward a destructive authoritarianism.[28]
- To coerce health-care providers' conscience, in the clinical situations discussed here, robs the polity, on the one side, of a clear voice for the meaning of sexuality,[29] marriage,[30] and family[31] as well as a transparent plan conducive to the healthy growth of the family[32] and imposes on all Americans, on the other, an LGBT 'ethic' and legal system.

28 Cardinal Ratzinger points out that the source of concern over the blunting of moral sensitivity so rampant under Marxist regimes was

> that those who lived in a system of deceit had lost much of their powers of perception. Society had lost the ability to feel compassion, and human emotions had withered away. An entire generation had become impervious to the good and was incapable of human deeds.... When conscience falls silent and we do nothing to resist it, the consequence is the dehumanization of the world and a deadly danger.
>
> *Values in a Time of Upheaval* at 83

29 Chai Feldblum, lesbian activist, is unequivocally committed to using government, through the power of its laws, to shape public opinion toward agreement that heterosexuality and homosexuality are equivalent moral goods. She claims that nothing short of this sort of moral equivalency will bring full equality to LGBT people. 'Gay Is Good: The Case for Marriage Equality and More', (2005) 17 *Yale Journal of Law & Feminism* 139–140.

30 The Congregation for the Doctrine of the Faith calls Christians to give witness to the moral truth regarding marriage by avoiding approval of homosexual acts and homosexual unions and by participating in the following actions: 'unmasking the way' that state tolerance, but not explicit legal recognition, of homosexual unions

> might be exploited or used in the service of ideology; stating clearly the immoral nature of these unions; reminding the government of the need to contain the phenomenon within certain limits so as to safeguard public morality, and above all, to avoid exposing young people to erroneous ideas about sexuality and marriage that would deprive them of their necessary defenses and contribute to the spread of the phenomenon.

'Considerations Regarding Proposals to Give Legal Recognition to Unions between Homosexual Persons', Part II, www.vatican.va/roman_curia/congregations/cfaith/documents/rc_con_cfaith_doc_20030731_homosexual-unions_en.html (accessed May 2017).

31 For example, in their evaluation of 49 empirical studies on same-sex or homosexual parenting, quantitative analysis experts Robert Lerner and Althea Nagai categorize the surveys' claim – that it makes 'no difference' whether a child has two heterosexual parents or two homosexual parents (two moms or two dads) – as inconclusive. Having identified at least one fatal flaw in each of the studies, they concluded that the papers (1) yield no reliable generalizations and (2) 'are no basis for good science or good public policy'. *No Basis: What the Studies* Don't *Tell Us About Same-Sex Parenting* (Marriage Law Project 2001), 3.

32 The Roman Catholic Church is one of the last mainline Christian denominations to maintain that the common good requires laws promoting and protecting traditional marriage as the basis of the family and the prime unit of society. Hence, the Congregation for the Doctrine of the Faith avers,

> [l]egal recognition of homosexual unions or placing them on the same level as marriage would mean not only the approval of deviant behaviour, with the consequence of making it a model in present-day society, but would also obscure basic values which belong to the common inheritance of humanity.

Supra at § 11. This ecclesial position could well be responsible for much of the gay rights rhetoric demanding that society, or at least the state, recognize that gay sex is the moral equivalent of heterosexual sex and that gay unions and their family-building efforts are as good for the culture as their heterosexual counterparts. See Chai R. Feldblum, 'Moral Conflict and Conflicting Liberties', in Douglas Laycock, Anthony R. Picarello, Jr., and Robin Fretwell Wilson, eds, *Same-Sex Marriage and Religious Liberty* (Rowman & Littlefield 2008), 123 and 'The Right to Define One's Own Concept of Existence: What *Lawrence* Can Mean for Intersex and Transgender People', (2006) 7 *Georgetown Journal of Gender & Law* 115.

## Protecting health-care rights of conscience against mounting threats

### *Phase one*

Conscientiously objecting health-care providers should educate their state lawmakers on the meaning of conscience. They should pique lawmakers' interest by listing the personal, professional, and societal fallout when government coerces the conscientious judgments of health-care providers.

### *Phase two*

Conscientiously objecting health-care providers should convince sympathetic state lawmakers to sponsor appropriate legislation to protect health-care rights of conscience. In other words, religious health-care providers should help their state representatives to draft and enact stand-alone comprehensive state health-care conscience protection statutes.

### *Phase three*

Conscientiously objecting health-care providers should dialogue with members of the same-sex advocacy community, aiming for a win-win resolution to liberty conflicts between homosexual patients and religious health-care providers.

They should emphasize that a liberal, tolerant society should not embrace coercion when other means are available. Coercing conscience does not merely harm the health-care provider. It also harms the patient, encouraging rancor and distrust between two private citizens (the provider and the patient). Dialogue, rather than coercion, is the only path capable of generating progress without inflicting serious harms.

When states enact robust safeguards for health-care rights of conscience, both sides win. Protecting diversity in the provider community, rather than forcing conscientious providers out of medicine, will maximize liberty and health-care options for all.

# 8 Preventing religious fundamentalism through higher education of faith leaders

*Clemens Steinhilber*[1]

## Introduction

Terrorist attacks perpetrated by pre- or anti-modern[2] religious fundamentalists have become a sadly common phenomenon. In the Western world, religious fundamentalism[3] has come to be associated almost automatically with Islam, although acts of violence committed in the name of religion are not unique to Islam. Religious fundamentalism also has a flourishing presence in Christianity, Judaism, Buddhism, and Hinduism.[4] While it is mainly movements within Islam that challenge us in our present life and political realities,[5]

1 This article is based on the author's doctoral thesis, 'Theologie an staatlichen Universitäten – Relikt oder Modell? Förderung des freiheitlichen Staatsethos durch integrative Feindpolitik' (Duncker & Humblot 2018).

2 Bassam Tibi, *Der Islam und Deutschland. Muslime in Deutschland* (2nd edn, Deutsche Verlags-Anstalt DVA 2001), 33 at 117 ff and 125 ff; Arnd Uhle, 'Die Integration des Islam in das Staatskirchenrecht der Gegenwart', in Hans Michael Heinig and Christian Walter, eds, *Staatskirchenrecht oder Religionsverfassungsrecht? Ein begriffspolitischer Grundsatzstreit* (Mohr Siebeck 2007), 299 at 326 ff; Hermann Lübbe, *Staat und Zivilreligion. Ein Aspekt politischer Legitimität* (ARSP 1981), 40 at 59; Hermann Lübbe, 'Religion nach der Aufklärung', in Hermann Lübbe, ed., *Philosophie nach der Aufklärung. Von der Notwendigkeit pragmatischer Vernunft* (1st edn, Econ 1980), 59; and Mark Juergensmeyer, *Die Globalisierung religiöser Gewalt. Von christlichen Milizen bis al-Qaida* (1st edn, Hamburger Edition 2009), 41.

3 I define religious fundamentalism here in accordance with the Six Country Immigrant Integration Comparative Survey (SCIICS) which compares the levels of structural and socio-cultural integration of Turkish and Moroccan immigrants in Germany, France, the Netherlands, Austria, Belgium, and Sweden by way of three interrelated attitudes: (1) that believers should return to the eternal and unchangeable rules laid down in the past, (2) that these rules allow only one interpretation that is binding for all believers, and (3) that religious rules should have priority over secular laws. See Ruud Koopmans, 'Fundamentalismus und Fremdenfeindlichkeit. Muslime und Christen im europäischen Vergleich', (2013) 142 *WZB Mitteilungen* 21.

4 See Mark Juergensmeyer, *Global Rebellion. Religious Challenges to the Secular State, from Christian Militias to al Qaeda* (University of California Press 2008); Mark Juergensmeyer, Margo Kitts, and Michael K. Jerryson, eds, *The Oxford Handbook of Religion and Violence* (Oxford University Press 2013); and Mark Juergensmeyer, *Terror in the Mind of God. The Global Rise of Religious Violence* (University of California Press 2001). See also Bruce Hoffman, *Terrorismus – der unerklärte Krieg. Neue Gefahren politischer Gewalt* (Fischer Taschenbuch 2006), 112 ff, 117 ff, 130 ff (Jewish terrorism), 137 ff (Christian terrorism), 159 ff (sects); Steve Bruce, *Fundamentalism* (Polity Press 2000), 1 ff and 5 ff; Bryan S. Turner, *Religion and Modern Society. Citizenship, Secularisation and the State* (Cambridge University Press 2011), 175; Lionel Caplan, ed., *Studies in Religious Fundamentalism* (1st edn, SUNY Press 1987); Friedrich Wilhelm Graf, *Die Wiederkehr der Götter. Religion in der modernen Kultur* (1st edn, C.H. Beck 2007), 48, 72, 80, and 172; and Otto Depenheuer, 'Wahrheit oder Frieden? Die fundamentalistische Herausforderung des modernen Staates', (1999) 33 *Essener Gespräche zum Thema Staat und Kirche* 5, fn 7. For manifestations of contemporary fundamentalism from an interdisciplinary perspective, see Heiner Bielefeldt and Wilhelm Heitmeyer, eds, *Politisierte Religion. Ursachen und Erscheinungsformen des modernen Fundamentalismus* (1st edn, Suhrkamp Verlag 1998).

5 For dimensions of Islamic fundamentalism in Western Europe, see Koopmans at 21. For the situation in Germany, see Detlef Pollack and Olaf Müller, *Religionsmonitor – verstehen was verbindet. Religiosität und Zusammenhalt in Deutschland* (Bertelsmann Stiftung 2013), 18 ff, www.bertelsmann-stiftung.de/fileadmin/files/BSt/

it is important to understand religious fundamentalism as a structural mode of religiosity in general, to avoid developing a generally negative attitude toward Muslims specifically. Unfortunately, confrontational language toward Muslims has become increasingly common. Legal and political discourse within Western societies has rediscovered the categories of the emergency and of the enemy,[6] categories which had long been considered taboo.[7] There are good reasons for this taboo, as I will show – even toward religious fundamentalists. Instead of excluding religious fundamentalists, Western societies should embrace them with a kind of parental love to ensure that their religiosity becomes moderate.[8]

In this article, I would like to outline a way to realize this admittedly ambitious objective. First, I will derive from modern state theory an argument for a positive, amicable, open, and inclusive attitude toward those we recognize as our enemies. Second, I will outline a preventive strategy to deal with religious fundamentalism without damaging our liberal convictions, which I call an 'integrative enemy policy'.[9] The solution I propose is the higher education of faith leaders as a measure for religious self-education.

## The problem religious fundamentalism presents for modern states

The problem that modern societies currently have with religious fundamentalists is not simply the violence as such, but the philosophical motivations underlying the violence. Religious fundamentalists are antagonistic to modernity.[10] They are willing to act in accordance with their convictions: to sacrifice their lives for the fervent pursuit of the goals of salvation in opposition to the secular ideology of order[11] and to fight against the secularism that Western societies believe to be a precondition of individual liberty and equality. In short, they oppose the ideological source of modern state theory in both their thoughts and their actions. Therefore, the crucial question arises of whether a modern secular state has adequate mechanisms to ensure the transformation of religious fundamentalism into secular faith.

---

Publikationen/GrauePublikationen/GP_Religionsmonitor_verstehen_was_verbindet_Religioesitaet_und_Zusammenhalt_in_Deutschland.pdf (accessed July 2017). For challenges fundamentalism poses to constitutional law and philosophy of law, see Friedhelm Hufen, 'Fundamentalismus als Herausforderung des Verfassungsrechts und der Rechtsphilosophie', (1992) 4 *Staatswissenschaften und Staatspraxis* (3) 455 at 456 and 460.

6 Carl Schmitt, *Der Begriff des Politischen. Text von 1932 mit einem Vorwort und 3 Corollarien* (Duncker & Humblot 1963). For a discussion of the friend-foe mode of thought, see Hasso Hofmann, *Legitimität gegen Legalität. Der Weg der politischen Philosophie Carl Schmitts* (Duncker & Humblot 2002), 94 ff.

7 For the German Basic Law's objective to eradicate a pessimistic emergency mind-set attributed to totalitarian regimes, see Rüdiger Altmann, 'Vorüberlegungen zum Ernstfall', in Anton Peisl and Armin Mohler, eds, *Der Ernstfall* (Propyläen Verlag 1979), 7 at 10 f and 14; Josef Isensee, 'Verfassung ohne Ernstfall: Der Rechtsstaat', in Anton Peisl and Armin Mohler, eds, *Der Ernstfall* (Propyläen Verlag 1979), 98 at 98 ff; and Wilhelm Hennis, 'Zur Begründung der Fragestellung', in Wilhelm Hennis, Peter Graf Kielmansegg, and Ulrich Matz, eds, *Regierbarkeit. Studien zu ihrer Problematisierung* (Klett-Cotta 1977), 9 at 11 and 17. For a refusal to think in friend-foe patterns see Otto Depenheuer, *Selbstbehauptung des Rechtsstaates* (Schöningh Paderborn 2007), 9 at 41, 53, 54 ff, and 59 ff. See also Steinhilber, § 5.

8 For this figurative paraphrase, see Patrice Rolland, 'La démocratie et ses ennemis', (1993) *La pensée politique* (1) 121, 133 ff.

9 For a detailed derivation and description of this concept, see Steinhilber, § 5, C. III., and § 7.

10 Ulrich Beck, *Die Erfindung des Politischen. Zu einer Theorie reflexiver Modernisierung* (1st edn, Suhrkamp Verlag 1993), 100 ff.

11 Bassam Tibi, *Islamischer Fundamentalismus, moderne Wissenschaft und Technologie* (1st edn, Suhrkamp Verlag 1992), 156; David M. Smolin, 'Regulating Religious and Cultural Conflict in a Postmodern America: A Response to Professor Perry', (1991) 76 *Iowa Law Review* 1067, 1094 ff.

The liberal, secular state faces a dilemma on this matter. As Ernst-Wolfgang Böckenförde,[12] a German legal scholar, political thinker, and former judge of the German Federal Constitutional Court (*Bundesverfassungsgericht*), formulates it,

> The liberal secularized state draws its life from presuppositions it cannot itself guarantee. This is the great risk it has made for the sake of liberty. On the one hand, as a liberal state it can only survive if the freedom it grants to its citizens is regulated from within, out of the moral substance of the individual and the homogeneity of society. On the other hand, it cannot seek to guarantee these inner regulatory forces by its own efforts – that is to say, with the instruments of legal coercion and authoritative command – without abandoning its liberalness.[13]

Böckenförde develops the paradox that the state, in an endeavor to uphold liberal democracy 'with the instruments of legal coercion and authoritative command', would disown the fundamental values underpinning it. In contrast to the absolutist state, the liberal democratic state is dependent on democratic convictions, on liberal civic virtues, on a unifying ethos, and on a sense of community among its citizens, and it cannot enforce those convictions because of its respect for those virtues.

Ultimately, religious fundamentalism disillusions our utopian expectations about the feasibility of this great and honorable modern adventure. As Stanley Fish has suitably said, '[i]f such doctrines are welcomed into the conversations, they may shut it down; if the door is closed to them, liberalism will seem to be exercising the peremptory authority it routinely condemns.'[14]

Against this background, answering the question of how a democratically constituted society can ensure its viability and defend itself against threats without breaking with its constitutive ideas seems quite difficult. The question remains: 'How does the liberal state deal with doctrines – like racial discrimination or religious intolerance – inimical to it and threatening to its survival?'[15] How can it create, sustain, and expand a liberal ethos among its citizens without violating that very ethos?

## Higher education as indirect steerage from within

A promising approach seems to be steerage from within individuals. Internal control accesses the inner attitudes of individuals and addresses the problem that modern states have with fundamentalist religiosity at its source. The state employs direct and indirect measures to influence individuals' religio-cultural identity. Direct measures include general influence on the mind with tools like appeals, information, warnings, consultation, state self-portrayals, and compulsory schooling. Indirect measures aim at a unifying liberal ethos by supporting societal actors and promoting the requirement of at least acceptance of the

12 For Böckenförde's political and legal thought, see Mirjam Künkler and Tine Stein, 'State, Law, and Constitution: Ernst-Wolfgang Böckenförde's Political and Legal Thought in Context', in Mirjam Künkler and Tine Stein, eds, *Constitutional and Political Theory. Selected Writings by Ernst-Wolfgang Böckenförde* vol. 1 (Oxford University Press 2017), I ff.

13 Ernst-Wolfgang Böckenförde, 'The Rise of the State as a Process of Secularization', quoted in Mirjam Künkler and Tine Stein, 'Böckenförde's Political Theory of the State', in Künkler and Stein, eds, 38 at 45. See Christian Joppke and John Torpey, *Legal Integration of Islam: A Transatlantic Comparison* (Harvard University Press 2013), 51 ff.

14 Stanley Eugene Fish, 'Mission Impossible: Settling the Just Bounds between Church and State', (1997) 97 *Columbia Law Review* (8) 2255, 2286.

15 Fish at 2286.

secular ideology of order. Indirect instruments are, for instance, promoting culture, religion, and fundamental rights.[16] It is on this indirect approach that I will focus.

The basic method of indirect steerage from within is the creation and strengthening of an open culture of dialogue and discourse. This is because openness to dialogue and discourse goes hand in hand with the consolidation of constitutional democracy's ideological values. The value of 'openness to dialogue and discourse', in turn, is created by pluralism, which relativizes the consciousness of individuals.[17] Peter Berger, a German-American sociologist, describes this as follows:

> As ever-wider areas of life lose their taken-for-granted norms, the individual must reflect upon and make choices among the alternatives that have become available. Indeed, modernisation can be described as a gigantic shift in the human condition from one of fate to one of choice.[18]

Berger calls this effect 'cognitive contamination'.[19] Therefore, we can conclude that indirect internal control has great potential for dealing with religious fundamentalism. If religious fundamentalists are engaged in discourse, they have taken their first step toward their reconciliation with Western Enlightenment norms.

The shining example of indirect internal control is higher education. Tertiary education represents the final stage of institutionalized, indirect state education. It stands for the highest form of societal penetration with cognitive reality. Thus, higher education turns out to be an excellent tool of modern religious policy.

## Modern academia's contribution toward creating modern religiosity

Religious fundamentalism is linked to a rejection of the modern pursuit, which is dedicated to progress as a part of the search for truth free of constraints – in particular in the religio-cultural area.[20] While religious fundamentalists may sometimes devote attention to science, for example, they arguably do so not for the sake of seeking truth and progress but, as Bassam Tibi, a German-Syrian political scientist and Islamologist,[21] describes it, to bolster an illusory dream of semi-modernity:[22]

> [They] recognise that they cannot prevail without adopting basic items of modernity, and thus they are poised to embrace instrumentally modern science and technology. At the same time they dismiss the human-based worldview and the secular values that underpin the instrumental modernity they are willing to adopt. Their splitting of modernity into techno-scientific instruments and culture is coupled with an inclination to adopt the one and simultaneously to dismiss the other.[23]

16 See Arnd Uhle, *Freiheitlicher Verfassungsstaat und kulturelle Identität* (Mohr Siebeck 2004), 422 ff and Steinhilber at § 7, C.II.
17 For these interrelations, see Steinhilber at § 8, B.III.2.
18 Peter L. Berger, 'Between Relativism and Fundamentalism', (2006) 2 *The American Interest* (1).
19 Peter L. Berger, *Sehnsucht nach Sinn. Glauben in einer Zeit der Leichtgläubigkeit* (Campus Verlag 1994), 44 ff.
20 Concerning fundamentalism in general, see Hufen at 457. ('Hermeneutik ist als Auslegungslehre der Wahrheit gefragt, als kritische Interpretationswissenschaft aber mit Verbot belegt'.)
21 Islamology as a social-scientific study of Islam and conflict in post-bipolar politics.
22 Tibi, *Islamischer Fundamentalismus* at 12–27, 137, and 165 and Tibi, *Der Islam und Deutschland* at 226–241.
23 Bassam Tibi, *Islam's Predicament with Modernity: Religious Reform and Cultural Change* (Routledge 2009), 33.

With regard to humanities, and in particular theology, religious fundamentalists oppose the liberal and modernist approach of a critical, historical view of scripture. Rather, they favor a literal interpretation of their sacred texts.[24]

### *Modern religiosity through internal discourse*

The reason for this refusal is quite obvious: modern science promotes a movement toward moral and religious individualization. Its dogma is autonomy of reason; its rite is the free examination of all claims to validity.[25] Modern academic research is based on communicative reason and ethics. Therefore, it favors an intellectual attitude, which does not believe in supernatural powers and effects and tries to explain all phenomena rationally.[26] Such a rational-academic attitude again corresponds to the value of individual freedom, which is the nucleus of the modern social order.[27] The noblest expression of its essence is the historical-critical method as the tool of modern humanities.[28] Historical-critical research stands for a political-ideological program and is accompanied by a process of religious education.[29] Thus, higher education serves as a pacesetter for hermeneutical self-reflection. It kick-starts a process leading toward an order-constructing belief system.

### *Academic education as an effective transformation strategy*

If religious fundamentalism is inimicable to modernity,[30] it is anathema to the modern university. Its basic characteristic is anti-science.[31] A respectful attitude to modern academic research therefore marks the boundary between anti-modern and modern belief systems. It draws the demarcation line between the competing secular and religious ideologies.

24 Jean-Paul Willaime, 'Le fondamentalisme protestant', in Émile Poulat, Jean-Paul Willaime, and Olivier Carré, eds, *Intégrismes, fondamentalismes, radicalismes religieux: Conférences du Cercle Condorcet de Vesoul, Paris 1990* (Ligue française de l'enseignement et de l'éducation permanent 1990), 11 at 15, rewords this concerning Protestant fundamentalism as follows: 'Les fondamentaliste croient à l'inspiration littérale des Écritures, pour eux la parole de Dieu est la Bible. Ils opposent à l'exégèse historico-critique qui, en analysant les textes bibliques selon les données philologiques et historiques, montre l'origine différente des passages d'un même livre, le contexte humain dans lequel ils ont été rédigés.'

25 Emile Durkheim, 'Der Individualismus und die Intellektuellen' (1898), in Hans Bertram, ed., *Gesellschaftlicher Zwang und moralische Autonomie* (1st edn, Suhrkamp Verlag 1986), 54 at 60 f.

26 Berger, Sehnsucht nach Sinn at 33.

27 For the correlation between academic research and modern thinking, see Hans Kelsen, 'Wissenschaft und Demokratie' (1937), in Matthias Jestaedt and Oliver Lepsius, eds, *Verteidigung der Demokratie. Abhandlungen zur Demokratietheorie* (Mohr Siebeck 2006), 238 ff.

28 For the operating principle of the historical-critical method, see Ernst Troeltsch, 'Ueber historische und dogmatische Methode in der Theologie', in Ernst Troeltsch, ed., *Zur religiösen Lage, Religionsphilosophie und Ethik* (Mohr Siebeck 1913), 729 at 730 ff and 735 ff. Troeltsch sees in the historical-critical method if applied to biblical research and church history a 'Sauerteig, der alles verwandelt und der schließlich die ganze bisherige Form theologischer Methoden zersprengt' ('leaven, which transforms everything, and which finally breaks up the whole present form of theological methods'). Troeltsch at 730. See also Gerhard Ebeling, 'Die Bedeutung der historisch-kritischen Methode für die protestantische Theologie und Kirche', (1950) 47 *Zeitschrift für Theologie und Kirche* (1), 1 ff.

29 Josef Blank, 'Das politische Element in der historisch-kritischen Methode', in Paul Neuenzeit, ed., *Die Funktion der Theologie in Kirche und Gesellschaft. Beiträge zu einer notwendigen Diskussion* (Kösel-Verlag 1969), 39 ff and 48 ff.

30 Tibi, Islamischer Fundamentalismus at 225.

31 Tibi, *Der Islam und Deutschland* at 233. See also Thomas A. Becker, 'Wege in die argumentative Gesellschaft. Wissensdynamik als zentrale Ressource der Modernisierung', (1991) 24 *Neue Zürcher Zeitung* (2/3) 29.

In response to the question of how a democratically constituted society can secure its survival and defend itself against threats without breaking with its constitutive ideals, we can state that training and socializing faith leaders and other disseminators – priests, imams,[32] chaplains, theologians, educators, lawyers, social workers, association representatives, and so on – within the realms of a plural discourse and the liberal spirit of a modern university may contribute to a transformation of fundamentalist religiosity into modern religiosity. Practicing an academic habitus goes hand in hand with modernizing religious belief. The function of religious leaders as disseminators contributes to the modernization of entire religious communities. Hence, higher education can create greater acceptance and ideally the affirmation of a secular, order-based ideology among religious fundamentalists. It serves as a measure of indirect state education introduced into religious self-education and serves therefore as an 'integrative enemy policy', and thus provides a way out of the modern state's dilemma.[33]

## Approaches to higher education of faith leaders in Europe

Against this background, European governments maintain an interest in the higher education of religious faith leaders, which is widely considered to be an important tool in the continuous fight against religious fundamentalism, and in particular the current challenges posed by radicalization in Muslim communities. Governments hope that by increasing the number of domestically and academically trained faith leaders, more moderate representatives will emerge who can help promote a liberal Islam and therefore further integration, dialogue, and mutual understanding both within and between religious and non-religious communities.[34] This is no inconsiderable task, not least because of the language barrier. To date, Islamic religious officials have largely come from Islamic countries of origin and/or received their training there – training that does not satisfy modern scientific standards – and thus they sometimes have only a limited grasp of the language of their host country.

States across Europe have adopted very different approaches toward the academic training of imams and other faith leaders. Besides the internal approach, which consists of denominational higher education of religious representatives, we can identify three external approaches to their higher education: civil and civic education, interfaith dialogue, and non-denominational religious studies.[35] A glance at Germany and Austria on the one hand

32 Rauf Ceylan, 'Religiöse Orientierungen und Einstellungen türkischer Imame. Am Beispiel neo-salafistischer, traditionell-konservativer und intellektuell-offensiver Imame', (2008) 16 *Zeitschrift für Religionswissenschaft* (2) 203, 203 ff.

33 For a detailed derivation and description see Steinhilber at § 8.

34 Dilwar Hussain and Henry Tuck, *The Education and Training of Islamic Faith Leaders in Europe: A Comparative Evaluation of Approaches in France and Germany* (Institute for Strategic Dialogue 2014), 4.

35 For the situation in Europe, see Francis Messner, ed., *Public Authorities and the Training of Religious Personnel in Europe. Proceedings of the XXVth Annual Conference Strasbourg/Klingenthal, 21–24 November 2013* (Editorial Comares 2015). For a brief overview, see Francis Messner, *La formation des cadres religieux musulmans* (Ministry of the Interior/Ministry of Education 2014), 9 ff and 14 ff, http://dres.misha.cnrs.fr/IMG/pdf/rapp_messner_version_diffusion.pdf (accessed July 2017). For initiatives in Europe, see also Pieter Sjoerd Koningsveld and Willem Drees, *The Study of Religion and the Training of Muslim Clergy in Europe. Academic and Religious Freedom in the 21st Century* (Amsterdam University Press 2007); Françoise Curtit and Anne-Laure Zwilling, 'L'enseignement de la théologie musulmane en Europe: Contexte et contenu', in Michel Deneken and Francis Messner, eds, *La théologie à l'université. Status, programmes et evolutions* (Éditions Labor et Fides 2009), 151 ff; Frank Frégosi, ed., *La formation des cadres religieux musulmans en France: Approches socio-juridiques* (Editions L'Harmattan 1998); Wolfram Weiße, ed., *Theologie im Plural.*

and at France at the other hand may illustrate the difference between a denominational and a non-denominational approach.[36]

## *Denominational approach: Germany and Austria*

### *Germany*

Under the German federal constitution (Basic Law [*Grundgesetz*]), religions and the State are separate. At the same time, they cooperate on a constitutionally secured basis (positive neutrality and tolerance).[37] In Germany, the academic training of religious personnel of religious congregations and teachers of religion for denomination-specific religious instruction at state schools is predominantly carried out at state universities. Confessional theology at state universities is integrated into the German system of amicable cooperation between the State and religion, as part of which the State supports all religious actors equally and, hence, is neutral in matters of religion and belief.[38]

In return for the State's offer to provide State-financed academic training for their functionaries, religious communities are generally expected to recruit their personnel from among the graduates of these programs. Thus, academic training at a public theology faculty becomes a condition for employment.[39] The State recognizes the religious community's authority over theological matters, and the religious community respects the State's insistence upon the methodologies of modern academic theology.[40]

Thus universities have a dual function: they are places for academic research, and at the same time, they train personnel for religious communities.[41] They are public institutions

*Eine akademische Herausforderung* (Waxmann Verlag GmbH 2009); Anna-Katharina Szagun, ed., *Die religiöse Dimension (in) der Gesellschaft und die Aufgabe der Theologischen Fakultäten* (Universität Rostock, Theologische Fakultät 1997); and Adrian Loretan, ed., *Theologische Fakultäten an europäischen Universitäten. Rechtliche Situation und theologische Perspektiven* (1st edn, LIT 2004). For international initiatives, see Conseil de l'Europe Assemblée parlamentaire, Recommandation 1396 'Religion et démocratie' (1999) and Recommandation 1720 'Education et religion' (2005).

36 For a comparison of the French and German approaches, see Hussain and Tuck.

37 For the legal sources and basic approaches to religion and belief in Germany, see Gerhard Robbers, 'Germany', in Gerhard Robbers, W. Cole Durham, Jr., and Donlu Thayer, eds, *Encyclopedia of Law and Religion* vol. IV (Brill-Nijhoff 2016), 141 ff.

38 For the German system of theology at state-run universities, see Wissenschaftsrat (Council on Science and the Humanities), *Recommendations on the Advancement of Theologies and Sciences concerned with Religions at German Universities* (2010) and Christian Waldhoff, 'Theologische Fakultäten an staatlichen Hochschulen', in Dietrich Pirson et al., eds, *Handbuch des Staatskirchenrechts der Bundesrepublik Deutschland* (Duncker & Humblot 2018), 8 ff and 16 ff.

39 Ernst-Lüder Solte, *Theologie an der Universität. Staats- und kirchenrechtliche Probleme der theologischen Fakultäten* (Mohr Siebeck 1971), 103 ff.

40 With respect to Catholic theology in particular, see Martin Heckel, *Die theologischen Fakultäten im weltlichen Verfassungsstaat* (Mohn Sieback 1986), 52 f and 228 f.

41 Heckel at 265 f; Ulrich K. Preuß, 'Art. 140 GG', in Rudolf Wassermann et al., eds, *Reihe Alternativkommentare. Kommentar zum Grundgesetz für die Bundesrepublik Deutschland* vol. 2 (3rd edn, Luchterhand 2001), 1549 ff (recital 43); and Dirk Herkströter, *Wissenschaftsfreiheit und Theologie. Ein Beitrag zu Entstehung, Verlauf und Stand der Diskussion um den Rechtsstatus theologischer Fakultäten* (doctoral dissertation, Gießen University 1996), 265–317. For a critical comment on the 'dual role' of theological faculties as both state and church institutions, see the *Lüdemann* decision of the German Constitutional Court: 'The wide-spread interpretation, according to which theological faculties occupy a "dual function" as state organisations with the purpose of carrying out church tasks … or, as the case may be, represented a joint matter of state and church

that also perform tasks for religious communities. This is often referred to as a *res mixta*, a 'joint venture' between state and religious community.[42] However, this does not mean that university theology is subordinated equally to the State and the religious communities on any given issue. Rather, there is a strict separation of competences.[43] The State and the religious communities cooperate, without being institutionally intertwined. The State is responsible for the secular, organizational aspects: equipping the theological institutions with finances, staff, and rooms, as well as ensuring academic standards. The religious communities, on the other hand, are responsible for aspects relating to the denominational content.

The rule on separation derives from the constitutional prohibition on institutional and functional links between the State and religious communities. This has its basis in the principle, enshrined in the Basic Law, that there be an amicable separation between the State and religion,[44] which in turn derives from the principle of the State's neutrality in religious and ideological matters.[45] The rights and obligations between the State and religious communities derive from the Basic Law, the constitutions of the various federal states (*Bundesländer*), statutory law, bylaws, and customary laws. They are also the subject of contractual agreements.[46]

... can at best be a description of the necessary cooperation between state and religious communities ... but it cannot give rise to a dual legal nature.' BVerfGE 122, 89, 111 f. Accordingly, these are not referred to as state and church institutions, but rather as state institutions, which also serve the purpose of fulfilling some church tasks.

42 Theological faculties are the prime example of a joint venture between state and church, a legal construct that has been known for centuries. Axel von Campenhausen, 'Theologische Fakultät und Landeskirche', in Joachim E. Christoph, ed., *Gesammelte Schriften* (Mohr Siebeck 1995), 211. For a brief overview of this dominant constitutional law view of 'joint matters' with a focus on theology at public university faculties, see Martin Heckel, *Die theologischen Fakultäten im weltlichen Verfassungsstaat* (Mohr Siebeck 1986), 25 ff and 30 ff. See also Alexander Hollerbach, 'Theologische Fakultäten und staatliche pädagogische Hochschulen' (§ 56), in Ernst Friesenhahn, Joseph Listl, and Dietrich Pirson, eds, *Handbuch des Staatskirchenrechts der Bundesrepublik Deutschland* vol. 2 (Duncker & Humblot 1995), 549 at 560 and Hermann Weber, 'Theologische Fakultäten und Professuren im weltanschaulich neutralen Staat – Staatskirchenrechtliche und rechtspolitische Aspekte', (2000) 15 *Neue Zeitschrift für Verwaltungsrecht* (8) 848, 851 f. Related to the concept of *res mixtae* and limiting the concept of 'joint matters' to its actual meaning, see also Dirk Ehlers, 'Die gemeinsamen Angelegenheiten von Staat und Kirche', (1987) 32 *Zeitschrift für evangelisches Kirchenrecht* 158, 180.

43 Heckel, *Die theologischen Fakultäten* at 29, 47 f, 51 f, 114, 203, 227, 300 ff, 328 ff, 343, 379 (bzgl. kirchlichen Hochschulen), and 380; and Martin Heckel, 'Der Rechtsstatus der theologischen Fakultäten im freiheitlichen, religiös neutralen Verfassungsstaat', in Klaus Schlaich, ed., *Gesammelte Schriften. Staat Kirche Recht Geschichte* vol. IV (Mohr Siebeck 1997), 946 at 966 f.

44 For a brief overview of possible ways in which the principle of separation could be implemented, see Peter Unruh, *Religionsverfassungsrecht* (Nomos 2009), recitals 141 ff.

45 Basic Law Art. 140 in conjunction with Weimar Republic Constitution Art. 136(1) and (4) and Art. 137(1), as well as Basic Law Art. 4(1) and (2), Art. 3(3)(1), and Art. 33(2).

46 Unruh at 275 ff (recitals 64 ff). A brief overview of the (state) church law is given in Stefan Korioth, 'Art. 140 GG', in Theodor Maunz, Günter Dürig, and Roman Herzog, eds, *Grundgesetz. Kommentar* (Beck 2014), recitals 22 ff and Michael Germann, 'Art. 140 GG', in Volker Epping and Christian Hillgruber, eds, *Grundgesetz: GG* (Beck 2014), recital 20. For the different legal sources of religious constitutional law in general, see Joseph Listl and Dietrich Pirson, eds, *Handbuch des Staatskirchenrechts der Bundesrepublik Deutschland* vol. I (2nd edn, Dunckel & Humblot 1994), 211–343 and Axel von Campenhausen and Peter Unruh, 'Art. 140 GG', in Hermann von Mangoldt, Friedrich Klein, and Christian Starck, eds, *GG III. Artikel 83 bis 146* (6th edn, Franz Vahlen 2010), 2123 recitals 41 ff.

Historically, the subjects taught included Catholic and Protestant theology, and then Orthodox, Old Catholic, and Jewish theology.[47] Islamic theology was established in the more recent past at various public universities, as a denominationally bound academic discipline. Chairs of denominational Islamic studies have been nominated at the state-run universities of Erlangen/Nürnberg, Münster/Osnabrück, Frankfurt/Gießen, and Tübingen.[48] These institutions received subsidies of EUR 40 million from the Federal Ministry for Education and Research, which started in 2011 and is expected to continue until 2020. Beginning in the winter semester of 2018/2019, Humboldt University in Berlin is planning to operate an institute for Islamic theology.

Given that Islam lacks an institutionalized organizational apparatus comparable to that of Christian churches, the question of who the State's partner should be for Muslim education is one that poses some difficulty. An advisory board model was developed as an interim solution.[49] In view of the fact that denominational Islamic theology is still quite a new discipline, academic standards are occasionally still in need of catching up. It is envisaged that the academic standards in research and teaching will be ensured in the medium term by dedicated, interdisciplinary exchange, motivation to acknowledge academic achievements within the academic disciplines, and by the academic freedom at public universities.

The newly created Islamic theology programs are similar in motivation to early Catholic theology programs at public universities, which were also originally established with a goal of mitigating fundamentalism.[50] Furthermore, theology at public universities has been serving as a neutralizing mechanism since at least the late nineteenth century in order to make religiousness compliant with the established order, whether in Prussia, the German Empire, the Weimar Republic, Nazi Germany, or the German Democratic Republic.[51]

## *Austria*

Austria is a secular state. Similar to Germany, the relationship between state and religion is characterized by an amicable institutional separation. The State, which is denominationally neutral and therefore avoids any identification with religious or philosophical belief, tolerates and supports the activities of the religious communities in public. In order to do this, the State makes available a legal framework separate from the State's core functions for the pluralistic inclusion of religion in society.[52]

47 For an overview of institutionalized academic theology in Germany, see Wissenschaftsrat, supra note 38 and Waldhoff, supra note 38 at recitals 8 ff and 16 ff.

48 For a brief overview about Islamic theology at state-run universities in Germany, see Waldhoff at recitals 59 ff.

49 See in this respect Christian Walter, Janbernd Oebbecke, and Antje von Ungern-Sternberg, eds, *Die Einrichtung von Beiräten für islamische Studien* (1st edn, Nomos 2011). For this reason, Wolfgang Loschelder considers Islamic theology unconstitutional. 'Und nun: Islamische Theologische Fakultäten an staatlichen Universitäten? – Kritische Fragen zu einem fragwürdigen Projekt', in Marten Breuer and Eckart Klein, eds, *Der Staat im Recht. Festschrift für Eckart Klein zum 70* (Duncker & Humblot 2013), 217 at 223 ff and 227.

50 See, for example, the Prussian 'Kulturkampf'. Solte, *Theologie an der Universität* at 101 fn 1. See also Ernst-Lüder Solte, 'Die deutschen katholisch-theologischen Fakultäten im Konflikt um die päpstliche Unfehlbahrkeit', in Karl-Hermann Kästner, ed., *Festschrift für Martin Heckel zum siebzigsten Geburtstag* (Mohr Siebeck 1999), 251 and Ernst Rudolf Huber, *Struktur und Krisen des Kaiserreichs* (2nd edn, Stuttgart 1982), 679 at 682 ff, 712 ff, and 717 ff.

51 See Steinhilber at § 8, B.III.5.

52 For the legal sources and basic approaches to religion and belief, see Richard Potz, 'Austria', in Robbers, Durham, and Thayer, eds, at 15 ff. and Richard Potz, 'Staat und Kirche in Österreich', in Gerhard Robbers, ed., *Staat und Kirche in der europäischen Union* (2nd edn, Nomos 2005), 426 at 429 f.

Even before the new Islam Law (see the following) came into force, Austria boasted a private institution for trainings teachers of Islamic religion at state schools, namely, the Islamische Religionspädagogische Akademie (Academy for Islamic Religious Pedagogy), which was set up in 1998. In 2005, this was converted to a private degree for teachers of Islamic religion, as per the Austrian Universities Act.[53] The task of further training for teachers is met by the private university course for Further Training in Islamic Religious Pedagogy.[54] Both programs are run by the Islamic Religious Community in Austria (IGGÖ). Since 2007, teachers of Islamic Religion for secondary schools have been trained in the master's course 'Islamic Religious Pedagogy' at the University of Vienna.

On 31 March 2015, the new Islam Law came into effect in Austria.[55] Part 5 of the Islam Law contains provisions on cooperation between the Islamic religious communities and the State. Section 24 governs the setting up of denominational Muslim theological studies at the University of Vienna, beginning 1 January 2016, for the purposes of theological research and teaching, and for the academic training of the leaders of the next generation of Islamic religious communities.[56] This ensures that the academic education of theological staff is guaranteed for Islam in the same way as for Catholic and Protestant churches[57] and puts Islam on equal footing in that regard.[58] Each Islamic 'religious society' as defined under the Law is to have its own branch of studies.[59] As in Germany, the appointment of professors shall be agreed upon with the respective Muslim religious societies.[60] The Austrian government is providing subsidies for the setting up of the 'theological studies' envisaged in Section 24 of the Islam Law. A bachelor's degree in 'Islamic Theology' is set to be offered at the University of Vienna from autumn 2017.

To be clear, this academic training is not practical, professional training qualifying someone to become an imam. Such training must be organized by the Muslim religious communities themselves. However, the academic training can help prepare for this. Graduates might also start working in social or youth work, offering pastoral care in hospitals, or in academia.

### *Non-denominational approach: France*

The French system of *laïcité* is traditionally regarded as a strict separation between religion and state.[61] *Laïcité* is guaranteed by the Constitution[62] and implies state neutrality, religious

53 See www.irpa.ac.at (accessed July 2017).

54 See www.ihl.ac.at (accessed July 2017).

55 Bundesgesetz über die äußeren Rechtsverhältnisse islamischer Religionsgesellschaften – Islamgesetz 2015 [Federal Law Regarding the External Legal Relations of Muslim Religious Communities – Islam Law 2015], StF: BGBl. I No. 39/2015. This law replaced the Islam Law of 1912.

56 446 der Beilagen XXV. GP – Regierungsvorlage [government bill] – Erläuterungen zum IslamG 2015, Zu § 24 (3).

57 Protestant Law Sec. 15.

58 446 der Beilagen XXV. GP – Regierungsvorlage [government bill] – Erläuterungen zum IslamG 2015, Zu § 24(1).

59 Islam Law Sec. 24(2).

60 Islam Law Sec. 24(4). 446 der Beilagen XXV. GP – Regierungsvorlage [government bill] – Erläuterungen zum IslamG 2015, Zu § 24(2).

61 For the legal sources and basic approaches to religion and belief in France, see Francis Messner, 'France', in Robbers, Durham, and Thayer, eds, 120 at 122 f. See for a comparison of French and German approaches to state neutrality regarding religion Yoan Vilain, 'Verfassungsprinzipien', in Nicolas Marsch, Yoan Vilain, and Mattias Wendel, eds, *Französisches und Deutsches Verfassungsrecht. Ein Rechtsvergleich* (1st edn, Springer 2015), 45 at 64 ff.

62 Constitution of 4 October 1958 Art. 10 and preamble.

freedom, and pluralism.[63] This separation regime derives, in particular, from the first two articles of the 1905 Law on Separation of Church and State. First, the law guarantees the free exercise of religion. Second, religious communities may not receive official recognition or (generally speaking) receive funding from the State.[64] Apart from the department of Guiana and the overseas territories, the separation regime of the law of 1905 does not apply in the eastern departments Upper Rhine, Lower Rhine, and Moselle.[65] These latter eastern departments were under control of the Second German Reich from 1870 to 1918. Following their return to France, however, the status quo, i.e. the regime of 'Old France'[66] as progressively amended by German ecclesiastical law, was largely maintained.[67] Accordingly, with the exception of the Faculté de Théologie Catholique et Protestante (University of Strasbourg)[68] and the Centre Universitaire de Théologie Catholique in Metz (University of Lorraine), there is no state-sponsored denominational theology. Theological education is provided by private universities.[69]

In view of France's fairly strict secularism, one might assume that there would be no current or past state initiatives for training Muslim leaders, but that is far from the truth.[70] Since the late 1980s, French governments have been trying to influence the training of the *cadre religieux musulman*. The aim has been to create an *islam de France* through educating the religious leaders *à la française*, to create a core group of 'modernist Muslims'.[71] The *Bureau central des cultes* (Central Worship Office), part of the Ministry for the Interior, has primary responsibility, but the Ministry for Education and Research and the Ministry for Immigration and National Identity are also involved.

That said, the plan to establish Islam as a non-denominational academic discipline at universities and to have the Muslim elites educated there has so far not had much success. Not even the attempts to establish an Islamic theological faculty in Strasbourg comparable

63 Constitutional Council, No. 2012-297, QPC (21 February 2013).

64 See Arts. 1 and 2 of the 1905 Law:

> Article 1. La République assure la liberté de conscience. Elle garanti le libre exercice des cultes sous les seules restrictions édictées ci-après dans l'intérêt de l'ordre public.
>
> Article 2. La république ne reconnaît pas, ne salarie ni ne subventionne aucun culte. … Pourront toutefois être inscrites auxdits budgets les dépenses relatives à des services d'aumônerie et destinées à assurer le libre exercice des cultes dans les établissements publics tels que lycées, collèges, écoles, hospices, asiles et prisons. Les établissements publics du culte sont supprimés, sous réserve des dispositions énoncés à l'article 3.

65 Messner, 'France', at 125.

66 Law of 18 Germinal year X for Christian faiths and 1808 decrees for Jewish faith.

67 For the local law in Alsace-Moselle, see Messner, 'France', at 133 ff and Francis Messner, 'Public Funding of Faiths According to Local Law in Alsace-Moselle', in Francis Messner (ed.), *Public Funding of Religions in Europe* (Routledge 2015), 83 ff.

68 Michel Deneken, 'Contenu et methode de la discipline théologique dans les universities publiques francaises: l'exemple de Strasbourg', in Michel Deneken and Francis Messner, eds, *La théologie à l'université. Status, programmes et evolutions* (Éditions Labor et Fides 2009), 35 at 35 ff.

69 L731 Code de l'éducation – Titre III. See Francoise Curtit and Anne-Laure Zwilling, 'L'enseignement en théologie et sciences des religions dans les établissements d'enseignement supérieur en France: Ce que révèlent les programmes de formation', in Deneken and Messner, eds, at 17 ff.

70 The following broad outline of the developments in France is based on Anne-Laure Zwilling, 'L'enseignement de l'islam dans les universités en France: Une histoire mouvementée', in Michel Deneken, ed., *Droit et religion en Europe. Ètudes en l'honneur de Francis Messner* (Presses Universitaires de Strasbourg 2014), 239 at 240 ff; Franck Frégosi, 'La problématique de la formation des cadres religieux musulmans en France: Au croisement des logiques politique, academique et communautaire', in Deneken, ed., at 443, 448 ff.; Frégosi, ed.; and Hussain and Tuck at 7 ff.

71 See *Le Monde*, 28 and 29 November 2014, quoted in Zwilling at 244.

to the Catholic and Protestant theological faculties, which began in the 1970s, have been successful.[72] Opposition from within the university system, from politicians, from society, and from the Islamic associations has affected the viability of these efforts.

After decades of unsuccessful attempts to set up educational institutions and programs for specifically training religious staff in matters of Islam, France focuses today on non-denominational higher civil and civic education (*formation civile et civique*), particularly within the setting of *formation continue*, or training programs, rather than traditional university degree programs. There are several academic programs, financed by public-private partnerships, aimed at improving the civic education of Muslim faith leaders that have received the support of the French government. These are mostly year-long *diplôme universitaires* (DU), *certificats*, and master's programs.

Following the terrorist attacks in 2015, the French government showed renewed interest in developing an *islam républicain*, in creating a cultural and religious organization that would encourage a strand of Islam compatible with the values of the Republic. This was partly realized when the *Fondation de l'islam de France* was set up on 6 December 2016, with the former minister for the interior, Jean-Pierre Chevènement, as its president. This secular non-profit foundation intends to use cultural, social, and educational projects to improve knowledge and a better understanding of Islam as a religion and culture within French society, but also among Muslims themselves. One point of emphasis is university research in the field of Islamology and on the secular education of imams, for example by subsidizing their participation in the aforementioned programs. It is also envisioned that Muslims themselves will set up a central religious organization to finance mosques and the theological training of imams,[73] but due to disputes among the different French Muslim associations, this has not yet been set up.

## Is a denominational or a non-denominational approach preferable?

Germany, Austria, and France are all pursuing the same promising idea. The two approaches chosen – denominational academic theology on the one hand (Germany/Austria), or a civic education on the other (France) – subject religious beliefs to the pressure of modernization, to translate their fundamentalist beliefs into modern thinking compatible with European values. They pursue the project of modernizing fundamentalist elements by integrating them into the academic discourse. That said, ensuring a denominational academic theological education is probably the more suitable approach in order to attain the goal of religious transformation as quickly and sustainably as possible. First, non-denominational education only reaches the religious consciousness from an external perspective without any religious authority or legitimacy. Only a denominational framework deemed religiously legitimate by the believer himself promises the ethical self-civilization necessary for the transformation of individuals. Second, it is doubtful that the non-denominational approach of one-year academic programs

72 The legal basis for this would have been provided by Article 33 of the Loi sur l'enseignement supérieur of 1875. The Catholic and the Protestant faculties in Strasbourg were also founded on the basis of this legal provision. See Francis Messner, 'L'enseignement de la théologie à l'université publique: L'exemple de la création d'une faculté de théologie musulmane à Strasbourg', in Frégosi, ed., at 141 ff.

73 For a brief description, see Anne-Bénédicte Hoffner, 'La Fondation de l'islam de France es créée', *La Croix*, 6 December 2016.

can sufficiently effect the desired transformation. It is too much to expect the desired socialization in what is effectively a study period of nine months. Countries should aim for study programs, ideally at the undergraduate level, with a duration of several years. The shorter programs may work as an interim solution for religious leaders who already hold office.

## Challenges and critiques

### *Would religious fundamentalists actually attend higher education programs?*

Whether any such denominational or non-denominational approaches to modernizing the attitudes of religious communities through higher education will work depends on the willingness of the religious communities to engage with academic education. Any voluntary programs initiated by the state can only succeed if they are wholly embraced by the religious communities, to the extent that they will become involved in developing the programs, encourage their staff to attend them, and employ the graduates.

This raises the initial question what interest fundamentalist religious communities might have in such programs. After all, the religious groups we are most interested in providing the training to are the ones most likely to reject it. Opponents of such programs within the Muslim communities are manifestly unlikely to accept these programs.[74] Even among who might be more open to these programs, no religious community likes the state to tell it what to believe and whom to employ as religious personnel.

One way of persuading religious groups to embrace these academic programs might be if they are presented not as methods of transformative religious education, but rather as attractive offers of state support for religious minorities that include not only education but also support for religious, cultural, and basic human rights. To embrace these programs, Muslim communities must be convinced that the programs would also provide Muslims with organizational, institutional, social, and financial advantages, putting them on equal footing with other religious communities. Islamic religious communities would also need to be convinced that the denominational theology offered at public universities is their own rather than a state imposition.

Austria's Islam Law, Sections 11 and 18, provides another mechanism for increasing the willingness of Islamic religious communities to employ the graduates of Islamic theology study programs offered at public universities. The State limits the ability to provide pastoral care in the armed forces, prisons, hospitals, and other comparable institutions to those holding such degrees or comparable education. In addition to professional suitability, it also requires personal suitability including at least three years of relevant professional experience and sufficient command of the German language.[75] The limiting of careers in pastoral care to those who have completed these programs is a significant enticement to them.

### *Efficacy: does higher education actually de-radicalize faith leaders?*

Perhaps the most significant proof of the effectiveness of theology taught at state universities is that while Christian churches in Germany initially opposed any interference by modern academia with their religious denominations, they now embrace modern academia even to the

74 On the inner conflicts within German Muslim communities concerning Islamic theology at state universities, see Steinhilber at § 8, B.IV.2.

75 Islam Law Secs 11(1) and (2) and 18(1) and (2).

point of excluding non-academic theology from the discourse.[76] Today, theology is accepted without question as an academic discipline in Germany.[77] The justification for theology to be taught at state universities is no longer questioned by the majority consensus; it is merely acknowledged as a necessity.[78] The dominant political, legal, and religious actors are all agreed that academic theology forms the basis of solid, socially constructive religiosity, and at the same time, it prevents fundamentalism. Accordingly, the discourse is no longer framed by the question of whether there should be academic theology, but merely by questions of where and how.

As soon as religious communities no longer question the fundamental justification of academic theology, i.e. as soon as the 'whether' is no longer asked, academic theology has fulfilled its purpose. The respective religious communities have arrived in modernity. They appreciate the values of equality, liberty, tolerance, and pluralism. Or, to put it another way, religious communities have integrated into the secular framework of the legal order. If one looks at the history of Catholicism and Protestantism in Germany, one sees that the internal divide between fundamentalist and liberal interpretations of religion has been largely resolved in favor of the latter, which also supports a secular society. There is reason to hope that just as the large German churches have overcome historical divisions and now draw their religious staff almost exclusively from graduates of public universities, teaching denominational theology at public universities can over time contribute towards the overall modernization and liberalization of Islam in Germany.

Of course, this is no panacea. It is questionable to what extent university-trained religious personnel still have influence at a time when radicalization of persons tends to take place online.[79] And religious people might be more easily encouraged to affirm the social order when that social order is inherently compatible with their religious beliefs,[80] which is not self-evident in the case of some forms of Islam. On the other hand, we should not underestimate the salutary influence of integration into a modern society such as Germany's, offering gentle but sure encouragement to moderation rather than radicalization. Even if there is no certain recipe for moderating all religious views to conform to democratic norms, efforts in that direction can strengthen the moderate forces within Muslim communities in their fight against religious fundamentalism. Non-denominational or civic programs can achieve this less effectively or not at all, but they could at least increase the societal pressure to modernize from outside.

### *Is the transformation strategy of higher education paternalistic and a violation of religious freedom and non-interference by the state?*

Some would accuse the proposed transformation strategy of being paternalistic and violating religious freedom and the principle of non-interference by the state. Yes and no.

76 Steinhilber at § 8, B.IV.2.b.

77 See Steinhilber at § 9, B.I.1.

78 For rare critical views on the prevailing legal opinion, see Gerhard Czermak, *Religions- und Weltanschauungsrecht. Eine Einführung* (Springer 2008), recitals 393 ff; Ludwig Renck, 'Verfassungsprobleme der theologischen Fakultäten', (1996) *Neue Zeitschrift für Verwaltungsrecht* 333 ff; Erwin Fischer, *Volkskirche ade! Trennung von Staat und Kirche. Die Gefährdung Religions- und Weltanschauungsfreiheit in der Bundesrepublik Deutschland* (4th edn, IBDK 1993), 311 ff; Erwin Fischer, *Trennung von Staat und Kirche. Die Gefährdung der Religions- und Weltanschauungsfreiheit in der Bundesrepublik* (3rd edn, IBDK 1984), 307 ff; and Johannes Neumann, 'Theologische Fakultäten', in *Trennung von Staat und Kirche. Thesen der Humanistischen Union*, (Humanistische Union 1995), 31 at 31 ff.

79 See Frégosi at 461 ff.

80 For example, Bahá'í. For the Bahá'í Faith's legal status in Germany, see Emanuel Vahid Towfigh, *Die rechtliche Verfassung von Religionsgemeinschaften. Eine Untersuchung am Beispiel der Bahai* (Mohr Siebeck 2006).

From a meta-perspective, which does not interrelate with the discourse it describes, we can admit that it is paternalistic and that it does infringe the religious neutrality of the state. Simply put, the state aims at transforming fundamentalist religiosity into modern religiosity, and thus manifestly interferes in religious matters.

On the other hand, from an insider's perspective – that is to say, with a view from within the system of law, human rights, the modern state, etc. – this transformation strategy appears as a generous offer by the state to promote religious freedom. Offering study programs that affirm and proactively teach the value of religious freedom in the modern liberal sense enhances the overall commitment of the society to religious freedom.

Admittedly, the assumption of a meta-perspective, which does not interrelate with the discourse it describes, is more theoretical than practicable, because perhaps religious fundamentalists reading this article would introduce meta-reflections in the participation discourse. Bearing this in mind, this article runs contrary to the political goal of religious integration. By presenting academic theology, or indeed education in a wider sense, as a transformation strategy, it alerts pre- or anti-modern Muslims to the fact that these university programs are aimed at changing their religiosity. However, this destructive effect is counterbalanced by the constructive contribution to changing awareness in the context of religious fundamentalism. After all, it shows that free societies urgently require effective integration strategies to be developed consciously. This is the weak point of a dual-perspective approach.[81] Nevertheless, I allow myself this academic luxury.

## Conclusion

The strategies adopted in Germany, Austria, France, and elsewhere follow the same basic approach of utilizing the higher education sector to deal preventatively with religious fundamentalism. Any such approach is based on the convincing assumption that at the moment religious fundamentalists engage in academic discourse they enter a transformation process toward liberal thinking. Higher education puts fundamentalist thinking under gentle pressure to modernize. Although higher education of faith leaders is not a panacea, it does represent an intelligent, inclusive, and preventative approach to solving the modern state's dilemma in combatting religious fundamentalism.

81 For the necessity for considering religious fundamentalism, see Steinhilber at § 5. Chapter, C.

# 9 Religious freedom and places of worship

## Religious buildings in Europe and the United States

*Maria Luisa Lo Giacco*

### Worship buildings and local identity

Since the middle of the last century, there has been a growing process of urbanization throughout the world. In 2014, the United Nations Population Report found that more than half (54%) of the world population lives in urban areas (in 1950 it was 30%), and that number is estimated to rise to 66% by 2050.[1] This process of urbanization is mainly due to migration, which is at the same time a major cause of the cultural and religious pluralism that now characterizes towns and cities, and not only in Europe.[2] If this trend continues, in the year 2050 two thirds of the world's population will live in towns and cities, and those towns and cities will be pluralistic, with different cultures and religions coexisting in close proximity to one another.

The increasing phenomenon of pluralistic urban areas is not merely a manifestation of cultural and religious change; it also concerns the architecture and urban planning of diverse urban areas.[3] In European towns and cities, religious changes are taking place in environments that were long characterized by a certain degree of cultural and religious homogeneity, and that homogeneity helped to form the urban landscape. One challenge in the decades to come is to create physical urban spaces where inhabitants belonging to different religions and cultures may live together peacefully and avoid conflict between different identities.

Such changes do not happen painlessly. Sometimes, even the simple request to build a place of worship of a religion considered alien to the cultural heritage becomes a source of suspicion and hostility, and if the request comes from Islam, the reaction often leads to conflict. As Pierluigi Consorti writes, the conflicts that often occur in European towns over requests to build mosques are 'representative of many of the conflicts of religiously divided societies in Europe'.[4] The word 'mosque' tends to be associated with 'conflict',[5] as does

1 United Nations Department of Economic and Social Affairs, 'World Urbanization Prospects: The 2014 Revision, Highlights' (2014), UN Doc ST/ESA/SER.A/352, available at https://esa.un.org/unpd/wup/Publications/Files/WUP2014-Highlights.pdf (accessed 27 February 2017).

2 See Mario Ricca, *Culture interdette. Modernità, migrazioni, diritto interculturale* (Bollati Boringhieri 2013).

3 Maria Chiara Giorda, 'I luoghi religiosi a Torino. Le religioni nei contesti urbani contemporanei', (2015) 23 *Quaderni di diritto e politica ecclesiastica* (2) 340.

4 Pierluigi Consorti, 'The "Mosque Affaire" in European Divided Societies. The Florence Case: A New Participatory Model', in Marcello Mollica, ed., *Bridging Religiously Divided Societies in the Contemporary World* (Pisa University Press 2015), 154.

5 Consorti at 161.

the word 'minaret'. Specifically, 'the minaret appears to have become the ultimate symbol of the conflict about Islam, or rather around its visible manifestation in the public space.'[6]

It seems paradoxical that secular societies should battle over the subject of religious buildings. The possibility of building a space in which to worship freely, individually, or collectively is closely linked to the exercise of religious freedom guaranteed in Article 9 of the European Convention on Human Rights (ECHR). However, buildings – like clothing – have become symbols of a cultural identity that must be defended in the name of secularism: 'Veils, turbans, crosses, churches and minarets… are branded as ideal scimitars to protect identity and at the same time to disguise what the secularists really want to preserve or are frightened of being altered in some way.'[7] Those who oppose the construction of religious buildings belonging to minority religions do so in the name of a cultural identity manifest in the historical development of European towns around the church and its bell tower.[8] Many of the recent legislative measures across Europe limiting the ability to build mosques or minarets are based on the alleged need to protect the cultural and religious identity of a territory.

Without denying the role played by Christianity in forging European identity, it is also true that European towns and cities were built over the centuries or even millennia with the influence of different cultures that all left their mark. The city of Rome is a striking example of the multicultural, multi-religious development of many European cities. It is the iconic heart of Catholicism, yet the Christian basilicas stand next to the monuments of ancient pagan Rome. Tourists take pictures of the dome of the Great Synagogue next to the bell tower of the basilica that houses the remains of the Apostle Bartholomew. The minaret of the Great Mosque of Parioli rises in the skyline, competing in height with the dome of St. Peter. All over Europe, this pattern is repeated. Granada and Seville, two of the most beautiful cities in Spain, owe their distinctiveness to their Islamic architecture. Such cities, in their diversity, are representative of European identity: historical cities are 'witness to interculturality'.[9]

In such an environment, the fear of adding new or other cultural references seems paradoxical. Rather than defending the identity of cities, this type of protectionist attitude produces cultural impoverishment: 'In the light of history, the valorisation of expressions of various confessions, even in the urbanistic context, represents an enrichment factor intended to be enjoyed by all and not only by the narrow circle of the faithful.'[10]

It is noteworthy that controversial requests to build places of worship do not come only from the Islamic religion. In the 1996 case of *Mannousakis and Others v. Greece*,[11] the European Court of Human Rights adjudicated a case involving the Congregation of Jehovah's Witnesses, for whom Greek law made the construction, or even the use, of buildings for worship very difficult. Other minority religions faced the same difficulties under

6 Stefano Allievi, 'Moschee in Europa. Conflitti e polemiche, tra fiction e realtà', (2010) 18 *Quaderni di diritto e politica ecclesiastica* (1) 155.

7 See Mario Ricca, *Pantheon. Agenda della laicità interculturale* (Torri del Vento 2012), 22.

8 See Luciano Zannotti, 'I luoghi della convivenza religiosa e del pluralismo culturale', (2010) 18 *Quaderni di diritto e politica ecclesiastica* (1) 75.

9 Ricca, *Pantheon* at 450.

10 Mario Ricca, 'Crisi della sovranità, decentramento, fattore religioso. Un caso paradigmatico: l'edilizia di culto tra localismo democratico e polivalenza giuridica del territorio urbano', in *Studi in onore di Gaetano Catalano* vol. III (Rubbettino 1998), 1164.

11 *Manoussakis and Others v. Greece*, App. No. 18748/91 (ECtHR, 26 September 1996).

Greek law. The Strasbourg Court declared the Greek legislation to be discriminatory, recalling that the possibility to build and to have places of worship is closely linked to the exercise of religious freedom guaranteed by Article 9 of the ECHR. This principle was recently reaffirmed in another case concerning Jehovah's Witnesses,[12] in which the Court acknowledged that while states may restrict this right if necessary to protect public order, states must commit themselves 'à maintenir un véritable pluralisme religieux, inhérent à la notion de société démocratique' ('to maintain a true religious pluralism, inherent in the notion of democratic society'). In other words, in the view of the Strasbourg judges, religious pluralism is an essential feature of democracy and buildings for worship are an essential feature of religion; the logical conclusion is that there must be pluralism among religious buildings.

Beyond concerns about protecting the identity of a territory, hostility to requests to build places of worship is sometimes based on fears concerning the long-term effect of the place of worship on the surrounding area. After all, the request to build a church or another religious building shows that the believers desire to be integrated into that place, making an investment for the future.[13] It is not uncommon for neighbors to fear that the presence of a certain place of worship could lead to a reduction in property values or a modification of business activities as new businesses related to the newly present religion displace old businesses.[14]

Concerns also include the protection of public order, especially regarding places of Islamic worship. In Italy and in many European countries, many people want firmer control of mosques in order to avoid radicalization or behavior not compatible with democracy, including support for terrorism.[15] Some perceive full religious freedom for Muslims as a danger to public safety and propose that restricting places of Muslim worship will mitigate this danger.[16]

In Italy, this fearful interpretation of religious pluralism has recently motivated a proposal for a more restrictive interpretation of Articles 8 and 19 of the Italian Constitution, relating to religions other than Catholicism and to individual religious freedom. It has been said that these articles do not take into account the dangers of the Islamic religion, a religion that 'poses a risk to public security and to the values of Western civilization'.[17] Supporters espouse a strict limitation on the possibility of opening Islamic worship sites, pointing to the examples of similar Swiss and Austrian legislation, in contrast to the countries of southern Europe whose permissiveness it is claimed will subject them to massive Islamic immigration.[18]

12 *Association de Solidarité avec les Temoins de Jehovah et Autres c. Turquie*, App. Nos 36915/10 and 8606/13 (ECtHR, 24 May 2016).

13 See Zannotti at 84.

14 See Ricca, *Pantheon* at 450–451.

15 See Gianfranco Macrì, 'Islam e questione delle moschee. (Brevi riflessioni)', in Nicola Fiorita and D. Loprieno, eds, *La libertà di manifestazione del pensiero e la libertà religiosa nelle società multiculturali* (Firenze University Press 2009), 221.

16 See Nicola Fiorita, 'Come un'introduzione', in Francesco Dal Canto, Pierluigi Consorti, and Saulle Panizza, eds, *Libertà di espressione e libertà religiosa in tempi di crisi economica e di rischi per la sicurezza* (Pisa University Press 2016), 175–176.

17 Luciano Musselli, 'Edilizia religiosa, Islam e neogiurisdizionalismo in Europa. Alcune note sul nuovo "Islamgesetz" austriaco e sul divieto di edificare minareti in Svizzera', (2015) 23 *Quaderni di diritto e politica ecclesiastica* (2) 442.

18 Musselli at 455.

The Swiss example refers to the Swiss referendum of 2009, approved by 57.5% of voters, which introduced a paragraph banning the construction of minarets into Article 72 of the Federal Constitution. The rule was justified by the need to preserve the Swiss landscape from foreign elements that would transform its identity; in fact, it mainly affects the symbols of Islam, whose values are claimed to be incompatible with those of Swiss democracy.[19] It is interesting to note that at the time of the referendum, in the whole of Switzerland there were only four mosques with minarets.

Austria was the first European country to legally recognize the Islamic religion in the 1920s, because at that time the Balkan part of the Austro-Hungarian Empire had a Muslim population. In fact, in 1979 the government authorized the construction of a mosque with a minaret. Recently, however, a new law prohibited the construction of buildings that are not homogeneous with the landscape. It is not a law against mosques *per se*; a Buddhist pagoda or a Hindu temple is not an architectural element typical of the alpine landscape either. Then again, while in theory the law affects all religious minorities of recent settlement in Austria,[20] due to the growing population of Muslims there would likely be significantly more demand for mosques than for other non-homogeneous religious buildings.

Measures adopted in Austria and Switzerland have echoed in Italy, not only in the news, but also in parliamentary discussions. During the last legislature, a bill was presented dealing with the construction of places of worship, which included the obligation to seek the opinion of the local population by referendum before authorizing the construction of a place of worship of a religion that does not have an agreement with the State. It is hard to overstate the absurdity of a law that would subject the exercise of religious freedom by a minority to the majority opinion, an opinion easily be influenced by political or ideological motivations.[21]

Proposals and legislative acts of this kind, as well as being contrary to constitutional principles, ironically present a social danger and a risk to healthy religious pluralism. Politics and discriminatory laws produce in those who suffer these laws a 'feeling of exclusion' that is likely to benefit the more radical and extreme religious groups.[22] If this manner of protectionist reasoning were to be welcomed across Europe, European cities would risk becoming 'more and more places of conflict instead of places of welcome, becoming territories where communities live separated from each other'.[23] In countries where the Islamic presence is more numerous and longstanding, and where implemented 'intercultural policies have effect',[24] fear fades and coexistence appears not only possible but even an asset. Perhaps a change in the city's skyline is not too high a price to pay to prevent 'the formation of ghettos, of resentment, of hate and marginality'.[25]

19 See Vincenzo Pacillo, '"Die religiöse Heimat". Il divieto di edificazione di minareti in Svizzera ed Austria', (2010) 18 *Quaderni di diritto e politica ecclesiastica* (1) 207.

20 See Pacillo at 221.

21 See Natascia Marchei, 'Gli edifici dei "culti ammessi". Una proposta di legge coacervo di incostituzionalità', (2010) 18 *Quaderni di diritto e politica ecclesiastica* (1) 109–117.

22 See Silvio Ferrari, 'Libertà religiosa e sicurezza nazionale in Europa dopo l'11 settembre', (2005) 13 *Quaderni di diritto e politica ecclesiastica* (1) 182.

23 Zannotti at 91.

24 Allievi at 150.

25 Nicola Fiorita, 'La moschea, il consiglio comunale e il diritto di libertà religiosa', (2010) 18 *Quaderni di diritto e politica ecclesiastica* (2) 463.

## The Italian case: regional laws and the interventions of the Constitutional Court

The Italian case deserves special attention on the European scene. The Constitution stipulates that building construction, including construction of buildings for worship, is the purview of regional legislation. Over the years, however, regional laws on worship buildings have provoked the intervention of the Constitutional Court on several occasions.

The first of these interventions concerned a law of the Abruzzo Region limiting the granting of regional contributions for the construction of worship buildings only to the Catholic Church and to the religious confessions that had entered into agreements with the State on the basis of Article 8 of the Italian Constitution.[26] In 1993, the Constitutional Court reiterated that state secularity does not prohibit the government from providing economic benefits in such cases, but held that this law constituted unjustifiable discrimination among religions.[27] The Court then focused on the definition of 'religious confession' and, having ruled out the possibility of resorting to the simple criterion of self-qualification, stated that the confession must be established in light of some criteria, such as previous public recognition, statute, or common agreement. Once the nature of the religious confession has been established, the only aspects that the Region can assess in the decision on the granting of contributions are the substance and social impact of the applicant's confession and the acceptance by the latter of the conditions and constraints on the use of the funds.[28]

After the 1993 ruling, other Regions were under pressure to change their laws that were in conflict with the Court's ruling.[29] The Court could, in fact, have ordered that the illegality of the Abruzzo law be extended to those laws of other Regions which were similar to the one of Abruzzo.[30] Failure to do so was criticized by some who, aware of the inertia of regional legislators, argued that the Court had 'been short-sighted, not foreseeing the adverse effects of the limits of its decision'.[31] A few years later, the Constitutional Court had to intervene again concerning a law in the Lombardy Region that, like that of Abruzzo, limited the granting of regional contributions for the construction of worship buildings to religions with agreements with the State.[32] The Court again declared the law unconstitutional.[33]

In this second judgment, concerning the Lombardy law, the Court reaffirmed the principles already established in 1993, reiterating the close link between the exercise of religious freedom and access to public funding for worship buildings, and again focused on the question of the definition of 'religious confession'. The Court declared the unconstitutionality of the Lombard law in limiting the granting of public contributions to worship buildings to the Catholic Church and other religious confessions with state agreements. The Court also held that state agreements 'are not and cannot be a condition imposed by public powers on Confessions in order for them to enjoy the freedom of organization and of action... nor

26 Law No. 29/1988.

27 Judgment No. 195 of 27 April 1993. In (1993) 1 *Quaderni di diritto e politica ecclesiastica* (3) 693–697.

28 See Maria Luisa Lo Giacco, *Le competenze delle regioni in materia ecclesiastica* (Cacucci 2004), 57–60.

29 See Riccardo Acciai, 'La sent. n. 195 del 1993 della Corte Costituzionale e sua incidenza sulla restante legislazione regionale in materia di finanziamenti all'edilizia di culto', (1993) *Giurisprudenza Costituzionale* (3) 2160–2165.

30 In accordance with Law No. 87 of 11 March 1953.

31 Valerio Tozzi, 'Edilizia di culto (libertà delle confessioni)', in Raffaele Botta, ed., *Diritto ecclesiastico e Corte costituzionale* (Edizioni Scientifiche Italiane 2006), 347.

32 Law No. 20 of 1992.

33 Judgment No. 346 of 16 July 2002.

to avail themselves of favourable rules concerning religious confessions'.[34] The Court thus rejected the argument that only a religion that had entered into an agreement with the State could be considered a 'religious confession', emphasizing that concluding agreements with the State is not within the means of all religious confessions.

It is interesting to note that the Court did not actually define 'religious confession', a difficult matter in a multicultural society that would deserve more attention. Instead, the Court merely rejected a definition that would limit 'religious confessions' to those religious groups that had concluded agreements with the State. More than 20 years ago, in a work about the reconstruction of the concept of a 'religious confession' in a comparative approach, Silvio Ferrari wrote that it is possible to 'survive' even without a clear legal notion of 'religious confession'.[35] However, the Italian version of secularism – the so-called open, positive secularism – legitimizes the intervention of public authorities in favor of religion, and therefore requires some means to separate what is religion from what is not.[36]

Often, the language of regional and local authorities can appear aggressive toward religious minorities. In the past, this harshness was mainly addressed to the so-called 'new religious movements' or to the Jehovah's Witnesses, the religious confession that challenged the two Laws of the Abruzzo and Lombardy Regions as noted earlier. More recently, a climate of 'increased local Islamophobia'[37] has provoked legislative interventions that are discriminatory toward Islam and not easily reconciled with constitutional principles.

I refer, in particular, to the Lombardy Region Law No. 3 of 3 February 2015,[38] which its authors defined as an 'anti-mosque law'. The explicit intention was to 'contain, if not to totally prevent, the construction within the Region, of places of worship belonging to the Islamic religion'.[39] The law manifestly ignored the principle that government action affecting a religious confession must protect the individual religious freedom of the adherents of that confession.[40] In ruling on the Lombardy law in 2016,[41] the Constitutional Court pointed to the close link between the right to religious freedom and the possibility of building places of worship. The impediments placed on a religion in the construction

34 Italian Constitutional Court, Judgment No. 346 of 16 July 2002, in (2003) 11 *Quaderni di diritto e politica ecclesiastica* (3) 686–688. See Luigi D'Andrea, 'Eguale libertà ed interesse alle intese delle confessioni religiose: brevi note a margine della sent. cost. n. 346/2002', (2003) 11 *Quaderni di diritto e politica ecclesiastica* (3) 667–685.

35 See Silvio Ferrari, 'La nozione giuridica di confessione religiosa (come sopravvivere senza conoscerla)', in Vittorio Parlato and Giovanni Battista Varnier, eds, *Principio pattizio e realtà religiose minoritarie* (Giappichelli 1995), 19–47.

36 Maria Luisa Lo Giacco, 'Riflessioni sulla difficile interpretazione delle parole "Religione" e "Religioso" nel diritto delle società multiculturali', (2015) *Annali del Dipartimento jonico in sistemi giuridici ed economici del Mediterraneo* vol. III, 267–283 and 'Hidden Meanings of the Words "Religion" and "Religious" in Legal Discourse', (2016) 209 *Semiotica. Journal of the International Association for Semiotic Studies/Revue de l'Association Internationale de Sémiotique* 341–356.

37 Giancarlo Anello, 'Passato e futuro della minoranza musulmana in Italia, tra islamofobia e pluralismo pragmatico-giuridico', (2016) *Stato, Chiese e pluralismo confessionale. Rivista telematica* (32) 4, available at www.statoechiese.it.

38 Modifying Articles 70 and 72 of Law No. 12.

39 Marco Parisi, 'Uguaglianza nella libertà delle confessioni religiose e diritto costituzionale ai luoghi di culto. In merito agli orientamenti della Consulta sulla legge regionale lombarda n. 2/2015', (2016) *Diritto e Religioni* (2) 211 and Giuseppe Casuscelli, 'La nuova legge lombarda sull'edilizia di culto: di male in peggio', (2015) *Stato, Chiese e pluralismo confessionale. Rivista telematica* (14), available at www.statoechiese.it.

40 See Giovanni Di Cosimo, 'Sostegni pubblici alle confessioni religiose, tra libertà di coscienza ed eguaglianza', (1993) *Giurisprudenza Costituzionale* (3) 2169.

41 Judgment No. 63 of 24 March 2016, (2016) 24 *Quaderni di diritto e politica ecclesiastica* (3) 644–654.

of its places of worship are in fact obstacles to the exercise of the religious freedom of the individual believers of that religion.

The Court also found numerous other aspects of the Lombardy law to be unlawful, noting that although the issue of building of places of worship is properly within the jurisdiction of the Region, the regional government cannot introduce 'provisions that hinder or compromise freedom of religion'. The Court struck down rules requiring approval by a regional body appointed by the Regional Council for the construction of worship buildings of confessions without state agreements. The Court noted that such a body had not yet been instituted after more than a year since the law came into force, making the construction of new religious buildings impossible for religious confessions that did not have agreements with the State. The Court also declared unlawful a provision allowing revocation of the agreement between a religious confession and the local authority if activities were carried out in the place of worship other than those provided for in the agreement. The Court held that provision to be contrary to Article 19 of the Italian Constitution because it interfered with the freedom of a religious confession to pursue activities other than those strictly linked to the worship.[42] The Court also found unconstitutional the obligation to install video surveillance equipment connected to law enforcement in worship buildings belonging to confessions without agreements. The Court did not deny that the exercise of religious freedom may be limited or regulated when it is necessary to protect public safety, but held that these measures were not within the purview of a local authority. On the other hand, the Court upheld the provisions allowing for the possibility of a local referendum and requiring new buildings to conform to the architectural characteristics of the Lombard landscape.

The judgment of unconstitutionality against much of the Lombardy law has not resolved the difficulties for Islamic communities of obtaining permits for the construction of mosques in the Lombardy Region. In fact, there is still a requirement for municipalities to adopt urban development plans for religious facilities, a long and difficult urban planning document, the lack of which has rendered useless all the projects already developed and financed by various Islamic communities on land which, prior to the law, had been declared suitable for new places of worship.[43]

In sum, the 2016 judgment on the Lombardy law hit an exposed nerve in the jurisprudential, cultural, and political debate on religion: what space must be afforded to Islam in Italian society, what limits can legitimately be put on recognition of Islam, and what is the balance between religious freedom and safeguarding the public?[44]

It was with the stated purpose of safeguarding the public that another Region, Veneto, passed Law No. 12 of 12 April 2016. Article 2 of this law obliged places of worship to use the Italian language for all the activities carried out within the building not 'strictly related

42 Giancarlo Anello, 'Freedom of Religion vs. Islamophobia: Lombardy's "Anti-Mosque Law" is Unconstitutional', Verfassungsblog, 2 April 2016, available at http://verfassungsblog.de/freedom-of-religion-vs-islamophobia-lombardys-anti-mosque-law-is-unconstitutional/ (accessed 15 February 2017).

43 See Simone Gorla, 'Legge "anti-moschee" in Lombardia, lo scontento delle associazioni religiose', *La Stampa*, 13 July 2016, available at www.lastampa.it/2016/07/13/italia/politica/legge-antimoschee-in-lombardia-lo-scontento-delle-associazioni-religiose-tskIfxVdOG3iQxmcLg5npL/pagina.html (accessed 15 February 2017) and Francesca Oliosi, 'La Corte Costituzionale e la legge regionale lombarda: Cronaca di una morte annunciata o di un'opportunità mancata?' (2016) *Stato, Chiese e pluralismo confessionale. Rivista telematica* (33) 28, available at www.statoechiese.it.

44 *See* Angelo Licastro, 'La Corte costituzionale torna protagonista dei processi di transizione della politica ecclesiastica italiana?', (2016) *Stato, Chiese e pluralismo confessionale. Rivista telematica* (26), available at www.statoechiese.it.

to ritual practices'. The idea underlying the provision was that within certain places of worship (Islamic, of course), the faithful use foreign languages (namely, Arabic) to spread fundamentalist doctrines or, worse, to organize terrorist attacks. The Constitutional Court declared the requirement of using the Italian language in places of worship to be illegal,[45] emphasizing that the Regional Assembly had gone beyond its jurisdiction in urban planning to 'ensure the balanced and harmonious development of its population centres'. Above all, the Court held that the use of one's own language is a fundamental right of the person guaranteed by the Constitution, stressing the importance of language as an 'element of individual and collective identity'.[46]

It would be unrealistic and naïve to expect to block the spread of a religion by hindering the construction of places of worship or by obliging the faithful to express themselves in the local language. These measures seem to be more populist than political, if by 'political' we mean intended to manage the problems of coexistence in a multicultural society. While places of worship may be important to religious believers, religion does not live in buildings; it does not have 'specific places to exist so that, if you want, you can keep it away'.[47] In the case of Islam, there is no precise definition of a place of worship or a prescribed architectural pattern of mosque; the mosque is where the faithful pray. What really matters is the prayer, not the place where it is carried out.[48] Laws such as those approved in some Regions are not only unconstitutional, at least in part, but useless. Rather than blocking the spread of the Islamic religion, they merely strike at the legitimate right of the faithful to have a place of worship.

The difficulties of the Italian Regions in managing religious worship buildings are a manifestation of a general crisis in Western democracies – local instances of a broad and painful process of cultural and religious change and accommodation.[49] A policy that truly seeks to manage religious pluralism cannot ignore the fact that relations among cultures and religions are played out in urban settings. The task of the legislator is to ensure that these relationships take place in a spirit of respect and mutual acceptance. Using religion as a populist tool to suppress those who are different hinders, rather than helps, the development of shared values necessary to mitigate confrontation.[50]

## Religious places and buildings in the United States: the Religious Land Use and Institutionalized Persons Act

In the United States, the Religious Land Use and Institutionalized Persons Act of 2000 (RLUIPA) deals with religious buildings. The first part of the law protects land use for

45 Judgment No. 67 of 7 April 2017.

46 See Giancarlo Anello, *Teologia linguistica e diritto laico* (Mimesis 2015).

47 Mario Ricca, 'Laicità interculturale. Cos'è?' in Gianfranco Macrì, Marco Parisi, and Valerio Tozzi, eds, *Diritto e religione. L'evoluzione di un settore della scienza giuridica attraverso il confronto fra quattro libri* (Plectica 2012), 60.

48 See Giancarlo Anello, 'Categorie ermeneutiche dei diritti religiosi e libertà di culto', in Macrì, Parisi, and Tozzi, eds, 330–337 and Giancarlo Anello, 'The Holy Word Does Not Come Strictly in Italian: Another Islamophobic Law Stopped in Northern Italy', Verfassungsblog, 10 April 2017, available at http://verfassungsblog.de/the-holy-word-does-not-come-strictly-in-italian-another-islamophobic-law-stopped-in-northern-italy/ (accessed 15 April 2017).

49 See Ricca, 'Crisi della sovranità' at 1166.

50 See Alberto Fossati, 'Le nuove norme, asseritamente urbanistiche, della Regione Lombardia sulle attrezzature religiose', (2015) 23 *Quaderni di diritto e politica ecclesiastica* (2) 439.

religious purposes, while the second part is devoted to protecting the religious freedom of persons who are detained or otherwise held in public institutions.[51]

Until 1990, the US Supreme Court required the government to demonstrate a compelling governmental interest in order to justify restricting individual religious freedom. In 1990, the Supreme Court essentially lowered the standard for the government to justify interference with religious exercise, holding that a government measure may be constitutional even if it interferes with religious freedom so long as it is a neutral law of general applicability – that is, not aimed at interfering with religion. RLUIPA was part of the US Congress's response to this ruling, aiming to protect religious freedom beyond the protection available under the Constitution as interpreted by the Supreme Court.[52] RLUIPA followed other legislative measure of the US Congress on religious freedom, including the Religious Freedom Restoration Act of 1993 (RFRA).[53] RLUIPA takes up the principles of RFRA in stating that a local measure regarding land use may limit religious freedom only if the local authority can prove that there is a compelling governmental interest and that the chosen measure is the least restrictive means of furthering that compelling governmental interest.

Jurisprudence in the United States before RLUIPA failed to acknowledge the central role of places of worship for the free exercise of religion. In a 1988 case in which a Baptist group had been prevented from building a church in an agricultural area,[54] a federal appeals court made a distinction between 'freedom to believe', which is absolutely protected by the Constitution, and 'freedom to act', which can be limited by public authorities. In essence, the court ruled that land use laws do not interfere with religious freedom because they do not interfere with the freedom to believe. The court concluded that 'there is no infringement of the Church's religious freedom. A church has no constitutional right to be free from reasonable zoning regulations nor does a church have a constitutional right to build its house of worship where it pleases.'[55]

Other cases in which US courts ruled against religious land use included the case of a rabbi who had asked to be allowed to turn his home into a synagogue and was told he could go and pray elsewhere,[56] and that of a Jehovah's Witnesses group whose request to build a prayer hall was refused on the basis that they could build it elsewhere.[57] In yet another case,[58] a court rejected the appeal of a Christian group that had rented a building in a residential zone and wanted to transform it to better suit their worship needs. Local authorities had denied the permit on the basis that this transformation would disturb the local population. The court held that it is the right of local authorities to determine land use, and that there was no discrimination because other religions had also been forbidden to build in the same zone.

51 See Maria Luisa Lo Giacco, 'La libertà religiosa dei detenuti nelle carceri degli Stati Uniti. Riflessioni a margine del caso *Holt v. Hobbs*', (2016) *Diritto e Religioni* (21) 166–190.

52 See Ira C. Lupu and Robert W. Tuttle, 'The Forms and Limits of Religious Accommodation: The Case of RLUIPA', (2010/2011) 32 *Cardozo Law Review* (5) 1853–1888.

53 The federal RFRA has limited application since the Supreme Court case of *City of Boerne v. Flores*, 521 U.S. 507 (1997), but many states have enacted their own RFRAs.

54 *Messiah Baptist Church v. County of Jefferson*, 859 F.2d 820 (10th Cir. 1988).

55 A dissenting judge disagreed, stating that '[t]he place of worship is central to the first amendment concept of free exercise as essentially the only place of religious assembly and the central place for the expression or religious speech.' McKay, J., dissenting.

56 *Grosz v. City of Miami Beach*, 721 F.2d 729 (11th Cir. 1983).

57 *Lakewood, Ohio Congregation of Jehovah's Witnesses, Inc. v. City of Lakewood*, 699 F.2d 303 (6th Cir. 1983).

58 *Christian Gospel Church, Inc. v. City and County of San Francisco*, 896 F.2d 1221 (9th Cir. 1990).

Historically, the courts decided in favor of religious land use only in cases of clear discrimination or hostility.[59] One federal appeals court case[60] concerned an Islamic organization that was repeatedly denied permission to build an Islamic center in an area where there were several religious buildings, including a large Pentecostal center and five other Christian churches. The court concluded that the ban was unlawful because it was discriminatory, forbidding the construction of an Islamic center in an area where there were religious buildings of other denominations. Notably, however, the court held that there was no violation of the religious freedom of Muslims because the ordinance did not prevent them from praying elsewhere, and congregational prayer is only recommended and not compulsory in Islam.

By strengthening protections for religious land use, RLUIPA has changed the principles by which land use restrictions are judged. Section 2(a)(1) applies the 'strict scrutiny' test to the cases of land use involving religious groups:

> No government shall impose or implement a land use regulation in a manner that imposes a substantial burden on the religious exercise of a person, including a religious assembly or institution, unless the government demonstrates that imposition of the burden on that person, assembly or institution: (a) is in furtherance of a compelling governmental interest; and (b) is the least restrictive means of furthering that compelling governmental interest.

Section 2(b) prohibits discrimination against religious organizations in land use:

1 Equal terms. No government shall impose or implement a land use regulation in a manner that treats a religious assembly or institution on less than equal terms with a non-religious assembly or institution;
2 Non-discrimination. No government shall impose or implement a land use regulation that discriminates against any assembly or institution on the basis of religion or religious denomination.

RLUIPA enforcement causes specific problems for judges. First, in order to decide if there is a substantial burden on religious exercise, courts must decide what is meant by 'religious exercise' and 'substantial burden'. The law itself provides some guidance, defining 'religious exercise' as 'any exercise of religion, whether compelled by, or central to, a system of religious belief'.[61] While this definition is not crystal clear, it is less thorny than defining 'substantial burden', which has had various interpretations in courts. Certainly there would be a 'substantial burden' if a land use regulation made religious exercise impossible or severely limited it. One interpretation would consider it a 'substantial burden' for a religious group to be forced to change its behavior or to violate its beliefs. Some courts have found a 'substantial burden' when a regulation was arbitrary, or targeted exclusively at religious organizations, or apparently neutral but actually damaging to religious actors. For religious organizations, it is often difficult to prove that a land use regulation produces a 'substantial burden' on religious exercise. Sometimes applicants have to prove that they have no other valid options for building elsewhere.

59 See Angela C. Carmella, 'Land Use', in Boris I. Bittker, Scott C. Idleman, and Franck S. Ravitch, eds, *Religion and the State in American Law* (Cambridge University Press 2015), 511.
60 As in the case of *Islamic Center of Mississippi, Inc. v. City of Starkville*, 840 F.2d 293 (5th Cir. 1988).
61 On the problem of the legal definition of 'religion' and 'religious', see Lo Giacco, 'Hidden Meanings'.

Once a substantial burden is proved, the court must determine whether the local regulation advances a compelling governmental interest and whether there are less restrictive means of achieving that interest.[62] The 'compelling government interest' test, also known as 'strict scrutiny', is considered the most demanding test in American constitutional law.[63] Nevertheless, even under RLUIPA, there have still been cases of failure to protect religious organizations in their legitimate requests for place of worship.

Post-RLUIPA cases include *Elsinore Christian Center v. City of Lake Elsinore*,[64] in which a federal court adjudicated the request of a Christian congregation to convert a supermarket into a worship center. The local authorities denied a permit, stating that a supermarket was more useful because it created jobs and tax revenue. The court noted that if such a justification were accepted, RLUIPA would be rendered moot because prohibition of land use for religious purposes would effectively always be justified. The court did consider ensuring an acceptable quality of life for residents of the area to be a compelling interest, but found that local authorities had not shown that the refusal was the least restrictive way to achieve that interest.[65] In another case, *Midrash Shepardi, Inc. v. Town of Seaside*,[66] a federal court applied the non-discrimination principle rather than the 'substantial burden' provision. Various congregations of Orthodox Jews had requested to use property in a commercial district where religious buildings had been prohibited but private clubs and associations were allowed. The court of appeals ruled that the zoning provision was unlawful because it prohibited religious groups while allowing similarly situated non-religious organizations.

There continues to be widespread debate about whether RLUIPA has struck the right balance between government interests and free religious exercise in the area of land use.[67] Marci Hamilton underlines the inherently local aspect of land use laws, noting that 'there is nothing more local than land, and state and local communities have been entitled to significant autonomy in crafting their land use priorities.'[68] It would be a departure from the norm, it is claimed, for the federal government to interfere with local authorities' ability to design local land use strategies. There are those who point out that federalism, the basis of the American legal system, is based on the idea that 'on many issues, local control is more likely to achieve better results for the public good than federal control,'[69] and land use is one of those issues. Hamilton also accuses RLUIPA of violating the First

62 See Carmella at 514–526.

63 See *Sherbert v. Verner*, 374 U.S. 398 (1963) and *Wisconsin v. Yoder*, 406 U.S. 202 (1972). See also Caroline R. Adams, 'The Constitutional Validity of the Religious Land Use and Institutionalized Persons Act of 2000: Will RLUIPA's Strict Scrutiny Survive the Supreme Court's Strict Scrutiny?', (2002) 70 *Fordham Law Review* (6) 2366–2367, available at http://ir.lawnet.fordham.edu/flr/vol70/iss6/19 (accessed 15 February 2017) and Maria Luisa Lo Giacco, 'La tutela della libertà religiosa negli U.S.A. Il Religious Freedom Restoration Act', in Raffaele Coppola and Luca Troccoli, eds, *Minoranze, laicità, fattore religioso. Studi di diritto internazionale e di diritto ecclesiastico comparato* (Cacucci 1997), 245–264.

64 291 F. Supp. 2d 1083 (C.D. Cal. 2003).

65 Interestingly, after its extensive analysis confirming the government's violation of RLUIPA, the court still dismissed the plaintiff's claim on the basis that RLUIPA was unconstitutional because Congress lacked constitutional authority to enact it. This was overturned by the Ninth Circuit Court of Appeals, which upheld RLUIPA and reversed the lower court's decision. No. 04-55320 (9th Cir. 2006).

66 366 F.3d 1214 (11th Cir. 2004).

67 See Jerold L. Waltman, *Religious Free Exercise and Contemporary American Politics: The Saga of the Religious Land Use and Institutionalized Persons Act of 2000* (Continuum 2011).

68 Marci A. Hamilton, 'The Constitutional Limitations on Congress's Power over Local Land Use: Why the Religious Land Use and Institutionalized Persons Act Is Unconstitutional', (2009) 2 *Albany Government Law Review* (2) 368.

69 Marci A. Hamilton, 'Federalism and the Public Good: The True Story Behind the Religious Land Use and Institutionalized Persons Act', (2003) 78 *Indiana Law Journal* (1) 321.

Amendment by creating a privileged class of land owners.[70] Some also argue that existing general laws and the intervention of local courts would be sufficient to prevent discriminatory land use.[71]

On the other hand, defenders of RLUIPA point to local rules that have in fact posed obstacles to the building, enlargement, and renting of places of worship. Religious buildings are often subject to problems in the permit process because of unpopularity due to their effects on traffic (too much in residential zones, too little in commercial zones), their tax-exempt status that prevents local governments from collecting tax revenue on the land, or the unpopularity of the religion itself. But, proponents argue, building churches is a 'core First Amendment activity' that must be protected even if unpopular.[72] Defenders of RLUIPA also note that pre-RLUIPA courts sometimes shied away from considering the merits of land use matters so as to respect the autonomy of local authorities,[73] leaving open the question of how effective judicial redress would be in cases of discriminatory land use regulations without RLUIPA.

There is no doubt that RLUIPA is an especially useful protection for minority religions. Cases involving Jews, Muslims, Buddhists, and Hindus account for 34% of RLUIPA litigation, while only about three percent of the US population belongs to these religions. There is a documented tendency of local authorities to use urban planning to exclude or limit the rights of certain minority religious groups,[74] which often encounter difficulties when they seek to set up a place of worship.[75] Although it is sometimes true that land use rules are primarily concerned with the preservation of the environment and the reduction of problems like traffic, pollution, and noise, 'it is also true that such reasons are often used as a façade for invidious discrimination. Also, it is far more frequent that minority faiths and those that are unfamiliar to local residents suffer from such intolerance.'[76]

Thus, in US law we find the same tendency observed in Europe, namely, the attempt to limit the construction of worship buildings when the request comes from religions

70 Hamilton, 'Constitutional Limitations' at 368 and 371.

71 Hamilton, 'Constitutional Limitations' at 368–409; Ashira Pelman Ostrow, 'Judicial Review of Local Land Use Decisions: Lessons from RLUIPA', (2008) 31 *Harvard Journal of Law & Public Policy* (2) 717–760; Lara A. Berwanger, 'White Knight?: Can the Commerce Clause Save the Religious Land Use and Institutionalized Persons Act?', (2004) 72 *Fordham Law Review* (6) 2355–2401, available at http://ir.lawnet.fordham.edu/flr/vol72/iss6/4 (accessed 15 February 2017); and Evan M. Shapiro, 'The Religious Land Use and Institutionalized Persons Act: An Analysis under the Commerce Clause', (2001) 76 *Washington Law Review* (4) 1255–1288. See also Roman P. Storzer and Anthony R. Picarello, Jr., 'The Religious Land Use and Institutionalized Persons Act of 2000: A Constitutional Response to Unconstitutional Zoning Practices,' (2001) 9 *George Mason Law Review* (4) 929–1000.

72 Douglas Laycock and Luke W. Goodrich, 'RLUIPA: Necessary, Modest and Under-Enforced', (2012) 39 *Fordham Urban Law Journal* (4) 1021–1022. But Marci Hamilton argues that '[t]here was no alleged evidence of discrimination offered by anyone other than a self-interested religious organization.' Marci A. Hamilton, 'RLUIPA Is a Bridge Too Far: Inconvenience Is Not Discrimination,' (2012) 39 *Fordham Urban Law Journal* (4) 963.

73 Anthony C. Zecca, Jr., 'A Decade Since 9/11: Religious Land Use Discrimination and the Continued Need for Protective Judicial Mechanism under RLUIPA', (2011) 21 *Temple Political & Civil Rights Law Review* (1) 275–281.

74 See Carmella at 513.

75 See Thomas E. Raccuia, 'RLUIPA and Exclusionary Zoning: Government Defendants Should Have the Burden of Persuasion in Equal Terms Cases', (2012) 80 *Fordham Law Review* (4) 1856.

76 Roman P. Storzer and Blair Lazarus Storzer, 'Christian Parking, Hindu Parking: Applying Established Civil Rights Principles to RLUIPA's Nondiscrimination Provision', (2013) 16 *Richmond Journal of Law and the Public Interest* (2) 296.

considered strange, foreign, or dangerous.[77] Since 11 September 2001, land use controversies involving Islam have increased alongside rising anti-Islamic sentiment, interfering with the construction of mosques and Islamic schools. In 2012, the Civil Rights Division of the Department of Justice issued a report documenting dozens of attempts to hinder the construction or transformation of mosques and Islamic centers.[78] RLUIPA provides timely protection for the civil rights of Muslims in America at a time of particular challenge.[79]

77 See Laycock and Goodrich at 1025–1032.

78 US Department of Justice, 'Confronting Discrimination in the Post-9/11 Era: Challenges and Opportunities Ten Years Later', 19 October 2011, 3, available at www.justice.gov/sites/default/files/crt/egacy/2012/04/16/post911summit_report_2012-04.pdf (accessed 10 July 2017).

79 See Eric Treene, 'RLUIPA and Mosques: Enforcing a Fundamental Right in Challenging Times', (2012) 10 *First Amendment Law Review* (Winter) 332 and Zecca at 291–292.

# 10 The religious precinct

## The inequalities of equality law in religious property

*Sarah Hayes*[1]

### Introduction

The 'religious precinct' is a place in which both worship and community activities take place. It may be used at different times for corporate worship, private prayer, church meetings, and, for example, as a drop-in center, the meeting place for a parent and toddler group, a food bank, a job club, and a community café. As people from the wider community participate in activities, the faith group whose space it is must decide whether its worship space is open to those coming to participate in activities which appear to have nothing to do with worship. Where the religious precinct is a single-roomed building, opening it up to community activities at all evidences the decision which has been made. Where sites are more complex, comprising many rooms in one building or many buildings, the host religious community may have a choice about which parts of its precinct it makes accessible, although, of course, some layouts may require people to pass through a worship space to access other parts of a building. Where those who come to participate are of another faith, they may request permission to pray or exercise other religious practices. The host religious community may be faced with the dilemma of whether to facilitate another religious community's religious practices within its religious space or preserve religious separateness within its precinct. Understandings of sacredness, theologies of place, hospitality, and community responsibility inform how a religious community chooses to respond.

Although the host religious community is usually able to make its own decisions about those responses, the way it delivers the services it provides and how they are funded may introduce aspects of equality law which narrow its choices. Whereas the host religious community may understand its community activities as an expression of faith, perhaps of divine love for the surrounding community, equality law, aided by other areas of law, imposes lines between religious and secular activities. What is religious and what is secular is determined by the law's understanding of the nature of the activity, rather than either the religious provider's understanding of that activity or its motivation for doing it. The law's approach often requires religious groups to treat their precincts not as religious property subject to internal regulation, but simply as the backdrop to both religious and secular community activities to which different rules apply. This assumption of the secular nature of community activities leads, in turn, to the use of equality law as a tool for securing the rights of individuals to manifest their religious rights without any consideration of whether communal rights of manifestation should also be taken into account.

This stark division between religious and secular activities is unintelligible to many religious communities, and creates an artificial separation. They may understand an invitation to participate in community activities to be an expression of religious faith, the fulfillment of religious obligation, or an opportunity for the participant to connect with the divine. There are, for example, many approaches to the provision of food through a food bank. A religious group may consider that it has such a strong theological imperative to feed

1 This chapter is based on the author's doctoral research and forthcoming thesis.

the hungry that if it does not do so, its identity as a religious community is undermined. It may understand the provision of food to be a divine blessing to all people of which it is a steward and must pass on to others to ensure that they too are blessed. More simply, it may understand feeding the hungry to be a divine command which must be fulfilled. A religious community might establish a food bank in fulfillment of any of these religious understandings of its role. It might consider that the delivery of such an activity from the religious precinct commutes an ordinary activity into a religious one, or it might consider the religious nature of the activity to imbue the space in which it takes place as religious. Where either of these is the case, there is a conflict between the law's understanding of the community activity as secular and the religious community's treatment of it. Requiring the religious group to treat such community activities as secular infringes religious freedom and undermines a group's ability to govern its own religious activities.

This is not to say that equality law is ignorant of religion's requirements. Indeed, it identifies circumstances in which it allows exemptions in a religious context from laws which would otherwise apply. However, those exemptions reflect the legislator's, rather than the religions', views of what constitutes 'the religious'. Further, they fail to appreciate inequalities arising from different religions' allocation of roles to its ministers. These may result in a practice carried out by a minister of religion in one context being subject to an exemption, while in another, the same practice carried out on behalf of a religious community by a lay person is beyond the exemption's reach. The exemptions fail too to take account of the inequalities experienced by a religious community which, driven perhaps by its theology of hospitality, opens its doors to community activity in such a way that people of other faiths may pray within its precinct. It may find that nearby religious communities use the exemptions to exclude members of one gender, but that its policies allow those excluded from manifesting faith within their own religious precincts to manifest faith within its, another faith community's, precincts.

This chapter explores the inequalities created by equality law within and between religious precincts. Its particular focus is on the United Kingdom's Equality Act 2010. It considers inequities arising from the Act's provisions concerning the gender exemption exercisable by a minister of religion, working with co-religionists, and the Public Sector Equality Duty. It concludes by proposing some steps that might alleviate the current situation in which equality law sometimes contributes to, rather than alleviates, inequalities within religious groups, or sacrifices the communal religious freedoms of a host religious community in favor of the individual religious freedoms of guests or employees.

## The context

The historical and contemporary engagement of religious communities in social provision is well documented,[2] albeit that there seems to be relatively little empirical evidence from religious communities themselves about this provision. For centuries, religious groups in the United Kingdom have provided wide-ranging social support to communities through, for example, education, health care, and alms to the poor. As the United Kingdom has moved from a mono- to a multi-faith society, incoming as well as established faith groups have engaged in meeting social needs.[3] Those developments run parallel to the developing

2 For a brief historical and contemporary overview, see, for example, Rana Jawad, *Religion and Faith-Based Welfare: From Wellbeing to Ways of Being* (The Policy Press 2012), 33–128. See also Frank Prochaska, *Christianity and Social Service in Modern Britain: The Disinherited Spirit* (Oxford University Press 2006) and Linda Woodhead and Rebecca Cato, eds, *Religion and Change in Modern Britain* (Routledge 2012).

3 Jawad provides examples of welfare and social action contributions from a wide variety of religious actors in the United Kingdom. However, Pathik Pathak and Derek McGhee note the challenges to minority faith

relationship between government and faith communities, most noticeably in the closing years of the last century and in this,[4] and have led government to perceive religious groups, as members of the faith sector,[5] as significant, almost commonplace,[6] allies in delivering social welfare and achieving community cohesion.[7]

Government expectation is that faith communities can assist in building community cohesion – that is, bridging divisions based on ethnicity, faith, or culture that create dysfunctionality and stunt community growth. It is expected too that they are able to reach those otherwise hard to reach, and are resilient to the challenges of provision.[8] Since the inception of the language of community cohesion in 2001,[9] government attempts to nurture community cohesion have developed to the point that it is now 'a ubiquitous agenda across the activities of the local state',[10] albeit that some challenge it as a theoretical construct inadequate to counter the real economic and social difficulties experienced within neighborhoods.[11] However the understanding of, language around, and purpose of community cohesion is evolving, it is clear that it remains a focus of central and devolved government policy,[12] local authority strategy,[13] school policy,[14] policing,[15] and local communities.[16]

---

engagement and their primary focus on overseas aid, questioning the ubiquity of provision from all faiths in the United Kingdom currently. See Pathik Pathak and Derek McGhee, '"I thought this was a Christian thing?" Exploring Virtuous and Exclusionary Cycles in Faith Based Social Action', (2014) 50 *Community Development Journal* (1) 40–54 at 52.

4 For a brief history of government engagement with faith communities in its community cohesion strategies in the early part of this century, see Robert Furbey, 'Beyond "Social Glue"? "Faith" and Community Cohesion', in John Flint and David Robinson, eds, *Community Cohesion in Crisis? New Dimensions of Diversity and Difference* (The Policy Press 2008), 119–137 at 122–123. For a more comprehensive analysis, see Adam Dinham, *Faiths, Public Policy and Civil Society: Problems, Policies and Controversies* (Springer 2009).

5 For an explanation of the evolution of discourse from 'religion' to 'faith', see James A. Beckford, 'The Return of Public Religion? A Critical Assessment of a Popular Claim', (2010) 23 *Nordic Journal of Religion and Society* (2) 121–136 at 126.

6 Elaine Graham, *Between a Rock and a Hard Place: Public Theology in a Post-Secular Age* (SCM Press 2013), 21.

7 Graham. For a European perspective see José Luis Romanillos, Justin Beaumont, and Mustafa Sen, 'State-Religion Relations and Welfare Regimes in Europe', in Justin Beaumont and Paul Cloke, eds, *Faith-Based Organisations and Exclusion in European Cities* (The Policy Press 2012).

8 Office of the Deputy Prime Minister, *Community Cohesion: Seven Steps* (Home Office 2005), 3.

9 See http://tedcantle.co.uk/about-community-cohesion/#ccrs (accessed 25 April 2017). See also Ted Cantle, *Community Cohesion: A New Framework for Race and Diversity* (Palgrave Macmillan 2008).

10 Charles Husband and Yunis Alam, *Social Cohesion and Counterterrorism: A Political Contradiction?* (The Policy Press 2011), 50.

11 See generally Flint and Robinson, eds, in particular David Robinson's chapter 'Community Cohesion and the Politics of Community'.

12 Welsh Assembly Community Cohesion Delivery Plan 2016–2017, available at http://gov.wales/topics/people-and-communities/communities/communitycohesion/?lang=en (accessed 21 June 2017).

13 Some local authorities include a community cohesion plan within a suite of strategy documents; others consider community cohesion to be their strategy. For an example of the latter, see Manchester City Council's strategy document, available at www.manchester.gov.uk/download/meetings/id/20756/5_community_cohesion (accessed 3 May 2017). For the former, see, for example, Lancaster County Council's Equality, Cohesion and Integration Strategy 2014–2017, available at www.lancashire.gov.uk/media/399212/Equality-Cohesion-and-Integration-strategy-2014-17-final-April-14.pdf (accessed 3 May 2017).

14 An internet search of school community cohesion policies produces numerous examples.

15 One example is the strategy for Oldham 2016–2019, available at www.oldhampartnership.org.uk/wp-content/uploads/2015/01/CSCP-Plan-2016-19.pdf (accessed 3 May 2017). Another is the Community Cohesion Awards offered by the Bedfordshire police; see www.bedfordshire.police.uk/about_us/news/latest_news/2017/170210_-_communities_thanked.aspx (accessed 3 May 2017).

16 Many communities run community cohesion awards – for example, Coventry; see www2.warwick.ac.uk/about/community/newsandevents/news/communitycohesion16/ and www.asianimage.co.uk/news/15268575.FUSION_2017__Community_Cohesion_Award_Finalists/ (accessed 3 May 2017).

Religious groups, acknowledged 'simultaneously as a problem and a solution',[17] are perceived as significant in many local communities and important in initiating cohesive activities.[18] They have been invited to participate in national discussions to set agendas,[19] shape guidance to local authorities,[20] become bridgebuilders and make links between and within communities,[21] as well as facilitate dialogue about and between religious groups at local, regional, and national levels.[22] Central government has released funding to support these initiatives[23] and utilizes the networks and organizational structures of religious groups to achieve its ends.[24] Funding has been allocated to promote the development of relationships across faith and ethnic barriers,[25] build faith communities' capacity,[26] and motivate volunteering.[27] Alongside this, regional statutory bodies, such as government and police authorities, often partner with religious groups to deliver focused local services.[28] Whether supported by statutory bodies or not, the range of services offered by religious groups includes food banks, debt advice, children's centers, family contact centers, drop-in centers, and a plethora of general community activities.[29] Some choose to fund activities delivered by others, while other groups use their own resources or enter collaborations with others to meet identified need within their local communities.

Significant for the purposes of this chapter are the premises from which religious groups deliver such services. Although there is no data that reliably evidences how many religious precincts serve as facilities for community use or as sites of social action or welfare delivery, such evidence as is available suggests that religious precincts are a

17 Furbey at 119.

18 Louise Casey, *The Casey Review: A Review into Opportunity and Integration* (Department for Communities and Local Government, 2016), 1.71, available at www.gov.uk/government/uploads/system/uploads/attachment_data/file/575973/The_Casey_Review_Report.pdf (accessed 24 May 2017).

19 For a brief review of government's structured relationship with faith communities prior to the coalition government, see David Cheetham, Douglas Pratt, and David Thomas, eds, *Understanding Interreligious Relations* (Oxford University Press 2013), 376.

20 See, for example, Local Government Association, *Working with Faith Groups to Promote Health and Well-Being* (January 2017) and Christians in Parliament, *Faith in the Community: Strengthening Ties between Faith Groups and Local Authorities* (2013).

21 Department for Communities and Local Government (DCLG), *Face to Face and Side by Side* (Community and Local Government Publications 2008).

22 See Rita Fentener et al., *Faith Groups and Government* (Community Development Foundation 2008). See also the role of the Faith-Based Regeneration Network in Cheetham et al., eds, at 373–375.

23 See infra notes 25–27.

24 Furbey at 127.

25 The Near Neighbours program receives funding from Department of Communities and Local Government, and has the dual objectives of social interaction (that is, the development of positive relationships in multi-faith and multi-ethnic areas) and social action (that is, enabling people of different faiths, including no faith, and different ethnicities to come together to improve their local neighborhoods). It was established in 2011 with a DCLG grant of GBP 3 million, and has received further funding in 2014 (GBP 3 million) and most recently in 2016 (GBP 1.5 million).

26 Daniel Singleton, ed., *Faith with Its Sleeves Rolled Up* (Faith Action 2013), 28. The Faith Communities Capacity Building Fund 2006–2008 received GBP 13.8 million and received a further sum of GBP 7.5 million in 2008.

27 'Together in Service', a DCLG initiative from November 2013 providing a fund of GBP 200,000 to support multi-faith volunteering.

28 Cited as significant partners in faith group activities in Cinnamon Network, *Cinnamon Faith Action Audit* (May 2015), available at www.cinnamonnetwork.co.uk/wp-content/uploads/2015/05/Final-National-Report.pdf (accessed 21 April 2017). In its Faith Audit, the Cinnamon Network identifies government, the police, and health authorities as statutory partners.

29 Cinnamon Network.

significant resource in many communities.[30] Although religious groups often engage directly in provision, they may also form separate legal entities through which to meet community need. This may be to enable members of the wider community to become appropriately involved in management structures, to satisfy the requirements of funders, or simply to clarify and maintain the boundaries between worship and community engagement. Where religious groups establish such separate legal entities, they may embed religious values within their legal and management structures, and may retain involvement in, or control of, decision-making – for example, by ensuring that the religious group has a certain number of places on a management board or entitling its members to also be members of the newly established organization. Where these organizations become occupants of the religious precinct, whether under formal or informal occupation agreements, they extend the means by which a religious group may communally manifest its religious belief that it has a responsibility to support those in need from its religious precinct.

## Social action and religion

Where religious groups engage with government and other partners to deliver wide-ranging social and welfare benefits within their local communities, the parties may have different perceptions of the relationship between the activities and religion. Whereas meeting others' social and economic needs may be for a religious group a religious duty or enacted expression of doctrinal truth,[31] it may for a non-religious partner simply be a sensible use of resources it considers otherwise underused to benefit the wider community. Whereas a religious group may understand its provision of benefits to be inseparable from spiritual value, its regulator, the Charity Commission, is interested in measuring the tangible rather than the metaphysical, considering this an objective evaluation. The effect is a tendency to evaluate the benefit of religious organizations by those outputs most easy to measure. This contributes to a culture of disinterest in how who delivers an activity shapes it, giving preference to the evaluation and measurement of functional outputs. Some activities thereby become separated in the institutional narrative from the spiritual values that mold them and imbue them with their distinctive value.

These different perceptions inform both how equality law is applied and how religious groups respond to its interpretation. The purpose of this section is to briefly examine religious belief as a catalyst for social action and welfare benefit, and, as an example of the State's approach, to consider the role of such delivery in attaining charitable status. It concludes by considering social action as communal religious practice that deserves protection under Article 9 of the European Convention on Human Rights (ECHR). Later on, this paper will examine whether applying equality laws to church social action is a legitimate derogation from religious groups' Article 9 rights.

30 For an indication of the amount of social action in which religious organizations are engaged, see Adam Dinham and Matthew Francis, eds, *Religious Literacy in Policy and Practice* (Policy Press 2016), 109.

31 See the example of Pathways Ltd. in Andrew Williams, Paul Cloke, and Samuel Thomas, 'Co-Constituting Neoliberalism: Faith-Based Organisations, Co-Option, and Resistance in the UK', (2012) 44 *Environment and Planning A* (6) 1479–1501, 1490–1493. See also Chris Baker and Hannah Skinner, *Faith in Action: The Dynamic Connection between Spiritual and Religious Capital* (William Temple Foundation 2006) (updated 2014), 11.

### *Religious belief*

Although some claim that the primary motivation for religious groups' engagement in service delivery is proselytization, many groups do not identify their motivations in this way.[32] A recent report from New Philanthropy Capital (NPC) distinguishes between 'dimensions of faith', which determine the extent to which faith influences an organization's choice of activities and structures, and the explicit or implicit communication of faith from within a given structure. It suggests that there is not necessarily a correlation between organizations whose religious beliefs motivate their choice of projects and activities undertaken, and the communication of faith to beneficiaries.[33] The report underlines the desire of many religious charities to engage in service delivery as a product of religious belief, not necessarily as a vehicle to promote it.

Such findings are in accord with a view that engagement in service provision is the product of doctrine, teaching, and practice which have together established a 'heritage of values centred on generosity, altruism, philanthropy and care for the poor and needy'.[34] That heritage frames, informs, and motivates believers' behaviors across many religious faiths.[35] While there are circumstances in which these principles are not borne out by adherents' behaviors, perceiving faith groups only as organizational conveniences for the distribution of aid without acknowledging their spiritual dimensions diminishes their value and impoverishes their contribution.

### *Religion and public benefit*

Although not all religious organizations engaged in worship are registered as charities, many are either registered or excepted from registration[36] and so are subject to charity law.[37] Further, some religious precincts are the subject of charitable trusts. Where they are not, activities that take place within religious precincts may still be subject to charity law even where the land is not. The meaning of 'public benefit', for which purposes a charity is established,[38] is therefore of concern to those managing many religious precincts.

32 For a general discussion from a Christian perspective, see Paul Cloke, Samuel Thomas, and Andrew Williams, 'Radical Faith Praxis? Exploring the Changing Theological Landscape of Christian Faith Motivation', in Justin Beaumont and Paul Cloke, eds, *Faith-Based Organisations and Exclusion in European Cities* (The Policy Press 2012), 105–126.

33 Rachel Wharton and Lucy de las Casas, *What a Difference a Faith Makes: Insights on Faith-Based Charities* (NPC 2016), 9–10, available at www.thinknpc.org/publications/what-a-difference-faith-makes/what-a-difference-a-faith-makes_npc/?post-parent=18631 (accessed 4 May 2017).

34 Kerry O'Halloran, *Religion, Charity and Human Rights* (Cambridge University Press 2014), 479.

35 See Adam Dinham, *Faiths, Public Policy and Civil Society: Problems, Policies and Controversies* (Palgrave 2009), 61.

36 Churches and other religious charities maintained mainly or wholly for worship are excepted from registration if they have an income of less than GBP 100,000 and are linked to one of a list of identified bodies. For a list of the relevant bodies, see Guidance notes on 'Excepted charities', www.gov.uk/government/publications/excepted-charities (accessed 24 May 2017).

37 Other organizations are exempt from registration, usually because they are accountable to another body. For a brief overview of the current status of exempt charities, see Charity Commission Guidance, 'Exempt Charities (CC23)', available at https://www.gov.uk/government/publications/exempt-charities-cc23 (accessed 26 July 2017).

38 Mary Synge draws attention to the distinction between the legislative requirement that a charity's purposes are for the public benefit, and that it provides public benefit. Mary Synge, *The New Public Benefit: Making Sense of Charity Law?* (Hart Publishing 2015).

The statutory requirement that to be charitable, purposes must be for the public benefit, enshrines in the Charities Act 2011[39] a long-standing common-law assumption in England and Wales that charities do benefit the public.[40] Its predecessor, the Charities Act 2006, removed the presumption that religious groups, among others, were charitable. Achieving charitable status now requires evidence that an organization's purposes are for the public benefit. As organizations whose members worship or pray in private are not charitable,[41] the law does not endorse spiritual activity as beneficial *per se*. What is considered beneficial is either the transfer of benefits received by participants in spiritual activities to others with whom they mix,[42] or efforts to include those external to a religious group in its religious or, to others at least,[43] secular activities.[44] In assessing public benefit, the relative weight of participation in religious and secular activities, respectively, is now ambiguous,[45] and some question whether the public benefit test heralds the future reduction of religious benefit to a tangible secular measure.[46] Whether secular outputs will eventually be the primary measure of religion's measured public benefit or not, it is noticeable that in reporting their decisions on applications for charitable status the Charity Commission increasingly makes mention of the secular benefits contributed by religious organizations.[47]

### *Social action as a manifestation of religion*

The ECHR, incorporated into English law under the Human Rights Act 1998, protects not only the freedom of individuals, but of individuals collectively, to manifest their religion or belief.[48] The rights of manifestation are set out in Article 9 of the ECHR, preserving the right of all people to pursue internally as an absolute right whatever religion or belief they choose, and externally to manifest that religion or belief subject to national rights to restrict a manifestation where the limitation is prescribed by law, serves one of the legitimate aims identified in Article 9(2), and is necessary within a democratic society.[49] It is an

39 Charities Act 2011, § 4.

40 Kerry O'Halloran, Myles McGregor-Lowndes, and Karla Simon, *Charity Law and Social Policy: National and International Perspectives on the Functions of the Law Relating to Charities* (Springer 2008), 40.

41 *Gilmour v. Coats* [1949] AC 426.

42 *Neville Estates v. Madden* [1962] Ch 832.

43 See 'Social Action as a Manifestation of Religion', later.

44 See the Charity Commission's response to an application for charitable status by the Preston Down Trust, and their subsequent report, www.gov.uk/government/uploads/system/uploads/attachment_data/file/336112/preston_down_trust_full_decision.pdf and www.gov.uk/government/uploads/system/uploads/attachment_data/file/500364/preston_down_trust.pdf respectively (accessed 24 May 2017).

45 Robert Meakin, 'Gilmour v Coats Revisited: A Study in the Law of Public Benefit', Law & Religion UK, 28 November 2016, available at www.lawandreligionuk.com/2016/11/28/gilmour-v-coats-revisited-a-study-in-the-law-of-public-benefit/ (accessed 20 June 2017).

46 O'Halloran at 480.

47 See, for example, the recent decision concerning the Druid Network in which its environmental contribution appears to have been significant in the decision, available at www.gov.uk/government/uploads/system/uploads/attachment_data/file/324236/druiddec.pdf (accessed 25 April 2017).

48 ECHR Art. 9(1): 'Everyone has the right to freedom of thought, conscience and religion; this right includes freedom to change his religion or belief and freedom, either alone or in community with others and in public or private to manifest his religion or belief, in worship, teaching, practice and observance.'

49 ECHR Art. 9(2): 'Freedom to manifest one's religion or beliefs shall be subject only to such limitations as are prescribed by law or are necessary in a democratic society in the interests of public safety, for the protection of public order, health or morals, or for the protection of the rights and freedoms of others.' See Russell Sandberg, *Law and Religion* (Cambridge University Press 2011), 82.

important principle of Convention rights that there is a fair balance between 'the demands of the general interests of the community and the requirement of the protection of the individual's fundamental freedom right'.[50] Proportionality is an essential principle in determining a fair balance, requiring that state interference be justified by the legitimate aim pursued.[51] In determining what is legitimate, the state, subject to European supervision,[52] is entitled to take account of local circumstances and so exercise a 'margin of appreciation' in its interpretation of the convention's requirements.[53] The right to freedom of religion or belief is as absolute 'in community with others' as it is for an individual 'alone'.[54] However, the manifestation of belief may be the legitimate subject of state interference.

Although it is accepted that the establishment and maintenance of a place of worship is intrinsic to a communal freedom to manifest religion,[55] there is otherwise relatively little case law concerning the protection of communal rights of manifestation under Article 9. One categorization of legitimate internal uses of a place of worship includes worship, teaching, and meeting the internal cultural needs of a religious community.[56] However, little, if any, consideration has been given to whether a manifestation of religion which engages with the wider community is a legally defensible communal manifestation under Article 9 ECHR.[57]

In the context of individual rights, it is established that an action emanating from a religious duty may constitute a manifestation.[58] There is no equivalent clarity in relation to lawful activities offered by a religious group for the benefit of the wider community. Intrusive proclamations of the religious community's existence[59] may be prohibited.[60] The European Court of Human Rights has held that land generating funds surplus to a religious community's needs, that is not 'necessary for... religious practice and worship' is deemed secular and not relevant to the manifestation of religion.[61] The implication of this is that land generating funds essential to a religious community's needs may be a manifestation of religion, and that activities 'necessary for... religious practice and worship' comprise only those that support the internal life of the religious community, even when activities carried out in fulfillment of religious doctrine support those outside of the religious community. In the current circumstance, it is not that activities generate funds which is at issue, but the activities themselves. It remains to be seen whether, for example, the generation of funds to pay for such activities by the renting out of surplus space might

50 *Sporrong and Lannroth v. Sweden*, App. Nos 7152/75 and 7152/75 (ECtHR, 23 September 1982), § 69.
51 *Handyside v. the United Kingdom*, App. No. 5493/72 (ECtHR, 7 December 1976), § 49.
52 *Handyside*, § 49.
53 *Buckley v. the United Kingdom*, App. No. 20348/92 (ECtHR, 29 September 1996), § 75.
54 ECHR Art. 9(1).
55 See Noel G. Villaroman, 'The Right to Establish and Maintain Places of Worship: The Developments of its Normative Content under International Human Rights Law', in Silvio Ferrari and Sabrina Pastorelli, eds, *Religion in Public Spaces: A European Perspective* (Routledge 2016) (first published by Ashgate 2012), 321.
56 See Villaroman at 314.
57 For a consideration of the provision of goods and services as religious freedom or practice, see Jane Calderwood Norton, *Freedom of Religious Organizations* (Oxford University Press 2016), 174 ff.
58 *X and Church of Scientology v. Sweden*, App. No. 7805/77 (ECtHR, 5 May 1979).
59 Villaroman at 314.
60 For the criteria against which noise emanating from a religious activity will be assessed, see *R (on the application of Hackney LBC) v. Rottenberg* [2007] Env. L.R. 24, § 23. See also *Soltau v. De Held* [1851] 61 ER 291 and R.H. Bloor's comments in 'Clocks, Bells and Cockerels', (1995) 3 *Ecclesiastical Law Journal* (17) 393–397.
61 *Holy Monasteries v. Greece*, App. Nos 13092/87 and 13984/88 (ECtHR, 1 September 1997).

itself be considered a manifestation of religion and, if so, what the impact on domestic charity law might be.

In the context of an individual believer, manifesting practices need not be religious duties prescribed by articles of faith, but may be action which 'give[s] expression to religion or belief in any way',[62] and so be an expression 'of the way of life connected to the religion or belief'.[63] There must be 'a sufficiently close nexus between the act and the underlying belief',[64] and there is no requirement for a behavior or expression motivated or inspired by religion to be in 'a generally recognised form', or mandated by any central authority within the religion.[65] It is not open to the state to evaluate the legitimacy of a religious belief or how a belief is expressed,[66] only to determine whether an identified act has a sufficiently close nexus with religion or belief. Provided the belief is cogent and important, the individual's chosen expression of their belief may be protected, subject to legitimate interventions.

When these principles are applied to the communal manifestation of religion, it appears that practices such as hospitality,[67] giving relief to those in need,[68] or facilitating the development of good relationships within a community[69] may be as much a manifestation of religion as religious worship. There is no requirement that the expression is stated to be, or indeed is, in fulfillment of a prescribed religious duty. It is sufficient that the activity emanates from a community's understanding of its obligations. It is, for example, sufficient that running a food bank is motivated by a community's desire to express divine care for people in need or is the means through which the community fulfills a universal or congregationally chosen obligation to give a percentage of the community's income to those in need.

If it is accepted that in some circumstances social action or the delivery of welfare benefit is a manifestation of religion, any interference by the state requires a convincing justification. The state would need to show that such provision by a religious organization is contrary to English law, and that it is necessary in a democratic society to restrict or prevent it in order to protect public safety, public order, or others' health, morals, or rights and freedoms.

If the harm feared is that in providing benefits religious groups inappropriately promote the religious beliefs of the group's adherents and so infringe others' rights, this is a matter to be determined in each case. Interference is justified where improper pressure is exerted on people in distress or need, or where material or social advantages are offered in return for religious participation.[70] In dealing with an appeal from a social worker dismissed for

62 Norman Doe, *Law and Religion in Europe: A Comparative Introduction* (Oxford University Press 2011), 50, citing Netherlands, HR 13 April 1960, NJ 1960, 436.

63 Doe at 50, citing the German Constitution BVerf G£ 24, 236 (246).

64 *Eweida and Others v. United Kingdom*, App. Nos 48420/10, 59842/10, 51671/10, and 36516/10 (ECtHR, 15 January 2013), § 82.

65 *Eweida*, § 82.

66 *Manoussakis v. Greece*, App. No. 18748/91 (ECtHR, 26 September 1996), § 47 ('The right to freedom of religion as guaranteed under the convention excludes any discretion on the part of the state to determine whether religious beliefs or the means used to express such beliefs are legitimate.'). See also *Eweida*, § 81.

67 See Letty M. Russell, *Just Hospitality: God's Welcome in a World of Difference* (Westminster John Knox Press 2009) and Chris Shannahan, *A Theology of Community Organizing: Power to the People* (Routledge 2013), 147.

68 Shelina Janmohamed, *Generation M: Young Muslims Changing the World* (I.B. Tauris 2016), Malcolm Brown, ed., *Anglican Social Theology Today* (Church House Publishing 2014), and Shmuly Yanklowitz, *The Soul of Jewish Social Justice* (Urim Publications 2014).

69 Jawad at 145. See also Shannahan at 139 ff.

70 *Kokkinakis v. Greece*, App. No. 14307/88 (ECtHR, 25 May 1993).

giving a Bible and speaking about personal religious beliefs to service users contrary to their wishes, the U.K. domestic courts have distinguished between an individual's lawful manifestation of religion and their inappropriate communication of it.[71]

U.K. domestic courts have held that activities such as inviting a Muslim colleague to attend church services and praying with her when she wanted neither,[72] a manager organizing a Bible training day which employees of a nursery felt obliged to attend,[73] and the unsolicited distribution of printed and digital material pertaining to personal beliefs to colleagues[74] go beyond an individual right of manifestation and infringe others' rights. If similar boundaries are mapped onto a communal manifestation of religion through social and welfare activities within a local community, it becomes clear that although there may be justification for intervening when provision becomes a vehicle for proselytization, there is no such justification where the provision itself is a manifestation of religion. It is equally clear that it is impossible to assess whether provision is appropriate or not, except by considering each circumstance individually.

A prerequisite for considering whether an interference is justified is to determine whether the interference is prescribed by domestic law, and whether the actions in question have breached that law.

## Equality Act 2010

The role of equality law, notably the Equalities Act 2010, in the balancing of individual and collective religious rights with other characteristics identified and protected by the Act[75] has been extensively explored. Much of that exploration has focused on the manifestation of religion in the workplace,[76] circumstances in which a religious employer may select employees from an identified faith group,[77] and the requirements of the Public Sector Equality Duty.[78] However, little attention has been paid to the effect of these provisions on access to religious precincts. Where worship and community activities take place within the same or adjacent precincts, significant considerations include the Act's provisions governing the services offered by a minister of religion, selective engagement with co-religionists, and a religious organization's relationship with a public body. The first three of the following subsections identify relevant aspects of those provisions. The fourth explains the nature of the religious precinct and its relationship to the Equality Act.[79]

71 *Chondol v. Liverpool City Council* [2009] All ER (D) 155 (Feb) [23].

72 *Wasteney v. East London NHS Foundation Trust* [2016] ICR 643.

73 *Grace v. Places for Children* [2013] WL 6865214.

74 *Power v. Greater Manchester Police Authority* [2011] EWCA Civ 534.

75 Equality Act 2010 s 4 identifies age, disability, gender reassignment, marriage and civil partnership, pregnancy and maternity, race, religion or belief, sex, and sexual orientation as protected characteristics.

76 See, for example, Lucy Vickers, *Religious Freedom, Religious Discrimination and the Workplace* (2nd edn, Bloomsbury 2016) and Andrew Hambler, *Religious Expression in the Workplace and the Contested Role of Law* (Routledge 2015).

77 Vickers, *Religious Freedom, Religious Discrimination and the Workplace* at 175–177 and 183–185.

78 Lucy Vickers, 'Promoting Equality or Fostering Resentment? The Public Sector Equality Duty and Religion or Belief', (2001) 31 *Legal Studies* (1) 135–158 at 145–149 and Julian Rivers, 'Promoting Religious Equality', (2012) 1 *Oxford Journal of Law and Religion* (2) 386–401.

79 The Equality Act 2010 provides an exemption concerning the use of religious premises by, or their disposal to, persons otherwise protected under the sexual orientation characteristic. This exemption is not of relevance to this chapter.

### *Services offered by a minister of religion*

The Act provides that a minister of religion may restrict the services he or she provides 'only to persons of one sex' or make provision separately 'for persons of each sex' where this is necessary to comply with doctrinal beliefs or to avoid conflict with the strongly held religious convictions of a significant number of the religion's followers.[80] The exemption applies only to services offered in fulfillment of a minister of religion's functions carried out on behalf of an organized religion, at a place occupied or used for those purposes.[81] A minister of religion is defined as 'a minister of religion, or other person, who performs functions in connection with the religion and holds an office or appointment in, or is accredited, approved or recognised for the purposes of a religious organization in relation to the religion'.[82] An organized religion is one which practices or advances the religion or teaches the practice of religion, enables members of the religion to receive benefits or participate in activities within the religion's framework, or fosters or maintains good relations between persons of different religions.

Government guidelines explain that acts of worship do not constitute 'services' under the Act, and so require no exemption.[83] This is consistent with a general unwillingness by, for example, the courts to comment on the legitimacy of religious rites.[84] However, it leaves open the question of what other actions might fall within the 'function' of a 'minister of religion' and so enjoy the exemption.

Whom a religion appoints as a minister and what form such authorization takes differ among religions. Differences reflect the respective religions' theologies of ministry, their cultural origins, and the way in which each role is developing within British culture.[85] Groups' governing documents and the terms of contracts between them and their ministers vary, making it virtually impossible to identify any functions as common to ministers across religions or to categorize all ministers as responsible for every activity within their community. Roles vary not only between religions but between groups within the same religion.

The roles of a Sikh granthi and a Muslim imam serve to illustrate the point. A granthi is appointed by a local management committee,[86] often has no formal training,[87] is the custodian of the gurdwara, and in that capacity, is responsible for its religious services – although not its teaching[88] – and the upkeep of the building.[89] In contrast, an imam has theological

80 Equality Act 2010, Schedule 3, s 29.
81 Equality Act 2010, Schedule 3, s 29.
82 Equality Act 2010, Schedule 3, s. 29(2).
83 Equality Act 2010, Explanatory Notes, § 742, available at www.legislation.gov.uk/ukpga/2010/15/notes/division/3/16/20/7/6 (accessed 24 April 2017).
84 This is well illustrated by courts' approaches to property disputes within religious groups. See Julian Rivers, *The Law of Organized Religions* (Oxford University Press (2010), 96–100.
85 For a brief overview of the development of the role of the imam 'in the context of a diasporic community', see Mohamed Keshavjee, *Islam, Sharia and Alternative Dispute Resolution: Mechanisms for Legal Redress in the Muslim Community* (I.B. Tauris 2013), 105–106. On the developing role of the imam, see also Alison Scott-Baumann and Sariya Cheruvallil-Contractor, *Islamic Education in Britain: New Pluralist Paradigms* (Bloomsbury 2015), 65 ff.
86 Gurharpal Singh and Darshan Singh Tatla, *Sikhs in Britain: The Making of a Community* (Zed Books 2006), 84.
87 Gerald Parsons, ed., *The Growth of Religious Diversity: Britain from 1945, Volume 1: Traditions* (Routledge 1993), 234.
88 Which may be undertaken by a gyani where one is available. For the role of the gyani, see Parsons at 234.
89 W.H. McLeod, *The A–Z of Sikhism* (Scarecrow Press 2009), 76.

training and is responsible for leading prayers, preaching, and teaching on a daily basis and for conducting weddings and funerals. He may, among many other things, be responsible for community liaison and for pastoral and social activities.[90] All these activities are considered part of the individual's ministerial role within the religion. Adding the many roles of rabbis, Hindu priests, Christian ministers, and officiants of other religions expands even further the list of functions that could trigger the exemption.

Given the diversity of ministerial roles in religions, if the Act's wording is to be taken literally then the exemption has a disparate impact for different religious groups. In the example given earlier of a granthi and an imam, a literal interpretation would mean, for example, that within the Muslim community social activities and activities amounting to liaison with the local community which are hosted within a religious building could be segregated on grounds of gender under the exemption, whereas identical activities in a gurdwara would not because they are not the responsibility of the granthi. If the only interpretation available is a literal one, it depends entirely on what each religion, and indeed each congregation within each religion, requires of its minister to understand what can be subject to the exemption. It is inevitable that in a multi-faith context, such legislative flexibility creates inequalities between religious groups.

Further, where local resources enable more than one minister to be appointed, ministers may be appointed to carry out functions more usually carried out by others, potentially creating inequalities between richer and poorer congregations. Where the difference between congregations is simply that a minister in a poorer congregation has to do all the work, whereas in a richer one it can be spread between a greater number of ministers, the legislation creates no inequalities. However, if the employment of more ministers enables tasks to be undertaken which simply cannot be carried out by one person, the employment of those additional ministers brings within the exemption activities which would not otherwise be covered.

In explaining the exemption, the government's interpretative guidance cites as its only example that 'a synagogue can have separate seating for men and women at a reception following a religious service.'[91] It is not clear what aspect of this scenario qualifies it for the exemption. Is it the fact that the reception is ancillary to a religious rite at which the rabbi has officiated? Is it an assumption that the rabbi himself organized the reception as part of his duties? Is it an assumption that a rabbi is responsible for all activities within the group whether or not he carries them out himself? Even if it were possible to identify which aspect of the sample scenario qualified it for the exemption, this would provide neither absolute clarity nor equality of application among religions. If only activities ancillary to a minister's performance of religious rites were eligible for the exemption, the exemption would apply only to activities associated with religious rites at which a minister had officiated. It is unclear why ancillary activities should be exempted based solely on whether a minister officiated in the religious event itself. A wedding reception on a site for which a minister of religion has responsibility looks exactly the same as a reception where the minister is a part-time employee with no general responsibilities for community activity on the site. Observers may question why segregation is permitted at one event but not the other when they appear to be identical.

90 Scott-Baumann and Cheruvallil-Contractor at 65.

91 Equality Act 2010, Explanatory Notes, § 743, available at www.legislation.gov.uk/ukpga/2010/15/notes/contents (accessed 24 April 2017). Confusingly, the provision is explained by Blackstone's Guide as 'designed to deal with ancillary issues such as separate seating arrangements in places of worship'. John Wadham et al., eds, *Blackstone's Guide to the Equality Act 2010* (Oxford University Press 2012) § 5.103.

In contrast, the Equality and Human Rights Commission provides as its sole example of how the legislation works, 'running a shelter for homeless people or holding a mother and toddler group'.[92] This choice of example is confusing because it is so rarely the case that a minister is responsible for running such activities, and so suggests that the legislation is not to be interpreted solely in light of what a minister does, but should extend beyond activities which fall within a minister's direct responsibilities, to include those under the minister's overarching management responsibility, or those ancillary to any preaching, teaching or pastoral function, or none of the above. It is unclear what aspect of that activity qualifies it for the exemption, but it is clear that if the illustration correctly represents how the legislation is to be interpreted, it encompasses many activities which are not part of a minister's obvious function. This could result in, for example, situations where a parent and toddler group run by one congregation is lawfully accessible only by either female or male parents or caregivers, while that run by a different congregation in an adjacent building is accessible to both. In other words, a member of the public could be excluded from one religious precinct, but not the other simply because of different local interpretations of the exemption.

### *Working only with co-religionists*

The Equality Act protects a person's right not to be directly or indirectly discriminated against because of their religion or belief. However, in some circumstances, it allows an organization to be selective about the recipients of services delivered or about who it employs, on the grounds of religion or belief. The provisions in each case are briefly considered later.

#### *Service delivery*

The Act provides that a religious organization may restrict the provision of goods, activities, or services on the basis of, *inter alia*, religion or belief[93] when the organizations' purposes are not commercial, are to practice or advance or teach the practice of the religion, support members of the religious group or foster good relations between people of different faiths,[94] or when members of the religion would be offended if it were not so restricted.[95]

Religious organizations often engage in service delivery that is expressly intended for all people irrespective of their religion or belief, or indeed any other protected characteristic. The issue in that case is not about who may access whatever provision is offered, but whether those accessing that provision within the religious precinct may there manifest a religion or belief which is not that of the host religious group.

Some expressions of religion are more easily accepted than others. For example, religious groups often wrestle with the extent to which members of other religious groups should be permitted to pray in the host religious group's spaces. Where a religious building is used by

92 Equality and Human Rights Commission, *What Equality Law Means for Your Voluntary and Community Sector Organization (Including Charities and Religion or Belief Organizations)* (2016), 21, available at www.equalityhumanrights.com/en/publication-download/what-equality-law-means-your-voluntary-and-community-sector-organisation (accessed 25 April 2017). In fact, these activities might well be single sex under alternative provisions enabling provision to people of one sex or another where that is appropriate for the activity.

93 Equality Act 2010, Schedule 23, s 2(3).

94 Equality Act 2010, Schedule 23, ss 2(1) and (2).

95 Equality Act 2010, Schedule 23, s 2(6).

the wider community, activities may span the Muslim community's prayer times. The host religious community must decide whether it is acceptable for people from another faith to pray within its religious precinct. Some groups will not allow the prayers of another faith to be said anywhere within their precinct, whereas others allow them in a hall or a room set aside for the purpose, but not in a worship space. Similar decisions arise where, for example, a drama group from one religious faith performs in the religious precinct of another and it is its habit to pray before a performance, or where there is a wedding celebration of one religious tradition in part of the spacious precinct of another. Groups wanting to extend hospitality to people of all faiths and none are conflicted between their understanding of their religious obligations to meet community need and offer hospitality, and a sense that their own religious practices are compromised by others' manifestations of belief within their space.

### *Employment*

Employees' rights to religious non-discrimination are generally protected under the Equality Act.[96] Notwithstanding this, a religious organization may restrict itself to employing co-religionists if it can demonstrate either that there is an occupational requirement serving a legitimate aim[97] or that the organization's ethos justifies the employment of people of a particular faith.[98] The restriction must be appropriate and necessary for the achievement of the aim,[99] and the principles of proportionality require each job to be carefully considered to assess whether the exception is justifiable.

The ethos exception could mean that a religious workplace may require all staff to share the religion, even in positions for which religion is not a defining aspect of the job, such as custodians or caterers.[100] However, where an organization decides that some roles should be undertaken by co-religionists while others need not be, any argument that the organization's ethos requires employment of co-religionists for certain roles may be weakened.[101] This is particularly the case where the roles which the organization considers need to be occupied by a person of one religion cannot be defined as religious. For example, an organization may decide that although the role of a receptionist is not of itself religious, it is important that the person greeting visitors is representative of its values, although it has no similar views about employees catering or carrying out administrative roles. Where a role appears to have no objectively measurable religious requirement, it may prove difficult to justify requiring the employee to be a co-religionist unless the organization uniformly insists that all employees be co-religionists to protect the organizational ethos. In other words, for an organization to ensure that such roles are occupied by co-religionists, it must ensure that it can satisfy the ethos requirement and to do so requires the creation

96 Note that volunteering has been held not to be an occupation for the purposes of the Act, and to some extent volunteers' rights to religion are therefore not protected. *X v. Mid Sussex Citizens Advice Bureau* [2012] UKSC 59. Note that this volunteerism situation was distinguishable from some volunteering contracts, as the claimants received no expenses, had no set hours of work nor any obligation to undertake the work, and the volunteering role was not associated with any future opportunity for employment.

97 Equality Act 2010, Schedule 9, s 1(1).

98 Equality Act 2010, Schedule 9, s 3.

99 *Bilka-Kaufhaus v. Weber von Hartz* [1986] ECR 1607.

100 Vickers, *Religious Freedom, Religious Discrimination and the Workplace* at 176.

101 *Sheridan v. Prospects for People with Learning Disabilities*, Case No. 2901366/06 (Employment Tribunal, 13 May 2008) and *Hender v. Prospects for People with Learning Disabilities*, Case No. 2909090/06 (Employment Tribunal, 13 May 2008).

of a religiously homogeneous workplace. As explained, it is possible for a religious organization to desire both a religiously mixed working environment and one in which certain roles not normally seen as having a religious requirement are nevertheless performed by co-religionists. The regulations effectively foreclose this possibility.

### *Public-sector collaboration*

Local authorities have various interpretations of their duties in contracts with religious organizations. Some fear that by contracting with a religious group, the statutory body is funding proselytization; in reality, NPC's recent research endorses the notion that statutory engagement may actually lead a religious group to weaken its religious identification.[102] Even if they are controversial, such collaborations are not unusual and we can analyze how they function in practice.

The Equality Act provides that in carrying out its public functions,[103] a public authority must have *due regard* to the need to eliminate discrimination, victimization, or harassment in connection with a protected characteristic, and create equality of opportunity and promote good relations among people of differing beliefs.[104] There are differing views about how the duty should be interpreted.[105] The legal requirement itself is weak, requiring nothing but 'due regard'; it makes no pre-determination of the outcome in any given situation. This duty is applicable not only where a local authority provides services directly, but also where it facilitates the provision of services, facilities, or benefits: for example, in collaboration with a third-sector organization such as a religious group.[106] Notwithstanding this duty, a religious organization in such a relationship continues to be eligible for the exemptions discussed earlier.[107]

However, the requirement to exercise 'due regard' may affect a public authority's willingness to enter into collaborative arrangements with religious organizations. This could arise where a public body thinks the religious organization's actions may prevent individuals exercising their religious freedoms when participating in activities, so jeopardizing the public body's perception of its ability to eliminate discrimination, victimization, or harassment. So, for example, a local authority may be unwilling to fund a youth club held in a mosque, a church, or a gurdwara if the religious community on whose premises the club is to be run insists that any paid staff must be of their religious faith group. The public body may view this as discriminating against people of another or no faith. Similarly, it may be unwilling to fund a lunch club that segregates men from women, or is provided solely for either men or women, if the reason for the segregation is religious. Where it takes such a view, a public body may draft a contract so that the exemption rights are excluded.

If such clauses are inserted without any consideration of how, and whether it is appropriate, to balance the religious organization's communal rights against those of individuals, the public body has not fulfilled its duty of 'due regard'. Rather, it has decided that individual religious rights take precedence over communal religious rights. Where clauses require an organization to act without discrimination with respect to each of the characteristics protected under the Equality Act, the religious organization must decide whether to withdraw

102 Wharton and de las Casas at 29.

103 Equality Act 2010, s 31(3) includes services within an authority's public functions.

104 Equality Act 2010, s 149.

105 See, for example, Vickers, 'Promoting Equality or Fostering Resentment?' and Calderwood Norton at 187.

106 Equality Act 2010 s 212(4).

107 Equality Act 2010 s 28(2)(b).

from the contract and preserve its ability to apply exemptions under the Act, or to enter the contract and sacrifice its ability to apply the exemptions.

Where a religious organization seeks funding from a public body, it is perhaps reasonable that it should choose between the funder's conditions and its way of working. However, where a public body wants assistance from a religious organization because of the quality of its service, is it appropriate for it to dictate how the service should be delivered? Should the religious organization be trusted to continue to deliver the service in a way it knows to be effective, even if its method of delivery invokes exemptions which the local authority usually considers compromise individual religious freedoms? For example, if a public body wants a religious organization to extend its successful children's center or youth provision to encompass a wider geographical area, it may object to some of the roles being filled by people from that religious group. However, the religious organization may identify its successful delivery as partly, or wholly, due to the employment of staff aligned with its values. This may make no objective sense to the public body, but nonetheless in changing the way the organization works, the public body may be reducing the possibility of it continuing to offer successful provision. In such circumstances, everyone loses. The public body cannot utilize the benefits of the group's activities, recipients go without adequate services, and the religious organization is unable to fulfill its obligations to serve the wider community.

Where a religious group does not provide services which would otherwise have been given to a minority group, the way in which a local authority exercises its responsibility to have 'due regard' has resulted in one section of the community suffering inequality of provision. Where a support service is threatened with the withdrawal of funding and, for example, has offered opportunities to elderly people that enable them to network with others, or to children excluded from school so that they can overcome challenges and reintegrate into mainstream education, it may be legitimate to argue that the rights of these small groups are prejudiced if the provision is withdrawn.[108] Even where provision has not been previously made, it would seem pertinent for a local authority to take into account who else could make provision for the people concerned if a particular organization does not offer to meet their need. Where the only possible provider is a religious organization working with marginalized groups in a difficult-to-reach area, it should carefully consider whether giving precedence to individual religious rights over communal religious rights has the effect not only of creating an imbalance between religious rights but of denying members of the wider community provision and so denying them fundamental rights. The public body's actions will have accentuated, rather than relieved, public need.

## *The Equality Act and the religious precinct*

The religious precinct is private land. The identity of the legal person who is the private landowner varies according to the religious group for which the land is held. Setting aside the Church of England, in which a precinct's legal title may be held by more than one ecclesiastical person including its minister of religion, precincts are often held on trust by a local, regional, or national body on behalf of a local congregation. That local congregation is represented by a local management body which, among other things, deals with the day-to-day running of the precinct. In some cases, a minister of religion may be a member of that local body, but in many cases is not. In other arrangements, land is held by individuals acting as

108 *R (Kaur and Shah) v. London Borough of Ealing* [2008] EWHC 2062 (Admin).

trustees for a local congregation, or a faith group is managed by a body incorporated for the purpose. Where this is the case, it owns and manages land along with other assets. It would be unusual for a minister to be an individual land-holding trustee; membership of a managing board is more common.

In none of these structures, apart from the Church of England, does a minister of religion have individual capacity as a landowner to exercise control over entry to, or use of, a religious precinct. Where a minister is a member of a management body and/or an employee,[109] a minister may have delegated authority to act on the landowner's behalf. However, in many situations neither the landowner nor the minister would consider it appropriate for the minister to be responsible for the building.

Where the land is held on trust, the trust's provisions dictate its use. Where not held on trust but the asset of a charity, it must be used in fulfilment of that charity's purposes. The status of land ownership within the Church of England is complex but broadly requires that the precinct is held for ecclesiastical purposes. Where, rarely, the land is neither held in trust nor subject to charitable or ecclesiastical jurisdiction, its use is a matter for its owners or subject to any agreement within the landowner.

The statements of purpose, whether directed at the land under trust as a specified use or as stated purposes of an organization accepted by the Charity Commission as charitable, determine how a religious group is bound to use its land. Trust and charitable purposes can be restricted to worship and the teaching of faith to the religion's members, children, or those wishing to become members. Sometimes they are more broadly framed as supporting the internal needs of the religion's adherents, educating others about its beliefs, and building bridges in communities, or more broadly still as carrying out activities in accordance with its doctrines or ethos. Most broadly of all, they may simply be stated as the advancement of the identified religion.

The trusts imposed on land, charitable purposes, or any agreement within the landowner are expressions of a religious group's self-understanding. Whether those expressions are focused solely on the sustenance of the religious community or include an outward focus may be indicators of a group's security, or a carefully structured articulation of its beliefs about its communal purpose. Religious groups inevitably vary in their interpretations of statements of purpose, and those interpretations become more critical where standardized statements of purpose, as encouraged by the Charity Commission, are adopted. For example, a purpose 'for the advancement of religion' may for one group mean that it focuses on supporting the internal life of the religious community, for another that compliance with its doctrines or ethos requires externally focused activities to be accompanied by an explanation of adherents' beliefs, and for another that an offer to meet need is made without any explanation of why. It is not possible to understand a religious group's understanding of how it should use its assets from a brief review of its credentials as a religious organization.

The provisions of the Equality Act impose obligations and confer rights on legal persons, making little reference to the premises on which such obligations and rights are practiced. A minister of religion, for example, may restrict participation in activities even though he or she has no power over the building in which they take place. The only reference to property relevant to the provisions discussed is its use as a qualifying reference for a minister's functions which may be subject to the gender exemption. The effect is that the religious precinct forms a backdrop against which rights and obligations are exercised. The law is indifferent

109 For a detailed consideration of the legal status of a minister of religion, see Rivers, *The Law of Organized Religions* at 108–146.

to any variations in access which it creates. It takes no account of the character of the religious precinct as land dedicated to use for religious practices in fulfillment of doctrinally driven purposes, or of any contribution the land may make to legitimizing communal acts as manifestations of religion.

## Inequalities and challenges

### *Inequalities*

Where the provisions of the Equality Act identified earlier are applied differently in one religious precinct than in another, the inequalities may seem to relate to the precincts rather than the activities which take place within them. If differences in ministers' roles and religious communities' theology result in people of one gender being excluded from an activity in one building, but invited into a similar activity in another, it appears that, for example, women are excluded from some sorts of religious buildings while permitted entry to others. Where activities to which everyone has access are offered by a religious community which either chooses, or is contractually obliged, to ensure that individual participants can manifest their religion by, for example, praying, people excluded from their own religious precinct because of their gender are able to pray within another religious group's precinct. Where that religious group has entered into a contract with a public body that prevents it employing people of its own faith, and so delivering the service in a way which it considers to be in alignment with its faith, it may consider itself restricted in exercising its communal religious rights while others are permitted to secure their individual freedoms.

These inequalities arise from the combined effects of compliance with Equality Law, religious groups' differing theological stances and, in separate or sometimes the same situation, a public body's choices about the interpretation of its responsibilities. The inequalities created are accentuated by ambiguities in the meaning of 'a minister of religion', the all-or-nothing nature of religious exemptions within employment law, and too narrow an interpretation of a public body's obligation to have 'due regard'. Although religious bodies' theologies are unlikely to change, some changes to the law and its application may reduce the inevitability of inequalities within and between religious precincts.

### *Challenges*

There are no easy solutions to the inequalities identified, not least because some arise from religious groups' differing interpretations of their religious obligations. Those choices are complicated further by groups' differing theologies of sacredness of space. These may identify some places as sacred spaces set apart from worldly intrusion[110] or consider community provision to be consistent with, or even a contributor to,[111] an area's sacred character. It should also be noted that although many religious groups do not acknowledge any part of their precinct as sacred, this does not mean that they necessarily view, or are legally obliged to view, precincts as only neutral backdrops to activities, devoid of theological or doctrinal

110 For one conception of the sacredness of space, see Mark Barrett, 'The Monastery as Sacred Space', in Steve Brie, Jenny Daggers, and David Torevell, eds, *Sacred Space: Interdisciplinary Perspectives within Contemporary Contexts* (Cambridge Scholars Publishing 2009).

111 See, for example, Sara Miles, *Take This Bread: A Radical Conversion* (Canterbury Press 2012) (previously Penguin Random House 2008).

significance.[112] The trusts to which land is subject may necessitate religious use, as may charitable objects, and it is not open to external institutions or other persons to interpret for a religious group what constitutes religious use. Notwithstanding that, state and other institutions find it administratively convenient to use and measure the functional benefits derived from religious organizations' land assets, such a reductionist view denies a religious group the ability to fully realize its religious expression through the use of its precinct. The law's failure to acknowledge that religious activity is broader than activities which support the internal life of religious communities, and institutional perceptions of religious motivations for external engagement, perpetuate the often false separation of religious spaces into those used for religious and those used for secular purposes.

In addition, ambiguity within the legislation creates uncertainty and an inequality of application between religions. It is unclear what is meant by a minister of religion's functions: whether these include only activities undertaken by a minister and ancillary to religious rites; activities ancillary to religious rites carried out by anyone, including a minister; or any activity which falls under the ambit of a minister's managerial functions. Further difficulties arise from the obligation on a public body to have 'due regard' in the elimination of discrimination, victimization, or harassment. The flexibility created by such a weak obligation as 'due regard' is only effective if well used. Where that flexibility gives a public body freedom to use standardized contracts which prescribe the individual freedoms to be accommodated with little regard for whether in any given case the communal rights of a religious organization delivering services should be taken into consideration, the contracts have become an inflexible instrument. That inflexibility negates the purpose for which flexibility is given, creating a situation in which only individual freedoms are considered and there is not due regard to achieving all religious freedoms. In other words, it is unhelpful for one religious right to automatically trump another.[113]

Another challenge arises where a religious group wants to preserve the possibility of employing co-religionists in the future, considers that its view of whether a post is religious or not may be challenged, and so employs co-religionists for all posts under the ethos provisions, even for positions that are not identifiably religious. The religious group may be very willing not to appoint co-religionists to many posts, but want the freedom to determine which posts are religious rather than for that decision to be made by an external body. This may, in turn, cause problems to a public body which, because of its view of what is religious, perceives the organization as unwilling to work with people of another, or no, faith. An impasse is reached, with the religious organization fearful of not being able to deliver services as effectively as it believes it can, and a public body mistrustful of a religious organization's willingness to fully engage with society. Religious organizations should feel free to determine which roles need to be undertaken by people of their own faith to ensure the delivery of a service in fulfillment of a contracting body's requirements while employing others in roles where religious motivation and values are not essential.

To redress legislative and policy-driven imbalances between individual and communal rights to manifest religion, state actors need a level of religious literacy that equips them to understand when social action is delivered in fulfillment of religious doctrine or belief,

112 See John Inge, *A Christian Theology of Place* (Ashgate 2017) for a consideration of place as sacramental rather than sacred. See also Jean Holm and John Bowker, eds, *Sacred Places* (Continuum 1994) and Patrick A. Desplat and Dorothea Schultz, eds, *Prayer in the City: The Making of Muslim Sacred Places and Urban Life* (Transcript 2012).

113 Sandberg at 127.

whether that relationship affects the quality or nature of provision, how other factors affect delivery, and the role of the religious precinct within a religious group's self-understanding.

Currently, legislative provisions and policies relate to activities and the legal actors involved in them, but not the precincts themselves. It seems to be assumed that the precinct is a neutral place within which a range of activities may take place, and one in which only those which the state considers to be religious must be recognized as such. Although in other contexts the state expresses itself as reluctant to evaluate what is, and is not, religious, in this context it exercises no such restraint. In making its own determination about activities, the state fails to understand the significance of a precinct within the life of a religious community, even one with no theology of the sacredness of space, and the problems which may arise for a religious group in fragmenting the uses of its space between that which is recognized as religious and that deemed externally to be secular. Where religious groups seek state support for their activities, it is perhaps acceptable that they should have to make choices about the relationship between belief, activities, and their precincts. However, where the state requires the assistance of religious groups, the current system results in the unavailability of resources which might otherwise be engaged in collaborative activity.

A beneficial contribution to institutional literacy on these issues would be a qualitative or quantitative study which purposefully explores how significant these issues are to religious organizations and how they affect their decisions to engage the religious precinct in social action or welfare provision. The results of this research would form the basis for discussions with public bodies, as well as policy makers and legislators, to develop a legal landscape in which increased institutional religious literacy increases the availability of resources which public bodies wish to use, but religious communities are uncertain about releasing for wider community use.

# 11 Freedom of/for/from/within religion in prison

## A taxonomy of the Strasbourg jurisprudence

*Jeroen Temperman*[1]

## Introduction

More than 60 complaints by prisoners alleging freedom of religion or belief violations have been put before the European Court of Human Rights (the 'Strasbourg Court') and before the former European Commission of Human Rights (the 'Commission'). While this is not the place to engage with all of those cases,[2] the here-selected Strasbourg jurisprudence lends itself perfectly to illustrate all the fascinating dimensions of the right to freedom of religion or belief – from the individual to the collective dimension, from the state's negative to the state's positive obligations, from the freedom to have and manifest a religion to the freedom to not have anything to do with religion, that is, from freedom *of* religion to freedom *from* religion, and so on.

Most of the Strasbourg case law squarely falls within the freedom *of* religion or belief category, that is, jurisprudence revolving around the permissibility of certain religious manifestations inside the confines of the prison walls. Also, the very need on the part of secular authorities to establish whether or not a certain action or inaction amounts to a religious manifestation in the first place may impact the freedom of religion.

On the freedom *for* religion,[3] it will be demonstrated that while many of the questions the Strasbourg Court has to settle directly impact core *individual* religious liberties, some cases do in fact touch upon the *collective* aspect of religious freedom, the freedom to practice religion together with others, including the role of organized religion.

Freedom *from* religion in prison is significant since this literally 'captive audience' may be subject to religious coercion coming from both the prison authorities (possibly in tandem with members of the dominant religion) and/or from fellow prisoners.[4] Here relevant case law is more scant, yet a number of important observations can be made under this heading.

1 The title is a play on the Fourth ICLARS Conference entitled 'Freedom of/for/from/in Religion: Differing Dimensions of a Common Right?', held 8–11 September 2016, at St. Hugh's College, Oxford, where this paper was presented.

2 For the full report, see Jeroen Temperman, 'Freedom of Religion or Belief in Prison: A Critical Analysis of the European Court of Human Rights' Jurisprudence', (2017) 6 *Oxford Journal of Law and Religion* (1) 48–92. The present chapter draws on that more comprehensive article.

3 In the words of the Fourth ICLARS Conference description, '*Freedom for religion*… concerns the institutional side of this right (what was once called "libertas ecclesiae").' www.iclars.org/event.php?event=13.

4 In the words of the Fourth ICLARS Conference description, '*Freedom from religion*, that is the right to live one's life without being compelled to perform religious acts'.

Freedom *within* religion,[5] finally, shows up in the Strasbourg jurisprudence each time regulations imposed by secular authorities potentially impact the internal *religious autonomy* of a religious community.

## Freedom *of* religion in prison

The bulk of prisoners' religious liberty cases before the Strasbourg Court are classic freedom of religion or belief cases, that is, cases concerning complaints by prisoners alleging unacceptable interferences with their freedom to practice their religion or belief. Many such cases revolve around church attendance, clergy visits, possession and use of religious items, facilitation of religious rituals, and religious dietary requirements. For the purposes of illustrating this most familiar and least controversial of dimensions, this section will discuss a selection of church attendance and clergy visits cases specifically.

On the issue of prison chapel attendance, the Strasbourg court has found clear-cut violations in a number of cases. Take for instance the case of *Igors Dmitrijevs v. Latvia*, which concerned the applicant's impossibility to take part in religious services while in pre-trial detention.[6] In the view of the Strasbourg Court, any such obstacle to attending church services in prison indeed minimally amounts to an interference with the right to freedom of religion or belief. Crucially, the Court observed that Latvia at the time had no law in place governing the exercise of religious rights during pre-trial detention. Accordingly, the interference with the applicant's rights had no basis in positive law and hence amounted to a breach of Article 9. Similarly, in *Kuznetsov v. Ukraine* the Court found a violation of the applicant's religious rights by dint of the legality principle.[7]

Being barred from attending religious services may also amount to a breach on more substantive grounds. Interestingly, whereas most Article 9 complaints have been dismissed by the Court (typically for failure to prove the interference), no less than an Article 3 complaint (inhuman and degrading treatment) proved successful. In *Gavrilovici v. Moldova*, the European Court of Human Rights expressly lists the 'inability to...go to church' as one of the reasons – admittedly, the list of examples of harsh treatment was considerable in this case – why his treatment in prison 'attained a level of severity so as to constitute treatment contrary to Article 3 of the Convention'.[8]

Occasionally, sound safety concerns are at stake and refusals could, under the right circumstances, legitimately be made by prison authorities. In *Marek Glínski v. Poland*, the responding state could come up with sound arguments why the applicant was denied permission to attend a five-day Jehovah's Witnesses congress.[9] The applicant had served only a part of his 25-year term for murder, and considering that only two years prior he had planned a prison escape, he could justifiably be considered a high-risk case.[10]

In the older case of *Childs v. United Kingdom*, revolving around an inmate who was usually denied permission to attend prison church service, security concerns were equally

5 In the words of the Fourth ICLARS Conference description, '*[F]reedom in religion* concerns the rights that the faithful (and sometimes not so faithful) are entitled to enjoy within their religious communities.'

6 *Igors Dmitrijevs v. Latvia*, App. No. 61638/00 (ECtHR, 30 November 2006).

7 *Kuznetsov v. Ukraine*, App. No. 39042/97 (ECtHR, 29 April 2003).

8 *Gavrilovici v. Moldova*, App. No. 25464/05 (ECtHR, 15 December 2009), § 44.

9 *Marek Glínski v. Poland*, App. No. 59739/08 (ECtHR, 11 February 2014).

10 These facts are explained not in the judgment but in the more detailed Statement of Facts and Questions (under 6), http://hudoc.echr.coe.int/eng?i=001-111160 (accessed July 2017).

clearly at stake.[11] Not only was Childs a convicted murderer, responsible for multiple killings, he moreover had previously testified against other criminals. Hence, his leaving his cell could very well have a disruptive effect, also causing a situation in which it was hard for the prison authorities to guarantee his own safety. The Commission considered 'disturbances' likely given the applicant's 'background'.[12] Arguably, there was still a duty incumbent upon the authorities to ensure his religious rights, but whether that positive duty went as far as allowing him to attend church service with, for instance, heightened personal security protection is questionable. Such a scenario would not only be quite demanding, but more importantly might endanger others, notably the prison guards who would be forced to protect him against potential attacks from other inmates.[13] The Commission took into account that the applicant could at least be regularly visited by the prison chaplain, an indication that the responding state had positively endeavored to ensure his religious rights to the furthest extent possible.

Generally speaking, whenever church attendance in prison is denied (for instance for sound security reasons), it would appear to be all the more important to facilitate having at least regular access to a clergy member of the inmate's church. In sum, the Strasbourg jurisprudence suggests that *access to prison chapel services* and *individual access to a member of the clergy* could function, depending on the facts of the case and the security or other interest at stake, as interchangeable.[14]

Being denied regular access to a minister of religion may amount to a breach of the Convention. Accordingly, in *Poltoratskiy v. Ukraine* the Strasbourg Court agreed with the applicant that Ukraine's reluctance to facilitate clergy visits amounted to a violation of Article 9.[15]

It is far from clear what constitutes regular visits, how long those visits ought to last minimally, or, indeed, what should roughly be the quality of these inmate-clergy conferences. Case law in this area is scant and not fully crystalized. The older case of *M. v. United Kingdom* is a good illustration of what arguments could, at least in theory, legitimize far-reaching interferences with the right to manifest a religion in prison.[16] The applicant was in isolation and under strict surveillance. He was deemed psychopathic, highly dangerous, and untreatable. On account of his violent past, he was not permitted to attend church services. The security risk was far from abstract: he had killed both in and out of prison. Hence, an argument in favor of a restriction based on the 'rights of others' was rather straightforwardly made. Still, though, being in isolation and barred from church services, it was all the more important to find ways to accommodate his religious needs in alternative ways. Accordingly, at the applicant's request, he was occasionally visited by a Catholic priest. These visits, however, took place with the priest outside the steel mesh door of the cell. The applicant claimed that this made it impossible to take Communion in a manner consistent with his beliefs (a number of other forms of ill-treatment were alleged also). The Commission concluded that while these conditions were severe, they did not amount to a breach of the Convention.

11 *Childs v. United Kingdom*, App. No. 9813/82 (ECtHR, 1 March 1981).
12 *Childs* at § 4.
13 Carolyn Evans, *Freedom of Religion under the European Convention on Human Rights* (Oxford University Press 2001), 151.
14 *Childs* at § 4. The former Commission expressly took into account the fact that 'the applicant at least receives regular visits from the prison Chaplain who prays with the applicant.'
15 *Poltoratskiy v. Ukraine*, App. No. 38812/97 (ECtHR, 29 April 2003).
16 *M. v. United Kingdom*, App. No. 9907/82 (ECmHR, 12 December 1983).

This finding of no violation may very well have been fostered by the fact that the applicant chiefly complained under Article 3, suggesting that the overall harsh treatment amounted to 'mental torture'. The Commission did not wish to go quite as far as that. It would have been interesting to hear the Commission's views on whether it was strictly necessary, under Article 9, to conduct these clergy visits in this manner. Obviously, the safety of the priest warranted measures that affected, if not ruled out, a personal, face-to-face meeting. That said, there do exist modalities in between the one the prison had chosen and a face-to-face meeting, such as convening meetings in a conference room with a glass partition. In fact, the prisoner did sometimes leave his cell, namely for his weekly bath, albeit accompanied five prison officers. Taking religious freedom seriously may mean acknowledging that for certain inmates regularly speaking to a priest may be as important as, if not more important than, having a weekly bath. That said, it must be reiterated that the applicant staked the case perhaps too strongly on Article 3.

Recently, the Grand Chamber of the Strasbourg Court had an opportunity to comment upon the quality of clergy visits in the case of *Mozer v. Moldova*.[17] The applicant was imprisoned for fraud in a Moldovan prison, where he was refused visits by a Norwegian pastor, and the government provided no explanation whatsoever for the refusal. Interestingly, a 'presidential adviser' had already determined that the denial was contrary to the Constitution of Moldova and its laws. More to the point, eventually the requested visit took place but with a guard present. The right to have access to representatives of one's religion should naturally include the specific right to have private, confidential conferences. Given the fact that religious practitioners may feel a need to discuss intimate aspects of their religious faith, troubles of the conscience, and indeed actually wish to 'confess' – in both the religious and secular sense of the word – to a representative member of their faith, it is hard to see how privacy rights can be severed from religious rights. Yet the Grand Chamber, while holding that the refusal to allow the prisoner a pastoral visit with no justification was a violation of Article 9, did not comment upon whether the supervised visit that eventually took place was of sufficient quality.

Another freedom of religion question that has repeatedly popped up in the Strasbourg jurisprudence revolves around whether genuine religious practice requires knowledge of religions one does not adhere to. The applicant in *X. v. Austria*, for example, was a Buddhist prisoner who complained about having been denied access to certain publications he deemed necessary 'for a further development of his philosophy of life (*Welstanschauung*)'.[18] The prison's refusal was upheld by the Commission, which reasoned that 'Article 9 does not oblige a Contracting Party to put at the disposal of prisoners books which they consider necessary for the exercise of their religion or for the development of their philosophy of life'. The request was legitimately refused since it boiled down to a financial and administrative burden for the institution, suggesting that the answer could have been different in case the applicant had offered to purchase them himself (personally or through family or friends).

On the other hand, another part of the same decision showed that the burden on the institution was not the only important factor. The applicant also wanted a subscription to *Weltmission*, a Catholic magazine. He had offered to pay the 30 Austrian schillings to cover the subscription himself, seeing this as 'part of the charity to which he is morally obliged'.

17 *Mozer v. Republic of Moldova and Russia*, App. No. 11138/10 (ECtHR Grand Chamber, 23 February 2016).
18 *X. v. Austria*, App. No. 1753/63 (ECmHR, 15 February 1965).

The Commission agreed with Austria that Catholic publications are not necessary reading for a Buddhist:

> The Commission has been informed that this periodical is edited by a Roman Catholic organization; whereas it follows that by the refusal the Applicant, being himself of Buddhist faith, has not been, in any way, restricted in the exercise of his religion.

It is difficult to see how the Commission is in a position to judge what does and what does not belong to the practice of the Buddhist faith. It is far from unimaginable that a religious practitioner immerses him- or herself in religious comparative studies as part of their religious practice. At any rate, the Commission's response did no justice to the fact that the prisoner made his request as an act of (religious) charity. All in all, and especially since Mr. X was willing to bear the costs himself, it is rather unclear which ground for limitation justifies the restriction on Mr. X's religious manifestation.

In the recent case of *Kovaļkovs v. Latvia*, the Strasbourg Court took a more robust approach. The responding state had denied that Kovaļkovs was in fact a member of the Hare Krishna movement.[19] Questioning the sincerity or genuineness of a complainant's religious faith serves to cast doubt as to whether the criteria for 'victim status' under the Convention (and hence admissibility) are satisfied. The government thought that it had found proof of insincerity on the part of the applicant in the fact that in the past the applicant had followed a distance-learning Bible course. Obviously, that fact alone cannot disprove the sincerity of one's belief. First, an adherent to religion *y* may have a genuine interest in learning more about religion *x*, as in the case of Mr. X earlier. Second, a person may change one's religion, including in prison. The Court takes this opportunity to underscore the point that 'in no way can a person's choice to educate himself – be it on religious or other topics – be objectively held to affect that person's belief system.'[20] In short, the Strasbourg Court did not discern any special reasons to doubt the applicant's sincerity simply because he had researched other religions.[21]

## Freedom *for* religion in prison

Some of the aforementioned freedom of religion or belief cases already touched upon the freedom to observe religious practices together with others, showing how inextricably linked the different dimensions of this right may be. The need of individuals to seek religious fellowship with coreligionists invokes the collective aspect of freedom of religion or belief of which freedom *for* religious organizations is a part.

In addition to prison chaplaincy, another area where one could conceive of a meaningful 'freedom for religion' in prison is the area of nutrition. More specifically, where complying with the religious dietary needs of prisoners is burdensome for prison authorities (on account of the variety of different diets for instance), one could imagine modalities where religious organizations are cont(r)acted to help out. The case of *D.S. and E.S. v. United Kingdom* concerned, among other matters, this question.[22] The case revolved

19 *Kovaļkovs v. Latvia*, App. No. 35021/05 (ECtHR, 31 January 2012), § 57.
20 § 57.
21 Note that the applicant did not go on to win his case; no Article 9 violation was pronounced eventually.
22 *D.S. and E.S. v. United Kingdom*, App. No. 13669/88 (ECmHR, 7 March 1990).

around orthodox Jewish inmates who requested kosher food, but who were instead put on a vegan diet. In this case, an organization called the Society of Welfare of Jewish Prisoners had offered to prepare kosher food for strictly Orthodox prisoners, but this was refused by the Home Office. The offer made by the Society seems eminently suitable and clearly fulfilling an urgent demand. The Commission, however, argued that the refusal to take this organization up on its offer did not breach the Convention.[23]

It should be noted that in the meantime, the Strasbourg jurisprudence on religious dietary requirements is among the most crystallized of all of its case law on prisoners' freedom of religion – jurisprudence that outlines a crucial advisory role for religious organizations. In the landmark case of *Jakóbski v. Poland*, the responding state was reproached by the Strasbourg Court for not having consulted a Buddhist organization on dietary rules.[24] Specifically, the 'Buddhist Mission' in Poland should have been consulted on the issue of what dietary requirements flow from the Mahayana branch. From the Court's strong criticism of the Polish prison authorities one could distill no less than an actual *positive obligation* to consult religious authorities in the event of emerging questions about how to accommodate the religious precepts of a particular belief.

Similarly, in *Vartic v. Romania* the Strasbourg Court reproached the responding state for apparently not acting upon the advice on dietary requirements actually given by a Buddhist organization (and by the prison's doctor).[25] During the domestic proceedings leading up to this case, Romanian judges dismissed Vartic's complaints largely in light of the fact that sufficient expertise had been sought. Yet the Strasbourg Court points out that from the submissions made by Romania, it was not at all clear whether the authorities had in fact acted upon the advice rendered by the 'Group of Buddhist Meditation'; indeed, the government of Romania was deliberately vague about what the advice consisted of.

Conversely, such a consultation process may also establish that an alleged religious duty *cannot* be regarded as such according to expert opinion on the religious doctrine and practice concerned. Thus, in *Kovaļkovs v. Latvia*, the information obtained from members of the Riga Vaishnavist (Hare Krishna) congregation – which was to the effect that incense burning is not under all circumstances required of followers – effectively dismantled this part of the applicant's freedom of religion complaint.[26] The fact that a certain act is not a hard and fast religious duty does not mean that the denial thereof does not engage the right to freedom of religion or belief. However, the Court rightly noted that the qualification of an act as a non-essential manifestation of religion impacts the balancing exercise. More specifically, this qualification impacts the necessity and proportionality of the interference, especially when the rights of others are at stake.[27]

## Freedom *from* religion in prison

When the 'rights and freedoms of others' (meaning in our context other prisoners and occasionally wardens) limitation is invoked by states and accepted by the Strasbourg Court as a legitimate and necessary restriction on a certain manifestation of religion, what in

23 It should be noted that the complainant was denied standing for failure to comply with the admissibility criteria.

24 *Jakóbski v. Poland*, App. No. 18429/06 (ECtHR, 7 December 2010), § 52.

25 *Vartic v. Romania (No. 2)*, App. No. 14150/08 (ECtHR, 17 December 2013), §§ 44–55.

26 *Kovaļkovs* at §§ 18 and 68.

27 § 68.

fact typically happens is that the 'freedom from religion' of other inmates is upheld at the expense of the freedom *of* religion of the religious prisoner. Obviously, this is not always the case. When security and the rights of others are at stake, for instance, those 'rights of others' rather refer to the right to bodily integrity, and in extreme cases the right to life.

While the Strasbourg Court has not yet extensively dealt with the freedom from religion in prisons, the European Prison Rules, adopted by the Council of Europe, do contain a comprehensive prohibition of coercion: 'Prisoners may not be compelled to practise a religion or belief, to attend religious services or meetings, to take part in religious practices or to accept a visit from a representative of any religion or belief.'[28]

Arguably, the recent case of *Kovaļkovs v. Latvia* contains minor traces of 'freedom from religion'. The applicant, a member of Hare Krishna, wished to burn incense sticks in his cell; however, the latter were confiscated on account of both safety concerns and concerns about the rights of others. In the latter respect, the Court emphasized that a point 'to be taken into account in that regard is other prisoners' *wish not to be disturbed* by the applicant's performance of religious rituals'.[29] The Court concludes that 'the burning of incense sticks typically creates a powerful odour which is not pleasant to everyone and which might be disturbing to other prisoners.'[30] Obviously, the judgment did not engage with freedom from religion as protection against religious coercion, but against what other prisoners might experience as a nuisance.

The *Kovaļkovs* case does contain one other interesting freedom from religion dimension – or rather a freedom from forced dealings with non-religionists or persons of other faiths. The applicant contended that due to the constant swearing by and the 'immoral lifestyles' of his fellow inmates, he could not concentrate on his religious duties, like meditation and religious studies. Therefore the applicant had requested to have access to isolated facilities in which to pursue his religious duties. The refusal thereof was not found to be in breach of the Convention. The Strasbourg Court considered that 'having to pray, read religious literature and to meditate in the presence of others is an inconvenience, which is almost inescapable in prisons, yet which does not go against the very essence of the freedom to manifest one's religion.'[31]

## Freedom *within* religion

Choices made by prison authorities in the area of collective religious exercise – denominationally specific prison services, availability of religious representatives of some but perhaps not all religions adhered to by prisoners – may touch upon questions of *equal* religious freedom. The European Prison Rules provide on this point:

> The prison regime shall be organised so far as is practicable to allow prisoners to practise their religion and follow their beliefs, to attend services or meetings led by approved representatives of such religion or beliefs, to receive visits in private from such representatives of their religion or beliefs and to have in their possession books or literature relating to their religion or beliefs.[32]

28 European Prison Rules, Rule 29.3. See Committee of Ministers of the Council of Europe, Recommendation Rec(2006)2 of the Committee of Ministers to Member States on the European Prison Rules, adopted by the Committee of Ministers on 11 January 2006, containing the (revised) European Prison Rules in the appendix.

29 *Kovaļkovs* at § 64 (emphasis added).

30 § 68.

31 § 67.

32 European Prison Rules, Rule 29.2.

The Strasbourg Court is under no mandate to enforce these Rules, but may very well, and indeed has referenced them in its case law.[33] While the Rules (unlike the UN equivalent)[34] do not subject the right to private clergy visits to any numerical requirement in relation to the prison population, the official commentary does move in that direction:

> If a prison contains a *sufficient number of prisoners of the same religion*, an approved representative of that religion should be appointed. If the number of prisoners justifies it and conditions permit, such appointment should be on a full-time basis. Such approved representatives should be allowed to hold regular services and activities and to pay pastoral visits in private to prisoners of their religion. Access to an approved representative of a religion should not be refused to any prisoner.[35]

Still though, there is a difference between permanently appointing representatives of different religions and making sure that access to a representative of a minority religion is guaranteed if and when the need arises. The Rules do not rule out that – 'so far as is practicable'[36] – prison authorities are under a positive obligation to make such visits possible by drawing on external representatives.

The Strasbourg case law, however, is not conducive to construing such a specific right to meetings with a representative of one's specific religious *denomination*. The case of *X. v. Federal Republic of Germany* revolved around a complaint made by a prisoner about not having access to an Anglican priest.[37] The European Commission of Human Rights rejected the claim as 'there [was] no evidence that a Protestant pastor or facilities for worship in the Protestant religion [was] not available to the Applicant.'[38] Thus, the Commission suggested that if there is access to church representatives and services roughly compatible with the prisoner's religion, the state has discharged its obligations in this regard, especially where the religion (or specific denomination) in question is not widely practiced in the country concerned. Again, while this ruling may be compatible with international soft-law prison rules, the Commission's complete disregard of denominational significance and preference is striking. This may very well be due to the fact that this was an early decision.

Presently, after such judgments as *Metropolitan Church of Bessarabia* (firmly endorsing denominational choice as an integral aspect of freedom of religion or belief),[39] the European Court of Human Rights might rule differently.[40] Of course, denominational choice in liberty may be different from denominational choice in captivity; put differently, interferences with denominational choices that cannot be legitimatized in

33 See, e.g., *Jakóbski v. Poland*, supra note 32 at § 26.

34 'If the prison contains a sufficient number of prisoners of the same religion, a qualified representative of that religion shall be appointed or approved. If the number of prisoners justifies it and conditions permit, the arrangement should be on a full-time basis.' Resolution 70/175 'United Nations Standard Minimum Rules for the Treatment of Prisoners (the Nelson Mandela Rules)' (17 December 2015), UN Doc A/Res/70/175, Rule 65(1).

35 European Prison Rules Commentary, Rule 29.2 explanation (emphasis added).

36 Rule 29.2.

37 *X. v. Federal Republic of Germany*, App. No. 2413/65 (ECmHR, 16 December 1966).

38 *X. v. Federal Republic of Germany* at 'The Law'.

39 *Metropolitan Church of Bessarabia and Others v. Moldova*, App. No. 45701/99 (ECtHR, 13 December 2001).

40 See also Paul Taylor, *Freedom of Religion: UN and European Human Rights Law and Practice* (Cambridge University Press 2005), 224–225.

the former context could perhaps under some circumstances be justifiable in the latter context. The crucial question from a human rights law perspective is whether or not it is proportionate to altogether refuse to facilitate a visit by, for example, an Anglican priest rather than merely a Protestant one. Again, it is one thing not to appoint one on a full-time basis (the applicant was most likely quite alone in his demand); it is another to deny *ad hoc* visits by a local Anglican priest, should there be one. Arguably, the applicant overplayed his hand somewhat by demanding 'facilities for worship according to the rites of the Church of England'.[41]

Another striking example of how prison life may limit the freedom 'within' religion is provided by the recent case of *Florin Andrei v. Romania*.[42] From the Court's judgment in this case, it may be distilled that although prisoners have a right to access to clergy, there is no specific right to see a priest on a particular day of the prisoner's choosing, for instance because the prisoner urgently wants to take part in the rite of confession. The applicant had wanted to go to confession on a day significant within Eastern Orthodox liturgics (the facts of the case refer to 15 August, so presumably it concerned the feast of the Dormition of the Theotokos, analogous with the Assumption of Mary in Catholicism). The case is perhaps more complicated than the insensitive approach of the Court suggests. Arguably, confessions of faith on important feast days, and celebrations together with fellow practitioners and representatives of religion, form core elements of religious practice and are hence integral to the free manifestation of religion. That is to say, any state-imposed obstacle to the observance of religious feast days outside the prison context could very well lead to a determination of an interference with the freedom to manifest a religion – that interference in turn either being justifiable or not. It is not at all evident that this should be any different as regards the religious rights of prisoners.

These types of cases beg the question if and to what extent secular authorities (in the first instance the prison authorities, and at a later stage, courts) are competent to identify what amounts to important – worthy-of-protection – religious celebrations. While it may come with imprisonment that not each and every minor holy day or feast can be celebrated together with other members of the religion, the feast at stake in this case does in fact belong to one of the so-called 'great feasts' in Orthodoxy. Hence, the implicit concern that accommodation would amount to an administrative nuisance does not necessarily justify interferences here; also, one may expect the Strasbourg Court to assess the necessity of interferences in this area rather more diligently.

## Concluding remarks

As far as the promotion of the freedom *of* religion or belief of prisoners is concerned, the European Court of Human Rights has been particularly steadfast in the area of respect for religious dietary requirements. While basic religious manifestations such as chapel attendance or clergy visits can be restricted in the interest of public safety in accordance with the Convention, the Strasbourg Court at times may be expected to make a more robust assessment of the necessity of restrictions imposed by states. On the freedom *for* religion, in certain cases there may be a profound role for religious organizations, either as direct providers or facilitators of religious freedoms (such as in the area of providing

41 *X. v. Federal Republic of Germany* at 'The Facts'.
42 *Florin Andrei v. Romania*, App. No. 33228/05 (ECtHR, 15 April 2014).

nutrition in accordance with religious tenets) or as advisors as to what exact religious duties do – and do not – emanate from the religion or belief in question. It has been observed that there are remarkably few freedom *from* religion cases yet put before the Strasbourg Court. Finally, some of the cases that were categorized as freedom *within* religion cases show that seemingly neutral treatment of the relevant facts of a case on the part of courts, including descriptions and assessments of the religious manifestation at stake, in fact meddle in doctrinal religious debates (e.g. what are important feast days and which are not). Third-party expert advice may serve here to defuse this issue.

# Part III

# Emerging regional contexts

# 12 Islamic Preaching Board Laws of Kano, Borno, and Niger States

## A constitutional and human rights assessment

*Ahmed Salisu Garba*

### Introduction

This paper assesses the Islamic Preaching Board Laws of Kano,[1] Borno,[2] and Niger[3] States in relation to the Constitution of the Federal Republic of Nigeria 1999 and other democratic norms that relate to free exercise rights. I argue that these laws can succeed only insofar as they are compatible with the Constitution and other democratic norms that relate to free exercise of religion. Second, I propose that the judicial mechanism used by the European Court of Human Rights (ECtHR or 'Strasbourg court') to review claims of infringement of free exercise is more suitable to the Nigerian environment than other alternatives such as that of the United States.

Nigeria is a highly religious country and home to many religions, so religion is a very sensitive matter that government at all levels is aware of and interested in accommodating.[4] Islam and Christianity are the two major religions at the national level. In states where Christians are in the majority, the state government identifies more with Christianity and likewise for Islam in states where Muslims are in the majority.[5]

Twelve states in the Muslim-majority northern region of Nigeria have implemented Sharia law alongside civil law in their jurisdictions. Eleven of these states, and two others, have also enacted Islamic Preaching Board Laws. The functions of these boards are generally to examine intending Islamic preachers and to issue preaching licenses to those qualified. The laws also criminalize preaching without a license or in contravention of its content. The composition of the Islamic preaching boards is determined by the government, and in practice they are mainly composed of representatives of dominant religious groups.

The three states I focus on were the first in northern Nigeria to enact Preaching Board Laws.[6] They also each experienced unique challenges with local Islamic religious groups –Maitatsine in Kano, Boko Haram in Borno, and Darul Islam in Niger, among

1 Kano State Religious Preaching Edict of 1985, repealing and replacing earlier laws.

2 Borno State Islamic Religious Preaching Law of 2010, repealing and replacing earlier laws.

3 Niger State Islamic Religious Preaching Edict of 1985, repealing and replacing earlier laws.

4 Rosalind I.J. Hackett, 'Regulating Religious Freedom in Africa', in *Sharia, Family, and Democracy: Religious Norms and Family Law in Pluralistic Democratic States* (2011) 25 *Emory International Law Review* (2) 853–879.

5 Ahmed Salisu Garba, 'Nigeria's Religion-State Relation and its Legal Implications for Freedom of Religion', in Pieter Coertzen, M. Christian Green, and Len Hansen, eds, *Religious Freedom and Religious Pluralism in Africa: Prospects and Limitations* (Sun Media Stellenbosch 2016), 157–175.

6 Other states with Preaching Board Laws include Sokoto, Bauchi, Plateau, Kaduna, Katsina, Jigawa, Kebbi, Yobe, Zamfara, Gombe, Yobe, and Nassarawa. The Kaduna State Religious Preaching Law, which regulates both Islamic and Christian preaching and is currently being much discussed, is not discussed here because this paper focuses on states that regulate Islamic preaching only.

many others. But the fact that the laws were enacted democratically by state legislatures and that they were a response to unique challenges does not automatically make them valid from a constitutional or human rights perspective.[7] I attempt to answer important questions about the Islamic Preaching Board Laws of these states, such as how justifiable are the Preaching Board Laws in the states under study? What criteria can be adopted to determine their reasonability? And how have they agreed or disagreed with free exercise rights in a democratic Nigeria?

These questions are critical, because Article 45 of the Nigeria Constitution allows interference with the right to free exercise of religion only by a 'reasonably justifiable law in a democratic society'. If and when the judiciary decides upon the constitutionality of these laws, it inevitably engages in the exercise of discretion to determine what is 'reasonably justifiable', and discretion has been found to be susceptible to bias especially where it involves groups whose ideologies disagree with that of the majority. For example, research has shown that courts handling cases involving dissident groups in particular tend to accept otherwise inadmissible when such evidence supports their preconceived bias against such groups.[8] This study intends to provide perspective and analysis that could be useful for the judiciary to discharge its function in as unbiased a manner as possible.

The overall aim of this paper is to recommend a judicial standard of review for the resolution of conflicts between citizens' free exercise rights and the regulatory power of the State in a democratic Nigeria – in other words, to clarify the ambiguity in the meaning of the phrase 'reasonably justifiable law in a democratic society', thereby minimizing the likelihood of arbitrariness and misapplication of the Preaching Board Laws.

## Theoretical frameworks

The controversy over Preaching Board Laws in some states of northern Nigeria and attempts to re-enact them in Katsina, Niger, and more recently in Kaduna State have been portrayed as a clash between, on one side, the government alarmed by the alleged threat of provocative religious preaching and religious 'hate speech', and on the other hand religious and human rights groups seeking to protect the free exercise rights of citizens.

Scholars have taken a variety of attitudes toward restrictions on religious preaching. Some support government regulation of free exercise rights including restrictions on the right to engage in religious propagation or preaching, arguing generally that the government is justified in regulating uncivil or inflammatory religious speech as threat to public order.[9] Others argue against such restrictions as incompatible with democracy, suggesting that the

7 Yasuo Hasebe and Cesare Pinelli, 'Constitutions', in Mark Tushnet, Thomas Fleiner, and Cheryl Saunders, eds, *Routledge Handbook of Constitutional Law* (Routledge 2013), 1–19.

8 See James T. Richardson, 'Religious Diversity, Social Control and Legal Pluralism: A Socio-Legal Analysis', in Giuseppe Giordan and Enzo Pace, eds, *Religious Pluralism: Framing Religious Diversity in the Contemporary World* (Springer 2014), 31–47. See also 'Regulating Religion: A Sociological and Historical Introduction', in James T. Richardson, ed., *Regulating Religion: Case Studies from Around the Globe* (Kluwer Academic/Plenum Publishers 2004), 1–15.

9 See, for example, Audrey Peltze, 'A Survey of Constitutional Challenges to Municipal Regulation of Religious Solicitation and a Suggested Legislative Compromise', (1982) 11 *Fordham Urban Law Journal* (4); Kenneth Lasson, 'Incitement in the Mosques: Testing the Limits of Free Speech and Religious Liberty', (2005/2006) 27 *Whittier Law Review* (3); and Isaac Terwase Sampson, 'Religious Violence in Nigeria: Causal Diagnosis and Strategic Recommendations to the State and Religious Communities', (2012) 12 *African Journal on Conflict Resolution* (1).

restrictions themselves are discriminatory against minority religious groups and can incite violence against them[10] or that they violate human rights norms of secularity, free religious exercise, and proportionality.[11] These are based on the religious economy thesis which posits that in a free market of ideas, religious ideas should be allowed to compete with one another in the available public space so that in the end the truth prevails. A final category of scholarship does not support or oppose such restrictions *per se*, but views them from the perspective of balancing mechanisms or proportionality tests in resolving conflicts between the regulatory power of the state and the free exercise rights of citizens.[12]

## Overview of Islamic Preaching Board Laws in Northern Nigeria

Regulation of Islamic preaching is an old phenomenon in northern Nigeria.[13] In the late eighteenth century, the rulers of Gobir sought to control the preaching of Usman dan Fodio, who would later rebel and launch a successful jihad against Gobir. Measures taken against Usman dan Fodio and his followers included restricting Islamic preaching, barring conversion to Islam, ordering all convertees to return to their former religions, and forbidding the wearing of turbans and veils.[14] Nevertheless, the jihad beginning in 1804 would eventually give rise to a new administration in northern Nigeria headed by Usman dan Fodio.

Another significant attempt to regulate Islamic preaching took place under the colonial administration in 1926, as a reaction to incessant disagreements between the dominant Islamic groups in the region – essentially between the Qadiriyya and Tijjaniyya Sufi orders – in addition to friction associated with the emergence of new Islamic religious groups in the region, such as the Ahmadiyya and the Wahhabiyya.[15] Moreover, the region had witnessed an increase in Christian missionaries against the wishes of the northern emirs, who were Muslims.[16] As a result, the colonial government directed the governors of Kano, Zaria, Sokoto, and Niger to issue proclamations to control religious preaching in their areas. This

10 See, for example, Brian J. Grim and Roger Finke, *The Price of Freedom Denied* (Cambridge University Press 2011) and Monica Duffy Toft, Daniel Philpott, and Timothy Samuel Shah, *God's Century* (W.W. Norton 2011). See also Auwalu Anwar, *Gardawa, Ulama and the State of Northern Nigeria: The Maitatsine Phenomenon, 1962–1985* (dissertation, University of Maiduguri 1997) and Haruna Wakili, *The Phenomenon of Revolts and Riots in Kano, 1983–1995: An Historical Perspective* (dissertation, Bayero University Kano 1997).

11 See, for example, Sam Amadi, 'Kaduna Anti-Preaching Law: A Regulatory Misstep', *This Day Newspaper* weekly pullout, 19 April 2016, 7 and Inibehe Effiong, 'Kaduna Preaching Bill: Resolving the Constitutional Controversy', *Punch Nigeria*, published in three installments on 1 April 2016 at 20, 4 April 2016 at 26, and 5 April 2016 at 23.

12 See, for example, T. Jeremy Gunn, 'Possible Limitations on the Freedom of Religion or Belief', in John Witte, Jr. and M. Christian Green, eds, *Religion & Human Rights: An Introduction* (Oxford University Press 2012), 254–268; Aharon Barak, *Proportionality: Constitutional Rights and Their Limitations* (Cambridge University Press 2012), 2–7; and Robert Alexy, *A Theory of Constitutional Rights*, trans. Julian Rivers (Oxford University Press 2002).

13 Abubakar Gwandu, 'Aspects of the Administration of Justice in the Sokoto Caliphate and Shaykh Abdullahi ibn Fodio's Contribution to It', in Syed Khalid Rashid, ed., *Islamic Law in Nigeria* (Islamic Publications Bureau 1986), 10–27.

14 Ricardo Rene Laremont, *Islamic Law and Politics in Northern Nigeria* (Africa World Press 2011), 64–65.

15 Wakili at 38–45.

16 Funso Afolayan, 'Religion and Politics in Colonial Nigeria: The Life and Career of Sir Walter Miller, 1782–1952', in Julius O. Adekunle, ed., *Religion in Politics: Secularism and National Integration in Modern Nigeria* (Africa World Press 2009), 37–66.

was contained in a circular signed by the acting secretary of the Northern provinces.[17] The injunction against preaching applied to everyone, not only Muslims or particular sects. These strict restrictions on religious preaching of all kinds existed in these states through the 1950s.

In 1960, when Nigeria became independent, the new constitution provided for the first time full liberal rights including freedoms of religion, expression, and association. Notwithstanding the constitutional guarantees, a third attempt to control religious preaching occurred soon afterwards with the establishment of Islamic Religious Preaching Boards, likely as a consequence of a form of gerrymandering against minority religious groups in the region. The recurrent pattern throughout the Northern Region in the 1960s and 1970s was that the *Ulama* of the dominant local Islamic groups persuaded the government to form councils – again composed of representatives of the dominant sects – with the authority to restrict preaching by minority sects.[18]

## *Kano*

Government regulation of Islamic religious preaching began in Kano in the 1960s when the *Ulama* of the dominant Sufi orders persuaded the Emir of Kano to convince the state government to regulate the preaching of the minority Gardawa. The first preaching board law in Nigeria was the Kano Local Government Authority (control of Qur'anic Interpretation and Admonishing) Rules 1970, also called the Kano State Local Government Authority Law No. 3 of 1970. It established the 'Interpretation and Admonishing Committee of Kano Local Government Authority' and required intending Islamic religious preachers to obtain permits, except for preaching to students in schools or other buildings. It penalized violation of the law with fines or up to six months' imprisonment.

In spite of the existence of this law that was, in theory, intended to minimize religious tensions in the region, the 1970s saw many skirmishes between members of the Izala and Tariqa Islamic groups. That era also saw the Gardawa Islamic groups re-emerge under Muhammadu Marwa Maitatsine, a peripatetic preacher who engaged in ferocious public preaching against other Islamic groups in the region. In 1980, the Maitatsine movement engaged in a militant uprising in Kano State, which the Nigerian Army quickly suppressed. It is unclear why the Islamic Preaching Board Law then in operation had not been used

17 Hale H. Middleton, 'Memorandum to Residents; Kano, Zaria, Sokoto and Niger. Missionary Activities in Muslim Centres', 13 December 1926. For example, the resulting proclamation of the Emir of Kano at the time reads as follows:

> Salutations to the people of the whole land of Kano, District Heads, Village Heads and peasantry, religious scholars and the entire male and female population of the land, as well as to the strangers (inhabiting the jurisdiction). Know that this is a decree from us to you. Let no man amongst you preach, no matter who he may be, in a city, on a road, or in towns, or in wards of towns, or in hamlets or villages. Whosoever wishes to preach, let him go to his mosque to preach there. Or let him preach in his house. Whoever shall disobey this decree and does what we have forbidden, let him blame no one but himself for what will befall him. Written in friendship on Friday the 3rd of Rajab, 1345 A.H.
>
> (7 January 1927)

Copies of these documents are on file with the author.

18 See Laremont at 3. See also Mohammad Sani Umar, 'Changing Islamic Identity in Nigeria from the 1960s to the 1980s: From Sufism to Anti-Sufism', in Louis Brenner, ed., *Muslim Identity and Social Change in Sub-Saharan Africa* (Indiana University Press 1993), 154–178.

to control Maitatsine, given that his violent preaching had been apparent since 1973, or to control the earlier Izala and Tariqa confrontations.

The Kano State Council for Islamic Affairs Law 1982[19] repealed the 1970 law. Section 1 established the Kano State Council for Islamic Affairs under which committees were formed. It gave the governor enormous power: first, he appointed all members of the committee. The preaching board was comprised of 17 people all 'learned in Islamic Religious Knowledge', representing various constituencies: a chairman, three representatives of religious organizations from Kano City, one to represent the State Ministry of Education, one to represent the business interests, one from each area demarcated for the eight emirs in the State, one to represent the Council of Chiefs, one to represent the Department of Islamic Studies of Bayero University and other higher Islamic institutions, and a legal practitioner learned in both Islamic and common law. Second, he paid them such sitting and traveling allowances as he may determine. Third, it gave the governor power to give directions to the Council of a general or specific character concerning their responsibilities under the law.

The law was designed to promote religious stability in the state and to 'check religious activities'. The functions of the Council were to advise state and local governments on religious affairs and 'on ways to check religious activities', public enlightenment on Islamic religious matters through publications and the mass media, regulation of religious organizations through issuance of regulations and registration of religious organizations, and regulation of 'admonishing and interpretation' through issuance of regulations and permits.

The law provided for statutory standards for the grant of preaching permits and required applicants for registration, whether individuals or organizations, to comply with the provisions of the law and the conditions and regulations imposed by the Council. Permits were issued by the Council on such conditions and terms and in such manner as it deemed fit, and could be revoked where the organization or preacher failed to comply with the provisions of the law or with the conditions and regulations imposed by the Council or both, or on the basis of public interest. Upon revocation, the person was required to cease to admonish or interpret any Islamic religious text.

The law also provided prohibitions and penalties. It provided that no group could function as a religious organization unless it was registered, and that a valid permit was required for an admonisher to admonish or an interpreter to interpret any Islamic religious text orally in any language. Violations were penalized with fines, imprisonment, or both.

This law was repealed and replaced by Section 20 of the Kano State Religious Preaching Edict of 1985.[20] This 1985 law is still in operation in Kano State. It establishes Emirate Committees for Islamic Religious Preaching with memberships of at least seven people: a chairman and not fewer than six other members, all 'Islamic religious scholars of high repute'. As under the 1983 law, the governor appoints all the members, but this time in consultation with the Emirate Council, and pays them such allowances as he may dim fit. The governor may also make regulations for giving effect to any provisions of the law.

The law also establishes Local Government Subcommittees for Islamic Religious Preaching with memberships including the Chief Executive Officers of the Local Government Council as chairman, all District Heads in the Local Government Council, the Divisional Police Officer in the Local Government Area, the Chief Imam in the headquarters of the Local Government Area, the Education Officer in charge of Islamic Education in the

19 No. 7 of 1983, Kano State of Nigeria Laws for the Year 1983 – Supplement Part A, Secs. 43–47.
20 Kano State Law No. 7 of 1985, Cap 124 Laws of Kano State 1991.

Local Government Council, the Social Welfare Officer in charge of the Local Government Council, and two other members who shall be Muslims of high repute and well versed in Islamic religious matters. Except in the case of *ex officio* members, the members of the subcommittee are appointed by the Commissioner for Local Government in consultation with the Committee.

The function of the Emirate Committees is that, in cooperation with all other Committees of the State, they are to establish a uniform standard and practice for examination and qualification of Islamic religious preachers; to receive applications for preaching permits, to examine applicants, and to grant permits to those who qualify; to open and keep a register of preachers with their names and particulars; to revoke permits as appropriate; to receive applications for preaching permits and forward to the Emirate Committee; to keep a register of all holders of preaching permits in the Local Government Area; to monitor movement and activities of every holder of a preaching permit in the Local Government Area; and to cause the arrest of any person preaching without a permit or contrary to the conditions of his permit.

In terms of statutory standards for grant of a permit, the Committee may grant the application if it is satisfied that an applicant has the requisite knowledge and experience to be a preacher of Islamic religious injunctions; the applicant must be a Muslim scholar of high repute and capable of complying with the conditions attached to the preaching permit. Furthermore, the Committee may, in satisfying itself with respect to the qualification of the applicant, examine the applicant orally, in writing, or in such other manner as the Committee may consider fit. The Committee may, where it considers necessary, endorse on the permit such conditions or restrictions to which the holder shall be subject, including limiting the holder to preach with respect to a subject matter or period.

The Committee is empowered to revoke permits if it is satisfied that the preacher has violated the conditions attached to the preaching permit or any provisions of the law, if the preacher has obtained the preaching permit by fraudulent means, or if it is in the public interest to do so.

One innovation of the 1985 law is the provision on geographical reach of permits. It provides that a preaching permit shall entitle the holder to preach in the Local Government Council to which it relates or any part thereof as may be specified in the permit. But the Committee may, where it considers necessary, endorse on the permit a limitation restricting the preacher to preach only in any town or village, or a specified number of towns or villages.

On prohibitions, the law provides that no person shall preach any Islamic religious injunctions in any public place without a lawful preaching permit. All preaching shall be conducted in a calm and orderly manner, without preaching acrimony or abuse, including not publicly insulting or seeking to excite contempt of any religious denomination in such manner as may likely lead to disorder or breach of the peace.

As penalties, the law provides that any preacher who preaches without a valid permit, preaches in violation of any conditions or order imposed pursuant to the law, or publicly insults or seeks to excite contempt of any religious denomination in such manner as may likely lead to disorder or breach of the peace, shall be punished with imprisonment of not less than three years for a first offense, and not less than five years and a fine for the second or third offense.

### *Borno*

The Boko Haram movement started in Borno State in 2002 and later grew into a violent insurgency that threatened Nigeria and Africa at large, until the government introduced new strategies to confront it and largely eradicated it as of 2016. Like Kano, Borno State had its own Islamic Preaching Board Law in operation when Boko Haram erupted in the state. In fact, Borno State had enacted Islamic Preaching Board Laws in 1977 and again in 1981 apparently to control minority Izala preachers coming 'to criticize and make trouble'.[21] The Board, whose composition was similar to that of Kano, was to determine the qualification of preachers and to issue licenses to preach specific subjects. In theory, the Board did not discriminate based on sect but only ensured that a preacher was qualified to preach his chosen subject. Nevertheless, there were complaints of religious discrimination from those who had been refused licenses or had their licenses revoked.

In 2010, the new Borno State Islamic Religious Preaching Law was enacted in reaction to the Boko Haram problem. The Board consists of a chairman, one representative from each Emirate Council, six representatives of *Ulama* to be recommended by the Emirate Councils and approved by the governor, six other persons appointed by the governor on their personal merits, a representative of the Ministry for Religious Affairs, and a representative from each registered Islamic organization. Under Section 5, the functions of the Board are to determine and regulate the qualification required for any person to become an Islamic preacher or a Qur'anic interpreter and submit recommendations to the appropriate Emirate Council of satisfactory application received by them; to conduct examinations and set standards for any person desirous of becoming an Islamic religious or a Qur'anic interpreter; to compile and approve sets of Islamic religious poetry, songs, or literature that may be permitted in mosques or in public places; to regulate and determine the type of Islamic religious poetry, songs, or literature to be approved for public consumption and dissemination in public preaching or places of worship; and to carry out any other function that may be referred to it by the Council of *Ulama* in the state or by the state government.

Under the various laws in place since 1981, the Islamic Preaching Board has issued about 500 licenses.[22] Many people have preached without licenses and have not been prosecuted, including Boko Haram founder Muhammad Yusuf. Yusuf was apparently also on the board of the Borno State Sharia Implementation Committee in 2003 and had been collecting his allowances up to the time he was extrajudicially killed,[23] and he served on religious committees in Yobe State for which he collected salaries from the government while at the same time preaching that it was forbidden to do so. It is unclear why the government did not apply the preaching law to Yusuf long before Boko Haram's violent insurgency and Yusuf's assassination.

### *Niger State*

The first law on religious preaching in Niger State was enacted in 1979. The Islamic Religious Preaching Edict of 1985 replaced that law and remains the law in the state. Niger State's law, unlike others, also requires the licensing of *Mallams* (Islamic scholars), registration of their Islamic schools, and regulation of their movement.

The law provides for a board headed by a chairman, to be appointed by the governor, who shall be a person of unimpeachable character and unquestionable integrity and well versed in Islamic religious matters and reputed to be strictly adhering to Islamic religious

21 Sheikh Goni Mohammed Saad Ngamdu (North East Zonal Coordinator and Borno State Secretary General of Jama'atu Nasril Islam), in an interview with Philip Ostien on 12 May 2012. Copy on file with the author.

22 As of 2012.

23 Kadi Abubakar Imam (Kadi at the Sharia Court of Appeal, Maiduguri and the secretary of the management committee of the mosque of Al-Amin Daggash where Yusuf used to preach once a week), in an interview with Philip Ostien on 12 May 2012. Copy on file with the author.

teachings. The Board also consists of one person learned in Islamic religious matters to represent each Emirate Council, one person each to represent various Ministries such as Education and Justice, and two other persons learned in Islamic religious matters to be appointed by the governor.

The Board's functions are to determine and regulate the qualification, competence, and sincerity of any person to become an Islamic religious preacher or Mallam; to conduct examinations and set standards for any person desirous of becoming an Islamic religious preacher or a Mallam; to issue licenses and certificates to qualified Islamic religious preachers and Mallams; to exercise control over the movement of Islamic religious preachers and Mallams; to register all Islamic religious organizations in the State; to prescribe terms and conditions on licenses and certificates; to regulate and determine the types of Islamic religious poetry or songs to be approved for public consumption and dissemination in public places of worship; and to render advice to the Emirate Councils on Islamic religious matters.

Despite the existence of the law, the State has been reluctant to enforce it. For instance, the peaceful group Darul Islam was founded in 1993 as 'a pious community that was isolated as much as possible from the rest of the sinful world',[24] and gradually grew in number to about 4,000 people. They acquired land for their settlement from the government of Niger State legally, and mainly engaged in farming. They applied Maliki Sharia in all civil and criminal matters among themselves with the exception of *hudud* punishments: serious cases were handled by excommunication or by the police. They had their own *qadi* (Islamic judge), their own Islamiyya schools where they taught their children both Islamic and Western education, and their own hospitals. They were well known to the government of Niger State and had a peaceful disposition including in their religious preaching style, but they never sought licenses to preach and teach under the law.

In the heightened concern for security after the Boko Haram uprising in July 2009, the government of Niger State dislodged Darul Islam on 15 August 2009, raiding their settlements, detaining them in camps, and sending them back to their states of origin. The same government also dislodged another minority religious group, the Nibrassiya Huda Islamic group, in 2008. It is important to note that all this happened without any recourse to the Islamic Religious Preaching Board Law that was in operation in the state, which in theory could have intervened much earlier to avoid later conflicts.

## Constitutional framework

Section 38(1) of the Constitution of the Federal Republic of Nigeria 1999 (as amended) protects citizens'

> freedom of thought, conscience and religion, including freedom to change his religion or belief, and freedom (either alone or in community with others, and in public or private) to manifest and propagate his religion or belief in worship, teaching, practice and observance.

24 Philip Ostien, 'A Survey of the Muslims of Nigeria's North Central Geo-Political Zone', NRN Working Paper No. 1 (Nigeria Research Network (NRN)), Oxford Department of International Development.

Section 39(1) further provides that 'every person shall be entitled to freedom of expression, including freedom to hold opinions and to receive and impart ideas and information without interference.' and Section 40 provides that 'every person shall be entitled to assemble freely and associate with other persons.'

These rights are not absolute. Section 45(1) of the Constitution allows the State to derogate from them through laws that are 'reasonably justifiable in a democratic society (a) in the interest of defence, public safety, public order, public morality or public health; or (b) for the purpose of protecting the rights and freedoms of other persons'. This leaves plenty of room for the standard array of penal and other legislation that states may use to restrict citizens' enjoyments of these rights. This limitation clause is the basis of each state's authority to enact Preaching Board Laws.

Questions remain, however, about to what extent the state can legitimately restrict the enjoyment of free exercise of religion particularly. And since courts in Nigeria have not yet reviewed the constitutionality of the Preaching Board Laws in Nigerian states, it is unclear what criteria or judicial review mechanism would be employed in such a case. In addition to the question of whether the Islamic Religious Preaching Boards currently operating in these states comply with the Constitution of Nigeria, there are real questions about their compatibility with standard international human rights norms.

### *Judicial review in Nigeria*

In Nigeria, courts will generally invalidate a law that contravenes constitutionally protected fundamental rights, unless it is allowed by the limitation clause in Article 45 allowing laws that are 'reasonably justifiable in a democratic society (a) in the interest of defence, public safety, public order, public morality or public health; or (b) for the purpose of protecting the rights and freedom or other persons'. The Constitution does not define terms like 'reasonably justifiable' or 'public morality', however, leaving it to the courts to define them.

The approach of the Nigerian courts so far has been shapeless, so it is very difficult to predict what might happen if Religious Preaching Board Laws were challenged in courts. On matters of religion generally, the courts have shown an inclination toward American-style jurisprudence on judicial review of laws designed to limit free exercise rights. The case of *Medical and Dental Practitioners' Disciplinary Tribunal v. Okonkwo*[25] concerned a patient's rejection of blood transfusion because of his religious beliefs as a Jehovah's Witness. The Nigerian Supreme Court held that

> The right to freedom of thought, conscience or religion implies a right not to be prevented, without lawful justification, from choosing one's life, fashioned on what one believes in, and a right not to be prevented, without justification. The sum total of the rights to privacy and of freedom of thought, conscience or religion which an individual should be left alone to choose a course for his life, unless a clear and compelling overriding state interest justifies the contrary. The law's role is to ensure the fullness of liberty when there is no danger to public interest. Ensuring liberty of conscience and freedom of religion is important component of that fullness.[26]

25 (2001) 19 WRN 1.
26 *Medical and Dental Practitioners' Disciplinary Tribunal* at 25.

It is clear that the Supreme Court is attempting to set down a criterion for evaluating a state's restriction on freedom of religion. The phrase 'clear and compelling overriding state interest' echoes the 'strict scrutiny' approach used by the Supreme Court of the United States. The Court went on to say that the 'law's role is to ensure the fullness of liberty when there is no danger to public interest'. The question remains, though, what constitutes a 'clear and compelling overriding state interest' or a 'danger to public interest' in a Nigerian environment. In the event of a conflict between the right to free exercise of religion and the government interest, courts will have to exercise discretion in answering these questions.

The lack of a clear judicial mechanism does not always result in decisions favorable to free exercise of religion. In a case currently before the Court of Appeal, a court in Lagos State held, astonishingly, that the wearing of the hijab by female Muslim students infringes on the right of non-Muslim students who will feel inferior to the hijab-wearing students.[27] In another case, the Court of Appeal refused to allow a Jehovah's Witness to deny a blood transfusion for her child, condemning her attitude as 'illegal and despicable which must be condemned in the strongest terms'.[28] The important point here is that the courts in these cases either applied the reasonability test without specifying what constitutes 'reasonable', or left the reasoning unclear. There is simply no specific legal device for testing the reasonability of restrictions on free exercise of religion in Nigeria.

## International judicial standards of review

In construing the meaning of terms like 'justifiable' and 'reasonable in a democratic society', Nigerian courts are entitled to look elsewhere for guidance. While comparative constitutional analysis itself has no authority, it yields insights that can be persuasive to judges and other officials in Nigeria responsible for interpreting constitutional norms. Former Chief Justice of the Supreme Court Bello held that

> It has long been a cardinal principle of our constitutional law that on account of the unique character and diversity of our Constitution, the courts should always endeavour to find solutions to constitutional questions within the Constitution through its interpretation, but the courts may seek guidance as persuasive authorities from decisions of the courts of other common law jurisdictions on the interpretation and construction of the provisions of their Constitutions which are in par material with the relevant provision of our Constitution.[29]

The Supreme Court of Nigeria here underscores the relevance of 'persuasive authorities from… other common law jurisdictions'. While virtually every kind of legal system grapples with this type of problem, other common law jurisdictions use similar interpretative techniques and are perhaps most likely to have similar understandings of key texts.

On the other hand, universal principles like freedom of religion can and should be implemented in diverse ways in different cultural and historical settings. There are a range of options open to Nigeria, and it need not confine its perspective to one type of jurisdiction, but rather seek any perspective that relates well to the Nigerian context.

27 *Asiyat Abdulkareem & Others v. Lagos State Government & Others*, ID/151M/13 (17 October 2014), 13–14.
28 *Esunabor v. Faweya*, (2009) All FWLR (Pt.478) 380.
29 *Ogugu v. The State*, (1998) 1 HRLRA 167 at 189.

Nigeria's culture, experience, and state-religion relations differ significantly from the United States, so it is somewhat surprising that the Supreme Court has seemed to favor the US approach. One salient difference is that unlike the Nigerian Constitution, the US Constitution has no derogation clause. Instead, there are various tests created by the courts and legislative bodies for when a government action may infringe the free exercise of religion. Besides being inapposite to Nigeria's Constitution, these tests are complex and somewhat unwieldy as tools of comparison. For these and other reasons, the United States may not be the ideal legal system on which to model Nigeria's jurisprudence.

The ECtHR takes an approach more suitable to the Nigerian environment. Articles 8–11 of the European Convention on Human Rights (ECHR) protect various rights subject to derogation clauses similar to those in the Nigerian Constitution. All of them – including Article 9 protecting freedom of religion, conscience, and belief – contain some variation on the standard formulation that the limitations must be 'necessary in a democratic society' in the interests of national security, public safety, the protection of health or morals, or the protection of the rights and freedoms of others.

Over the years, the Strasbourg court has articulated five steps to evaluating whether a state action is justified by the limitation clauses: (1) identify the right; (2) identify the intrusion; (3) consider whether the hindrance is prescribed by law; (4) determine what objectives, legitimate aims, or interests are sought to be protected by the interference; and (5) decide whether the intrusion is necessary in a democratic society – in other words, whether the state gives cogent reasons for the interference and those reasons are proportionate to the limitation of the applicant's enjoyment of his right. The Court has also incorporated principles of state neutrality and impartiality, as well as protection for religious pluralism, into its human rights rulings.

### *'Prescribed by law'*

The 'prescribed by law' requirement ensures that the law is accessible to the citizen and unambiguous so as to enable the citizen to control his conduct: he must be able to foresee, to a degree that is reasonable in the circumstances, the consequences of a given action under the law. For domestic law to meet these requirements, it must protect against arbitrariness by public authorities. The law must define the scope of official discretion and the manner of its exercise.

### *'Legitimate aim'*

Both public order and the protection of the rights and freedoms of others have been upheld by the Strasbourg court as legitimate aims that might justify interferences with religious freedom. The Court has upheld the refusal to grant approval for access to slaughterhouses for the purpose of ritual slaughter, requiring state approval to set up a place of worship,[30] and refusing official recognition of a church[31] on grounds of public order. The Court has also recognized that some kinds of proselytism can be restricted in order to protect the rights of others.[32]

30 *Manoussakis and Others v. Greece*, App. No. 18748/91 (ECtHR, 26 September 1996).
31 *Metropolitan Church of Bessarabia and Others v. Moldova*, App. No. 45701/99 (ECtHR, 27 March 2002).
32 See, for example, *Larissis and Others v. Greece*, App. No. 140/1996/759/958–960 (ECtHR, 24 February 1998) § 44. But see also *Kokkinakis v. Greece*, App. No. 14307/88 (ECtHR, 25 May 1993).

### *'Necessary in a democratic society': margin of appreciation*

What does 'necessary' mean? In *Handyside v. The United Kingdom*,[33] the Court explained that 'while the adjective "necessary"... is not synonymous with "indispensable", neither has it the flexibility of such expressions as "admissible", "ordinary", "useful", "reasonable", or "desirable"'. The notion of necessity implies that the interference corresponds to a pressing social need. States have a certain 'margin of appreciation' in assessing whether such a need exists, but it is for the Strasbourg court to give the final ruling on whether a restriction is reconcilable with the rights protected by the ECHR.

The doctrine of 'margin of appreciation' can be defined as the degree of respect or error which the ECtHR allows to legislative, executive, administrative, and judicial bodies before it declares state actions invalid derogations of rights under the ECHR.[34] The Court clarified the doctrine first in the *Handyside* case, in which the Court considered whether a conviction for possessing an obscene article could be justified under Article 10(2) as a limitation on freedom of expression necessary for the 'protection of morals'. The Court stated,

> State authorities are in principle in a better position than the international judge to give an opinion on the exact content of those requirements (of morals) as well as on the 'necessity' of a 'restriction' or 'penalty' intended to meet them.... Nevertheless, Article 10 (2) does not give Contracting States an unlimited power of appreciation. The Court... is empowered to give the final ruling on whether a 'restriction' or 'penalty' is reconcilable with freedom of expression as protected by Article 10. The domestic margin of appreciation thus goes hand in hand with European supervision.[35]

The Court reasoned that allowing a 'margin of appreciation' for local authorities' decisions respects their superior knowledge and understanding of the specific issues at stake. Furthermore, each member state maintains its own unique constitution, laws, and instrumentalities bearing upon the protection of basic rights. The Court might also have mentioned language differences among member states as another reason for a sort of default position of deference toward local authorities.

In one example of the Court's awareness of variations in local norms across Europe, in the case of *Otto-Preminger-Institut v. Austria*[36] the Court noted that '[a]s in the case of "morals" it is not possible to discern throughout Europe a uniform conception of the significance of religion in society... . Even within a single country such conceptions may vary.'[37] In this case, an organization had been prevented from showing a satirical film due to concerns of offending Roman Catholics. The Court recognized that '[i]t is in the first place for the national authorities, who are better placed than the international judge, to assess the need for such a measure in light of the situation obtaining locally at a given time'.

33 *Handyside v. UK*, App. No. 5493/72 (ECtHR, 7 December 1976).

34 See Nilufar Shahpanahi, *Margin of Appreciation in [the] Context of Freedom of Religion (Article 9 of the European Convention on Human Rights) in the Interpretation of the European Court of Human Rights* (LLM thesis, University of Toronto 2011).

35 *Handyside* §§ 48–49.

36 *Otto-Preminger-Institut v. Austria*, App. No. 13470/87 (ECtHR, 20 September 1994).

37 § 50.

While upholding the local authority's decision, it noted that the margin of appreciation cannot be a wide one, and that while interference with the right to freedom of expression may exceptionally be permitted, it must be narrowly interpreted.[38]

Scholars have criticized this doctrine, arguing that the idea that contracting states are better placed to assess local values and their application to particular cases reflects unacceptable moral relativism and compromises the universality of human rights.[39] After all, the Court's supervisory function by definition must reduce the discretion of the states. In fact, the Court acknowledges that the scope of margin of appreciation varies depending upon which interest is being protected. In *Sunday Times v. UK*,[40] the Court held that the scope of the margin of appreciation is more narrow when the interest at stake is 'maintaining the authority and impartiality of the judiciary', which is objectively ascertainable, in contrast to the interest of 'protection of morals', which is subject to a wide variety of interpretations.[41] The scope of margin of appreciation would be even greater in cases of public emergency.

In other words, the scope of the doctrine will be wide when there is no European consensus on a particular interest, particularly where the case raises sensitive moral or ethical issues – for example, regulating the wearing of religious symbols in educational institutions. At the other extreme, the margin of appreciation for state interference is reduced almost to a vanishing point in certain areas, particularly those concerning the right to human integrity – for example, issues concerning one's private life.[42]

The margin of appreciation doctrine thus serves to keep a tight rein on state conduct in some contexts and a looser rein in others. It essentially allows the state to make the initial assessment of whether the intrusion is justified.

### *Neutrality and impartiality*

The Strasbourg court has emphasized the role of the state to remain impartial in its treatment of religious groups, noting that 'a failure by the authorities to remain neutral in the exercise of their powers... must lead to the conclusion that the State interfered with the believers' freedom to manifest their religion'.[43] The Court explained that

> in exercising its regulatory power in this sphere and in its relations with the various religions, denominations and beliefs, the state has a duty to remain neutral.... [A]ny evidence that the state has failed to act in such a fashion in its dealings with religious bodies will require justification under Article 9(2) if it is not to amount to a breach of Article 9.[44]

Not only should states remain impartial in their dealings with religious believers and organizations, but the Court has gone even further to suggest that states are under positive obligations with regard to the freedom of religion and belief. The Court has said that the state

38 § 48.

39 Jill Marshall, *Personal Freedom through Human Rights Law?* (Martinus Nijhoff/Brill 2009), 42.

40 *Sunday Times v. The United Kingdom*, App No. 6538/74 (ECtHR, 26 April 1979).

41 § 28.

42 See, for example, *Dudgeon v. The United Kingdom*, App. No. 7525/76 (ECtHR, 22 October 1981) and *Odievre v. France*, App. No. 42326/98 (ECtHR, 13 February 2003).

43 *Hasan and Chaush v. Bulgaria*, App. No. 30985/96 (ECtHR, 26 October 2000) § 78.

44 *Metropolitan Church of Bessarabia* § 116.

serves as 'the impartial organizer of the exercise of various religions',[45] and that its role is to ensure a 'level playing field' among believers (and between believers and non-believers).[46] It is not simply that the state remains neutral and impartial in its dealings with religions and believers; the state must ensure that religious life within the state is neutral and impartial. The state is a 'facilitator' of organizational and individual religious freedom.

An alternative model, which seems to be the dominant model now, takes a different approach, emphasizing the need for the freedom of religion and belief to be understood in the broader context of a democratic society. The Court has said that while

> freedom of thought, conscience and religion is one of the foundations of a "democratic society"...it may be necessary to place restrictions on this freedom in order to reconcile the interests of the various groups and ensure that everyone's beliefs are respected.[47]

In that sense, the requirement for neutrality and impartiality is a justification for, rather than merely evidence of, infringement on religious freedom in certain cases.

## Evaluating Nigeria's Islamic Religious Preaching Board Laws

With the ECHR framework in mind, it is clear that the current Islamic Religious Preaching Board Laws are deeply flawed.

In a constitutional democracy governed by the rule of law, the state is expected to be neutral and should operate by laws of general application and not laws that target a specific religion.[48] The Islamic Preaching Board Laws of Kano, Borno, and Niger States are designed to regulate Islamic religious preaching only. Furthermore, the power to appoint members of the Preaching Boards vests generally with the governors of the various states, in consultation with emirate councils where they exist. Because these governors and emirate councils represent the majority sects, this results in laws enacted by majority Islamic groups with the aim of burdening minority Islamic religious groups. In Kano and Borno, for example, the composition of the boards favors the established Sufi Islamic religious groups.

Another major problem is that the laws enable discriminatory practices because they lack criteria to determine the acceptability of religious preaching. In this sense, they are not 'prescribed by law'. In the exercise of their discretion, the Boards are vulnerable to bias especially concerning groups whose religious ideologies disagree with those of the majority.[49] Other concerns include that these laws allow governments to 'legitimately' silence their critics, which kills the open debate upon which healthy democracy relies, and allow a select few voices to monopolize the discourse on religion.

Indeed, state regulation of religious preaching in Nigeria has been characterized by discrimination against minority religious groups that heightens rather than alleviates conflicts

45 *Leyla Şahin v. Turkey*, App. No. 44774/98 (ECtHR Grand Chamber, 10 November 2005) § 107.

46 *Kokkinakis* and *Larrisis and Others v. Greece*, App. Nos 23372/94, 26377/94, and 26378/94 (ECtHR, 24 February 1998).

47 *Kokkinakis* §§ 31 and 33.

48 John C. Reitz, 'Freedom of Religion and Its Limitations: Judicial Standards for Deciding Particular Cases to Maintain the State's Secular Role in Protecting Society's Religious Commitments', in Philip Ostien, Jamila Nasir, and Franz Kogelmann, eds, *Comparative Perspectives on Shari'ah in Nigeria* (Spectrum 2005), 180.

49 See Richardson.

in the region. Furthermore, government negligence in actually enforcing the Islamic Religious Preaching Board Laws sows confusion and indicates an absence of a democratic culture. Such laws have proven to be impotent at best, and harmful at worst. As they stand, they cannot possibly be said to meet the requirements of 'reasonably justifiable in a democratic society' as required by the Nigerian Constitution or the requirements of neutrality, impartiality, or protection of pluralism expected under international human rights norms. The Preaching Board Laws of the states under study need to be amended to agree with free exercise norms and to qualify as reasonably justifiable in a democratic Nigeria.

## Conclusion

The re-assertive nature of religion in the public domain in Nigeria and the world indicates the indispensability of religion as a consideration in the maintenance of public order and security at the global level.[50] Part of the local experience of Nigeria for the past 20 years has been managing crises related to religion, but neither the government nor any of the victims has approached the court for judicial determination of the conflict. If and when that happens, the courts will have a chance to introduce a robust standard of review that perhaps might guide Nigerian states, religious organizations, and believers toward avoiding such conflicts in the first place. If and when courts have to resolve questions of competing rights and interests, they should use a balancing mechanism that recognizes the current role of religion and the local experience of countries. In particular, courts need to consider the state-religion pattern of a country as a factor. In other words, it is probably not practical or necessary to insist that states such as Nigeria with long histories of particular state/religion relationships discard those relationships in favor of secularism. If the right balancing test is applied, a state can protect that relationship in a way consistent with the Constitution and international human rights standards.

50 See Toft, Philpot, and Shah, eds, at 207–223.

# 13 Freedom of religious beliefs or religious freedom? The recent case law of the Polish Constitutional Tribunal

*Piotr Szymaniec*

Issues related directly or indirectly to religious freedom have been discussed by the Polish Constitutional Tribunal in almost 40 rulings since 1991.[1] In the 1990s and at the beginning of the present century, the most important cases concerned such matters as religion in schools,[2] abortion and the right of a doctor to refuse to perform some medical interventions due to conscientious objection,[3] Christian values in the public media,[4] the concordat with the Holy See,[5] the right to substitute military service and the realization of religious freedom during military service,[6] and finally, the return of property confiscated from churches and religious associations during the communist era.[7]

This paper contains an analysis of the latest decisions of the Polish Constitutional Tribunal regarding religious freedom against the background of earlier constitutional case law. Religious freedom has been the subject of four recent judgments: a judgment concerning the constitutionality of criminalizing the insult to religious feelings,[8] a judgment on a doctor's right to conscientious objection to performing a medical procedure,[9] and two judgments with arguably opposing outcomes in relation to ritual slaughter.[10] The aim of this paper is to discern whether the Polish Constitutional Tribunal has developed a general attitude toward freedom of religion evident in its case law.

## The insult to religious feelings

The insult to religious feelings is a controversial issue in Polish criminal law.[11] Article 196 of the Polish Criminal Code defines the crime of insult to religious feelings as follows:

1 On some issues related to these judgments, see Jerzy Oniszczuk, *Konstytucja Rzeczypospolitej Polskiej w orzecznictwie Trybunału Konstytucyjnego* ['Constitution of the Polish Republic in the Jurisprudence of the Constitutional Tribunal'] (Zakamycze 2000), 406–409.
2 K 11/90 of 30 January 1991 and W 16/92 of 17 March 1993.
3 U 8/90 of 15 January 1991, U 1/92 of 7 October 1992, and K 26/96 of 28 May 1997.
4 K 2/93 of 17 August 1993 and resolution W 3/94 of 2 March 1994.
5 U 5/94 of 6 December 1994.
6 P 12/02 of 13 February 2003.
7 SK 25/02 of 8 November 2005 and SK 70/05 of 22 May 2007 (concerning the Baptist Church in the Republic of Poland and the Polish Autocephalous Orthodox Church, respectively).
8 SK 54/13 of 6 October 2015.
9 K 12/14 of 7 October 2015.
10 U 4/12 of 27 November 2012 and K 52/13 of 10 December 2014.
11 In the Polish Penal Code of 6 June 1997, Chapter XXIV contains the offenses against the freedom of conscience and belief: discrimination based on belief or irreligiousness (Art. 194), malicious obstruction of the performance of religious acts (Art. 195), and insult to religious feelings (Art. 196).

> Whoever offends the religious feelings of other persons by outraging publicly an object of religious worship or a place dedicated to the public celebration of religious rites, shall be subject to a fine, the penalty of restriction of liberty or the penalty of deprivation of liberty for up to two years.[12]

Assigning criminal responsibility for this crime includes determining (1) whether the persons injured by the crime have religious feelings and what the content of those feelings is,[13] (2) whether the behavior of the perpetrator was of a public character, and (3) whether the behavior of the perpetrator was offensive in nature.

This provision is controversial, because it shifts the focus from the objective behavior of the perpetrator to the subjective conviction of the person who believes that his or her feelings were offended (to use the more technical language of the Polish criminal law, the subjective feelings of the victim become part of the objective side of this crime, and so they are of the same importance as the behavior of the perpetrator which was manifested in the external reality). In addition, the maximum penalty for this crime (two years of imprisonment) is also criticized as excessive.

One of the most publicized applications of this criminal statute concerned a statement by the pop singer Doda (Dorota Rabczewska). In an interview in 2009, she said that she does not believe in the Bible because 'it is hard to believe in something that was written by someone plastered by wine and smoking some herbs' ('ciężko wierzyć w coś, co spisał jakiś napruty winem i palący jakieś zioła'). Reports to the prosecutor's office were filed by the president of the National Sect Protection Committee, Ryszard Nowak, and Polish Senator Stanisław Kogut on behalf of the conservative party 'Law and Justice'. In 2012, Doda was convicted of the offense of insult to religious feelings and sentenced to pay the penalty of PLN 5,000 (about GBP 1,000).[14] The court of the second instance upheld the judgment.[15]

12 Act of 6 June 1997, Journal of Laws 1997, No. 88, item 553, as amended, www.imolin.org/doc/amlid/Poland_Penal_Code1.pdf (accessed 5 September 2016). The translation was slightly modified by the author.

13 It is understood that this provision requires at least two persons injured by the crime. See Natalia Kłączyńska, 'Rozdział XXIV. Przestępstwa przeciwko wolności sumienia i wyznania' ['Chapter XXIV. Crimes against the Freedom of Conscience and Belief'], in Jacek Giezek, ed., *Kodeks karny. Część szczególowa* ['The Criminal Code: Specific Part'] (LEX. A Wolters Kluwer Business 2014), 509. See also Rafał Paprzycki, 'Czy bluźnierca jest przestępcą? Rozważania na temat znamienia "przedmiotu czci religijnej" przestępstwa obrazy uczuć religijnych – art. 196 k.k.' ['Is the Blasphemer a Criminal? Reflections on the Element "An Object of Religious Worship" in the Formulating of the Crime of Insult to Religious Feelings – Article 196 of the Criminal Code'], (2008) *Palestra. Pismo Adwokatury Polskiej* ['Palestra: The Journal of the Polish Advocates'] (5–6) 81–90; Marcin Berent and Jakub Strzelecki, 'Niejednoznaczność wykładni znamion czynów zabronionych a zasada nullum ctimen sine lege. Rozważania na przykładzie i wokół przestępstwa obrazy uczuć religijnych' ['The Ambiguity of Interpretation of Elements of Criminal Deeds and the Principle of *Nullum Crimen sine Lege*: Thoughts Concerning the Example of the Crime of Insult to Religious Feelings'], in Marcin Berent, ed., *Współczesne problemy prawa i ekonomii z perspektywy teorii i praktyki* ['Contemporary Issues of Law and Economics from the Perspective of Theory and Practice'] (Wydawnictwo Kurii Prowincjalnej Zakonu Pijarów 2013), 14–17; Wojciech Janyga, *Przestępstwo obrazy uczuć religijnych innych ludzi w świetle współczesnego pojmowania wolności sumienia i wyznania* ['The Crime of Insult to Religious Feelings of Other People in Light of the Modern Understanding of Freedom of Conscience and Belief'] (Wydawnictwo Sejmowe 2010), 154–242; and Łukasz Pohl and Stanisław Czepita, 'Strona podmiotowa przestępstwa obrazy uczuć religijnych i jego formalny character' ['The Subjective Side of the Crime of Insult to Religious Feelings and the Formal Character of that Crime'], (2012) *Prokuratura i Prawo* ['Prosecution and the Law'] (12) 72–81.

14 'Doda skazana za "naprutych winem autorów Biblii"' ['Doda Convicted for "The authors of the Bible plastered by wine"'], wprost.pl, 18 June 2012, www.wprost.pl/328978/Doda-skazana-za-naprutych-winem-autorow-Biblii (accessed 5 September 2016).

15 In Poland, there was another famous case concerning the insult to religious feelings, this time resulting in a complete acquittal. The rock star 'Nergal' (Adam Darski) tore a Bible to pieces during a concert in 2007,

The Constitutional Tribunal ruled that Article 196 of the Criminal Code was in conformity with the Constitution.[16] The Court declined to examine whether the statute's term of imprisonment met the condition of proportionality, because the singer had been sentenced to a fine rather than imprisonment.[17] After quoting extensively the views of authors on the crime of insult to religious feelings and previous court rulings, the Tribunal rejected the argument that the law was not sufficiently precise, finding that all the elements of the offense were adequately defined in the legal norm. Simultaneously, the Tribunal noted, 'The alleged "fluidity" in the meaning of the notion of 'object of religious worship' [as stated in the constitutional complaint] can of course refer to such creeds that are not widespread in a given society.'[18] In this enigmatic sentence, the Tribunal seemed to say that the 'objects of religious worship' are well known in the case of religions that are widespread in society, as opposed to the 'objects of religious worship' of the 'niche' religions that are less common. This seems to leave open the possibility that the former might therefore enjoy greater protection under criminal law.

The Court did not examine the so-called 'chilling effect' caused by the existence of the crime, i.e. whether the provision might be an excessive restriction on freedom of expression, even though that issue was highlighted in the constitutional complaint. For this reason, the Tribunal's judgment was criticized by some lawyers (for example, the first Polish Ombudsman, Professor Ewa Łętowska[19]). The Tribunal held only that the insult to religious feelings is not part of the essence of freedom of expression.[20]

The applicant also complained that Article 196 of the Criminal Code protects only religious beliefs and does not protect other beliefs, such as philosophical beliefs, and is therefore a case of unequal protection. The Constitutional Tribunal agreed with the applicant that 'Art. 196 of the Criminal Code protects freedom of religion, and it does not protect the non-religious worldview' but added, 'That is so, however, not because [the provision] favors freedom of religion, but because only religious feelings are the subject of protection

---

a video recording of which was put online, and Nergal's behavior was claimed to have offended religious feelings. The Regional Court in Gdańsk, upholding the judgment of a lower court, acquitted the singer on 20 February 2014. In the decision of 5 March 2015 (II KK 274/14), the Polish Supreme Court upheld the acquittal. The Court stated that the singer's behavior could not be considered a crime because it was not public. Admission to the concert was possible only after buying a ticket, and everyone who bought a ticket knew what kind of show to expect. The Court held that 'an act addressed to a person or a group of people who have voluntarily agreed to contact with content that can lead to insult to religious feelings' is not a crime. However, a person who publishes such content, for example on the Internet, may be liable for the crime of insult to religious feelings. See also the decision of 5 March 2015 (II KK 274/14), *Biuletyn Sądu Najwyższego* ['Bulletin of the Supreme Court'], No. 9/15 of 8 October 2015, sn.pl/orzecznictwo/Biuletyn_SN/Biuletyn_SN_9_2015.pdf (accessed 30 October 2016). The judgment of the Supreme Court shows the importance of analyzing all the circumstances of the accused person's behavior.

16 SK 54/13 of 6 October 2015. The Reasons for the Judgment are extensive (as is characteristic of the Polish Constitutional Tribunal's decisions), but one third of its content (10 of 33 pages) consists of a summary of the facts and arguments presented in the case.

17 SK 54/13, Reasons for the Judgment, 12. The Tribunal suggested only in a nonbinding way an amendment of the provision, reducing the maximum criminal liability. See Reasons for the Judgment, 33.

18 SK 54/13, Reasons for the Judgment, 24.

19 See Piotr Szymaniak, 'Prof. Łętowska: Trybunał Konstytucyjny kręci na siebie bat' ['Professor Łętowska: The Constitutional Tribunal Makes a Rod for Its Own Back'], *Dziennik. Gazeta Prawna*, 12 October 2015, prawo.gazetaprawna.pl/artykuly/899039,prof-letowska-trybunal-konstytucyjny-kreci-na-siebie-bat.html and Ewa Siedlecka, 'Prof. Ewa Łętowska: Nadmiar wsparcia państwa i prawa szkodzi religii' ['Professor Ewa Łętowska: Excess Support from the State and the Law is Harmful to Religion'], *Gazeta Wyborcza*, 31 October 2015, wyborcza.pl/magazyn/1,124059,19113378,prof-ewa-letowska-nadmiar-wsparcia-panstwa-i-prawa-szkodzi.html (both accessed 5 September 2016).

20 SK 54/13, Reasons for the Judgment, 28.

by Article 196.'[21] It can be asked, however, whether the exclusive protection of religious feelings does mean preference for religion. In the judgment, the Tribunal upheld broad protection of religious feelings by means of criminal law and at the same time implicitly admitted that such a protection will benefit in practice primarily the followers of 'mainstream' religions for whom there is no problem defining the 'objects of religious worship'.

## Conscientious objection of doctors

The conscientious objection of doctors and their right to refuse to perform specific medical treatments, such as abortion, due to convictions of conscience have occasionally arisen in the jurisprudence of the Polish Constitutional Tribunal since the early 1990s.[22] These issues became the subject of consideration in a judgment of 7 October 2015.[23] The National Medical Council – the organization of professional self-government for physicians – lodged the constitutional complaint and protested two aspects of the conscience clause in Article 39 of the Act of 5 December 1996 on the Professions of Doctor and Dentist: (1) the language restricting doctors' right to conscientious objection in situations where the delay in performing certain actions 'could lead to the danger of losing the patient's life, serious damage to the body or serious health disorder' and in 'other cases of urgency', and (2) the requirement that an objecting physician refer the patient to an alternative provider of the service.[24] The background of the complaint was the case of Professor Bogdan Chazan, the director of Holy Family Specialist Hospital in Warsaw, who in 2014 refused to perform an abortion in the case of a severe defect in the fetus (one of the few situations in which abortion is legal in Poland)[25]

21 SK 54/13, Reasons for the Judgment, 26.
22 See U 8/90 of 15 January 1991.
23 K 12/14.
24 Journal of Laws 2015, item 464.
25 The issue of abortion in Poland is regulated by the Act of 7 January 1993 on Family Planning, Human Embryo Protection and Conditions of Permissibility of Abortion (Journal of Laws 1993, No. 17, item 78, as amended), which was influenced by the social teaching of the Catholic Church. The law allows performing abortions only in certain exceptional cases, i.e. when there is a high probability of a grave and irreversible impairment of the fetus or an incurable life-threatening disease, when the pregnancy is a result of a crime (e.g. rape or incest), or when the pregnancy endangers the life or health of the pregnant woman (Art. 4a). See Ewa Weigend and Eleonora Zielińska, 'Das neue polnische Recht des Schwangerschaftsabbruchs: politischer Kompromiß und juristisches Rätselspiel' ['The New Polish Abortion Law: Political Compromises and Legal Riddles'], (1994) 106 *Zeitschrift für die gesamte Strafrechtwissenschaft* (4) 213–226. The law is referred to as the 'abortion compromise'; however, it can be seen as an uneasy compromise because the law has been criticized both by the right-wing political forces (according to whom it is too liberal) and by the left (for whom it is too conservative), and none of the political forces have been strong enough to impose a change in the law. Moreover, opinions are divided even within political factions. The October 2016 rejection of a bill in the Sejm that would have introduced more stringent antiabortion provisions is the sign of the stability of the 'compromise'. See 'Sejm odrzucił projekt ustawy antyaborcyjnej. 428 posłów głosowało, za odrzuceniem 352, przeciw 58, wstrzymało się 18' ['The Sejm Rejected the Project of the Anti-Abortion Bill: 428 Deputies Voted, 352 Deputies Were for the Rejection, 58 were Against, 18 Abstained'], Polskie Radio, 6 October 2016, www.polskieradio.pl/5/3/Artykul/1676660,Sejm-odrzucil-projekt-ustawy-antyaborcyjnej-428-poslow-glosowalo-za-odrzuceniem-352-przeciw-58-wstrzymalo-sie-18 (accessed 30 October 2016). It must be emphasized that the Constitutional Tribunal in the judgment of 28 May 1997 (K 26/96) pointed out that human beings enjoy protection even in the prenatal period, and, consequently, allowing the performance of abortion for such reasons as 'difficult living conditions' or a 'difficult personal situation' of the woman would lower the standard of the protection of life in a manner that would be drastic and unacceptable in a democratic state ruled by law. On this basis, the Constitutional Tribunal declared unconstitutional the Act of 1993 introduced by the Act of 30 August 1996 amending the law on family planning, protection of the human fetus, and conditions of permissible abortion and amending certain other acts (Journal of Laws 1996, No. 139, item 646; an amendment was

and refused to provide information about other hospitals where such a medical intervention could be performed.[26]

In explaining its judgment, the Tribunal emphasized the fundamental importance of freedom of conscience which includes both religious and non-religious beliefs. The Court laid out the basic reasons for respecting freedom of conscience. The first is 'to ensure freedom of adoption by a person the complex of views and moral, philosophical, religious, social rules, and to act in accordance with them; forcing to act contrary to conscience would be a violation of the inalienable dignity of a man.' The second purpose is to 'ensure that no one will force others to submit to the dictates which are considered by each person – in her conscience – to be valid'.[27] Therefore, freedom of conscience includes the ability to 'refuse the obligation imposed under the law with reference to scientific, religious or moral beliefs'.[28] The Tribunal held, however, that sometimes the realization of the conscience clause could lead to 'violations of the law and to chaos'.[29] The issue of this thread, however, was not developed in the reasoning.

Accepting the position of the Supreme Medical Council, the Tribunal challenged the view of the Attorney General and the Minister of Health that conscientious objection concerns only exceptional situations and is a 'privilege' of doctors that may be regulated by statute. According to the Tribunal, such a view is manifestly inconsistent with the standards of international law, as well as the right to freedom of conscience contained in Article 53 paragraph 1 of the Polish Constitution of 1997.[30] On this basis, the Tribunal ruled that Article 39 is unconstitutional because it overrides the doctor's conscience not only in situations where the delay in performing certain actions 'could lead to the danger of losing the patient's life, serious damage to the body or serious health disorder', which is justified, but in 'other cases of urgency', which the Court found to be too far-reaching a limitation on conscientious objection. The Tribunal also held that the requirement of a written notification to the superior by a doctor who intends to use the conscience clause is unconstitutional.

Unlike in the case of the judgment on the insult to religious feelings, in this case the Tribunal considered the chilling effect of the law. The Tribunal stated that the obligation to report to a superior

> may in some cases lead to restrict the freedom of conscience, especially when the employer is interested in hiring only a doctor who performs all the medical procedures. In such a situation, a doctor who applies for admission to work, in order to increase the chance of acceptance, indeed could refrain from exercising freedom of conscience.[31]

---

proposed by the left-wing coalition). See Krzysztof Wiak, *Ochrona dziecka poczętego w polskim prawie karnym* ['Protection of an Unborn Child in the Polish Criminal Law'] (Redakcja Wydawnictw Katolickiego Uniwersytetu Lubelskiego 2001), 186–202 and 225–227. The Constitutional Tribunal thus acted as the guardian of the 'compromise' of 1993.

26 On Bogdan Chazan, see 'Prof. Bogdan Chazan wydał oświadczenie' ['Professor Bogdan Chazan Issued a Statement'], wiadomosci.wp.pl, 10 June 2014, wiadomosci.wp.pl/kat,1342,title,Prof-Bogdan-Chazan-wydal-oswiadczenie,wid,16669183,wiadomosc.html?ticaid=118018 (accessed 30 October 2016).

27 K 12/14 of 7 October 2015, Reasons for the Judgment, 4.2.4.

28 4.4.1.

29 4.2.4.

30 4.4.2–3.

31 7.1.5.

Moreover, the Tribunal held that the obligation the law imposed on the doctor of informing the patient about the possibility of obtaining such a medical procedure from another doctor or medical entity was also unconstitutional. The Tribunal judged that informing the patient was too great a burden for a doctor invoking the conscientious objection clause. This point was in line with the position of the Supreme Medical Council that requiring a doctor to inform patients about the possibility of obtaining a medical procedure almost makes the doctor responsible for the procurement of this procedure. This point of the judgment aroused much controversy and was challenged in the dissenting opinion by Judge of the Tribunal Professor Sławomira Wronkowska.

This judgment is based on a very broad view of freedom of conscience. The question arises whether the same broad protection of freedom of conscience would be granted if the background of the case did involve conscientious objections that conformed to the teachings of the Catholic Church, which has a dominant position in Poland.

## Religious slaughter

In the case of ritual slaughter, there is a conflict between the right to freedom of religion and the duty of humane treatment of animals. Since the thirteenth and fourteenth centuries, Jews in Polish lands have exercised the right to perform ritual slaughter.[32] But regulations on the protection of animals were quickly introduced in Poland after it regained its independence after World War I. The first legal act concerning that matter was the regulation issued by the President of the Republic of Poland in 1928.[33] However, the act was silent about the definition of 'humane' killing of animals. Some argued that the humane treatment of animals meant the prohibition of ritual slaughter as practiced by the Jews[34] and two other small minorities, the Polish Tatars (Muslims)[35] and the

32 See Michał Rudy, Andrzej Rudy, and Paweł Mazur, *Ubój rytualny w prawie administracyjnym* ['Ritual Slaughter in Administrative Law'] (Kancelaria Prawna Result 2013), 23–26 and Sławomir Mroczkowski and Anna Frieske, *Prawna ochrona zwierząt gospodarskich* ['The Legal Protection of Farm Animals'] (Wydawnictwo Uczelniane Uniwersytetu Techniczno-Przyrodniczego 2015), 100.

33 Rozporządzenie Prezydenta RP z dnia 22 marca 1928 r. o ochronie zwierząt ['The Regulation of the President of the Republic of Poland of 22 March 1928 on Animal Protection'] (Journal of Laws 1932, No. 42, item 417).

34 In 1931, there were 3,113,000 Jews in Poland; by 1939, it had increased to 3,400,000. See Jerzy Tomaszewski, *Zarys dziejów Żydów w Polsce w latach 1918–1939* ['The Outline of the History of Jews in Poland 1918–1939'] (Wydawnictwo Uniwersytetu Wrocławskiego 1990), 9–12. The status of Jewish communities was determined by the Regulation of the President of the Republic of 14 October 1927 On the Legal Status of the Organization of Jewish Communities in the Republic with the Exception of Polish Silesia Province ['Rozporządzenie Prezydenta Rzeczypospolitej z dnia 14 października 1927 r. o uporządkowaniu stanu prawnego w organizacji gmin wyznaniowych żydowskich na obszarze Rzeczypospolitej Polskiej z wyjątkiem województwa śląskiego'] (Journal of Laws 1928, No. 52, item 500). See Tomaszewski at 37–41.

35 Tatars, professing mainly Sunni Islam, were brought to the lands of the Grand Duchy of Lithuania by the Grand Duke Vytautas (Witold) at the end of the fourteenth century. Then, between the first half of the fifteenth century and the beginning of the sixteenth century, Tatar settlements were also developed in the Mazovia region, which was one of the core Polish lands. The aim of bringing Tatars into Polish lands was to increase the military force. Tatars could freely practice their religion, and the vast majority of them belonged to the nobility (although they did not have the right to vote because they were not Christians). From the seventeenth century onward, the Polish Tatars did not use the Tatar language. See Artur Konopacki, *Życie religijne Tatarów na ziemiach Wielkiego Księstwa Litewskiego* ['The Religious Life of the Tatars in the Lands of the Grand Duchy of Lithuania'] (Wydawnictwo Uniwersytetu Warszawskiego 2010), 27–58. In the interwar period, the Tatar minority amounted to about 6,000 people. Tatars served in the Polish Army, and the special First Tatar squadron of the 13th Regiment of the Vilnius Uhlans was created in 1936. The Muslim Religious

Karaims.[36] Not infrequently, especially in the second half of the 1930s, when anti-Semitic attitudes increased in Polish society, the humane treatment of animals was a pretext to publish anti-Jewish commentary.[37]

The Act on the Slaughter of Farm Animals in Slaughterhouses was enacted on 17 April 1936.[38] The Act stated that the animals should be stunned before slaughter or in another way rendered unconscious before exsanguination.[39] The Act did not place a total ban on ritual slaughter as advocated by nationalist politicians at the time, but it did leave details of the conditions for ritual slaughter to be promulgated by regulations.[40] The Minister of Agriculture and Agrarian Reform, in consultation with the Minister of Religion and Public Education and the Minister of Internal Affairs, issued the regulation on the methods and conditions of ritual slaughter of farm animals on 26 August 1936.[41] It listed the conditions

Union was established in 1925, and the Act on the Relation of the State to the Muslim Religious Association in the Polish Republic was adopted by Parliament on 21 April 1936 (Journal of Laws 1936, No. 30, item 240). See Ali Miśkiewicz, *Tatarzy polscy 1918–1939* ['The Polish Tatars 1918–1939'] (Państwowe Wydawnictwo Naukowe 1990).

36 The Karaim minority in interwar Poland amounted to over 1,000 people living in a few religious communities in the Vilnius region and one in Vilnius. The Karaims were of Turkish origin, and they accepted a modified version of Judaism derived from the doctrine of Anan ben David (who taught in Babylonia in the eighth century). Karaims settled in the Grand Duchy of Lithuania at the end of the fourteenth century. See Waldemar Możdżonek, 'Karaimi – naród zapomniany' ['Karaims – The Forgotten Nation'], (2007) 5 *Forum Politologiczne* ['Political Science Forum'] 267–282; Szymon Pilecki, 'Karaimskie życie rodzinne, społeczne i religijne okresu międzywojennego, czas wojny, decyzje o przyjeździe do Polski' ['Karaim Family, Social and Religious Life during the Interwar Period, A Time of War, The Decisions Concerning Coming to Poland'], in Beata Machul-Telus, ed., *Karaimi* ['Karaims'] (Wydawnictwo Sejmowe 2012), 34–52; Andrzej Rykała, *Mniejszość religijna – mniejszość etniczna – wspólnota kulturowa. Uwagi na temat genezy, aktywności i tożsamości Karaimów w Polsce* ['Religious Minority – Ethnic Minority – Cultural Community: Remarks on Origin, Activity and Identity of Karaims in Poland'], (2011) 11 *Acta Universitatis Lodziensis Folia Geographica Socio-Oeconomica* 1–18. In 1936, the relations between the State and the Karaim Religious Association were regulated by a separate law, which remains valid today. See Act of 21 April 1936 on the Relation of the State to the Karaim Religious Association in the Polish Republic (Journal of Laws 1936, No. 30, item 241). It is worth pointing out that the Karaim Religious Association is one of 15 churches and religious associations that have their status regulated by statute. The total number of the Karaim minority in Poland is currently about 350 persons, whereas the Karaim Religious Association in Poland had 131 members as of 2008. See Lucyna Nowak et al., *Ludność. Stan i struktura demograficzno-społeczna. Narodowy Spis Powszechny Ludności i Mieszkań 2011* ['Population: Status and Demographic and Social Structure. The National Census of Population and Housing 2011'] (Główny Urząd Statystyczny [Central Statistical Office of Poland] 2013), 264 and 267; and Grzegorz Gudaszewski and Mariusz Chmielewski, eds, *Wyznania religijne. Stowarzyszenia narodowościowe i etniczne w Polsce* ['Religious Denominations: Ethnic and National Associations in Poland'] (Główny Urząd Statystyczny 2010), 20.

37 Such an attitude was presented by Father Stanisław Trzeciak (1873–1944), the author of several publications on ritual slaughter in the 1930s. See Stanisław Trzeciak, *Ubój rytualny czy mechaniczny? Opinia rzeczoznawcy wypowiedziana na posiedzeniu Komisji Administracji i Gospodarki Sejmu Polskiego 5.III.1936 r.* ['Ritual or Mechanical Slaughter? Opinion of an Expert Presented at the Meeting of the Committee on Administration and Economy of the Polish Sejm on 5 March 1936'] (Warszawa 1936); Stanisław Trzeciak, *Ubój rytualny w świetle Biblii i Talmudu* ['Ritual Slaughter in Light of the Bible and the Talmud'] (Warszawa 1935); and Rudy, Rudy, and Mazur at 28–31.

38 Journal of Laws 1936, No. 29, item 237.

39 Art. 1. This legal act, quite progressive for the times, indicated that the animal could not be introduced to the place of slaughter before the preparations for the immediate slaughter were complete. In addition, the exsanguination could only be started after complete loss of consciousness by an animal, and the flaying of an animal was not allowed until it had been declared dead (Art. 2 paras. 1–3).

40 Art. 5.

41 Journal of Laws 1936, No. 70, item 504.

required at the time of slaughter, as well as the possibility of limiting the number of ritual slaughter acts in proportion to the needs of the population. It also required an administrative license for performing the slaughter of meat for export.[42]

Subsequent attempts to ban ritual slaughter were made in 1938 and 1939. The Act on the Prohibition of Ritual Slaughter, which was to enter into force in 1942, was passed by the Sejm, but the Senate – the upper chamber of Parliament – could not pass it before the outbreak of World War II.[43] During the communist period, ritual slaughter was not forbidden in Poland but was performed only to fulfill the needs of the small Jewish and Muslim religious communities in a few places in Poland.

Ritual slaughter became a hot topic in public debate once again in 2012. It should be emphasized that current opponents of ritual slaughter rely only on arguments concerning the humane treatment of animals (including various positions on what humane treatment means). In the newspaper debate, much was written about the fact that both the Jewish communities and representatives of the Muslim Religious Association engaged in mass production of meat performed large-scale ritual slaughter for mass production of meat intended for export. Sometimes the debate turned very emotional; law professor and politician Genowefa Grabowska argued that ritual slaughter should be assessed simply as 'barbaric'.[44] However, unlike in the years before World War II, none of the voices in this debate can clearly be interpreted as anti-Jewish or anti-Muslim.[45]

The issue of ritual slaughter has risen to the Constitutional Tribunal frequently in recent years. It was the subject of two judgments[46] and two orders.[47] The view of some activists and journalists that ritual slaughter in Poland was on the industrial scale was undoubtedly important during debates in media on this matter.[48]

The first of the mentioned judgments concerned § 8 paragraph 2 of the Regulation of the Minister of Agriculture and Rural Development dated 9 September 2004 on the

42 Furthermore, the Regulation of 5 September 1936 on the Requirements for the Trading of Meat from Ritual Slaughter (Journal of Laws 1936, No. 70, item 505) required that retailers of meat from ritual slaughter obtain an administrative license. See Rudy, Rudy, and Mazur at 34–36 and Mroczkowski and Frieske at 100–104.

43 Tomaszewski, supra note 33 at 44.

44 On the public debate on ritual slaughter in Poland, see Rudy, Rudy, and Mazur, supra note 31 at 5–15.

45 Currently, the Jewish minority in Poland is very small, so its social impact is also limited. According to the census of 2011, 7,508 people consider themselves Jews, including those who claimed two national origins. Only some of these actively practice Judaism: the Union of Jewish Religious Communities in Poland counted 430 members in 2011. See Nowak et al. at 260–262 and Gudaszewski and Chmielewski at 24. As for the Muslim minority, the Muslim Religious Association in the Republic of Polish unites mainly the Polish Tatars, and since 1936, it has had its legal status regulated by statute. In 2008, it had 106 members (however, according to the census of 2011, 1,916 people claimed affiliation to the Tatar nationality). Four other Muslim religious communities were registered in the register of churches and other religious associations maintained by the Minister of Internal Affairs. Their members are Muslim immigrants or converts. These include the Association of Muslim Unity ['Organizacja Jedności Muzułmańskiej'] (Shia Islam, registered in 1990, 107 members in 2008), the Muslim League in the Polish Republic ['Liga Muzułmańska w Rzeczypospolitej Polskiej'] (Sunni Islam, registered in 2004, 110 members in 2008), the Muslim Association 'Ahmadiyya' ['Stowarzyszenie Muzułmańskie "Ahmadiyya"'] (Ahmadiyya Islam, registered 1990, 109 members in 2008), and the Islamic Assembly of Ahl-ul-Bayt ['Islamskie Zgromadzenie Ahl-Ul-Bayt'] (Shia Islam, registered 1990, 108 members in 2008). See Nowak et al. at 265 and Gudaszewski and Chmielewski at 22. Thus, the issue of ritual slaughter may directly concern fewer than 2,000 people in Poland.

46 U 4/12 of 27 November 2012 and K 52/13 of 10 December 2014.

47 P 34/13 of 24 February 2015 and K 32/14 of 3 November 2015.

48 This issue was highlighted in the dissenting opinion of Judge Wojciech Hermeliński to the judgment of 10 December 2014.

Qualifications of Persons Entitled to Professional Slaughter and on the Conditions and Methods of Slaughter and Killing of Animals,[49] which allowed ritual slaughter despite the fact that the Act on the Protection of Animals required rendering animals unconscious before slaughter. The Constitutional Tribunal held that this regulation exceeded the authority delegated to the ministry by the relevant statute, which clearly intended to prohibit slaughter of conscious animals.[50] Moreover, the argument of the Ministry of Agriculture that such a regulation was indicated by Directive 93/119/EC of 22 December 1993 on the Protection of Animals at the Time of Slaughter or Killing[51] was not accepted.

The constitutionality of a possible regulation of ritual slaughter was not considered by the Court, because Council Regulation (EC) No. 1099/2009 of 24 September 2009 on the Protection of Animals at the Time of Killing,[52] which allowed ritual slaughter,[53] was to enter into force on 1 January 2013. Consequently, after this date, ritual slaughter would be legal again, unless a different provision was to be adopted in Polish law (the Tribunal noted that the E.C. regulation allowing ritual slaughter did not prevent national legislation that might prohibit it). In fact, after 1 January 2013, the Polish Ministry of Agriculture notified the European Commission that ritual slaughter would remain prohibited. The Tribunal's judgment was highly criticized by Jewish organizations, as well as a small Muslim minority in Poland, mainly Polish Tatars.

The legal situation after the discussed judgment was changed by another judgment of 10 December 2014.[54] The proceedings were commenced by an application of the Union of Jewish Religious Communities in the Polish Republic, which challenged the Act on the Protection of Animals. In the judgment, the Tribunal held that the relevant provisions of the Act that precluded ritual slaughter were unconstitutional, but limited ritual slaughter only to slaughterhouses.[55] This decision was controversial because it jeopardized the ability of Muslims to perform ritual slaughter during the feast of Eid al-Adha (Kurban Bayrami).[56]

This decision of the Constitutional Court highlights the question of whether legislation (including EU law) may interfere with ritual slaughter or whether it is protected as part of the right to freedom of worship recognized by the State. Both the Jewish and Muslim communities in Poland have explicit legislative guarantees of freedom of worship: the Act of 20 February 1997 on the Relation of the State to the Jewish Communities in the Polish Republic[57] guarantees the 'free exercise of the principles of religion',[58] and Article 3 paragraph 2 indicates that 'Jewish communities govern themselves in their own matters by their domestic law'. Article 2 of the Act of 21 April 1936 on the Relation of the State to the Muslim Religious Association in the Polish Republic recognizes a similar right for Muslims.

49 Journal of Laws 2004, No. 205, item 2102, as amended.

50 The constitutionality of these provisions was challenged by the Attorney General.

51 OJ 340, 31 December 1993, 21.

52 OJ 303, 18 November 2009, 1.

53 Art. 4 para. 4.

54 K 52/13.

55 The Constitutional Tribunal found that Article 4 paragraph 4 of the Council Regulation (EC) No. 1099/2009 of 24 September 2009 on the Protection of Animals at the Time of Killing has superiority over Polish domestic law. According to that provision, ritual slaughter ('slaughter prescribed by religious rites') can be allowed by the Member States, 'provided that the slaughter takes place in a slaughterhouse'.

56 The Polish Tatars prefer the term 'Kurban Bayrami'.

57 Journal of Laws 2014, item 1798.

58 Art. 3 para. 1.

The Constitutional Tribunal's judgment seems to show that to some extent, such interference is nevertheless possible.

## Conclusion

It is difficult to discern a consistent attitude toward freedom of conscience and religion in the case law of the Polish Constitutional Tribunal. On the one hand, the Tribunal strongly protects freedom of conscience, manifesting itself in the right of a doctor to object to performing medical procedures that offend his conscience. On the other hand, far less protection is apparently given to freedom of worship as an element of freedom of religion (especially if the religious activities are performed by minority religious associations, as in the case of ritual slaughter). Moreover, the Tribunal upheld the wide protection of religious feelings by means of criminal law (the crime of insult to religious feelings), at least where the religious feelings reflect a mainstream religion. In recent years, therefore, it appears that the Tribunal has been somewhat less protective of the religious rights of relatively small religious associations and members of minority religious groups than of mainstream religious beliefs and practices.

Despite the somewhat incoherent understanding of religious freedom apparent in the case law, the core protection of freedom of conscience and religion, based primarily on Article 53 of the Constitution of 1997, seems to be stable. These protections are closely connected with the model of the relations between the State and churches and religious associations, determined by Article 25 of the Constitution, which is not a pure model of separation of church and state.[59] Most notably, the strong position of the Catholic Church affects, for example, the far-reaching – perhaps excessive – protection of religious feelings by means of criminal law[60] and the presence of a broad conscience clause for doctors. Yet despite some signs of preference for the dominant church, religious freedom is generally protected in Poland, and such situations as the attempt to ban ritual slaughter are exceptional.

59 See Paweł Borecki, *Geneza modelu stosunków państwo – Kościół w Konstytucji RP* ['The Origins of the Model of State-Church Relations in the Constitution of the Republic of Poland'] (Wydawnictwo Sejmowe 2008), 383–391; Ryszard M. Małajny, 'Regulacja kwestii konfesyjnych w Konstytucji RP (refleksje krytyczne)' ['Regulation of the Confessional Issues in the Constitution of the Republic of Poland (Critical Thoughts)'], in Roman Tokarczyk and Krzysztofa Motyka, eds, *Ze sztandarem prawa przez świat. Księga dedykowana Profesorowi Józefowi Wagnerowi von Igelgrund z okazji 85-lecia urodzin* ['With the Banner of Law throughout the World: Festschrift in Honor of Professor Wenceslas Joseph Wagner von Igelgrund on the Occasion of His 85th Birthday'] (Kantor Wydawniczy Zakamycze 2002), 289–304. In the literature, this model is sometimes called the model of 'friendly' separation between church and state.

60 It is worth pointing out that due to the completely different religious structure of society in the Czech Republic, the crime of the insult to religious feelings is absent in the Czech criminal law. The Criminal Code of the Czech Republic (Trestní zakonik 40/2009 Sb.) contains only one crime concerning religious freedom, i.e. the crime of forcing someone, by violence, threat of violence, or threat of other harm, to participate in a religious act or preventing someone, in the same way, from participating in a religious act (Sec. 176).

# 14 Christonormativity as religious neutrality

## A critique of the concept of state religious neutrality in Germany

*Armin Langer*

## Religious neutrality v. Christonormativity

### *The Ulusoy affair*

In the summer of 2015, Betül Ulusoy (age 26), a German Muslim law school graduate of Turkish origin, was denied a trainee job in the municipality of the district of Neukölln, Berlin. Although she was notified on 2 June of an offer to work at the city district of Neukölln, when Ulusoy went to the district on 3 June to sign the contract, she was denied the position because she was wearing a headscarf. Ulusoy was told that her scarf constituted an 'official business problem' that needed to be 'assessed'.[1] The city council pointed to Berlin's Neutrality Law that prohibits religious symbols in police forces, government services, and public schools. The law was passed in 2005 by the governing Social Democrats[2] in order to, theoretically, protect the 'religious neutrality of the state'.

Lawmakers argue that the Berlin Neutrality Law frees the state from religion, as in France under the concept of *laicité*. But no state is free from religion. Berlin is not a religiously neutral city, and Germany is not a religiously neutral country. Betül Ulusoy and the other Muslim women must put down the hijab in the name of state neutrality, but I argue that bans like this do not achieve neutrality at all. Rather, they reflect Europe's underlying Christonormativity.

A hundred years ago, the European elite was referring not to state neutrality but to Christianity as a requirement for participation in society. In the nineteenth century, German Jews, the only major non-Christian group at the time, were expected to give up their rituals, like head-covering, circumcision, or ritual slaughter, because these were rejected by the mainstream Christian society. Many Jews converted to Christianity in order to be accepted by society. Others decided to separate themselves from Europe and turned to Jewish Nationalism: Zionism.

Today, German lawmakers don't point to Christianity as a standard if someone wants to be involved in society, but to so-called state 'neutrality'. However, the ruling concept of this state neutrality is not plurality but homogenization – that is, the state does not retreat from religion, but rather enforces conformity with the underlying Christonormativity, to the detriment of non-Christians.

1 Enes Bayrakli and Farid Hafez, *European Islamophobia Report 2016* (SETA Foundation for Political, Economic and Social Research 2016), 192, www.islamophobiaeurope.com/.

2 The Social Democratic Party of Germany (*Sozialdemokratische Partei Deutschlands*, or SPD) is a Third Way political party in Germany.

Recognizing that so-called 'neutrality' is sometimes a manifestation of Christian norms might achieve a change in discourse on multiculturalism. Realizing what Europe's mainstream norms are might lead to a better understanding of the situation of those who have different norms. A peaceful coexistence is possible only on a basis of mutual understanding – which has to start with self-reflection.

### *The Berlin Neutrality Law*

An excellent example of the so-called religious 'neutrality' is the Neutrality Law of the State of Berlin. The law, introduced in the state senate in 2005 by a coalition of the Social Democrats and the democratic socialists,[3] prohibits 'any visible religious or ideological symbols that signal (to) the spectator an affiliation to a specific religious or ideological group and any noticeably religious or ideologically imbued garments'. The law categorically bars all public school teachers (including kindergarten teachers in the case of parental objections), police officers, judges, court officials, prison guards, district attorneys, and civil servants working in the judicial system from wearing visible religious or ideological symbols or garments. The same law forbids discrimination based on religion.[4]

Half of the German *Länder* (states) have no laws like the Berlin Neutrality Law. In these states, wearing religious symbols can be prohibited on a case-by-case basis if there is evidence that the person's behavior contravenes religious neutrality. But between 2004 and 2007, seven other *Länder* besides Berlin passed so-called neutrality bills. Many of them, for example those in Baden-Württemberg, Hessen, and Northern Westphalia, explicitly targeted Islamic symbols. These laws forbade all religious symbols in public offices except for Christian and Jewish ones, since these two cultures have, according to the argument for the bill, always been part of Western culture.[5] The discrimination against non-Christian and non-Jewish religious people is obvious in these cases.[6] After the complaints of a Muslim woman who had been denied a job at a public school because of her headscarf, the Constitutional Court of Germany proclaimed in January 2015 that a general ban on headscarves for teachers at state schools is not compatible with the Constitution and Northern Westphalia had to suspend its neutrality law.[7]

This 2015 decision by the Constitutional Court had no effect on the Berlin Neutrality Law, since Berlin's law doesn't explicitly differentiate between traditional Western religions and the 'non-Western' ones. Instead, the Berlin Neutrality Law forbids all religious symbols in public offices, making it theoretically compatible with the Constitution and the concept of equality.

3 The Left (*Die Linke*), also commonly referred to as the Left Party (*Linkspartei*), is a democratic socialist political party in Germany.

4 W. Cole Durham, Jr. et al., eds, *Islam, Europe and Emerging Legal Issues* (Ashgate 2012), 199.

5 I have to note that I strongly disagree with the statement that Judaism has always been a part of Europe. My opinion is based not only on the persecution of the Jews for 2,000 years on the European continent, but also on the fact that there is not a single Jewish thinker or writer who became part of Western culture without having been assimilated or baptized. This supposed 'Judeo-Christian' identity of Europe is, in my opinion, merely a political tool that instrumentalizes Jews to exclude Muslims from the society.

6 Ruth Wodak, Majid KhosraviNik, and Brigitte Mral, eds, *Right-Wing Populism in Europe: Politics and Discourse* (Bloomsbury Academic 2013), 66.

7 Constitutional Court of Germany, 'A General Ban on Headscarves for Teachers at State Schools Is Not Compatible with the Constitution', Press Release No. 14/2015 (13 March 2015), www.bundesverfassungsgericht.de/SharedDocs/Pressemitteilungen/EN/2015/bvg15-014.html (accessed 18 June 2016).

But theory and practice are not the same. Although the Berlin Neutrality Law seemingly treats all religious identities equally, in practice it discriminates against Muslims while hardly affecting Christians at all. According to a 2006 study of the Konrad Adenauer Foundation, 97% of German Muslim women who cover their heads consider it to be a religious obligation.[8] While the Jewish community of Berlin is very small and the number of halachically observant Jews is negligible, any observant Jews who did wish to work in government offices would likewise be required to remove the kippah or other religious covering. In contrast, the Berlin Neutrality Law allows the wearing of small pieces of jewelry, which would allow small crucifixes worn around the neck – one common way German Christians display their religion.[9] No wonder, then, that all the reports of discrimination under the Neutrality Law have affected Muslims, notably women, rather than Christians.

There have also been reports of private companies denying jobs to Muslim women with headscarves, referencing the Neutrality Law of Berlin. In 2009, the international NGO Human Rights Watch released a study on the effects of neutrality laws in Germany. Scholars and representatives of women's groups and Muslim groups interviewed suggested that headscarf bans by the state have generally aggravated discrimination against women who wear headscarves. A 2007 study by the Berlin State Equality Office indicates that the ban in Berlin affects women wearing headscarves in other employment sectors not covered by the law, and has an impact on the headscarf debate in general. Even Fritz Felgentreu, spokesperson at the time for legal affairs of the Social Democratic faction in the Berlin House of Representatives, acknowledged in 2008 that the danger of discrimination is real. However, as he pointed out, restrictions in the private sector based on the headscarf would be unlawful and the victims should go to court with these cases.[10]

In short, although the Berlin Neutrality Law is seemingly neutral and appears to treat all religions equally, its regulations are compatible with Christian theology but not with Islamic or Jewish ones. The law wasn't created in a vacuum, but in the context of certain norms that have been influenced by history. The terms 'neutral' or 'religious neutrality' might describe the law's purpose, namely, to avoid the appearance that the government favors any religion. In theory, this seems to be rational, as the separation of state and church made the emancipation of the religious minorities possible. But banning religious symbols in public office neither guarantees state neutrality – in fact, it discriminates against certain religious groups – nor contributes to respect and harmonious coexistence. For this reason, I suggest that the terms 'neutral' and 'religious neutrality' do not accurately describe the law's effects.

## *Christonormativity v. Christian hegemony*

In 1991, social theorist Michael Warner popularized the term *heteronormativity* to describe the belief that people fall into distinct and complementary genders with natural roles in life. Heteronormativity assumes that heterosexuality is the norm and that intimate relations are fitting only or mostly between people of opposite sexes. According to the theory, being heterosexual is so taken for granted that most people don't even realize the term has only

8 Frank Jessen and Ulrich von Wilamowitz-Moellendorf, eds, *Das Kopftuch – Entschleierung eines Symbols?* (Konrad-Adenauer-Stiftung 2006), 23–24.

9 Durham et al., eds, at 200.

10 Human Rights Watch, *Discrimination in the Name of Neutrality: Headscarf Bans for Teachers and Civil Servants in Germany* (2009), 50.

existed for just over 100 years. Heteronormativity thus describes 'how social institutions and policies reinforce the presumption that people are heterosexual and that gender and sex are natural binaries'.[11]

If a society is heteronormative, it doesn't necessarily mean that other sexual orientations are discriminated against. However, the non-heterosexual orientations are, at best, only tolerated, and never fully accepted. Even if in a country the institution of same-sex marriage is introduced and members of the LGBTQ community enjoy the same rights as their heterosexual counterparts, that doesn't mean that that particular society is not heteronormative but that the non-heterosexual orientations and institutions are tolerated. Only at the point where homosexuality or transsexuality is not considered to be 'other' can we speak of the end of heteronormativity.

To the analogy of the term heteronormativity, I suggest the usage of the term Christonormativity so we can better understand the nature of religious neutrality in a European context. Just like in the case of heteronormativity, where the mainstream discourse relates to a certain behavior as the standard, mainstream European society assumes that what it means by the term 'religious neutrality' is understood similarly by everyone. Christianity is so embedded in the European public discourse that it sets the norm; it defines everyday life for Christians and non-Christians alike, as I will present later. And as in the case of heteronormativity, Christonormativity doesn't necessarily force Christianity on the inhabitants of the country. A Christonormative society might very well tolerate other religious identities – or even embrace them. But it continues to view non-Christian norms as 'other'.

I have to note that I see a difference between Christonormativity and Christian hegemony, a distinction not always drawn by scholars in this field. One of the few books on the horizon that addresses these issues is Paul Kivel's *Living in the Shadow of the Cross – Understanding and Resisting the Power and Privilege of Christian Hegemony.* Kivel points out several examples from the United States where Christian traditions and values influence everyday life. He uses the term 'Christian hegemony' to refer to both the historical influence of Christian traditions and values on our contemporary narratives and the influence of current Christian organizations.

I find Kivel's terminology of 'Christian hegemony' too broad and would apply it only to the latter – the role of Christian institutions in society. A Christonormative environment, by contrast, is one whose traditions and values have historically been shaped by Christianity. Such a society, like the United States or Germany, might obviously promote and embrace Christian organizations and thus support Christian hegemony, but Christonormativity is only the foundation, not the building.

There is also a major difference between the group of people who actively participate in Christonormativity and those who participate in Christian hegemony. While most people who practice Christian hegemony also practice Christonormativity, the reverse is not true. To put it bluntly, virtually all Westerners practice Christonormativity simply by enjoying the weekend on Sunday, celebrating New Year's Eve on 31 December, etc. – they need not actually be Christians to do this. On the other hand, those participating Christian hegemony are linked to organized Christianity; they are members of Christian churches, church-run institutions, and lobby organizations close to the churches.

11 Victoria DeFrancisco, Catherine Palczewski, and Danielle McGeough, *Gender in Communication: A Critical Introduction* (Sage 2014), 16.

### *Different concepts of religiosity*

When Jan Stöß, the president of the Social Democrats in the State of Berlin, was asked by a journalist why he supports the Berlin Neutrality Law, he answered, 'Religion is a private issue.' According to Stöß, the Neutrality Law affects only the externalities but not the belief as such.[12] He emphasized that the Neutrality Law forbids all religious symbols, as did former interior senator of the State of Berlin, Ehrhart Köring, one of the legislators who presented the Neutrality Law in 2005: 'Muslim headscarves, Jewish skullcaps and Christian crosses may soon vanish from the workplace for a large number of the capital's public sector employees.... For us it was important not to differentiate between the religions.'[13] Unfortunately, the Berlin Neutrality Law *de facto* differentiates between the religions, since Stöß's and Köring's concept of religion which separates belief and 'externalities' (rituals) is itself a Christian concept.

One of the fundamental principles of Christianity has always been the emphasis on belief rather than rites. Jesus says, 'The sabbath was made for man, and not man for the sabbath,'[14] setting the focus of the law on meeting the individual's needs instead of on the ritual itself. In another passage, Jesus says,

> Love the Lord your God with all your heart and with all your soul and with all your mind. This is the first and greatest commandment. And the second is like it: Love your neighbor as yourself. All the Law and the Prophets hang on these two commandments.[15]

The founder of Christianity placed primary importance on inner aspects of religion rather than external rituals or requirements.

Christian theologies, especially the Protestant one, often place the emphasis on belief instead of rituals. The early doctrine articulated by Thomas Aquinas that salvation is possible by faith alone – *sola fide* – was later reintroduced by Protestantism, both Lutheran and Calvinist. Protestantism marked a major point in Christianity's turning inward to become a private matter, a question of personal conscience. In fact, one of the most common anti-Catholic critiques of the Protestant Reformers was that the Roman Catholic Church placed too much emphasis on the form of the sacraments instead of their meaning. Forms such as rituals or religious clothing were considered non-essential or even stigmatized as barbaric, primitive, or fundamentalist.[16] Jews, in turn, were considered worshippers of a barbaric god who demands primitive rituals like circumcision or ritual slaughter.

As noted earlier, one of the key arguments presented to oppose allowing religious symbols to be worn in public offices is that such a ban doesn't affect the individual's belief, which should be the proper locus of religion. For Christians, belief is the central question, an interior question, which doesn't have to be shown publicly.

However, this mainstream Christian concept is not found in all religions. For traditional Jews and Muslims, the interior level (belief) and the public level (practice, e.g. hijab) of religiosity are in cohabitation, or, in some cases, the focus is set on the latter only. In fact,

12 'Bei uns soll die Basis mitbestimmen', *Berliner Morgenpost*, 25 October 2015, www.morgenpost.de/berlin/article206327567/Jan-Stoess-Bei-uns-soll-die-Basis-mitbestimmen.html (accessed 1 September 2016).

13 Durham et al., eds, at 200.

14 Matthew 2:27.

15 Matthew 22:37–40.

16 Talal Asad et al., *Is Critique Secular? Blasphemy, Injury, and Free Speech* (Fordham University Press 2013), X.

Halachic Judaism posits the opposite: a Jew can have a place in the world to come without even believing in God, provided that he keeps the 613 commandments. The rabbis argued that belief is ideal, but it can't be forced and so it shouldn't be demanded. Many consider Judaism to be an orthopraxic religion which emphasizes the correct ethical and ritual practice as opposed to faith and grace.[17]

Since Christianity has different concepts of spirituality compared to Islam or Judaism, Christian-majority states err when they assume that they can apply the same notion of religiosity to Muslims or Jews. This ruling Christian concept might have worked seamlessly in more homogeneous European societies of the past, but our reality today is different and requires a more expansive notion of spirituality.

## The development of Christonormativity

### *The European-Christian symbiosis*

While acknowledging the religious complexity of European history, we can say that since the last days of the Roman Empire, Christianity has constituted the primary culture of the West. As Christianity spread, it came to constitute the mainstream discourse out of which the inexplicit, unconscious 'common sense' emerged.

For the greater part of two millennia, the European states were all confessional Christian states. Individuals were expected to follow the ruler's religion, at least if they aspired to any social standing. This influenced every aspect of culture, from arts and literature to sciences. Furthermore, the growth of kingdoms was at the same time regarded as the growth of Christianity. Thus, as Talal Asad points out, it was not merely Europe that the Ottoman Empire threatened but Christendom, since these two terms were used as synonyms.[18] Christendom was perceived as 'civilized', and its enemies were described as 'barbaric'.[19] The fourteenth-century Byzantine Emperor Manuel II Palaiologos infamously epitomized medieval prejudice against Islam: 'Show me just what Mohammed brought that was new and there you will find things only evil or inhuman, such as his command to spread by the sword the faith he preached.'[20] The Ottoman Empire's state religion, Islam, came to symbolize terror, with its demonic hordes of hated barbarians. Many Christian theologians actually criticized the treaties between European nations and the Ottoman Empire on the basis that Christians should not have pacts with infidels. The Ottoman Empire lurked as a threat on Europe's borders until the end of the seventeenth century.

We can see remains of this narrative to this day. Christianity is the core of European identity. When we hear the phrase 'European history', we don't automatically think of Jews (other than as victims) or about Muslims (other than being in Spain for a short period of time). In fact, we don't even think of Byzantium or Eastern Europe as much as we think of Rome and Western Europe. In many discourses, 'Europe' really stands for Western Europe and its form of Christianity.[21] Eastern Europeans realize this, which may be one reason politicians and historians from 'in-between' countries like the Czech Republic, Slovakia,

17 *Donald K. McKim, ed.,* Westminster Dictionary of Theological Terms *(Westminster John Knox Press 1996), 197.*

18 Talal Asad, *Formations of the Secular: Christianity, Islam, Modernity* (Stanford University Press 2003), 164.

19 Edward Said, *Orientalism: Western Conceptions of the Orient* (Penguin 1995), 59.

20 Ion Grumeza, *The Roots of Balkanization* (University Press of America 2010), 177.

21 Tone Bringa, *Being Muslim in the Bosnian Way: Identity and Community in a Central Bosnian Village* (Princeton University Press 1995), 167.

Poland, or Hungary emphasize that they are Central Europeans – i.e. closer to Western Europe – rather than Eastern Europeans. Muslims are either rejected by nationalists or tolerated by liberals, but never accepted as a natural part of Europe. Even Balkan Muslims, who have been part of Europe for centuries, often feel alienated from the continent. As Tone Bringa points out, Albanian, Bosnian, Bulgarian, Montenegrin, and Serbian Muslims are in some sense a contradiction, because Islam is foreign to the cultural definition of Europe.[22]

## *Christianity in state discourse*

Although Christianity doesn't play the same exclusive role in Europe that it used to, we find many proofs of its absolute relevance even today in our political establishment's discourses.

The first sentence of the Preamble of the Basic Law of the Federal Republic of Germany reads, 'Conscious of their responsibility before God and man,... the German people, in the exercise of their constituent power, have adopted this Basic Law'.[23] This reference to God sounds generic and inclusive. But given the historical context of this heavily Christian nation, it is hard to interpret the word 'God' as anything other than the Christian God. Some observant German Jews would not even write the word 'God', and the use of the singular rather than the plural does not represent German adherents to polytheistic religions. Furthermore, even if the references to God (*Gottesbezug*) could be interpreted as neutral among all religions, they would still exclude atheist citizens. Such references to God are found also in the constitutions of many German states, like the State of Baden-Württemberg, the Free State of Bavaria, and even the Free State of Thuringia, where the vast majority of the population are not members of any church.

Other countries of the European Union have similar references to God in the preambles. Some are even quite specific in invoking Christianity: the constitutions of the Czech Republic and the Republic of Slovakia refer to 'the spiritual heritage of Cyril and Methodius', two Byzantine Christian theologians. The Irish Constitution claims to be written 'in the Name of the Most Holy Trinity... from Whom is all authority and to Whom, as our final end, all actions both of men and States must be referred', and continues, 'We, the people of Éire, Humbly acknowledging all our obligations to our Divine Lord, Jesus Christ, Who sustained our fathers through centuries of trial'. The Hungarian and the Polish Constitutions emphasize the role of Christianity as building the identities of the two nations. All of these states, it should be noted, claim to be religiously neutral even as they pay special attention to certain religions in their foundational documents.

References to Christianity in the government context often include Christian symbols on official insignia. Christian symbols also adorn the flags of secular democracies like the Scandinavian states (Denmark, Faeroe Islands, Finland, Iceland, Norway, Sweden), all of which are based on the Danish flag, the *Dannebrog*, and as such contain a Christian cross, as does the national banner of Switzerland. The 'Union Jack', the flag of the United Kingdom, refers to three Christian patron saints: the patron saint of England, represented by the red cross of Saint George; the patron saint of Ireland, represented by the red saltire of Saint Patrick; and the patron saint of Scotland, represented by the saltire of Saint Andrew.[24]

22 Bringa at 7.

23 'Im Bewußtsein seiner Verantwortung vor Gott und den Menschen ... hat sich das Deutsche Volk kraft seiner verfassungsgebenden Gewalt dieses Grundgesetz gegeben'.

24 Jeroen Temperman, *State-Religion Relationships and Human Rights Law: Toward a Right to Religiously Neutral Governance* (Martinus Nijhoff 2010), 88.

Many German states have Christian symbols on their flags and coats of arms. The flag of the Free and Hanseatic City of Hamburg depicts a castle with three towers; on the middle tower, a cross recalls the fact that Hamburg used to be an archbishopric. The red cross on silver on the coat of arms of the Rhineland-Palatinate (*Reinland-Pfalz*) represents the Archbishop and Prince Elector (*Kurfürst*) of Trier, and the silver wheel on red, the so-called 'Wheel of Mainz', represents the Archbishop and Prince Elector of Mainz. The cross of the Archbishop and Prince Elector of Trier is also on the coat of arms of the Saarland. Yet even while displaying these symbols, all of these states forbid religious symbols in public offices (e.g. the Saarland explicitly forbids Muslim head-coverings in public offices), claiming to protect the neutrality of the state.

References to God in political discourse occur on a regular basis. In 2015, German Chancellor Angela Merkel referred to refugees fleeing to Germany as gifts of the Lord (*Herrgot*). In an article for the magazine of the German Lutheran Church, *Sonntagsblatt*, Merkel wrote that her belief in Jesus functions as her moral compass. When in December 2012 the former Federal Minister for Family Affairs, Kristina Schröder, said it doesn't matter whether people use the article 'der' (masculine) or 'das' (feminine) when referring to God, several members of the Conservative governing parties publicly expressed outrage that she would play with such holy terms, as one of the members of the German Bundestag described it. Both Merkel and Schröder are members of the party CDU (*Christlich-Demokratische Union Deutschlands*), the Christian Democratic Union of Germany, which has governed the Federal Republic of Germany since 2005 in coalition with the CSU (*Christlich-Soziale Union in Bayern*), the Christian Social Union of Bavaria. For more than a decade, Germany has been led by political parties whose very names claim Christianity as their foundation.

Besides Christian symbolism, one major example of the continuing influence of Christianity in Europe is the recognition of official (though not mandatory), state-sponsored Christian religions in many European nations: for example Catholicism in Liechtenstein, Malta, Monaco, and Vatican City; Anglicism in England; and Lutheranism in Denmark, Iceland, and Norway (until 2017).

To be clear, my purpose here is not to suggest that there should be no references to God or Christianity in the public sphere. I intend only to highlight them as evidence of the pervasive Christonormativity of modern Europe's political landscape.

### *Christianity in geography*

It would be nearly impossible to catalogue all the cities, districts, villages, and towns in Europe that have names of biblical origin or of Christian connotation. Even narrowing the focus to Germany alone, the list is daunting. I have collected a few examples – not meant to be exhaustive – and divided them into four categories:

1 Places with biblical names: Bethel, Jerichow, Jerusalem (district of Meiningen), Moabit (district of Berlin) ('Moab'), Montabaur ('Mount Tabor'), Salem (district of Lauenburg).
2 Places with names referring to biblical terminology: Eden (district of Diersbach), Engelsberg ('Mountain of Angels'), Engelsdorf ('Village of Angel'), Engelskirchen ('Church of Angels'), Engelstadt ('City of Angels'), Herrnhut ('the Lord's Watch'), Himmelpfort ('Gate of Heaven'), Himmelpforten ('Gates of Heaven'), Himmelreich ('Empire of Heaven'), Himmelspforten ('Gates of Heaven'), Himmelstadt ('City of Heaven'), Himmelsthür (district of Hildersheim) ('Gate of Heaven'), Höllental ('Valley of Hell'), Kirchengel ('Church Angel'), Lobetal ('Valley of Rejoicing'), Kreuzberg ('Mount of the Cross').

3 Places with names referring to biblical characters: Bad Marienberg ('Bath at the Mount of Mary'), Christdorf ('Village of Christ'), Christusgrün ('Green of Christ'), Hirten ('Shepherds'), Josefsthal ('Valley of Joseph'), Kasparzell ('Storage Place of Caspar'), Magdala, Mariaberg ('Mount of Mary'), Mariadorf ('Village of Mary'), Mariahütte ('House of Mary'), Marienberg ('Mount of Mary'), Marienfelde (district of Berlin) ('Field of Mary'), Marienmünster ('Monastery of Mary'), Marienthal (district of Zwickau) ('Valley of Mary'), Marienwerder, Melchiorshausen ('House of Melchior'), Sankt Pauli (district of Hamburg) ('Saint Paul'), Sankt Peter-Ording ('Saint Peter').
4 Places with names referring to Christian history: Allerheiligen ('All Saints'), Christenberg ('Mount of Christians'), Gelsenkirchen ('Church (on the River with the) Insects'), Heiligenberg ('Mount of Saints'), Heiligendamm ('Dike of Saints'), Heiligenhafen ('Port of Saints'), Heiligenkirchen ('Holy Church'), Heiligensee (district of Berlin) ('Sea of the Saints'), Heiligkreuz/Heiligenkreuz ('Holy Cross'), Kirchberg ('Mount of the Church'), Kirchhaslach ('Church-Haslach'), Klosterlechtfeld ('Field of the Monastery'), Lutheran ('Martin Luther'), Mönchengladbach ('Monks' River'), Münchberg/Müncheberg ('Mount of Monks'), München ('Monks'), Münchenbernsdorf ('Village of Monks'), Münster ('Monastery'), Münstermaifeld ('Monastery in Maifeld'), Neukirchen ('New Church'), Neunkirchen ('Nine Churches'), Neumarkt-Sankt Veit ('New Market-St. Vitus'), Nikolausberg ('Mount of St. Nicolaus'), Nikolausdorf ('Village of St. Nicolaus'), Oberkirch ('Upper Church'), Pfaffenhausen ('House of Priests'), Pfarrkirchen ('Parish Church'), Sankt Augustin ('Saint Augustine'), Sankt Bartolomä ('Saint Bartholomew'), Sankt Bernhard ('Saint Bernard'), Sankt Blasien ('Saint Blaise'), Sankt Egidien ('Saint Giles'), Sankt Englmar ('Saint Engelmarus'), Sankt Gangloff ('Saint Gangulphus of Burgundy'), Sankt Georg (district of Hamburg) ('Saint George'), Sankt Georgen im Schwarzwald ('Saint George in Schwarzwald'), Sankt Goar ('Saint Goar'), Sankt Goarshausen ('House of Saint Goar'), Sankt Ingbert ('Saint Ingobert'), Sankt Kilian ('Saint Kilian'), Sankt Nikolaus ('Saint Nicholas'), Sankt Wolfgang ('Saint Wolfgang'), Schwabmünchen ('Swabian Monks'), Tempelhof (district of Berlin) ('Court of the Templars'), Waldkirch ('Church of the Forest'), Waldmünchen ('Monks of the Forest').

This collection is not at all complete, but it provides a taste of the historical Christian influence on European geographical names. It should be noted that many of these towns, villages, and districts of cities have Christian symbols in their coat of arms, like crosses and depictions of churches or monks.

### *The Christian calendar*

Every year during Christmas, the Senate of Berlin places a huge Norwegian Christmas tree in front of the city council's spectacular building. Usually, the mayor inaugurates the tree in the presence of journalists and a crowd of Berliners. He or she ends the speech by wishing 'Merry Christmas' to everyone, and on the same evening the mayor's interns upload a jolly Christmas card to the mayor's Facebook page. The other district mayors of Berlin do the same. Some of Berlin's districts also place nativity scenes at the local city council buildings. Meanwhile, during all these Christianity-infused celebrations, under the Berlin Neutrality Law, not a single person working in the city council building is allowed to wear any religious symbols.

Good Friday, a Christian religious holiday commemorating the crucifixion of Jesus and his death at Calvary, is a widely instituted legal holiday in many Western countries. In Germany, dancing and horse racing are forbidden on Good Friday. The German association of public broadcasters, ARD, has since 1980 maintained a list of movies that are not allowed to be screened on this day, such as *Ghostbusters*, *Animal Farm*, and *Monty Python's Life of Brian*. Not even in the internationally acclaimed party city of Berlin, a city governed by the Berlin Neutrality Law, is it allowed to organize parties on this Christian holiday.

Not all evidence of Christonormativity in the European calendar is as obvious as the Christmas celebrations and Good Friday observances. Sometimes politicians will acknowledge the New Year's days of non-Christonormative cultures at other times of year – e.g. the Chinese New Year or the Jewish New Year – but the very fact that these holidays have to be referred to as 'Chinese' and 'Jewish' emphasizes that they are different from the 'normal' one. We do not call our New Year's Day the 'Christian' New Year, although that is what it is. The fact that everyone implicitly understands that is evidence of how taken for granted the Christian culture is. Other seemingly secular holidays such as Valentine's Day and Mother's Day have their own Christian roots in history.

Of course, none of these holidays is purely Christian. Many have non-Christian roots, and most have non-religious manifestations in the modern world, as these occasions have become part of the guiding culture (*Leitkultur*), not just religious observance. Yet even non-religious manifestations of a holiday like Valentine's Day or Christmas reflect traditions and values set historically by the Christian institutions that promulgated the holidays.

### *The impossibility of neutrality*

Seeing all these Christian symbols and references in official German contexts, one can't help asking: how can a state official who works for the City Council of the District of Kreuzberg ('Mountain of the Cross') in Berlin be religiously neutral? Under what definition of 'neutrality' could a teacher of a public school in Hamburg be called neutral when the coat of arms over the blackboard refers to the Roman Catholic Church? How could a policeman who swore his oath of office on the German Constitution which begins with a reference to God be religiously neutral? How can we say that official images and symbols represent entire communities or nations when they contain explicit references to religions that are not followed by a great many of the people they claim to represent?

Of course we cannot and should not try to erase history. People of non-Christonormative backgrounds in Germany have an obligation to respect its historical heritage and the rights of all citizens. A Shabbat-observant Jew should not rebel against the shops being open on Saturday, a traditional Hindu should not complain that the Berliner supermarkets are selling beef, and atheists may not demand that towns change their names to eliminate all references to their Christian heritage. But the natural corollary ought to be that the same respect is extended toward those of minority faiths. No one should be able to tell a Muslim woman who serves as a public clerk in the District of Kreuzberg ('Mountain of the Cross') to take off her head-covering in the name of religious neutrality. It is too late to be religiously neutral.

## The Jewish case of yesterday?

### *Integration v. assimilation*

'Integration is possible only through neutrality,' said Jan Stöß, president of the Social Democrats in the State of Berlin in a 2015 interview defending the Neutrality Law.[25] He claimed

25 'Nicht gegen den Islam', *Berliner Zeitung*, 28 September 2015, www.berliner-zeitung.de/berlin/interview-mit-jan-stoess-nicht-gegen-den-islam--sondern-fuer-gleichbehandlung-22303172 (accessed 1 September 2016).

that Muslim women can be integrated into German society only when they take off the head-covering in public offices. But as noted earlier, the Neutrality Law doesn't integrate anyone; it merely forces members of religious minorities to imitate the practices of the normative religion: Christianity. If they refuse, they are excluded from the system. Hence, the Neutrality Law is a tool not for integration, but for assimilation.

'Assimilation' is a word that is no longer used in mainstream German discourse because of its negative connotations, bringing to mind the (failed) historical attempts to assimilate the Jews of Germany. For centuries, the Jews in Europe have been perceived as the 'others'. By the end of the eighteenth century, if not earlier, Judaism had come to be perceived as a threat by all non-Jewish segments of society. For the anti-Semitic Conservatives, Jews represented society's every new tendency that caused insecurity (liberalism, capitalism, socialism); for the 'philo-Semitic' Liberals, Judaism was a reactionary identity that contradicted the Enlightenment idea of citizenship. Many of the European Enlightenment philosophers, such as Immanuel Kant, believed that Judaism was inferior to Christianity, and that the only way Jews – or 'Palestinians', as Kant called them – would escape their 'vileness' was through conversion.

The Humboldt brothers, influential German intellectuals, claimed that the rite of circumcision is the main issue that separates Jews from Western society and urged the Jews to abandon it. Both of them were Liberals who tried to encourage the Jews' assimilation. In 1831, Heinrich Paulus, professor of Oriental languages at the University of Heidelberg, wrote similarly that Jews must merge with Christians and discontinue circumcision, which served solely as a symbol of Jewish self-separation.[26] Other traditional Jewish rituals were also challenged, like the *Shechten* (ritual slaughter of animals). The opponents of Shechten were unshakable in their belief that the non-Jewish method of slaughter is more 'humane' than the Jewish one, and demanded that the Jews stop ritual slaughter.[27]

Of these attempts to eliminate Jewish practices, the German rabbi and author Ludwig Philippson wrote in 1872: 'This Equalization (*Gleichmacherei*) has only one goal: to create a political-social mush out of the human masses. It arises from the one-sidedness and ends as such; in the oppression of all free movements.'[28] Philippson played a role in the movement for Jewish enlightenment, the *Haskalah*, that emerged at the end of the eighteenth century. Philosopher Moses Mendelssohn, one of the main thinkers of the Haskalah, imagined a movement for Jewish integration, envisioning that Jews would be accepted by the Christian German society as Jews without having to give up their traditions. To reach this goal, the *Maskilim* (followers of the movement) made some compromises. They left the ghettos, started to speak German instead of Yiddish, and began to wear clothes similar to those of the rest of society.

Eventually Mendelssohn himself came to believe that despite all the efforts of the Haskalah, Jews would never be accepted by mainstream (Christian) German society unless they gave up their traditions, their language, and their religion.[29] Many Jews indeed chose what seemed the path of least resistance: assimilation, i.e. giving up Judaism. From the emergence of the Haskalah, assimilation had become the hope for normalization of Jews in

26 John M. Efron, *Medicine and the German Jews: A History* (Yale University Press 2001), 223.

27 Efron at 206.

28 '[Die] französische Gleichmacherei ohne Freiheit...will...einen politisch-sozialen Brei aus der Menschenmasse machen. Sie entspringt der Einseitigkeit und endet in solcher, in der Unterdrückung jeder freien Bewegung,' *Allgemeine Zeitung des Judenthums* (*AZJ*), 6 April 1872, 442.

29 Mattias Konzett, ed., *Encyclopedia of German Literature* (Fitzroy Dearborn 2000), 533.

Western and Central Europe. The generation before them had left Orthodoxy; finally a radical assimilation started, leading to mass conversions to Christianity. Some spoke of an epidemic of baptism among Jews in the nineteenth century. By the turning point between the nineteenth and twentieth centuries, almost all middle-class Jewish families in Berlin had converted to Christianity. In this way they gained access to public offices and social standing that had been inaccessible to them before.[30] The German poet Heinrich Heine was one of these Jewish converts to Christianity. Although he hesitated to join a group that had been oppressing his ancestors for centuries, he finally converted, calling the certificate of conversion to Christianity an 'entrance ticket to European culture'.[31]

### *The birth of Christonormative Judaism*

For Jews who wanted a less fraught relationship with the surrounding culture, there was a middle ground between small steps like dressing in Western clothing and reading German literature, and major changes like converting to Christianity. Some of the Maskilim realized that even if they left the ghettos and started reading Goethe next to the Talmud, they still would not be accepted by German society. So they created an 'updated' version of Judaism which they began to call Reform Judaism.

One of the pioneers of German Reform Judaism, philanthropist Israel Jacobson, founded the first Reform Jewish synagogue, the Hamburg Temple, in 1817. This synagogue introduced several radical changes in liturgy that reflected Christian norms. The language of the service became German instead of Hebrew and Aramaic, and the rabbis started to deliver long sermons on morals (also in German) instead of short Hebrew-language teachings on passages of the Tanach and the Talmud. Rabbis began to wear robes like their Christian 'colleagues', and services were accompanied by contemporary musical instruments commonly used in churches, such as organs or trumpets. The Brunswick Rabbinical Conference of 1844 officially abandoned the Sabbath Laws. Many Reform rabbis recommended that Jewish communities observe Shabbat on Sunday and appealed for an end to circumcision of newborns. Dietary laws were no longer considered to be obligatory. All this served to 'break down the barriers between Jewish and non-Jewish Germans',[32] albeit at the cost of Christianizing Judaism itself.

Early Reform Jewish thinkers reflected Christianity – especially Protestant Christianity – not only in liturgical aspects, but also in theology. The Reform rabbis started to abandon the concept of Jewish peoplehood and began to call themselves 'Germans of Mosaic faith', expressing full support for the German state. In 1845, the Frankfurt Rabbinical Conference decided to omit all the references to the return to Jerusalem and the rebuilding of the Temple from the prayers.

With these radical changes in Jewish practice, liturgy, and theology, Reform Jewish leaders created the Christonormative Judaism that might have been expected to be well received by mainstream German society.[33] But even these radical reforms didn't stop the deportations to

30 Werner Fölling, *Zwischen deutscher und jüdischer Identität – Deutsch-jüdische Familien und die Erziehung ihrer Kinder an einer jüdischen Reformschule im 'Dritten Reich'* (Springer Fachmedien 1995), 262.

31 Eliezer Ben-Rafael, Olaf Glöckner, and Yitzhak Sternberg, *Jews and Jewish Education in Germany Today* (Koninklijke Brill NV 2011), 22.

32 Steven Bayme, *Understanding Jewish History: Texts and Commentaries* (Ktav Publishing House 1997), 279.

33 I have to note that Reform Judaism today is much more traditional than in the nineteenth century. Except for synagogues of the Society for Classical Reform Judaism in the United States, most Reform Jewish synagogues today are keeping Shabbat and the dietary laws, and encourage circumcision.

the German death camps. Reforming Judaism to look more Christian simply did not achieve integration.[34]

Today, when voices demand a 'European' Islam, they actually mean a Christonormative Islam that places the emphasis on belief and not on rituals. Demanding that Jews become more Christian to participate fully in society did not work to integrate the Jews of the nineteenth century. It won't work with Muslims in the twenty-first century, either.

### *When integration is not possible: separatism*

> The idea of a general baptism is half jest and half earnest. I am permitted to say it, I who would not be baptised. But what about my son Hans? When I think of his future I am ready to admit that the pressure of his Jewishness will teach him much concerning humanity. But I ask myself whether I have the right to make life so superfluously difficult for him as it has become for me.

Theodor Herzl wrote this in 1893 in a letter to Baron Friedrich Leitenberger.[35] Herzl, who gave his son a typical Germanic name and didn't circumcise him, was embracing at the beginning of his career a complete desertion of Jewish identity – the program of full assimilation of the Jews. He himself came from a Reform Jewish family and wanted to be full member of Austro-Hungarian society.

Herzl was following the German Liberal agenda that we can see, for example, in the writings of Gustav Freytag, a Member for the National Liberal Party in the German Reichstag. Freytag opposed the anti-Semitic movement in Germany, because in his opinion, anti-Semitism hindered the process of Jewish disappearance. In the opinion of the contemporary Liberals like Freytag, assimilation was the key to end the Jews' persecution and isolation. In 1869, he wrote an essay evincing warm admiration for German-Jewish achievements in art and science, testifying to the Jewish potential once they were assimilated.[36]

However, after the Dreyfus affair, a notorious anti-Semitic incident in France, Herzl realized that Jews, no matter how assimilated they are, will be always perceived by non-Jews as Jews. Herzl came to reject his early ideas regarding Jewish assimilation and to believe that Jews must physically remove themselves from Europe. Thus, he began to develop the idea of political Zionism and came up with the idea of the *Judenstaat*, an independent state for Jews.[37]

It does not help to create a peaceful coexistence if only those acting like members of the mainstream society are fully recognized as citizens of that society. The demand for Christonormalization – hand in hand with anti-Semitism – led not to integration but to a separatist ideology, namely, Jewish nationalism or political Zionism. If a society wants the members of its minorities to be active and engaged citizens, it has to embrace them the way they are.

In 2015, when Ehrhart Körting, former interior minister of the State of Berlin and one of the core legislators who passed the Berlin Neutrality Law, was asked by the Berlin daily newspaper *Der Tagesspiegel* to evaluate the 10 years of the law, he was no longer enthusiastic about it: 'I'm not sure if this law didn't achieve the opposite of what we wanted, which was the emancipation of Muslim women and girls. On the contrary, it became an obstacle

34 Adolf Grünbaum, *Collected Works, Vol. I: Scientific Rationality, the Human Condition, and the 20th Century Cosmologies* (Oxford University Press 2013), 124.

35 André Chouraqui, *A Man Alone: The Life of Theodor Herzl* (Keter Books 1970), 62.

36 Jacques Kornberg, *Theodor Herzl: From Assimilation to Zionism* (Indiana University Press 1993), 20.

37 Victor Karady, *The Jews of Europe in the Modern Era: A Socio-Historical Outline* (Central European University Press 2004), 262.

for these women's integration in our society.'[38] Through personal meetings with several Muslim women, he realized that the law didn't help in integrating non-Christian people into German society as he originally intended, but in fact pushed them out. Muslim women would decline job offers at public schools before they would take off their head-coverings. Today, Körting supports removing the Neutrality Law and replacing it with a real integration policy that doesn't force Christian norms on non-Christian religious communities.

## Deconstructing Christonormative neutrality

My goal is not to criticize Christian norms *per se*, or to suggest that we discard them, only that we recognize that the West is not a religiously neutral entity. When members of German mainstream society speak of religious neutrality, their thinking moves along Christian norms and they imagine neutrality within Christian frames. Christianity is so embedded in the public discourse in Western Europe that it sets the norm. The dominant Christian heritage even influences religious discourse for non-Christians: I, for example, am a student of Jewish Theology, although most Jews would say that there is no such thing as theology in Judaism.

The neutrality offered by laws such as the Berlin Neutrality Law is only a kind of pseudo-neutrality that in fact forces the underlying Christonormativity upon non-Christonormative Berliners. Minority populations are asked to abandon aspects of their religious and cultural identity in order to have a place in society, not unlike how the Prussian society of a century ago required Jews to convert to Christianity if they wanted social access. Members of other faith traditions sometimes see only one way out of being marginalized: assimilation. But assimilation – that is, abandoning one's minority identity to conform with the prevailing culture – not only violates the integrity of the person but also provides a false hope of full acceptance in society. German Jews believed in the power of assimilation, but the horrors of the Shoah proved that it was not enough. Despite all their efforts, they were still regarded as foreign and undesirable.

In his essay 'Anti-Semite and Jew', Sartre writes that an anti-Semite and a representative of pseudo-neutrality have the same goal: a world without Jews.[39] There is reason to wonder if the goal of so-called neutrality laws in Europe is not actually religious neutrality, but a Europe without Muslims.

We need not try to erase the effects of two millennia of Christian dominance in Europe. We cannot create a new, non-Christonormative society out of whole cloth. But we can recognize that we live in a different epoch now than the one in which this Christonormativity formed. Individuals are not bound to follow the religion of their sovereign; we live in an unbundled age, in an age of fragmentation, to paraphrase Charles Taylor.[40] Every individual has the right to choose their own path. Instead of hindering that process, a truly neutral state should respect and empower it. We might eventually stop marginalizing non-Christians by telling them their religious practices are unwelcome even while they must tolerate the pervasive Christonormativity resulting from Europe's historical heritage. On the contrary, we might start to embrace them, creating a real inclusiveness in European society.

38 'Ich sehe mein Gesetz heute kritischer', *Der Tagesspiegel*, 13 March 2015, www.tagesspiegel.de/politik/ehrhart-koerting-zum-kopftuchurteil-ich-sehe-mein-gesetz-heute-kritischer/11502098.html (accessed 5 September 2016).

39 Jean-Paul Sartre, *Anti-Semite and Jew* (Schocken Books 1995), 55.

40 Charles Taylor, *A Secular Age* (Harvard University Press 2007).

# 15 Freedom of religious conscience and persuasion

## International law, domestic practice, and perspectives from Asia

*Li-ann Thio*

## Introduction

Religious conversion is a profound personal choice, entailing a fundamental reorientation in terms of relationships, meaning, and value. To followers of missionary religions, spreading their message through religious persuasion is integral to the right to manifest religious beliefs.[1] Religious proselytism and conversion are integral aspects of religious freedom, which rests on the core ideas of free conscience and voluntarism, and safeguards the right of all to have, not to have, or to change religious belief.

Religious freedom is facilitated by a constitutional state-religion arrangement oriented toward the religious 'free market', in which the government is impartial and makes room for religious groups to freely compete for and retain adherents through religious persuasion. Blasphemy, apostasy, and anti-propagation laws stand at odds with this religious liberty, embodying a 'protectionist' posture toward a favored religion, whether theistic or anti-theistic. Religious persuasion is pejoratively cast as deploying inappropriate methods of religious advocacy to win adherents from other ideologies.

Article 18 of the Universal Declaration of Human Rights (UDHR), the international human rights baseline, endorses voluntarism, explicitly recognizing that religious freedom 'includes freedom to change [one's] religion or belief'.[2] Early disquiet was expressed toward voluntarism by countries like Saudi Arabia, which abstained from voting to support the UDHR.[3] Certain Islamic nations assert that Muslims may not change their

1 Arcot Krishnaswami, 'Study of Discrimination in the Matter of Religious Rights and Practices' (1960), UN Doc E/CN.4/Sub 2/200/Rev 1.

2 On how Article 18 denotes a shift from the institutional protection of religious groups to individualized liberty of conscience, see Linde Lindkvist, 'The Politics of Article 18: Religious Liberty in the Universal Declaration of Human Rights', (2013) 4 *Humanity: An International Journal of Human Rights, Humanitarianism, and Development* 3, 429–447.

3 Article 1 of the Saudi Arabian Constitution (1992) identifies the Holy Quran and the Prophet's Sunnah (traditions) as the Basic Law; the State considers the UDHR contrary to Islamic law. The Constitution contains no religious freedom clause, and Article 34 requires citizens to defend 'the Islamic faith'. Notably, Foreign Minister Zafrullah Khan, an Ahmadi, voiced Pakistan's support for Article 18 before the General Assembly in 1948, citing a Quranic passage that supports free conscience ('Let him who chooses to believe, believe, and him who chooses to disbelieve, disbelieve') and pointing out that Islam was a proselytizing religion. See Mary Ann Glendon, *A World Made New: Eleanor Roosevelt and the Universal Declaration of Human Rights* (Random House 2001), 168. Khan later wrote, citing the Quran:

> [M]an is left to his own free choice in acceptance of the Truth. Faith is not commanded on the basis of authority, but is invited on the basis of understanding. (12:109) 'This is a Book that We have revealed to thee, full of blessings, that they may reflect over its verses, and that those gifted with understanding may

religion,[4] although dissenting Muslim perspectives exist.[5] Although religious freedom as embodied in Article 18 is considered by many to be binding international law,[6] dissonant voices clearly exist and challenge the universality of one of the oldest human rights norms.[7]

Today, alternative human rights declarations issued by the Organisation of Islamic Co-operation (OIC) and the Association for Southeast Asian Nations (ASEAN)[8] in 1990 and 2012, respectively, contain more restrictive religious freedom clauses. Article 10 of the Cairo Declaration on Human Rights in Islam (CDHRI)[9] states,

> Islam is the religion of true unspoiled nature. It is prohibited to exercise any form of pressure on man or to exploit his poverty or ignorance in order to force him to change his religion to another religion or to atheism.

This assumes the finality of the preferred divine religion and subjects all human rights to Shariah principles, including freedom of expression. This provision is incompatible with international law's guarantee of religious freedom and conscience.

Article 22 of the ASEAN human rights declaration (AHRD)[10] dilutes the more robust formulation in Article 18 UDHR, which includes the right to change religions and to

---

> take heed' (38:30). There is complete freedom to believe or to reject. 'Say to them: It is the Truth from your Lord therefore let him who will, believe, and let him who will, disbelieve' (18:30).... [T]hough the choice is free, the consequences of the choice follow in accordance with Divine law. No one is forced. Everyone must choose and seek the purpose of his life on the basis of faith or turn his back upon the Truth and destroy his soul, according to his choice.

Muhammad Zafrullah Khan, *Islam: Its Meaning for Modern Man* (2nd edn, Routledge 1980), 143–144, available at https://themuslimtimesdotinfodotcom.files.wordpress.com/2013/06/islam-itsmeaningformodernman.pdf (accessed July 2017).

4 'When a person who has reached puberty and is sane voluntarily apostatizes from Islam, he deserves to be killed'. *Reliance of the Traveller: A Classic Manual of Islamic Sacred Law* (Amana Corporation 1991), 595. In 1982, Rajai Khorasani, an Iranian official at the United Nations, stated that the UDHR was 'a secular understanding of the Judeo-Christian tradition' and that it was impossible for Muslims to implement it 'without contravening Islamic law'. David Littman, 'Universal Human Rights and "Human Rights in Islam"', *Midstream*, February/March 1999.

5 Karl Josef Parsch, 'Freedom of Conscience and Expression and Political Freedoms', in Louis Henkin, ed., *The International Covenant on Civil and Political Rights* (Columbia University Press 1982), 211. See Abdullahi An-Naim, 'Human Rights in the Muslim World: Socio-Political Conditions and Scriptural Imperatives', (1990) 3 *Harvard Human Rights Journal* 13. Surah 2:256 ('Let there be no compulsion in religion') is often cited in support of free choice in religion.

6 See Hurst Hannum, 'The Status of the Universal Declaration of Human Rights in National and International Law', (1996) 25 *Georgia Journal of International and Comparative Law* (1) 287.

7 Malcolm Evans, *Religious Liberty and International Law in Europe* (Cambridge University Press 1997).

8 This is composed of 10 Southeast Asian nations, excluding Timor Leste.

9 Cairo Declaration on Human Rights in Islam (5 August 1990). At least six of the 57 OIC members are from Asia (Malaysia, Indonesia, Pakistan, Bangladesh, Maldives, Brunei); Thailand is an observer state. See Robert Carle, 'Revealing and Concealing: Islamist Discourse on Human Rights', (2005) 6 *Human Rights Review* (3) 122–137, 131–133.

10 See Catherine Renshaw, 'The ASEAN Human Rights Declaration 2012', (2013) 13 *Human Rights Law Review* (3) 557–579. This reflects the regressive diminution of religious freedom in human rights instruments since the UDHR. Article 18 of the International Covenant on Civil and Political Rights (ICCPR) of 16 December 1966 includes the right to 'have or to adopt a religion' but makes no express reference to changing religion. The Human Rights Committee considers this implicit. See General Comment 22 on Article 18 (1994), UN Doc HRI/GEN/1/Rev.1, 35, which observes that 'manifest' also includes the 'freedom to prepare and distribute religious texts and publications'. Article 1 of the Declaration on the Elimination of All Forms of Intolerance and of Discrimination Based on Religion or Belief (25 November 1981), UN Doc

practice religion in community, in baldly stating: 'Every person has the right to freedom of thought, conscience, and religion. All forms of intolerance, discrimination and incitement of hatred based on religion and beliefs shall be eliminated.' The right to change or manifest one's religion goes unmentioned, although the preamble reaffirms commitment to the UDHR.

Some have argued that the freedom to change religious belief is a Western or Christian imposition on other cultures.[11] Certainly the premise underlying modern Western human rights norms regarding religious freedom is the Madisonian one: 'Religion… can be directed only by reason and conviction, not by force or violence,' and that religious freedom is 'an unalienable right' resting on 'the conviction and conscience of every man.'[12] That is, God creates the mind free and humanity has free will to choose who or what to believe in, or in other words, to exercise human agency in matters of conscience. This departs from the historical European practice of requiring subjects to adhere to their prince's religion (*cuis regio, eius religio*), based on the belief that political unity required religious unity. That notion has been superseded by the new orthodoxy, more compatible with the Madisonian view of religion based on conscience, that religious pluralism can secure political stability as citizens support a system that protects their freedoms.

This robust notion of religious liberty is severely truncated, however, without the freedom to hear alternative religious perspectives and change religious belief. This particularly affects the freedoms of religious minorities and individuals against a religious majority and the state that lends its power to a majority religion. The United Nations Special Rapporteur on Freedom of Religion or Belief in 2012 clarified that the right to conversion as part of the *forum internum* had 'the rank of an absolutely protected right'.[13] Accordingly, states have a duty to respect the right to convert by removing all punishment or administrative hurdles against converts, to protect this right against possible third-party infringement, and to 'promote a societal climate in which converts can generally live without fear and free from discrimination'.[14] Likewise, international human rights law opposes forcible attempts

---

A/RES/36/55, while mentioning the freedom to have a religion or belief of one's choice and not to be subject to coercion in this respect, does not expressly mention the right to change religion. See Donna Sullivan, 'Advancing the Freedom of Religion or Belief through the UN Declaration on the Elimination of Religious Intolerance and Discrimination', (1988) 82 *American Journal of International Law* (3) 387–520 and Natan Lerner, 'Proselytism and Change of Religion', in *Religion, Secular Beliefs and Human Rights* (2nd edn, Brill 2012), 119–166.

11 T.N. Madan argued that the formal concept of religious freedom is a 'modern idea, not more than three centuries old and western in origin'. 'Freedom of Religion', (2003) 38 *Economic and Political Weekly* (11) 1034–1041, 1034. He asserts that the UDHR 'represented the consensus of opinion among the Christian countries/secular states of the West' who then composed the majority of UN members. Madan at 1036. Arvind Sharma states that '[t]he concept of religious freedom cannot be divorced from the concept of religion,' alleging that Western conceptions of religious freedom which advocate openness to changing religion are a cover for predatory proselytism. *Problematizing Religious Freedom* (Springer 2012), 255.

12 James Madison, 'Memorial and Remonstrance against Religious Assessments, [ca. 20 June] 1785', *Founders Online*, National Archives, available at http://founders.archives.gov/documents/Madison/01-08-02-0163 (accessed July 2017).

13 Special Rapporteur on Freedom of Religion or Belief, Interim Report (13 August 2012), UN Doc A/65/207, § 19. The *forum internum* is protected, as coercion in this 'inner nucleus', such as being forced to conceal one's true position, 'can mean betraying oneself' which can 'undermine the preconditions for developing a stable sense of self-respect'. Report of the Special Rapporteur on Freedom of Religion or Belief (23 December 2015), UN Doc A/HR/31/18, § 19.

14 Special Rapporteur, Interim Report (13 August 2012), § 21.

at conversion, as distinct from persuasive methods, and recognizes the rights of the child and parents in this matter.[15]

The right to try to persuade another to accept a religious belief, often described as evangelism, propagation, or with pejorative connotations, proselytism,[16] is closely connected to the right to profess, to have, or change a religion. However, it belongs in the *forum externum*, where limits may be placed to protect competing interests like public order, morality, health, or the rights of others. Such limits cannot be absolute, but must instead be reasonable and proportionate.

This article addresses the challenges to the liberty of religious persuasion in international legal standards and state practice in Asia, where public religiosity is an accepted social feature, in contrast with more secularized societies in the post-Christian West.[17] It draws from selected jurisdictions where there are clear religious majorities and where religion has a strong socio-political presence, although the state practices some variant of constitutional secularism. It examines these issues in states where Islam (Malaysia), Buddhism (Bhutan and Sri Lanka), and Hinduism (India) dominate public life. Here, the contours of religious freedom are shaped through legislation regulating apostasy and propagation, and perspectives that demonize propagation as an act of intolerance rather than the byproduct of religious tolerance. In contrast, multi-religious secular states like Singapore view freedom of religious conscience as a key facet of secular democracy where the state seeks to secure peace in the face of inter-religious disharmony, rather than to protect revealed truth. It identifies the reasons why freedom of religious persuasion is viewed with chariness or suspicion by some and argues that despite the contentious nature of religious choice and persuasion, these liberties remain at the heart of religious freedom in a religiously plural world and are key to buttressing secular democracies in Asia and beyond.

## Motivations for restricting religious persuasion: a provisional orientation

Religious persuasion is an aspect of religious freedom as well as the human right to free expression and the right to practice one's own religion, and can be especially important for minority religions.[18] As part of the *forum externum*, even under liberal human rights regimes this liberty is not absolute and may be limited when necessary to protect others' rights and certain public interests.

Two broad choices are open to states in relation to the propagation efforts of religious groups. First, a state may secure religious profession as an individual choice and adopt a 'marketplace of religious ideas' approach that tolerates competition among religious groups. The state is agnostic on questions of ultimate concern and regulates religious expression to keep the peace rather than to protect ideology. Second, a state may adopt a more

15 John Witte, 'Human Rights and the Right to Proselytize: Inherent Contradictions', (2000) 94 *Proceedings of the ASIL Annual Meeting* 182–184.

16 Lawrence A. Uzzell, 'Don't Call It Proselytism', *First Things*, October 2004, www.firstthings.com/article/2004/10/dont-call-it-proselytism (accessed July 2017).

17 This is not to discount the post-secular quality of many Western societies which discredits the secularization thesis, grappling with the influx of highly religious immigrants. See, for example, Jürgen Habermas, 'Notes on a Post-Secular Society', signandsight.com, 18 June 2008, www.signandsight.com/features/1714.html (accessed July 2017).

18 See ICCPR Arts 18, 19 (freedom of expression includes the right to 'seek, receive and impart information and ideas of all kinds'), and 27.

'protectionist' stance as an advocate or defender of what it sees as religious truth, and accord more weight to group integrity than individual autonomy, pursuant to protecting public order and the state's religious character. This discriminates against non-official faiths, using methods ranging from banning religious persuasion and conversion to regulating and distinguishing legitimate evangelism from illegitimate proselytism.

Resistance to allowing efforts at religious persuasion can be categorized under four broad types. First, the relativist position views missionary faith as an imposed cultural preference and discounts the truth claims of such religions. Second, resentment toward colonial-era practices in which foreign groups imposed their faiths and undermined indigenous beliefs informs some attitudes. Third, persuasion by other faiths is seen to intrude upon the 'turf' of a religious group, threatening group cohesion through the loss of followers and the power base, and financial resources they provide. Lastly, religious persuasion is resisted where one presumes to already hold the final revelation or fears competition in the form of having one's faith questioned or misrepresented.

## Regulating religious persuasion in Buddhist-majority states: Bhutan and Sri Lanka

### *Bhutan*

The Kingdom of Bhutan had a theocratic government until 2008, when Bhutan's first written constitution was adopted, ushering in a democratic constitutional monarchy.[19] Three quarters of the 700,000 people in this *beyul* ('hidden land') are Vajrayana Buddhist, and the national mission is to preserve *buddhadharma* (the 'way of the Buddha').

Although the Constitution of Bhutan requires that religion remain separate from politics,[20] it identifies closely with and privileges Buddhism as a buttress for cultural identity and public values. The Preamble begins, 'We, the people of Bhutan, blessed by the Triple Gem [of Buddhism] [and] the protection of our guardian deities'. Article 3 requires that 'religious institutions and personalities... shall remain above politics,' yet it requires them to 'promote the spiritual heritage of the country', defined in Article 3 as Buddhism. Article 3 also provides that the Druk Gyalpo (the king) is the 'protector of all religions in Bhutan', but Article 2 requires him to be Buddhist and uphold the Chhoe-sid (dual system of Buddhism and politics). Under Article 3, the king appoints the Je Khenpo, or chief monk, who heads the Dratshang Lhentshog (Commission for Monastic Affairs), and monastic bodies like the Zhung Dratshang receive state funds. Article 9 obliges Bhutanese citizens to protect and respect the 'culture and heritage of the nation' and that state policy create conditions to enable 'a good and compassionate society rooted in Buddhist ethos and universal human values'. In official Bhutanese life, as in the Constitution, Buddhism is omnipresent. Schoolbooks are filled with stories about Buddhist saints, reflecting the intertwining of state and religion.[21]

19 Available at www.nationalcouncil.bt/assets/uploads/files/Constitution%20%20of%20Bhutan%20English.pdf (accessed July 2017).

20 Art. 3(3).

21 See generally Darius Lee, 'Here There Be Dragons! Buddhist Constitutionalism in the Hidden Land of Bhutan', (2014) 15 *Australian Journal of Asian Law* (1) 1–19 and Richard W. Whitecross, 'Separation of Religion and Law? Buddhism, Secularism and the Constitution of Bhutan', (2007) 55 *Buffalo Law Review* (2) 707, 710–711.

While the Constitution does privilege Buddhism, it expressly guarantees Bhutanese citizens the fundamental right to 'freedom of thought, conscience and religion. No person shall be compelled to belong to another faith by means of coercion or inducement.'[22] Fundamental rights may be subject to reasonable legal restrictions on various grounds, including the 'sovereignty, security, unity and integrity of Bhutan' and 'incitement to an offence on the grounds of race, sex, language, religion or region'.[23] Article 9 requires Bhutanese citizens to foster 'tolerance, mutual respect and spirit of brotherhood' among all people, 'transcending religious, linguistic, regional or sectional diversities'.

Despite the constitutional norm of tolerance, and despite the benefits to Bhutanese society from, for example, Jesuit contributions to the educational system, the Bhutanese government has a hostile attitude toward proselytizing religions like Christianity. The Bhutanese view of tolerance is predicated on the moral equality of all religions, rejecting any conception of absolute truth. In the absence of economic or military might, preserving Buddhism as the basis of a strong Bhutanese culture and unity is considered imperative. Proselytizing activity is seen as 'divisive' and importing foreign influences that threaten Bhutanese values.

In 1979, a parliamentarian obtained majority support for his call to prohibit the preaching of Christianity, noting that Catholic priests were doing this in schools. He argued that the Christian faith was 'not only contradictory to Buddhism' but would harm the unity of Bhutan in the long run. The Assembly passed a law stating:

a The Christians are not allowed to preach their religion in public.
b Only academic studies are to be taught in schools and no Christian religion and practice are to be taught.
c The Christians are allowed to practise their religion in their homes.
d Any person found preaching Christianity in public shall be expelled from the country.[24]

In 1982, this ban was extended to Islam and any other foreign religion. The National Assembly has demonstrated more acceptance of proselytizing Hindu sects, noting that 'since the Hindus and Buddhists worship almost the same gods and goddesses, there have been no problems so far.'[25]

Continuing disquiet with 'foreign religions' like Christianity was evident in a 2000 National Assembly debate over fears that the spread of Christianity would displace existing religions and affect Bhutan's peace and stability. The debate highlighted two main concerns about Christianity, whose adherents constituted two percent to three percent of the national population. First, Christian proselytizers condemned Buddhism and Hinduism, which 'hurts the sentiments of Bhutanese people'. Second, Christian evangelism disrupted familial and communal harmony, which 'a small country like Bhutan cannot afford'. Commenting

22 Art. 7(4).
23 Art. 7(22).
24 'Preaching of Christianity Prohibited', *Resolutions Adopted by the 51st Session of the National Assembly Held from 18th to 29th November 1979*, § 16, available at www.nab.gov.bt/assets/uploads/docs/resolution/2014/51st_Session.pdf (accessed July 2017).
25 'Regarding the Spread of New Sects of Hinduism', *Resolutions Adopted during the 65th Session of the National Assembly Held from 13 July to 24 July 1987*, § 13, available at www.nab.gov.bt/assets/uploads/docs/resolution/2014/65th_Session.pdf (accessed July 2017).

on a draft law on proselytism in 2003, the Home Minister considered the antagonistic histories of Catholics/Protestants and Shiite/Sunni Muslims, stating that Bhutan could not 'afford to have too many divisive entities'.[26]

Prime Minister Jigme Thinley, in a 2001 interview, identified two primary bases for opposing proselytism.[27] First, manifesting an ideological commitment to relativism, Thinley condemned as 'the worst form of intolerance' the belief that one had the correct, superior religion and had to correct the wrong, inferior religion of the other, noting also that this divided families and societies. Second, Thinley vilified proselytizers as targeting the poor and weak with cash and material inducements.

One solution identified by the Bhutanese government to combat proselytization of the poor was to raise the level of socio-economic development,[28] thus deterring their vulnerability to predatory proselytizing that would harm Bhutanese solidarity as a Buddhist polity. Eventually, in 2010, Section 463 of the Penal Code made it an offense to use 'coercion or other forms of inducement' to cause a person to convert from one faith to another. This fourth-degree felony carries a punishment of three to five years of imprisonment.

The Bhutanese government's hostile attitude toward religious persuasion flows from a protectionist outlook which seeks to insulate a favored religion from challenges. Indeed, the stated purpose of the 2007 Religious Organizations Act is to 'benefit the religious institutions and protect the spiritual heritage of Bhutan',[29] and minorities such as Christian groups have sought unsuccessfully to be registered under this Act. Religious propagation is seen as the antithesis of tolerance, and competition between religions is frowned upon in Bhutan.

### *Sri Lanka*

The 1978 Constitution[30] declares that Sri Lanka is a democratic socialist republic where sovereignty inheres in the People. Article 9 gives the 'foremost place' to Buddhism and obliges the State to 'protect and foster the Buddhist Sasana' while assuring to other religions the enjoyment of their fundamental rights. Article 10 recognizes that every person 'is entitled to freedom of thought, conscience and religion, including the freedom to have or to adopt a religion or belief of his choice'. Article 14(1)(e) recognizes the freedom of citizens, in public or private, 'to manifest his religion or belief in worship, observance, practice and teaching', subject to the usual list of public interests like national security or the rights of others in Article 15(7).

Sri Lanka has suffered from communal violence in a fractured society divided along ethnic and religious lines. Militant sectors of the majority Sinhalese Buddhists, constituting some 70% of the population, have unleashed violent attacks on minority religions like

26 'Chathrim to Govern Religious Practice', *Resolution of the 81st Session of the National Assembly of Bhutan* (2003), 69–70, available at www.nab.gov.bt/assets/uploads/docs/resolution/2014/81st_Session.pdf (accessed July 2017).

27 'Religious Conversion Worst Form of "Intolerance," Bhutan PM Says', Compass Direct News, 14 April 2011, www.christianpost.com/news/religious-conversion-worst-form-of-intolerance-bhutan-pm-says-49830/ (accessed 23 May 2018).

28 'Chathrim to Govern Religious Practice' at 70.

29 Anugrah Kumar, 'Christian Pastors Arrested in Buddhist Bhutan', *Christian Post*, 10 March 2014, www.christianpost.com/news/christian-pastors-arrested-in-buddhist-bhutan-115873/ (accessed July 2017).

30 Available at www.parliament.lk/files/pdf/constitution.pdf (accessed July 2017).

Muslims (9.7%), Christians (7.6%), and Hindus (12.6%),[31] causing deaths, the destruction of businesses, houses, and religious sites, and looting.[32] In the 2000s, militant Buddhism primarily targeted churches because of alleged aggressive proselytizing by Christian missionaries. In 2011, another wave of religious intolerance was directed at Muslims and their demands for halal food and animal slaughter, on the basis of allegations of Islamic radicalism.[33]

The 2015 presidential elections brought about regime change and the prospect of drafting a new constitution that would aim to promote ethnic reconciliation, among other goals.[34] Christian minorities have urged the adoption of a secular constitution, not in the sense of an irreligious society but one where people enjoy 'equal freedom… to pursue their spirituality and faith without the obstacle of a constitution that guarantees only one religion which can sometime assault others'.[35] The Chairman of the Public Representations Committee on constitutional reforms already considered Sri Lanka to be a secular state under the present constitution, as Article 9's protection of Buddhism is subject to Articles 10 and 14(1)(e) and nowhere does the present constitution state that Buddhism is the state religion.[36] He noted divisions over what status to accord Buddhism in the new constitution,[37] including comments by the Prime Minister indicating that Buddhism should retain its primacy. This has disappointed minority groups who fear that upholding the primacy of Buddhism rather than protecting ethno-religious diversity 'could lead to further suppression of and discrimination against minority religions and communities'.[38]

The impact of Article 9 on limiting religious persuasion is evident in the Sri Lankan Supreme Court case *Teaching Sisters of the Holy Cross in Menzingen v. Sri Lanka* (2003).[39] The Teaching Sisters had established orphanages and homes for the aged as well as schools, receiving some state assistance. They sought to incorporate a Catholic order whose first objective would be 'to spread knowledge of the Catholic Religion'. A petitioner challenged this bill as violating Article 10, as it sought to 'allure' persons to the Catholic faith by providing material benefits.

31 'Foremost Place for Buddhism in New Constitution, Says Ranil', *The Hindu*, 3 November 2016, www.thehindu.com/news/international/south-asia/Foremost-place-for-Buddhism-in-new-Constitution-says-Ranil/article16069387.ece (accessed July 2017).

32 Rohini Mohan, 'Sri Lanka's Violent Buddhists', *New York Times*, 2 January 2015.

33 Ranga Jayasuriya, 'Militant Buddhism and Shadowy Salafism: Govt. Should Fight Both', *Daily Mirror* (Sri Lanka), 29 November 2016, www.dailymirror.lk/article/Militant-Buddhism-and-shadowy-Salafism-Govt-should-fight-both-119881.html (accessed July 2017).

34 Such as preventing a return to civil war between the government and the Tamil minority, which lasted for 26 years until the government finally defeated the Tamil insurgency in 2009.

35 Sarath Iddamalgoda, quoted in 'Christians Urge Sri Lanka to Adopt a Secular Constitution', ucanews.com, 4 August 2016, www.ucanews.com/news/christians-urge-sri-lanka-to-adopt-a-secular-constitution/76760 (accessed July 2017).

36 'Sri Lanka Already a Secular State – Lal Wijenayaka', *Daily Mirror* (Sri Lanka), 5 October 2006, www.dailymirror.lk/116864/Sri-Lanka-already-a-secular-State-Lal-Wijenayake (accessed July 2017).

37 Benjamin Schonthal and Asanga Welikala, 'Buddhism and the Regulation of Religion in the New Constitution: Past Debates, Present Challenges, and Future Options', CPA Working Papers on Constitutional Reform, Working Paper No. 3, July 2016, available at http://sangam.org/wp-content/uploads/2016/10/CPA-Buddhism-and-the-regulation-of-religion-in-the-new-constitution-Working-Paper-3.pdf (accessed July 2017).

38 Sruthisagar Yamunan, 'Will Sri Lanka's New Constitution Retain the Mistakes That Led to 25 Years of Civil War?', Scroll.in, 7 November 2016, http://scroll.in/article/820709/will-sri-lankas-new-constitution-retain-the-mistakes-that-led-to-25-years-of-civil-war (accessed July 2017).

39 S.C. Special Determination No. 19/2003.

The Supreme Court discussed Indian jurisprudence, noting that the religious freedom guarantee in Article 10 of the Sri Lankan Constitution is not absolute and is more restrictive than Indian Constitution, which contains an express right to propagate religion.[40] It reviewed European Court of Human Rights cases[41] holding that in the context of superior-subordinate military relationships, a superior officer preaching to his men could involve 'compulsion'. They applied this reasoning to the Teaching Sisters, whose enterprises, such as running schools for children or homes for the aged, could involve teacher/student or doctor/patient relations.[42] It accepted the distinction drawn in the Strasbourg Court's *Kokkinakis* case between 'true evangelism' and the deformation of it or 'improper proselytism', which exerts 'improper pressure' through offering social and material inducements to people in distress or need and is inconsistent with free conscience.

The Supreme Court held that the activities of the Teaching Sisters could bring improper pressure to bear on distressed and needy people, noting that Article 10 protects freedom to adopt a religious belief by choice, not by improper inducement. The Court held that spreading one's religion is not a constitutionally protected right in Sri Lanka, and 'could hinder the very existence of the Buddha Sasana' or Buddhism. Thus the Court held that the bill articulating the corporation's objective as to 'spread knowledge of the Catholic religion' was inconsistent with Article 9. To put it more bluntly, Article 9 of the Constitution of Sri Lanka can subjugate the rights of religious minorities to the desires of the religious majority.

## Regulating religious persuasion in Hindu-majority states: India

While Hindus comprise some 80% of India's population,[43] the principle of secularism is a basic feature of the Indian Constitution.[44] Article 25 provides that all persons have the right 'to freedom of conscience and the right to freely profess, practice and propagate religion' subject to 'public order, morality and health'.

The brand of secularism in India may be described as ameliorative – that is, rather than separating religion from the State, it subjugates religious freedom to the service of social reform.[45] Article 25(2) empowers the states to regulate 'any economic, financial, political or other secular activity' that may be associated with religious practice and to require that Hindu religious institutions of a public character be open to all Hindu classes in the interests of social reform, particularly the eradication of religiously based hierarchies.

40 Art. 25(1).

41 *Larissis and Others v. Greece*, App. Nos 23372/94, 26377/94, and 26378/94 (ECtHR, 24 February 1998) and *Kokkinakis v. Greece*, App. No. 14307/88 (ECtHR, 25 May 1993).

42 However, the European Court in *Larissis* also found that civilians outside the military hierarchy whom the applicant attempted to convert were not subject to the same pressures as the airmen. The military hierarchy analogy applied to the *Teaching Sisters* case may be inappropriate; see Asanga Welikala, 'The Menzingen Determination and the Supreme Court: A Liberal Critique', available at www.cpalanka.org/wp-content/uploads/2007/8/Menzingen_Review.doc (accessed July 2017).

43 'Census 2011: Hindus Dip to Below 80 Per Cent of Population; Muslim Share Up, Slows Down', *The Indian Express*, 27 August 2015, available at http://indianexpress.com/article/india/india-others/indias-population-121-09-crores-hindus-79-8-pc-muslims-14-2-pc-census/ (accessed July 2017).

44 *Kesavananda Bharati v. State of Kerala* (1973) 4 SCC 225. The 42nd Amendment in 1976 formally constitutionalized secularism.

45 Gary Jacobsohn, *The Wheel of Law: India's Secularism in Comparative Constitutional Context* (Princeton University Press 2005), 94.

The inclusion of a constitutional right to propagation was largely the initiative of the Christian minority, for whom propagation was the litmus test of religious freedom. During constituent assembly debates, proponents of the religious propagation clause supported it on the basis that a secular state tolerates all religions, and preventing a person from propagating religious views is a form of intolerance. Furthermore, they emphasized the importance of protecting religious minorities.

Detractors from the religious propagation clause were largely from the Hindu community, whose resistance appeared to flow from a few primary objections. First, they chafed at the memory of colonial-era missionary activities and the related fear that the poor and vulnerable would be induced by pecuniary incentives to convert. Second, Hindu leaders were especially concerned that the conversion of the lower castes (*dalits*) to faiths like Christianity, which recognizes the intrinsic worth and equal dignity of all people, would entail the loss of their power base. Third, to some Hindus, all religions are equally valid, so there was no point in people changing faiths.

Supporters of the religious propagation clause had their own answers to such concerns. B.R. Ambedkar, a *dalit* and architect of the Indian Constitution who converted to Buddhism, observed, 'Why should you live under the fold of that religion which has deprived you of honor, money, food and shelter?' To him, there was nothing wrong with changing religions either for material ends or for matters of conscience; he himself rejected the caste system which 'was disinterested in the common man' and interested only in 'a class of Supermen (Brahmin)'.[46]

Eventually, a compromise formulation was settled upon, whereby Article 25 protected the right to propagate but not to convert others. This clause would apply to all propagating religious communities whether Hindu, Arya Samaj, Muslim, Jain, Buddhists, or Christian, on the understanding that coercive conversions were not protected.[47]

In the 1950s, various states enacted euphemistically entitled 'Freedom of Religion Acts' avowedly designed to restrict 'unethical' religious conversions and to preserve peace and harmony in religiously plural India, in reality driven by Hindus nationalism. Six states currently have anti-propagation legislation. For example, the Gujarat Freedom of Religion Act 24 of 2003 provides 'for prohibition of conversion from one religion to another by the use of force or allurement or by fraudulent means'. It states its rationale as deterring

> the anti-social and vested interest groups exploiting the innocent people [belonging] to depressed classes and will enable people to practice their own religion freely. It will also be useful to maintain public order and to nip in the bud the attempts by certain subversive forces to create social tension.[48]

Section 2 defines 'allurement' as the 'offer of any temptation' in the form of gifts or material benefits, financial or otherwise. The definition of 'force' includes 'threat of divine

46 'Dr. BR Ambedkar's Call for "Renunciation of Hinduism"', available at http://creative.sulekha.com/renounce-hinduism-dr-ambedkar_427611_blog (accessed July 2017).

47 On the constituent assembly debates on including the right to religious propagation, see Li-ann Thio, 'Caesar, Conscience and Conversion: Constitutional Secularism and the Regulation of Religious Profession and Propagation in Asian States', (2011) *Fides et Libertas: Journal of the International Religious Liberty Association* 127–159.

48 Available at www.minoritiesofindia.org/wp-content/uploads/2015/01/Gujarat_Freedom_of_Religion_Act.pdf (accessed July 2017).

displeasure or social excommunication', and 'fraudulent means' includes misrepresentation. Forcible conversion is punishable with up to three years of imprisonment and a fine of INR 50,000, which may be increased to four years imprisonment and INR 100,000 where the subject of conversion is 'a minor, a woman or a person belonging to the Scheduled Caste or Scheduled Tribe'.

The definitions in Section 2 are so broad that 'allurement' may capture even charitable acts like providing meals or a prayer of blessing, and 'force' could include any mention of hell or divine punishment. It is easy to imagine such a law being misused to stifle legitimate religious activities and peaceful religious persuasion as part of the right to manifest one's religion or belief. Furthermore, the UN Special Rapporteur on Freedom of Religion and Belief has noted that while there have been few convictions under such laws, they have adversely affected religious minorities, including fostering 'mob violence' against them. It was feared that these laws could become 'a tool in the hand of those who wish to use religion for vested interests or to persecute individuals on the ground of their religion or belief'.[49] Indeed, Hindu nationalism and the spread of the Hindutva ideology have fueled violent campaigns against Christians and Muslim minorities.[50]

In addition to anti-propagation laws, some states in India have attempted to require prior permission from designated state officials before one converts to another religion. The Special Rapporteur criticized this as 'unduly onerous' on the individual intending to convert and interfering with the private realm of individual belief, particularly where state officials are afforded protection against prosecution or legal proceedings for 'anything done in good faith' under the law.[51] For example, Section 4 of the Himachal Pradesh Freedom of Religion Act 31 of 2006 requires that a person intending to convert from one religion to another give at least 30 days prior notice to the district magistrate, who may make any enquiries into the matter he deems fit. Failure to give notice is punishable by fines up to INR 1,000. However, no such notice is required 'if a person reverts back to his original religion'; in other words, it does not apply to former Hindus re-converting to Hinduism. Another state's law excludes conversion to one's ancestral religion from the requirement of giving notice, which in practice means non-Hindus converting to Hinduism.[52] Critics argue that these acts are based on 'long-time propaganda by right-wing Hindu groups against Christian and Muslim minorities'.[53]

49 Report of the Special Rapporteur on Freedom of Religion or Belief (26 January 2009), UN Doc A/HRC/10/8/Add.3, § 50.

50 See, for example, 'Pastor Humiliated, Paraded Half-Shaven on Donkey on False Conversion Charges in U.P.', *Christian Today,* 31 January 2016, available at www.christiantoday.co.in/article/pastor.humiliated.paraded.head.half.shaven.on.donkey.on.false.conversion.charges.in.u.p/17834.htm (accessed July 2017).

51 Report of the Special Rapporteur (26 January 2009), § 49.

52 Section 2(b) of the Chhattisgarh Dharma Swatantraya Act of 2006 specifically excludes 'returning to one's forefather's religion or his origin religion' from the ambit of conversion.

53 World Evangelical Alliance, Universal Periodic Review: 13th session of the UPR Working Group, India (28 November 2011), 4, available at www.worldevangelicals.org/un/pdf/UPR2011-Anti-Conversion%20Laws%20in%20India.pdf (accessed July 2017). Hindu nationalism is well documented elsewhere. To take just one example, a 2006 amendment to the Gujarat Act grouped Jainism and Buddhism together within the category of Hinduism, causing strong opposition by members of those minority faiths who wanted to preserve their religious identity rather than have it subsumed in Hinduism. The Indian Supreme Court held that the 'Jain religion indisputably is not a part of Hindu religion' and Jains had the right to administer their own minority institutions. 'Minorities Protest against Gujarat's Conversion Law', *Times of India*, 21 September 2006, available at http://economictimes.indiatimes.com/news/politics-and-nation/minorities-protest-against-gujarats-conversion-law/articleshow/2011955.cms (accessed July 2017).

Anti-conversion legislation has had a mixed reception in the courts. The state High Court in *Evangelical Fellowship of India v. State of Himachal Pradesh* affirmed the right to transmit religious belief by peaceful propagation,[54] as freedom of conscience includes 'the very important right to change one's belief'.[55] It stated also that a civilized society could not permit conversions by force, fraud, or inducement, as the 'word of God cannot be spread either through the sword or by the use of money power'. A speaker may 'extol the virtues of the religion which he propounds' and question the beliefs of others in a civilized manner, but 'the right to propagate can never include the right to denigrate any other thought, religion or belief.' One can 'promise heaven' to the followers of one's faith but 'cannot say that damnation will follow if that path is not followed'.[56] Allowing conversions that are forceful, fraudulent, or by inducement would jeopardize 'the very being of our secular country' and 'lead India to total annihilation'.

While upholding states' authority to prohibit forceful conversions, the Court struck down the prior notice requirement as violating a person's right to privacy, as 'a person's belief or religion is something very personal to him' and a person had the 'right to keep his beliefs secret' subject to the larger public interest, which the Court noted was not synonymous with the majority interest. The Court could find no public interest that would justify the notice requirement; it would in practice not aid the state in discouraging forceful or fraudulent conversion, and in fact could open individuals wishing to change their religion to a number of harms.[57] The Court also criticized the 30-day window for providing notice as useless, as it is impossible to 'determine when the thought process of a person has changed'.[58]

The Court also struck down the exclusion of re-conversion to the 'original religion' as a violation of Article 14's non-discrimination clause and utterly irrational in practice, as there could be no justification for the notice requirement that would not also apply to many re-conversions. The Court also criticized the provision requiring a person who failed to give notice to pay a fine since it made criminals of the largely 'poor and the downtrodden'[59] who had been converted by force, fraud, or inducement. The Act should instead have targeted those seeking to convert others this way.

A religious majority insecure about losing adherents who convert to another faith may abuse their political clout to enact restrictive anti-conversion and anti-propagation laws, in the guise of 'religious freedom'. A preferable view of religious freedom is that religious persuasion does not violate free conscience but gives meaning to it. Propagating religion inherently goes beyond imparting knowledge; it seeks 'to produce intellectual and moral conviction leading to action, namely, the adoption of that religion. Successful propagation of religion would lead to conversion.'[60] While undoubtedly a state is justified in prohibiting

54 CWP No. 438 of 2011 (Judgment of 30 August 2012), available at www.adfmedia.org/files/EFofIndia-Decision.pdf (accessed July 2017). See also *Stanilaus v. State of Madhya Pradesh*, 1977 S.C.R. (2) 611. The Supreme Court had held that the right to transmit views did not extend to coercing belief or a 'fundamental right to convert any person to one's own religion' in the sense that if a person 'purposely undertakes the conversion of another person to his religion', as distinct from transmitting religious tenets, this would impinge on the 'freedom of conscience'. Indian jurist H.M. Seervai has critiqued this reading, arguing that rather than violating free conscience, propagation provides an opportunity to exercise free choice in relation to religious belief and affiliation. *Constitutional Law of India* vol. 2 (NM Tripathi Private Ltd 1993), 1287.

55 § 20.

56 §§ 15–16.

57 § 40.

58 § 42.

59 § 46.

60 Seervai at 1287.

acts of force or coercion, the laws in these cases go far beyond that, criminalizing even a believer's sharing of religious doctrines about the eternal consequences of actions. Furthermore, they seem to validate pre-existing animosities by the majority religion toward the minority religions. The common myth that trying to convert others is unconstitutional has caused 'the greatest public mischief' and prejudice against religious minorities in India; restrictive religious freedom laws serve primarily to entrench the political interests of dominant religious groups driven by fear of the loss of the Hindu culture and way of life.

## Regulating religious persuasion in Muslim-majority states: Malaysia

Under Article 3 of the Malaysian Constitution (1957), Islam is the 'religion of the Federation'. Islam enjoys preferential treatment, as evident in Article 12(2) which allows states to establish Islamic religious institutions, although Article 3 guarantees that 'other religions may be practiced in peace and harmony in any part of the Federation.' Article 11(1) provides that every person has the 'right to profess and practice his religion' as well as to propagate it. However, Article 11(4) allows state and federal laws to 'control or restrict the propagation of any religious doctrine or belief among persons professing the religion of Islam'.

One example of such a restriction is the Johor anti-propagation law, which provides that a person commits an offense if he 'persuades, influences, coerces or incites' or organizes any activity designed to influence a Muslim to become a follower of a 'non-Islamic religion' or to forsake or disfavor Islam.[61] This includes meeting with a Muslim to speak to him about a 'non-Islamic religion' or sending unrequested publications related to such religions. Punishment may include imprisonment for four years and a fine of MYR 10,000. The act defines 'non-Islamic religion' as 'Christianity, Hinduism, Buddhism, Sikhism, Judaism' or any of its offshoots, or any creed that includes the worship of 'some spiritual or supernatural being or power' with the aim of attaining 'spiritual enlightenment, spiritual protection or spiritual existence' and which Islam does not recognize as belonging to it.

It is clear from the historical record that Malaysia was meant to be a secular state and that Article 3 was ceremonial in nature.[62] Today, this is a contested issue within both the political[63] and judicial domains.[64] In political discourse, 'secularism' has become a synonym for 'anti-religion' or 'anti-Muslim', carrying the baggage of colonial hegemony and cast as a threat to Malay-Muslim nationalism. This is in some tension with the view of secularism articulated by the Federal Court in *Che Omar bin Che Soh v. P.P.*[65] as the separation of religion and politics, in contrast to the historical position of the sultans, who had headed both, and the relegating of Islamic law from general law to a particular law applied only to the

61 Control and Restriction of the Propagation of Non-Islamic Religions Enactment 1991 (State of Johor) No. 13 of 1991.

62 Joseph Fernando, *The Making of the Malayan Constitution* (MBRAS 2002), 162.

63 'DPM: M'sia Not a Secular State', *The Sun Daily*, 18 July 2007, available at www.thesundaily.my/node/169707; Clive Kessler, 'Enough of This Nonsense! Malaysia Was Created as a Secular State', *Malaymail Online*, 19 January 2016, available at www.themalaymailonline.com/what-you-think/article/enough-of-this-nonsense-malaysia-was-created-as-a-secular-nation-clive-kess; and Zairil Khir Johari, 'The Demonization of Secularism in Malaysia', *Malaysian Insider*, 17 June 2015, available at www.ucanews.com/news/the-demonization-of-secularism-in-malaysia-/73792 (all accessed July 2017).

64 See, for example, Li-ann Thio and Jaclyn Neo, 'Religious Dress in Schools: The Serban Controversy in Malaysia', (2006) 55 *International & Comparative Law Quarterly* (3) 871–888.

65 [1988] 2 MLJ 55, 55.

personal law of Muslims. Thus, when Article 3 allowed restrictions on propagation of religion among those professing Islam, this was confined to the specific matter of propagation.

However, judicial revisionism has imported Islam as a source of public law values into the adjudication of religious freedom questions, notably where Muslims desire to change their religion. This has severely reduced the scope of religious freedom for Muslims, particularly in apostasy cases where the main assumption is that changing religion is not an individual right, but a crime that endangers state security, where the religious unity of the majority religion is considered indispensable to social unity.

For example, the High Court[66] in *Lina Joy v. Majlis Agama Islam Wilayah*[67] held that freedom of religion under Article 11(1) does not include the freedom of a Muslim to convert away from Islam without first applying to the Syariah courts for a declaration of apostasy. The High Court asserted that the constitutional liberty embodied in Article 11(1) had to be qualified by Article 3(1)'s declaration that 'Islam is the religion of the Federation,' such that religious conversion for Muslims was under the exclusive jurisdiction of the Syariah courts. The defendant had not applied to the Syariah courts, unsurprisingly, as this course of action could have opened her to criminal sanctions including detention at a religious rehabilitation center. In other words, an application for such a declaration is not a mere formality but a risky step that inhibits Muslims from changing their religion.

While deferring the question of conversion to the Syariah court, the judge referred to Article 160(2), which defines a 'Malay' as someone 'who professes the religion of Islam, habitually speaks the Malay language and conforms to Malay custom'. The judge noted that from the perspective of civil courts, the plaintiff, an ethnic Malay, would remain 'in the Islamic faith until his or her dying days'. In other words, the High Court treated religious identity as a matter not of choice but of ascription.

The Court of Appeal upheld the judgment, noting that the Muslim community considered renunciation of Islam a 'very grave matter', as it was their responsibility 'to save another Muslim from the damnation of apostasy', making conversions a 'highly sensitive matter'.[68] The Federal Court, despite a strong dissenting judgment, confirmed that matters of conversion fell within Syariah court jurisdiction and declined to protect a constitutional right to change religion.[69]

Another aspect of Malaysia's protective stance toward Islam is the fact that, although members of non-Muslim religions may be legislatively barred from engaging in religiously persuasive speech with a Muslim, the State itself actively engages in the propagation of Sunni Islam. This entails the discriminatory treatment of all other faiths, as well as Islamic sects such as Shia Muslims or Al-Arqam whose views are considered heretical. Raids have been conducted by the religious authorities in the name of national security to arrest Shiites

66 The High Court is in fact a lower court, not to be confused with the Federal Court, which is the supreme court of Malaysia.

67 [2004] 2 MLJ 119. For a critical analysis of the constitutional issues, see Thio Li-ann, 'Apostasy and Religious Freedom: Constitutional Issues Arising from the Lina Joy Litigation', [2006] 2 MLJ i. For a response see Shamrahayu A. Aziz, 'Apostasy and Religious Freedom: A Response to Thio Li-ann', [2007] 2 MLJA 1.

68 Abdul Aziz Mohamad JCA, *Lina Joy v. Majlis Agama Islam Wilayah Persekutuan* [2005] 6 MLJ 193, 208.

69 *Lina Joy v. Majlis Agama Islam Wilayah* [2007] 4 MLJ 585 (Federal Court of Malaysia). See, however, the case of Rooney Redit, whose conversion from Islam to Christianity was upheld as a constitutional right by the High Court of Sarawak State. Although decided on narrow grounds particular to the situation, this decision offered some hope to advocates of Muslims who desire to convert to other religions but have been stymied by the civil courts' continued referring of the matters to the jurisdiction of the Syariah courts, which are at best unsure how to proceed and at worst may impose criminal punishment on the applicants.

observing holy days.[70] There have been aggressive state-directed institutionalized Islamic missionary activities among the indigenous Orang Asli, who are mostly animists. Programs designed to assimilate the Orang Asli into mainstream Malay society are synonymous with conversion to Islam. The Department of Orang Asli Affairs provides financial inducements to convert to Islam, in terms of better housing, work opportunities, health, transportation, and scholarships. The government builds multi-purpose halls, mosques, and religious schools in Orang Asli settlements, with religious officials present to guide the Orang Asli to the Islamic faith. The Department reportedly determines who is allowed to visit settlements, thereby controlling religious proselytizing and preventing hindrances to the Islamization program.[71] Activists report instances of 'forced assimilation and bullying' by the government in relation to Sunni Islamic proselytization of the Orang Asli.[72]

Such a protectionist attitude toward the favored religion, where conversion away from Islam can be a crime and religious persuasion by non-Sunni Muslims incurs legal sanctions, chills religious speech and withers religious liberty.

## Regulating religious persuasion in multi-religious states: Singapore

Singapore is a religious society but a secular state. From its inception, Singapore has affirmed the right of religious propagation under Article 15 of its Constitution.

In 2014, a Pew Research Center report ranked Singapore as the most religiously diverse country in the world.[73] More than 80% of Singaporeans profess a religious affiliation, with the major faiths being Buddhism-Taoism, Catholicism, Christianity, Sikhism, Hinduism, and Islam.[74] There is some degree of ethnic and religious conflation insofar as more than 99% of Malays are Muslims, although, unlike Malaysia, the Constitution does not ascribe the religious identity of Muslim to the Malay ethnic group.

When Singapore seceded from the Malaysian Federation on 9 August 1965, its Independence Constitution departed from the Malaysian constitutional ordering of state-religion relations. Unlike the Malaysian Constitution, it contains no confessional clause. It contains no express principle of secularity either, but it is clear that the Constitution was intended to endorse a model of multi-racial secular democracy where political authority flows from the Constitution and the people, and not any divine source. The Minister for Law and Development at the time of independence suggested that 'a nation based on one race, one language and one religion, when its people are multiracial, is one doomed for destruction.'[75] The Constitutional Commission at the time endorsed an even-handed

70 'Malaysia Shiites Harassed and Face Uncertain Future', Al Arabiya News, 12 February 2011, available at www.alarabiya.net/articles/2011/02/12/137299.html (accessed July 2017).

71 Toshihiro Nobuta, 'Islamization Policy towards the Orang Asli in Malaysia', (2007) 31 *Bulletin of the National Museum of Ethnology* (4) 479–495.

72 'Probe into Allegations that Malaysian Government Sanctions Forced Conversions', Lapidomedia.com, 31 August 2011, http://religiousliteracyinstitute.org/probe-allegations-malaysian-government-sanctions-forced-conversions (accessed 23 May 2018).

73 Pew Research Center, 'Global Religious Diversity', 4 April 2014, available at www.pewforum.org/2014/04/04/global-religious-diversity/ (accessed July 2017).

74 The 2010 Singapore Census (www.singstat.gov.sg) indicates the religious composition as Buddhists/Taoists 44.2%, Christians 18.3%, Islam 14.7%, Hinduism 5.1%, other religions 0.7%, and no religion 17%. A Singapore humanist society was formed in 2010. 'Carving Out a Space for the Non-Religious Here', *Straits Times*, 9 November 2010.

75 Minister for Law and National Development E.W. Barker, Singapore Parliament Reports, 22 December 1965.

treatment of religions by rejecting special measures for any particular religion, such as financial assistance for religious instruction.[76] The Commission also rejected a version of the restrictive Malaysian Article 11(4) which authorizes anti-propagation laws in relation to Muslims, as it would be 'inconsistent' in a 'democratic secular state' to single out a particular religion for special treatment. The Court of Appeal has described the Singapore model as one of accommodative secularism, which predicates religious freedom 'on removing restrictions to one's choice of religious belief'.[77]

When forging its national policy expressed in a white paper on shared values, the government rejected a reference to 'belief in God', departing from the Malaysian *Rukun-negara* and the Indonesia *Pancasila*. The government has declared that it has 'no theological views on who is heretical and who is not'.[78] It sees its function as being to 'hold the ring' so 'all groups can practice their faiths freely without colliding with one another in Singapore.'[79]

Article 15(1) of the Constitution protects the right to profess, practice, and propagate religion, and is subject to the Article 15(4) limitation clause protecting public order, health, and morality. Religious groups are not banned or regulated on the basis of their faith itself but for instrumental reasons. For example, the government has banned the Jehovah's Witnesses on the basis that their objection to compulsory military service is a threat to public order[80] in a polity where a premium is placed on 'racial and religious harmony'.[81]

Although the Constitution guarantees freedom of religious propagation, the government has provided soft guidelines on how to exercise this liberty, with an eye to maintaining religious equilibrium and civil peace. In 1965, Prime Minister Lee Kuan Yew urged Christians not to attempt to convert Muslims, assuring them that

> Singapore has many people with no religious guidance whatsoever, no religious beliefs.... I would say more than 70 percent are either vaguely agnostics or iconoclasts.... I see no need for going around looking for the 12 percent Muslims to try and convert them.[82]

Some legislation may indirectly chill religious propagation, like the 1989 Maintenance of Religious Harmony Act (Cap 167A) (MRHA), which empowers the Minister to issue a

76 Li-ann Thio, 'The Passage of a Generation: Revisiting the 1966 Constitutional Commission', in Li-ann Thio and Kevin Y.L. Tan, eds, *The Evolution of a Revolution: 40 Years of the Singapore Constitution* (Routledge-Cavendish 2009), 7–49.

77 *Nappalli v. Institute of Technical Education* [1999] 2 SLR 569.

78 This was in relation to a request by Muslim leaders to ban Al-Arqam, considered a deviant sect, in 1994. 'Certain Controls Necessary to Keep Peace', *Straits Times*, Sunday Review, 10 December 1995, 4. Exceptionally, the Muslim Affairs Minister in 2014 expressed a theological view in stating that ISIS was a 'deviant group' whose brutal methods were 'basically not Islam'. Olivia Siong, 'PM Lee Holds Dialogue with Religious, Community Leaders on Islamic State Threat', Channel NewsAsia, 29 November 2014.

79 Prime Minister Lee Hsien Loong, National Day Rally Speech 2009, available at www.nas.gov.sg/archivesonline/speeches/view-html?filename=20090826007.htm (accessed July 2017).

80 *Colin Chan v. PP* [1994] 3 SLR (R) 207.

81 On the importance of harmony, see Lee, National Day Rally Speech 2009. Countries like Sri Lanka are often invoked as an anti-model: '"Religious Peace must be maintained": Otherwise Things Will Never Be the Same If Conflict Breaks Out: BG Lee', *Straits Times*, 20 May 1996, 3; Home Affairs Minister S. Jayakumar, 54 Singapore Parliament Reports, 22 February 1990, Maintenance of Religious Harmony Bill, 1048 ('Sri Lanka was once held up as a model of peaceful coexistence of different religions. Now a holy war is taking place there.').

82 Transcript of the Prime Minister's Statement to Religious Representatives and Members of the Inter-Religious Council, 30 September 1965.

restraining or gag order to a religionist on various grounds, including 'causing feelings of enmity, hatred, ill-will or hostility between different religious groups'.[83] In theory, the law does not restrain propagation itself but only the manner in which it is done, in order to safeguard religious and racial harmony and inter-group relationships. Tensions may arise where 'aggressive proselytism' arouses the insecurity of religious groups whose members are targeted by missionaries of other faiths or where inflammatory language upsets religious sensitivities.

The MRHA came at a time when competition for religious followers was becoming 'sharper and more intensive', where more were turning to 'exclusive beliefs'.[84] The Hindu community considered itself vulnerable to strong influences stemming from 'more dominant religions', particularly proselytizing Christians, and supported the MRHA as a form of protection from aggressive conversion tactics.[85] Many Buddhists also viewed the MRHA as a form of protection from harassment and insensitive proselytizing.[86]

Aggressive proselytism is contrasted with softer forms of innocuous proselytism, the exemplar of which is the approach of friendly dialogue adopted by Soka Gakai, a Buddhist sect, as a religious project to spread global peace and the truth of the Lotus sutra. It eschews former tactics of *shakubuku* (harsh debate) and teaches proselytism through dialogue, predicated on a spirit of openness toward others. Its teachings on 'the dignity and equality of all life' have been said to 'resonate with the Singaporean ethos of treasuring diversity and aspiring for peaceful coexistence'.[87] The Singapore Soka Association has won state acceptance, being the only religious group that participates in National Day parades.

The white paper on the MRHA recognized that the constitutional liberty to proselytize was integral to missionary faiths like Christianity ('bearing witness') and Islam (*dakwah*). While it was 'legitimate' for a religious group to point out to its own followers how its belief system differed from or was preferable to other faiths, 'it is possible to go too far,' such as where preachers denounce others as 'misguided infidels and lost souls', potentially causing 'great umbrage to entire communities'; if they respond with 'equal virulence', this may escalate a social crisis.[88] The white paper sought to lay down soft norms to provide guidance, such as refraining from denigrating other religions. While these norms are non-binding, they are authoritative for interpreting the scope of constitutional protection and in shaping expectations of social conduct. The intent was to highlight the need to consider the sensitivities of religious groups and the delicacy of Singapore's multi-religious balance.

The annex to the MRHA white paper details religious trends which raised security concerns, such as where Hindus were perturbed by 'aggressive Christian proselytization' in the form of posters advertising Christian seminars pasted at temple entrances or the distribution of pamphlets to devotees entering temple precincts. In 1986, when Christian groups

83 Sec. 8(a). Restraining orders may also be issued under Section 9 against others who foster inter-religious ill will.

84 Maintenance of Religious Harmony white paper (Cmd 29 of 1989), § 10.

85 Select Committee Report, MRHA Bill, 20 September 1990, 13–20.

86 Some Buddhists have released a booklet advising fellow believers how to politely resist unwanted proselytism by saying 'no' with compassion, and to engage with others 'without insisting that others accept our point of view'. 'Agree to Disagree: Conversations on Conversion', 7, available at www.conversion.buddhists.sg (accessed July 2017).

87 Juliana Finucane, 'Proselytizing, Peacework and Public Relations: Soka Gakkai's Commitment to Interreligious Harmony in Singapore', in Juliana Finucane and R. Michael Feener, eds, *Proselytizing and the Limits of Religious Pluralism in Contemporary Asia* (Springer 2014).

88 § 16.

distributed booklets in Malay using the word *Allah* for God, Muslims accused them of misleading them as they consider *Allah* a term specific to Islam. In response, mosques put up lists of names of Muslims who had converted to Christianity, warning other Muslims to avoid them and other Muslim organizations put out booklets questioning cardinal Christian beliefs.

Clearly, while the government is not opposed to religious propagation *per se*, it considers 'aggressive preaching' problematic. In this regard, the Sedition Act (Cap 290) has been deployed as a tool against aggressive proselytism. The Sedition Act deals not only with inciting disaffection against the government, but also with the promotion of 'feelings of ill-will and hostility between different races or classes of the population of Singapore'.[89] 'Races or classes' has been broadly interpreted to include religious groups. Two cases involving offense to Muslims have been prosecuted under the Sedition Act: *Benjamin Koh v. PP*,[90] in which a blogger posted a pig's head with a halal logo, and *Ong Kian Cheong v. PP*,[91] in which a Christian couple distributed religious tracts criticizing Islam.

The latter case has been characterized as one of 'pushing your religion' on others, causing 'nuisance and offence'.[92] Without referring to the constitutional right to propagate religion,[93] the District Judge in *Ong Kian Cheong* chastised the couple for failing, as Singaporeans, to appreciate religious sensitivities, noting that in Singapore's multi-religious and multi-racial context, 'distributing tracts with callous, denigratory, offensive and insensitive statements on religion with aspersions on race' had a tendency to 'cause social unrest' and jeopardize racial and religious harmony.[94] Common sense required that spreading the faith in this context should be 'constrained by sensitivity, tolerance and mutual respect' for each other's faith.[95] While the couple, who were given a deterrent prison sentence, may have been insensitive, it is hard to see how the judge could characterize them as intolerant unless the very exercise of the constitutional right of religious propagation is intolerant. This would be to endorse relativism, a postmodern brand of intolerant tolerance that would chill as 'intolerant' speech one does not wish to tolerate.

In contrast to the case of the offense to Muslims, which resulted in prison sentences, the blogger posting cartoons offensive to Christians received only warnings.[96] The greater solicitude for Muslim feelings is perhaps attributable to the Article 152 constitutional duty to protect racial and religious minorities, particularly Malays, whose religion is predominantly Islam.

The Internal Security Department has also intervened where religious harmony is threatened. In 2010, it issued a stern warning to Pastor Rony Tan of Lighthouse Evangelism for a video uploaded on YouTube where Pastor Tan was seen interviewing a former Buddhist monk and nun and making disparaging remarks about central Buddhist tenets like reincarnation, meditation, and Nirvana. The warning elicited a personal apology to Buddhist and Taoist leaders, who accepted it and urged calm restraint. The Ministry of Home Affairs

89 Sec. 3(1)(e).
90 [2005] SGDC 272.
91 [2009] SGDC 163.
92 Lee, National Day Rally Speech 2009.
93 See Thio Li-ann, 'Contentious Liberty: Regulating Religious Propagation in a Multi-Religious Secular Democracy', (2010) *Singapore Journal of Legal Studies* 484–515.
94 [2009] SGDC 163, § 81.
95 § 82.
96 'Warning for Blogger Who Posted Cartoon of Christ', *Straits Times*, 21 July 2006.

affirmed this rapprochement, reiterating soft norms that one must not 'run down' other religions and be 'mindful of the sensitivities' of other faiths when preaching.[97] Deputy Prime Minister Wong affirmed constitutional freedoms in stating that while Singaporeans were 'free to propagate their religious beliefs', this must 'never be by way of insulting the religious beliefs of others'.[98] These norms depend on an ethos of tolerance and civility, rather than legal sanction *per se*. After this incident, the National Council of Churches affirmed Wong's statement and drew attention to a 2008 internal guide advising member churches that Christian evangelism in a multi-religious society should take care 'not to denounce other religions', and to respect the beliefs of others so as 'not to create or sow ill-will'.[99]

The government also values a relational approach when inter-religious disputes break out, supporting efforts to build friendly relations between Christians and Taoists, such as where the Prime Minister attended a Taoist Federation dinner where Taoist and Christian leaders performed Hokkien ballads after a falling-out. This reflects a valuation of racial and religious harmony, not merely public order (absence of disorder).[100] The High Court has noted that while Singapore is a secular society in that there is no single religion all Singaporeans subscribe to, it could still have shared values, declaring that 'forgiving those who have trespassed against us' was one such value.[101] Prudence and grace is a function of character and culture rather than law, which the government exhorts, but cannot compel. Freedom of religious persuasion must be accompanied by both a commitment to promote free conscience in the pursuit of religious truth, as well as to a civilized standard of mutual respect and tolerance.

## Concluding observations: why protect religious persuasion?

Religious persuasion requires commitment to both freedom of conscience and religious pluralism and tolerance. Religions vary in their attitudes toward these values. Madan has asserted that there would be no pluralism without plurality, that religious pluralism is a 'concession to empirical reality rather than a matter of orthodoxy'.[102] In this sense, religious freedom is itself a religious proposition.[103] Nonetheless, religious views can change over time. To take one simple example, long-standing Catholic theology driven by Augustine and Aquinas justified the use of force against heretics, which changed with the Second Vatican Council document *Dignitatis humane personae*, which teaches the right of all

97 Ministry of Home Affairs, Press Release, 8 February 2010 (statement in response to media queries on the Lighthouse Evangelism videos and comments made by Pastor Rony Tan of Lighthouse Evangelism). The Pastor's comments about Buddhism and Taoism were deemed 'highly inappropriate and unacceptable as they trivialized and insulted the beliefs of Buddhists and Taoists'. These could 'give rise to tension and conflict between the Buddhist/Taoist and Christian communities'.

98 'DPM Wong Says "Glad to Note" Pastor Tan Realized His Mistake', Channel NewsAsia, 10 February 2010.

99 National Council of Churches of Singapore, Statement of 9 February 2010 'In Response to Comments by Pastor Rony Tan', available at http://nccs.org.sg/2010/02/09/in-response-to-comments-by-pastor-rony-tan-9-february-2010/ (accessed July 2017).

100 'Song of Friendship', *Straits Times*, 4 December 2010 and Li-ann Thio, 'Relational Constitutionalism and the Management of Inter-Religious Disputes: The Singapore "Secularism with a Soul" Model', (2012) 1 *Oxford Journal of Law and Religion* (2) 446–469.

101 *Kalpanath Singh v. Law Society of Singapore* [2009] SGHC 190, § 23.

102 T.N. Madan, 'Freedom of Religion', (2003) 38 *Economic and Political Weekly* (11) 1034–1041, 1034.

103 Joseph Weiler, 'Ways Out of the Christian Ghetto', Mercatornet, 4 February 2011, available at www.mercatornet.com/articles/view/ways_out_of_the_christian_ghetto/ (accessed July 2017).

persons to be free from coercion in matters of conscience,[104] while insisting on the right not to be deterred from faith by 'unjust vexations on the part of others'.[105]

For 'protectionist' states which seek to protect religious orthodoxy, the justification for clamping down on religious persuasion is the fear of conversions which might impair majority group integrity and perhaps national identity, or the belief that religious unity buttress social strength. Religious propagation is seen as morally offensive, as it involves imposing 'personal preferences and culturally conditioned prejudices' on others.[106]

However, this goes against human rights values of openness, development, and choice and fossilizes religion and culture. For states which restrict religious freedom in the name of preserving social equilibrium where religious persuasion may stir social tensions, the relationship between religious pluralism and a democratic society is better appreciated. The rationales for protecting free speech apply equally to that of religious free speech conveyed by persuasion – we all communicate to persuade and influence our hearers, and there is an inseparable link between liberty of thought and expression; viewpoint diversity facilitates personal self-determination. It is consonant with democratic values to support an individual's right to pursue truth as dictated by reason and conscience, to disagree with orthodoxy, and to propagate that truth he decides to commit to.

Freedom of religious persuasion embodies respect for the full expression of religious conscience; in a religiously tolerant society which protects persuasive religious propagation, part of respecting each other involves seeing a fellow human being as part of a community who has the freedom to accept or reject notions of truth within a marketplace of ideas. The speaker's freedom to engage in religious persuasion also entails the hearer's freedom to reject these efforts, hopefully in the spirit of civility and self-restraint.[107]

The issue in this context is how to distinguish legitimate evangelism from illegitimate proselytism, rooted in a commitment to social unity in the face of religious diversity and the belief that God is not interested in coerced faith. State regulation of religious persuasion in this context where the state is agnostic on questions of religious truth is not about preserving substantive ideology but relates more to the style of propagation and prudential concerns of maintaining social harmony while allowing some latitude within the civil order between competing visions of truth. The state does not deliver the good of religion but provides the framework within which each person or group can practice and pursue the human good of religion, while preserving peaceful coexistence. Vigorous criticism of a belief system from which the target of persuasion is being wooed may spark an emotional reaction, hostility, or even violence where a community feels misrepresented or insulted, and it is tempting for states to intervene to keep civil peace. This caters to the outraged sensitivities of the Emotional Man, rather than the restraint of a Reasonable Man open to religious truth who can tolerate unpleasant views in the interest of truth-seeking, critical enquiry, and intellectual pluralism.

104 John T. Noonan, 'Principled or Pragmatic Foundations for the Freedom of Conscience', (1987) 5 *Journal of Law and Religion* (1) 203–212.

105 Walter M. Abbot and Joseph Gallagher, eds, *The Documents of Vatican II* (Association Press 1966), 600.

106 Wolfhart Pannenberg, 'How to Think about Secularism', *First Things*, June 1996, available at www.firstthings.com/article/1996/06/002-how-to-think-about-secularism (accessed July 2017).

107 See, for example, Board of Experts, International Religious Liberty Association, 'Guiding Principles for the Responsible Dissemination of Religion or Belief', 29 January 2000, available at www.irla.org/respdissemination (accessed July 2017).

A democratic society not only protects free speech in relation to inoffensive matters, but prizes free conscience and broad exposure to disparate ideas as necessary for informed beliefs. A relational society is composed of individuals concerned with sustainable relationships between different communities coexisting together, who appreciate the value of respectful persuasion and whose motive force is concern for the other's well-being as opposed to denigration and disagreeable disagreement. A mix of liberty and relationalism is needed for religious pluralism to succeed in religiously diverse societies, where religious liberty is valued, but appropriate attention given to religious harmony as a public good which supports rather than destroys religious freedom.

The alternative is either an oppressive form of state-enforced religious orthodoxy or pseudo-religious secular totalitarianism, both of which discriminate against and suppress competing views. Besides crushing liberty, bans on religious propagation may engender not community but a form of spiritual tribalization that may translate into social balkanization as well as the enshrining of relativism as public dogma in a post-modern, post-secular age.

# 16 Religious equality in the Peruvian Constitution

*Oscar Díaz Muñoz*

Understanding the right to religious equality in Peru and its current situation requires a little knowledge of history. As a Spanish territory, Peru was bound by the Constitution of 1812, which Spain adopted as part of the war of independence against the Napoleonic invasion.[1] In that document, due to the influence of the US Constitution of 1787 and the French Constitution of 1791, principles of democratic liberalism (such as national sovereignty and separation of powers) were combined with the traditional laws of the Spanish monarchy.

It is in the latter group that we find the religious component in the Spanish Constitution of 1812. The wars of religion, from the sixteenth century until the Peace of Westphalia in 1648, set at odds European states identifying as either Catholic or Protestant, contributing to the creation of the idea of confessional states. Thus, under the principle of *cuius regio, eius religio*, each king could impose his religion on his subjects. This situation, with different names in countries like France, Germany, or Austria, was called *regalismo* in Spain.[2]

All this explains why Article 12 of the Constitution of 1812 says,

> The religion of the Spanish nation is and will forever be the Catholic, Apostolic, Roman, the only true [religion]. The nation protects it by wise and just laws, and prohibits the exercise of any other.

Peru declared independence from Spain in 1821. Its first constitution, promulgated in 1823, was clearly influenced by the American Constitution, adopting, for example, the presidential system and the separation of powers. However, while the people of North America had adopted principles of religious freedom early on – Christian pluralism in the Bill of Rights of the Good People of Virginia in 1776, and religious freedom in the First Amendment to the national constitution in 1791[3] – Peru, on the contrary, kept in its first constitution a formula similar to that of the *regalismo* of the Spanish Constitution of 1812. Thus, Articles 8 and 9 of the first Peruvian Constitution of 1823 read:

> The religion of the Republic is Catholic, Apostolic, Roman, excluding the exercise of any other.

1 See Juan Vicente Ugarte del Pino, *Historia de las Constituciones del Perú* (Andina 1978), 23–36.
2 See Pedro Lombardía and Juan Fornés, 'El Derecho eclesiástico', in Javier Ferrer Ortiz, ed., *Derecho eclesiástico del Estado español* (Eunsa 1996), 45–46.
3 See David F. Forte and Matthew Spalding, *The Heritage Guide to the Constitution* (Regnery 2014), 399.

> It is a duty of the Nation to constantly protect it, by all means in accordance with the spirit of the Gospel, and a duty of any inhabitant of the State to respect it inviolably.

With some slight variations, this text would be repeated in the ten constitutions Peru would have in the following years, including the Constitution of 1933, so that Peru could be defined during this period as a confessional state, although the Constitution of 1860 was reformed in 1915 to allow the public practice of faiths other than Catholicism.[4]

And thus we come to the Constitution of 1979 which, in a section and terms similar to those of the current Constitution of 1993, enshrines (1) the fundamental right to religious freedom, (2) its limits under the principle of *greatest possible freedom and minimum necessary restrictions*, (3) religious equality, (4) the principle of secularity, and (5) the principle of collaboration between the State and religious denominations.

This re-orienting of the Constitution toward religious freedom is explained by the rise and internationalization of human rights, including freedom of religion, which occurred after World War II, as evidenced by the Universal Declaration of Human Rights of 1948 and the International Covenant on Civil and Political Rights of 1966, followed in the Americas by the American Convention on Human Rights of 1969 (Pact of San José).

To this historical context must be added the contribution to the reasoning and content of religious freedom given by the doctrine of the Catholic Church through *Dignitatis Humanae*, the Declaration of the Second Vatican Council in 1965, which states,

> 2. This Vatican Council declares that the human person has a right to religious freedom. This freedom means that all men are to be immune from coercion on the part of individuals or of social groups and of any human power, in such wise that no one is to be forced to act in a manner contrary to his own beliefs, whether privately or publicly, whether alone or in association with others, within due limits.
>
> The council further declares that the right to religious freedom has its foundation in the very dignity of the human person.... This right of the human person to religious freedom is to be recognized in the constitutional law whereby society is governed and thus it is to become a civil right.

And so we come to our current Constitution of 1993 which, in Article 2.3, acknowledges the fundamental right to religious freedom in the following terms:

> [Everyone has the right]... [t]o freedom of conscience and religion in an individual or collective manner. No person shall be persecuted on the basis of his ideas or beliefs.... Public exercise of any faith is free, insofar as it does not constitute an offense against morals, or a disturbance of the public order.

On the basis of the constitutional text, it can be said that the right to religious freedom in Peru has two components: (1) the freedom of faith, immune from any coercion (which protects both the believer and the agnostic or atheist), and (2) the freedom of religious worship.[5]

4 Constitution of 1860, Art. 4. See Domingo García Belaunde, *Las Constituciones del Perú* (Ministerio de Justicia 1993), 291.

5 See Pedro-Juan Viladrich and Javier Ferrer Ortiz, 'Los principios informadores del Derecho eclesiástico español', in Ferrer Ortiz, ed. at 144.

The Peruvian Constitutional Court has said that religious freedom, in its internal dimension, 'supposes the ability of self-determination of every person in accordance with their convictions and beliefs in terms of religious faith'.[6] In its external dimension, it involves freedom for 'the practice of religion in all its forms, individual or collective, public and private, with freedom for teaching, worship, observance and change of religion'.[7] The external dimension generates the principle of immunity from coercion, pursuant to which, according to our Constitutional Court, 'no person may be compelled to act against their religious beliefs.'[8] Additionally, the external dimension of religious freedom protects its exercise not only individually but also in association, or collectively.

The right to religious equality is specifically mentioned in the Constitution, which in Article 2.2 provides: '[Everyone has the right]... [t]o equality before the law. No person shall be discriminated against on the basis of... religion.'

The Constitutional Court of Peru has explained that not all differential treatment is contrary to the right to equality, because 'we are before a fundamental right that does not consist in the right of people to demand equal treatment, but in being treated in like manner to those who are in the same situation.'[9] This, applied to the right to religious equality, has allowed the Constitutional Court to say,

> Equality... does not mean uniformity. Therefore, in order to determine whether in a particular case there is an issue with the *right-principle of non-discrimination or of religious equality*, we must, in the first place, determine whether we are facing unequal treatment based on objective and reasonable justifications; or unequal treatment which is arbitrary, capricious and unjustified, and therefore discriminatory.[10]

As regards religious equality, we should recall the Declaration on the Elimination of All Forms of Intolerance and of Discrimination Based on Religion or Belief (the 'Declaration'), adopted by the United Nations General Assembly in 1981, which includes not only the personal or individual dimension of the right to religious freedom, but also its collective dimension, acknowledging the rights of religious groups as such, which states must protect. Article 7 of the Declaration says it intends to ensure that the rights and freedoms enshrined in it be acknowledged 'in national legislation in such a manner that everyone shall be able to avail himself of such rights and freedoms in practice', which makes clear that the Declaration sees such rights as a minimum that the law of each state should guarantee to any religious group, regardless of the system of relations between the state and religious denominations.

I would finally like to refer to two principles of the Peruvian Constitution that directly affect religious equality. I mean the principle of secularity and the principle of cooperation between the State and religious denominations, both contained in Article 50, which reads:

> Within an independent and autonomous system, the State recognizes the Catholic Church as an important element in the historical, cultural, and moral formation of Peru, and lends the Church its cooperation.

6 STC 6111-2009-PA/TC, fundamento 11.
7 STC 6111-2009-PA/TC, fundamento 11.
8 STC 3372-2011-PA/TC, fundamento 11 and STC 3283-2003-AA/TC, fundamento 19.
9 STC 0048-2004-PI/TC, fundamento 59.
10 STC 6111-2009-PA/TC, fundamento 22.

> The State respects other denominations and may establish forms of collaboration with them.

Under the secularity principle, 'the State defines itself as lay or radically incompetent as regards religious faith and practice, not being competent to coerce or even concur, as one more subject, with the religious faith of citizens.'[11] Nevertheless, our Constitutional Court has stated that secularity does not mean a negative attitude of the State toward religion:

> [T]he fact that there is a neutrality of the State in religious matters does not mean that public authorities have to develop a kind of persecution of religious phenomena or any religious manifestation. Secularity is incompatible with the State seeing itself as an advocate or protector of a certain religious denomination, but it is also incompatible with a State that promotes atheism or agnosticism or banishment from the public sphere of all expressions of a religious nature. The incompetence of the State as regards religious faith and practice does not mean the promotion of atheism or agnosticism with the removal of religious symbols from the public sphere or the imposition of an anti-religious ideology, ignoring the traditions that are part of the historical, cultural and moral formation of Peru.[12]

Thus, the Constitutional Court has said that 'religious freedom can be affected both by a confessional State, and by a "secularist" State hostile to religion.'[13]

As regards the principle of collaboration between the State and religious denominations, the Constitutional Court has said that the Constitution considers the religious component in Peruvian society important and, therefore, in the aforementioned Article 50 it provides for State collaboration with the Catholic Church and enables the State to establish forms of collaboration with other religious denominations. Thus, as the Constitutional Court has said, 'Article 50 of the Constitution indicates a double content for the State: the establishment of relations with religious denominations, and that the relations be collaborative'.[14] The Religious Freedom Act No. 29635 of 2010, Article 15, has developed Article 50 of the Constitution with regard to the possibility of the State signing collaboration agreements with religious bodies, for which it requires them to be in the Registry of Religious Entities of the Ministry of Justice, 'having become deeply rooted, with a national scope and offering guarantees of stability and permanence due to the numbers of their adherents and activities'.

The signing of cooperation agreements between the State and religious denominations represents, as highlighted by the Constitutional Court, 'the most important way to realize the principle of cooperation'.[15] The Agreement of 1980 between the Peruvian State and the Holy See is an international treaty and, to date, the only collaboration agreement between the Peruvian State and a religious denomination in Peru.

The Constitutional Court has stressed that the State 'can also enter into collaboration agreements with different religious denominations other than the Catholic Church, in

11 STC 6111-2009-PA/TC, fundamento 25.
12 STC 6111-2009-PA/TC, fundamento 28.
13 STC 6111-2009-PA/TC, fundamento 28.
14 STC 6111-2009-PA/TC, fundamento 30.
15 STC 6111-2009-PA/TC, fundamento 32.

accordance with Article 50 of the Constitution'.[16] In such agreements, denominations may agree with the State to receive its collaboration in areas such as religious instruction in public schools, the granting of tax benefits like those provided for non-profit organizations, or the State allowing religious assistance in public establishments such as the armed forces, hospitals, and prisons.

It is important to point out that the explicit mention of the Catholic Church in the Constitution and the generic mention of other faiths is an example of the special treatment that the Constitution acknowledges to the Catholic Church in light of its great social reach, and the important role it has played in the historical, cultural, and moral formation of Peru. It cannot be understood as discrimination against other denominations, but, on the contrary, as an extension of the paradigm of the treatment of religions in general. That is, the juridical recognition enjoyed by the Catholic Church – due to its greater rootedness and organic complexity in Peruvian society – can be extended to the rest of the generically alluded-to denominations, provided that they exhibit similar characteristics.[17]

We can conclude, as our Constitutional Court has, that the term 'collaboration' used in the Constitution (joined to the principle of secularity) indicates that

> our constitutional model reflects neither the system of union nor of absolute separation between the State and religious groups. The collaboration between the State and religious groups is a meeting place as far from union as it is from a lack of communication between both spheres.[18]

The Peruvian constitutional model indicates, therefore, what the Spanish Constitutional Court has called 'healthy secularity', in which the Constitution, after having made a declaration of neutrality, values the religious component present in society and at the same time requires public authorities to keep like collaborative relationships with the Catholic Church and other denominations.[19]

16 STC 6111-2009-PA/TC, fundamento 33.
17 See Viladrich and Ferrer Ortiz at 141.
18 SSTC 3372-2011-PA/TC, fundamento 13 and 6111-2009-PA/TC, fundamento 31.
19 See STC of Spain 101/2004, 2 June 2004, fundamento 3. See also Alfonso Ruiz Miguel and Rafael Navarro-Valls, *Laicismo y Constitución* (Fundación Coloquio Jurídico Europeo 2009), 105.

# Index


Abruzzo Region (Italy) 115
Adams, John 21
Affordable Care Act (US) 33
Ahdar, Rex 49
Ahmadiyya 159
*Ahtinen v. Finland* 41n9, 43n22, 48, 51
Alba, Richard 82–6
Ambedkar, B.R. 205
American Bar Association Model Rules of Professional Conduct 34
American Constitution 29
American Convention on Human Rights of 1969 (Pact of San José) 218
Americans with Disabilities Act (ADA) 35
*Animal Farm* 191
Aquinas, Thomas 186
Argentine Constitution 80
Arieli, Yehoshua 56
Årsheim, Helge 45, 47
Asad, Talal 54, 187
assimilation: defined 192; *vs.* integration 191–3
Association for Southeast Asian Nations (ASEAN) 197
Austria: higher education of faith leaders in 104–5; Islamic religion in 114; Islam Law 105, 108; Universities Act 105

Bagehot, Walter 67
Balkin, Jack 22
*Benitez* case 90
*Benjamin Koh v. PP* 213
Berger, Benjamin 46–7
Berger, Peter 99
Berlin Neutrality Law (Germany) 183–4, 186
Bhutan: Constitution 200–1; regulating religious persuasion in 200–2; Religious Organizations Act 202
Bill of Rights (US) 27
Bishops' Conference (US) 43
Böckenförde, Ernst-Wolfgang 98
Boko Haram 157, 162–3
Borno: Boko Haram 157, 162–3; Islamic Preaching Board Laws 157, 162–3
Borno State Sharia Implementation Committee 163
Bradley, Gerard 23
Brunswick Rabbinical Conference 193
Buddhism 96, 199–210

Cairo Declaration on Human Rights in Islam (CDHRI) 197
Calabresi, Guido 15
California Proposition 8 31–2
Calo, Zachary 54
Castro, Martin 34
Cathedral of Notre Dame, Rouen 24
Catholic Family and Human Rights Institute 70; *see also* Center for Family and Human Rights
Catholicism 109, 112–13, 152, 189, 210, 218
Center for Family and Human Rights 70; *see also* Catholic Family and Human Rights Institute
*Centre Universitaire de Théologie Catholique in Metz* (University of Lorraine) 106
Charities Act 2006 (UK)130
Charities Act 2011 (UK) 130
Charity Commission (UK) 140
Chazan, Bogdan 175
*Che Omar bin Che Soh v. P.P.* 208
Chevènement, Jean-Pierre 107
*Childs v. United Kingdom* 145–6
'chilling effect' 174
Christian calendar 190–1
Christian hegemony: *vs.* Christonormativity 184–5; defined 185
Christianity 27, 44, 68, 96, 186–7; calendar 190–1; and Europe 112; and European-Christian symbiosis 187–8; in geography 189–90; and Nigeria 157; in state discourse 188–9
Christians 28, 94n30, 184–7, 201, 203, 206, 210n74, 211–14
Christonormative Judaism 193–4
Christonormative neutrality 195
Christonormativity: *vs.* Christian hegemony 184–5; development of 187–91; *vs.* religious neutrality 182–7

*Chronicle of Higher Education* 33
Church of England 63, 68, 139–40
*City of Boerne v. Flores* 90
Civil Rights Act, California 90
Civil Rights Commission 34
Clinton, Hillary 34, 36
Commission *see* European Commission of Human Rights
Committee on the Rights of the Child (UN) 73
community: Christian 44; integration in 84–5; political 5, 20, 23–4; same-sex advocacy 95; social 40
'compelling government interest' test 121
conscientious objection of doctors 175–7
Consorti, Pierluigi 111
Convention on the Elimination of all Forms of Discrimination Against Women (CEDAW) 59, 61
co-religionists: employment 137–8; service delivery 136–7
Convention on the Rights of the Child (UN) 73
Council of Europe 150

Danbury Baptists 30
dan Fodio, Usman 159
Darul Islam 157, 164
Dauvergne, Catherine 80–1
Declaration of Independence 28
Declaration on Religious Freedom 18, 21
Declaration on the Elimination of All Forms of Intolerance and of Discrimination Based on Religion or Belief 58, 219
*Der Tagesspiegel* 194
*Dignitatis humanae* 18, 23, 218
discrimination 8, 34; employment 25, 35; gender 60, 87; sexual orientation 88, 90
doctrine of 'margin of appreciation' 168–9
Doda 173
*D.S. and E.S. v. United Kingdom* 148–9
Due Process Clause of the Fourteenth Amendment 90
Durand, Jorge 83

Ebaugh, Helen Rose 83–4
Eich, Brenden 32
*Elsinore Christian Center v. City of Lake Elsinore* 121
Emirate Committees for Islamic Religious Preaching 161–2
Employers' Office of the Church *(Kirkon työmarkkinalaitos)* 43
*Employment Division v. Smith* 89
Enlightenment 29
Equality Act 2010 125, 133–41; public-sector collaboration 138–9; and religious precinct 139–41; services offered by a minister of religion 134–6; working only with co-religionists 136–8
Equality Acts (UK) 72
Equality and Human Rights Commission 136
equality law: and Equalities Act 2010 133; and religious communities 125
Esau, Alvin 46, 47, 52n77
Establishment Clause of the First Amendment 7, 10n29, 29–30
Europe: and Christianity 112; higher education of faith leaders in 101–7; ministerial exception and 'secular' laws 45–8; mosques in 111–12; religious buildings in 111–18; theological and legal perspectives from 39–55
European-Christian symbiosis 187–8
European Commission of Human Rights 144
European Convention on Human Rights (ECHR) 49–50, 64, 67, 71–2, 112, 113; Article 9 128, 130–1
European Court of Human Rights 8, 39, 49, 67, 112; and freedom for religion in prison cases 144, 148–9; and freedom from religion in prison cases 144, 149–50; and freedom of religion in prison cases 144, 145–8; and freedom within religion in prison cases 145, 150–2
European human rights system: discussion within 48–53; ministerial exception 48–53
'European' Islam 194
European Prison Rules 150
European Union (EU) 63
*Evangelical Fellowship of India v. State of Himachal Pradesh* 207
Evangelical Lutheran Church of Finland 39; Church Election Order (*Kirkon vaalijärjestys* (416/2014)) 40; Church Order (*Kirkkojärjestys* (1055/1993)) 40; future legal arrangements of 39–44
Evans, Carolyn 50
*Everson v. Board of Education* 30

*Faculté de Théologie Catholique et Protestante* (University of Strasbourg) 106
faith leaders, higher education de-radicalizing 108–9
Family Watch International 71
Feldblum, Chai 89
Felgentreu, Fritz 184
*Fernández Martínez v. Spain* 48, 49, 50, 52, 53
Ferrari, Silvio 116
Finland: Church Act (*Kirkkolaki* (1054/1993)) 40, 42, 51; ministerial exception and 'secular' laws 45–8; theological and legal perspectives from 39–55
Finnish Constitution 43
First Amendment (US) 4, 19–20; Establishment Clause of 7, 10n29, 29–30; Free Exercise Clause 25, 36;
Fish, Stanley 98
*Florin Andrei v. Romania* 152

*Fondation de l'islam de France* 107
Foner, Nancy 82, 84–6
*forum externum vs. forum internum* 7
'Four Freedoms' speech 1
Fourteenth Amendment 90
France: *Bureau central des cultes* (Central Worship Office) 106; Dreyfus affair 194; higher education of faith leaders in 105–7; *laïcité* 182
freedom for religion 4–5, 15–24; in prison 144, 148–9
freedom from religion 6–7; human rights imperative 62; in international human rights law 56–62; in prison 144, 149–50; secular constitutionalism 61–2
freedom of conscience 90–1
freedom of religion 2–4; burdens imposed on others by 71–4; in prison 144, 145–8
'Freedom of Religion Acts' 205
freedom within religion 7–9; in prison 145, 150–2
free exercise of religion: First Amendment and 35; importance of 29–31
French Revolution 86
Freytag, Gustav 194
fundamental rights: immigration as an experience of 79–86

Garnett, Richard 5
Garvey, John 17
*Gaudium et spes* 23
*Gavrilovici v. Moldova* 145
Georgetown University 36
German Empire 104
Germany: Berlin Neutrality Law 183–4; Christianity in state discourse 188–9; concepts of religiosity 186–7; higher education of faith leaders in 102–4; Ulusoy affair 182–3
*Ghostbusters* 191
Ginsburg, Ruth Bader 35–6
*Goldman v. Weinberger* 10n29
Good Friday 190
Great Mosque of Parioli (Italy) 112
Great Synagogue (Italy) 112
Gujarat Freedom of Religion Act 24 (India) 205
Gushee, David 34

Hagan, Jacqueline 83–4
Hamburger, Philip 30
Hamburg Temple (Germany) 193
Hamilton, Marci 121
Hand, Learned 23
*Handyside v. The United Kingdom* 168
Hare Krishna movement 148, 150
*Haskalah* 192
health-care conscience 87–95
health-care providers: harms of coercing the conscience of 91–4; personal harms 91; professional harms 92–3; public harms 93–4
Heine, Heinrich 193
Herzl, Theodor 194
heteronormativity 184–5
higher education of faith leaders: approaches to 101–7; in Austria 104–5; denominational approach 102–5, 107–8; in Europe 101–7; in France 105–7; in Germany 102–4; non-denominational approach 105–8
Himachal Pradesh Freedom of Religion Act 31 (India) 206
Hinduism 96, 204–8
Hines, Barbara 80
*Hobby Lobby* case 24, 36
homophobia 34
Hood, Anna 50
Horwitz, Paul 24
*Hosanna-Tabor Evangelical Lutheran Church and School v. Equal Employment Opportunity Commission* 25, 35–8, 45, 45n33
Humanism 64
Human Life International 71
human rights: religious challenges to the universality of 60–1
Human Rights Act 1998 (UK) 130
Human Rights Committee (UN) 59, 64
Human Rights Council's (HRC's) Special Rapporteurs on Freedom of Religion or Belief 59

*Igors Dmitrijevs v. Latvia* 145
imam 134–5
immigration 79–86
Immigration and Refugee Board of Canada (IRB) 80
India: Constitution 204; regulating religious persuasion in 204–8; secularism 204
inequality: and religious precinct 141–3
insult to religious feelings 172–5
integration: *vs.* assimilation 191–3; and neutrality 191–2
International Consortium for Law and Religion Studies (ICLARS) 1, 3
International Convention on the Protection of the Rights of All Migrant Workers and Members of Their Families of 1990 (UN) 79–80
International Covenant on Civil and Political Rights (ICCPR) 58–9, 64, 218
international human rights law: freedom from religion in 56–62
international judicial standards of review: doctrine of 'margin of appreciation' 168–9; 'legitimate aim' 167; neutrality and impartiality 169–70; and Nigeria 166–70; 'prescribed by law' 167

International Labour Organisation (ILO) 52
International Organization of the Family 70–1
intolerance 34
ISIS 63, 211n78
Islam 26, 38, 96, 112; in Austria 114; and land use controversies in the United States 123; in Malaysia 208–9; in Nigeria 157; and place of worship 118
Islamic Preaching Board Laws: of Borno 157, 162–3; evaluation of 170–1; of Kano 157, 160–2; of Niger State 157, 163–4; in Northern Nigeria 159–64; theoretical frameworks 158–9
Islamic Religious Community in Austria (IGGÖ) 105
*Islamische Religionspädagogische Akademie* (Academy for Islamic Religious Pedagogy) (Germany) 105
Islamophobia 34
Italy: Constitution 113, 117; Constitutional Court 115–18; regional laws on worship buildings 115–117
Izala 160

Jacobson, Israel 193
*Jakóbski v. Poland* 149
Jefferson, Thomas 6, 27–8, 30
Jehovah's Witnesses 113, 116, 119, 166
Jews 9, 57
Judaism 9, 96
*Judenstaat* 194

Kagan, Elena 35, 36
Kano State (Nigeria): Council for Islamic Affairs Law 161; Emirate Committees for Islamic Religious Preaching 161–2; 160 Islamic Preaching Board Laws 157, 160–2; Local Government Authority Rules 1970 160; Local Government Authority Law No. 3 of 1970 160; Maitatsine 157; Religious Preaching Edict of 1985 161
Kant, Immanuel 192
Karaims 178
Kennedy, Anthony 37, 90
Kivel, Paul 185
Knoll, Benjamin 82, 85
Konrad Adenauer Foundation 184
Koppelman, Andrew 20
Körting, Ehrhart 186, 194
*Kovalkovs v. Latvia* 148, 149, 150
*Kuznetsov v. Ukraine* 145

Laborde, Cecile 52
laws originating in religious doctrine 68–71
Lee Kuan Yew 211
Leigh, Ian 49
Leitenberger, Friedrich 194
Lerner, Natan 64–5
Levitt, Peggy 82
LGBT individuals 57, 94
*libertas ecclesiae* 4
*Lina Joy v. Majlis Agama Islam Wilayah* 209
Little Sisters of the Poor 33
*Lombardi Vallauri v. Italy* 48
Lombardy Region (Italy): and Constitutional Court 116–17; Law No. 3 116–17; and worship buildings 115–16
Lund, Christopher 45
Lutheranism 44

Madison, James 19, 27, 82
Mahmood, Saba 54
Maintenance of Religious Harmony Act (Cap 167A) (MRHA) (Singapore) 211–12
Maitatsine 157
Maitatsine, Muhammadu Marwa 160–1
Malaysia: Constitution 208; and Islam 208–9; regulating religious persuasion in 208–10
Mallams 163–4
*Mannousakis and Others v. Greece* 112
Manuel II Palaiologos 187
*Marek Glínski v. Poland* 145
*Maskilim* 192
Massey, Douglas S. 83
McConnell, Michael 29–30
McGoldrick, Dominic 49
*Medical and Dental Practitioners' Disciplinary Tribunal v. Okonkwo* 165
Melamed, Douglas 15
Mendelssohn, Moses 192
Menjívar, Cecilia 82, 84–5
*The Merchant of Venice* 57
Merkel, Angela 189
*Metropolitan Church of Bessarabia* 151
*Midrash Shepardi, Inc. v. Town of Seaside* 121
migration; and urbanization 111
minaret 112
ministerial exception: discussion within European human rights system 48–53; Europe 45–8; Finland 45–8; and 'secular' laws 45–8
Monet, Claude 15
*Monty Python's Life of Brian* 191
mosques; *see also* worship buildings: in Europe 111–12; in Singapore 213
*Mozer v. Moldova* 147
Mozilla Corporation 32
Murray, John Courtney 21
Muslim Religious Association (Poland) 179, 180
Muslims 97, 106, 107–8, 113–14, 122, 159–60, 162
*M. v. United Kingdom* 146

National Church Council *(Kirkkohallitus)* (Finland) 42, 43–4
Nazi Germany 104
neutrality: Christonormative 195; impossibility of 191; integration *vs.* assimilation 191–3; state 182
Nibrassiya Huda Islamic group 164
Nigeria: Constitution 157; and Christianity 157; constitutional framework 164–6; and international judicial standards of review 166–70; and Islam 157; Islamic Preaching Board Laws 159–64; judicial review in 165–6; religions in 157
Niger State: Darul Islam 157, 164; Islamic Preaching Board Laws 157, 163–4; Islamic Religious Preaching Edict of 1985 163; Mallams 163–4; Nibrassiya Huda 164
North America 81–3
Novak, David 3–4
Nowak, Ryszard 173

*Obergefell v. Hodges* 32
'object of religious worship' 174
*Obst v. Germany* 48
*Ong Kian Cheong v. PP* 213
Organization of Islamic Cooperation (OIC): [previously Organization of the Islamic Conference] 60–61, 197
Ottoman Empire 9
*Otto-Preminger-Institut v. Austria* 168

PA-SOGI laws 89, 91
Paulus, Heinrich 192
Penn, William 30
Perich, Cheryl 35
Perry, Michael 18
Peru: Constitution 217–21; Constitutional Court 219
Philippson, Ludwig 192
Poland: Act on the Prohibition of Ritual Slaughter 179; Act on the Protection of Animals 180; Act on the Slaughter of Farm Animals in Slaughterhouses 178; conscientious objection of doctors 175–7; Constitution of 1997 176; Criminal Code 172, 174; insult to religious feelings 172–5; religious slaughter 177–81; Supreme Medical Council 176
*Poltoratskiy v. Ukraine* 146
Pope Emeritus Benedict XVI 21
Pope John Paul II 93n26
positive secularity 5
'prescribed by law' requirement 167
Protestantism 27, 109
public accommodations/sexual orientation and gender identity (PA-SOGI) laws 87; regnant judicial interpretation of 90–1
public benefit: defined 129; and religion 129–30
public-sector collaboration: Equality Act 2010 138–9; and religious organizations 138–9
public sector equality duty 133

Qadiriyya 159
Quebec's Charter of Values 81, 86

Rabczewska, Dorota *see* Doda
racism 34
religion(s): challenges to universality of human rights 60–1; freedom for 4–5, 15–24; freedom from 6–7; freedom of 2–4; freedom within 7–9; global implications of separating politics from 38; importance of 26–9; and public benefit 129–30; and social action 128–33
*Religion, Secular Beliefs and Human Rights* (Lerner) 64
religiosity concepts 186–7
religious autonomy 8
religious belief 129, 199
religious buildings: in Europe 111–18; in United States 118–23
religious communities: and equality law 125; religious *vs.* secular activities 124–5; in United Kingdom 125–8
'religious confession' 115–16
religious conscience: and freedom of religious persuasion 215; and Singapore 199
religious conversion 196
religious denomination 151
religious equality: in Peruvian Constitution 217–21
'religious exercise' 120
religious feelings: insult to 172–5
religious freedom 34, 196; American understanding 26–31; in Article 18 of UDHR 196–7; Hosanna-Tabor 31–8; immigration as an experience of 79–86
Religious Freedom Restoration Act (RFRA) 90, 119
religious fundamentalism: challenges and critiques 108–10; denominational or non-denominational approach 107–8; higher education as indirect steerage from within 98–9; higher education of faith leaders in Europe 101–7; modern academia and modern religiosity 99–101; preventing through higher education of faith leaders 96–110; problem presenting for modern states 97–8
religious groups; *see also* religious organizations: autonomy 49; funding for 127; in United Kingdom 127
Religious Land Use and Institutionalized Persons Act of 2000 (RLUIPA) (US) 118–23
religious liberty 23, 34, 198
religious neutrality *vs.* Christonormativity 182–7

religious organizations; *see also* religious groups: funding from public body 139; and public-sector collaboration 138–9
religious persuasion: importance of protecting 214–16; motivations for restricting 199–200; regulation in Buddhist-majority states 200–4; regulation in Hindu-majority states 204–8; regulation in multi-religious states 210–14; regulation in Muslim-majority states 208–10
religious precinct: defined 124; Equality Act 2010 (UK) 125, 133–41; inequalities and challenges 141–3; social action and religion 128–33
religious slaughter 177–81
Renaissance 86
residual theocracy 67; *see also* 'soft theocracy'
Revolutionary War 27
*Reynolds v. United States* 30
ritual slaughter 177–81
Rivers, Julian 49
Roberts, John 27
*Roe v. Wade* 87
Roman Catholics 63
Romanian Orthodox Church 52
Roosevelt, Franklin D. 1–2; State of the Union Address 1

Sabbath Laws (Judaism) 193
same-sex marriage 37, 87
Sandberg, Russell 41, 48
Schröder, Kristina 189
*Schüth v. Germany* 48
Second German Reich 106
Second Vatican Council 9, 18, 23
secular constitutionalism 61–2
'secular' laws 45–8
*Separation of Church and State* 30
separatism 194–5
sexism 34
sexual freedom 37
sexual liberty claims: clinical cases 87–9; health-care conscience and 87–95
sexual morality 31–5
*Shechten* 192
*Siebenhaar v. Germany* 48
Sikh granthi 134
*Sindicatul "Păstorul cel Bun" v. Romania* 48, 50, 52
Singapore: Constitution 210–11; Maintenance of Religious Harmony Act (Cap 167A) (MRHA) 211–12; regulating religious persuasion in 210–14
Smith, Stephen 32
social action: as a manifestation of religion 130–3; and religion 128–33
social involvement 85–6
sodomistic sex 87
'soft theocracy' 67; *see also* residual theocracy
Sri Lanka: Constitution 202; regulating religious persuasion in 202–4
state neutrality 182
Stöß, Jan 191
Strasbourg Court *see* European Court of Human Rights
'strict scrutiny' 121
Stutzman, Baronelle 89
'substantial burden' 120
*Sunday Times v. UK* 169
Supreme Court of California 90
Switzerland 114, 188; referendum of 2009 114

Tan, Rony 213
Tariqa Islamic group 160
Tatars, Polish 177
Taylor, Charles 195
*Teaching Sisters of the Holy Cross in Menzingen v. Sri Lanka* 203–4
Thinley, Jigmi 202
Tibi, Bassam 99
Tijjaniyya 159
*Travaš v. Croatia* 48, 50, 53
*Trinity Lutheran Church of Columbia, Inc. v. Comer, Director, Missouri Department of Resources* 36n54

*Ulama* 160
Ulusoy, Betül 182–3
United Kingdom: Equality Act 2010 125, 133–41; and religious communities 125–8; religious groups in 127
United Nations 70; Population Report 111; Special Rapporteur on Freedom of Religion or Belief 198
United States: importance of free exercise 29–31; importance of religion 26–9; religious buildings in 118–23; 'religious exercise' 120; Religious Land Use and Institutionalized Persons Act of 2000 (RLUIPA) 118–23; status of religious freedom in 25–38
Universal Declaration of Human Rights (UDHR) 56, 58, 67, 196–7, 218; Article 18 of 4
universality of human rights: religious challenges to 60–1
University of Vienna 105
urbanization, and migration 111
US Commission on Civil Rights 34
US Congress 33, 119; and protection of conscience rights 90
US Constitution 4, 5; and protection of health-care rights of conscience 89
US Equal Employment Opportunity Commission (EEOC) 35
US Supreme Court 8, 19, 25

*Vartic v. Romania* 149
Vienna Convention 60
Vienna Declaration 56
Volokh, Eugene 34

Wahhabiyya 159
Wallace, Max 67
Warner, Michael 184
Washington, George 28
Weiner, Isaac 54
Williams, Roger 6
Women in the World Summit 34
World Youth Alliance 71
worship buildings; *see also* mosques: and Abruzzo Region 115; laws in Europe 115; and Lombardy Region 115–16

*X. v. Austria* 147
*X. v. Federal Republic of Germany* 151
*X v. Mid Sussex Citizens Advice Bureau* 137n96

Yusuf, Muhammad 163

Zionism, political 194

For Product Safety Concerns and Information please contact our EU representative GPSR@taylorandfrancis.com Taylor & Francis Verlag GmbH, Kaufingerstraße 24, 80331 München, Germany

**Batch number: 10726294**

Printed by Printforce, the Netherlands